Blood and Iron

Blood and Iron

Letters from the Western Front

Hugh Montagu Butterworth

Edited and with an Introduction
by Jon Cooksey

Pen & Sword
MILITARY

First published in Great Britain in 2011 by
Pen & Sword Military
an imprint of
Pen & Sword Books Ltd
47 Church Street
Barnsley
South Yorkshire
S70 2AS

ISBN 978 1 84884 297 7

A CIP catalogue record for this book is
available from the British Library

Typeset in Ehrhardt by Phoenix Typesetting, Auldgirth, Dumfriesshire

Printed and bound in England by CPI Antony Rowe, Chippenham and Eastbourne

Pen & Sword Books Ltd incorporates the imprints of Pen & Sword Aviation, Pen &
Sword Maritime, Pen & Sword Military, Wharncliffe Local History, Pen & Sword
Select, Pen & Sword Military Classics, Leo Cooper, Remember When, Seaforth
Publishing and Frontline Publishing.

For a complete list of Pen & Sword titles please contact
PEN & SWORD BOOKS LIMITED
47 Church Street, Barnsley, South Yorkshire, S70 2AS, England
E-mail: enquiries@pen-and-sword.co.uk
Website: www.pen-and-sword.co.uk

Contents

Foreword

The First World War claimed an incomprehensible number of lives. For anyone who has been to Ypres and gazed at the Menin Gate it is difficult to grasp the fact that the pattern on the walls is in reality name upon name of those who made the ultimate sacrifice. And if that wasn't tragic enough, you then need to travel to Tyne Cot cemetery which, at first, seems no different to countless other Commonwealth War Graves except that it includes a large memorial wall also covered with names – those names for whom there wasn't room on the Menin Gate.

For every name there is a story, a family, a life with all its ups and downs, twists and turns. Every now and then one of those 'names' speaks to us from beyond the memorial and in this case it is Hugh Montagu Butterworth through the letters he penned while serving with the Rifle Brigade on the Western Front. Then as the pieces of that life and family are painstakingly fitted together, as Jon Cooksey has done so diligently, the name develops a character and a personality we begin to care about. As the story develops other connections and associations are made which touch nerves and tug at strings. The final effect can mean very different things to different readers.

For me, the connections with Hugh's story are the Rifle Brigade and Wanganui Collegiate School. The Rifle Brigade in which Hugh served during the war was amalgamated in 1958 with the Oxfordshire and Buckinghamshire Light Infantry and the King's Royal Rifle Corps to form the Green Jackets Brigade. They later became the Royal Green Jackets in 1966 and in 2007 the 1st Battalion changed again into the 2nd Battalion The Rifles, at which point The Queen appointed me their Royal Colonel. The connection may seem tenuous, but in our regimental system the lineage is clear and the sense of family palpable.

The more striking connection is with Wanganui Collegiate School and the fact that we were both on the teaching staff there and attached to Selwyn House. The similarity stops abruptly there, for Hugh was considerably more gifted than me both on the sports field and in the classroom. I was merely helping out for a couple of terms while Hugh was a rather more permanent fixture and evidently had a far more beneficial impact on the educational life of his charges than I ever had. While university was my reason for returning to Britain, Hugh's was a far higher calling.

The next time I am at a Commonwealth War Graves cemetery or memorial, a Remembrance or Anzac Day event or find myself at the Menin Gate again I will recall

Hugh's name, his service, the Rifle Brigade and perhaps more significantly the other 162 boys and staff of Wanganui Collegiate School who gave their lives in the Great War. My life, my experiences, my possibilities may be different to theirs, but then I wouldn't have been able to enjoy any of them if Hugh and all those names had not fought and died. We will never forget them.

Edward

HRH The Earl of Wessex KG, KCVO

Preface

By Hugh M. Butterworth

Some of my earliest memories are of my half-brother Hugh. A photograph of a curly headed boy leaning against a trellis in a pose popular with photographers of the period stood on the sideboard in our family home in Devon. Gradually I came to know more about him; he had been killed in the war – he had died at Ypres – near Hooge – and his name was on the Menin Gate.

Regrettably the photograph did not survive the family's wartime upheavals but fortunately his letters, which appeared in a book published by his great friend John Allen in New Zealand in 1916, did. Over the years it became apparent that the *Letters from Flanders* were virtually unknown; the Museum at Winchester which looks after the records of the 9th Battalion, the Rifle Brigade had no knowledge of them and instantly copied them. They were unknown even to the Imperial War Museum.

Twenty-five years ago I made enquiries of a friend in the printing industry but the cost of reprinting the *Letters* was clearly prohibitive. I have always felt that they deserved a wider audience as Hugh's qualities and sense of humour come through so strongly amd the poignancy of the final letter is palpable.

I am thus extremely grateful to all those who have helped in the production of this book. My thanks go to staff at the Wanganui Collegiate School, New Zealand, Marlborough College, Wiltshire, The Master and Fellows of University College, Oxford and particularly to the historian Jon Cooksey, without whose help and enthusiasm this project would never have been completed. I am especially grafeul to HRH The Earl of Wessex for providing such a moving Foreword.

I had always wanted to visit the Menin Gate and one day in June 1960 I found myself in Ostend. I took the train to Ypres and booked in at the Station Hotel. I walked through the town and for the first time experienced the mildly curious sensation of seeing my name upon the stone panels of that awesome monument.

During dinner at the hotel, the manager came round to each table asking the diners whether they would attend the ceremony at the Gate. After dinner I strolled through the town and stood under the central arch. There were only seven of us present, four now are only shadowy figures, but I remember the other couple carried a wreath from The Essex Salient Circle.

Nothing seemed to be happening as the minute hand on my watch moved steadily towards eight o'clock. Then I noticed that two men had arrived and were removing their cycle clips. They took off their raincoats and I saw that they were in uniform and that they carried bugles. They were joined by two policemen and the four chatted quietly together.

Then the two policemen took up position in the road on either side of the Gate. One stopped a car coming from the town and the other, two vehicles which had come from the direction of the Menin Road. The policemen turned inwards and saluted as the Last Post began to sound. In a few moments it was all over and we slowly drifted away. Perhaps because of this experience, although I have attended the big ceremony in November and I am grateful to all those who take the trouble to honour those who died, I prefer to avoid the big occasions. I suppose that I have one more ambition left and that is to attend the ceremony – presumably on a cold, wet January evening – as the sole mourner, and, as the bugle notes die away across the Salient towards the Bellewaarde Ridge, to remember Hugh and wonder what might have been.

Hugh M. Butterworth
Braunton
Devon
2011

Acknowledgements

When I set out to research the historical and contextual introduction to this reprint of Hugh Montagu Butterworth's letters from Flanders, little did I realise that it would take me well beyond my usual bounds of grubbing around in various military records and archives. I have done a good deal of that of course, as Hugh's letters deal exclusively with his very short – just four months – period of service before he was killed in action in September 1915, but the work has taken me into realms that have been unfamiliar territory. I have found myself straying into areas of family and institutional history, into cricket and tennis archives; to Lord's, the MCC and the All England Club at Wimbledon and to consulting sporting experts as well as those who have a deep knowledge of the military aspects of the Great War as it was fought on the Western Front in 1915.

This book, therefore, would not have been possible without the wholehearted support, help, advice, enthusiasm and encouragement of a great many people with a deep knowledge of and expertise in their particular historical field. In particular, I must thank the second Hugh Montagu Butterworth for instigating the project, for it was his emotional reading of Hugh's last letter almost on the spot where his half-brother disappeared for ever in 1915 that opened my eyes to the possibility of a reprint. During the course of my subsequent research I spent time tracking down Hugh Butterworth's academic and sporting history and consulted numerous archival collections. The help and assistance I received was at all times prompt, courteous and unfailingly supportive and I must record my gratitude to the following, in no particular order, who went out of their way to answer a range of queries, send material and discuss and comment on drafts: Terry Rogers, Honorary Archivist Marlborough College; Dr Robin Darwall-Smith, Archivist University College, Oxford and author of the definitive history of that ancient institution; Margaret Mardall and Catherine Smith of the Charterhouse School archives; Roger McDuff, previously Headmaster of Hazelwood Prep School in Surrey, and his PA Samantha Dalziel; John Hamblin, who had already researched Hugh for his own project, for the sight of valuable documents; Pam White for information on the Warde family of Squerryes Court; Michael Barlow, author of the biography of Hugh's cousin George Butterworth, for his help on the Butterworth family tree and in tracing Hazelwood material; and Christine Clement, genealogist of New Zealand.

Accessing archival material half a world away is always a challenging prospect and I owe a particular debt of gratitude to Richard Bourne, Curator and Archivist of the

Wanganui Collegiate School Museum in New Zealand, for without his terrific enthusiasm and his desire to help in any way from the other side of the world, the story of Hugh's time as a schoolmaster in New Zealand would have been sketchy at best. My thanks go to him and to Rob van Dort, also of Wanganui Collegiate School, who helped with the gathering of photographic material. Thanks also to Donal Raethel, archivist with Archives New Zealand in Wellington, who, with a friendly 'Kia ora', managed to get Hugh's probate documents to me in double-quick time.

I am indebted to Graham McKechnie, sports journalist for the BBC and sometime off-spinner, with whom I have worked on several projects and who served as a sounding board for all my theories and queries regarding the sporting life of both Hugh and his father.

In terms of understanding Hugh's military life and his service with the 9th Battalion of the Rifle Brigade in Ypres during the summer and autumn of 1915, many have given of their time and knowledge to help clarify various issues. Special mention must be made of several people who really did go out of their way to provide me with material from which to make a judgment.

Andy Pay must surely rank as Britain's 'Mr Rifle Brigade'. He has been a tower of strength during our many conversations regarding a regiment with a fine military tradition and has loaned sheaves of original documents and constructively criticised drafts. Quite frankly what Andy does not know about the Rifle Brigade during the Great War is probably not worth knowing. It has been my good fortune to have had his support. I also had the good fortune to be able to call on the expertise of Terry Denham in arriving at the casualty figures of the 9th Battalion, the Rifle Brigade for the period 25 September–12 October 1915.

In a very similar vein, Ralph Whitehead in the United States has provided another strong pillar to lean on for information, images and sage advice regarding the German accounts of the regiment and division that opposed Hugh's battalion on 25 September 1915. Ralph expended an enormous amount of energy and put in a great deal of work on my behalf and I always looked forward to his emails. I looked forward also to emails from Sebastian Laudan in Germany. Sebastian too spent a lot of his valuable time either translating or discussing some of my theories on the German troop movements post-25 September 1915 and for that I am grateful. Alastair Fraser also helped by sending information on German units. I would like to record my sincere thanks for all their efforts.

Malte Znaniecki was also very kind in supplying German images. I should like to express my appreciation to Aurel Sercu, living near Ypres in Belgium, who was kind enough to offer to give up his valuable time to photograph the battlefield around Railway Wood as it is today – in fact I believe he made two trips.

Iain McHenry, also living and working in Belgium, gave freely of his time and made sure I had sight of several key documents relating to the work of 177 Tunnelling Company of the Royal Engineers, about which he is an acknowledged expert. Peter

Barton too was always willing to discuss the operations of the tunnellers on the Bellewaarde Ridge and helped in supplying several images of the front lines in September 1915.

Thanks must also go Nigel Steel, historian at the Imperial War Museum in London and to Alan Wakefield and David Parry of that institution's photographic archive for their help in tracing prints of the aerial photographs I had seen referred to in operation orders issued prior to the battle.

Taff Gillingham is always a trusted point of reference. I can almost see him crack a wry smile on the other end of the line when I ring him with another question about 'buttons, buckles and badges' but he and his 'chums' are always spot on. Thanks Taff for indulging me! Chris Baker, ex-Chairman of the Western Front Association and founder of the hugely respected Long, Long Trail website, is also a trusted voice. I am grateful to Chris for checking some early drafts and for his comments on them, as I am to commissioning editor Rupert Harding for his never less than sound good sense. Thanks also to my copy editor Alison Miles whose eagle-eye enabled me to make several improvements to the text and no doubt spared me a few blushes in the process.

Peter Donnelly, Curator at the King's Own Royal Regiment Museum, Lancaster, assisted with enquiries regarding John Allen's military service, and Jon Wilkinson and Jordan Szabo at Pen and Sword Books have again developed some super artwork.

It is with great sadness that I record my thanks to the late lamented Lieutenant Colonel Will Townend RA retired. An unrivalled artillery guru who really helped clarify for me the assembled weaponry of the 14th (Light) Division and 2 Group Heavy Artillery before his untimely death on 6 April 2010, Will was a valued colleague and friend. I and many others will miss him terribly.

I am especially indebted to HRH The Earl of Wessex for contributing his most thoughtful Foreword on his connection with Hugh.

My wife Heather and daughter Georgia have continued to indulge my often anti-social working habits and I thank them again for their patience and understanding. If anyone who has been kind enough to help in any way has been missed out, please be assured that it has not been intentional. To those affected please accept my sincere apologies.

In all instances every effort has been made to seek appropriate permissions where necessary but if, inadvertently, these have been overlooked then I or the publishers should be pleased to hear from copyright holders. If any errors or omissions remain in the text then they are entirely due to oversights on my part.

Jon Cooksey
Snitterfield
Warwickshire
2011

Hugh Montagu Butterworth
Born 1 November 1885
Died in Battle 25 September 1915

'I'm not particularly afraid of death, but I dislike the thought of dying because I enjoy life so much, and I want to enjoy it such a lot more. This dug-out life gives one plenty of time to think, I tell you, and the danger is, one gets down to a minor key and stays there. . . . Anyway I feel that I've expiated every crime I've ever committed. I fancy that when we warriors fetch up at the Final Enquiry they'll say, "Where did you perform?" We shall reply. "Ypres salient." They'll answer, "Pass, friend", and we shall stroll along to the sound of trumpets and sackbuts.'

Letter from the Front near Bellewaarde, Ypres, 16 July 1915

Blood and Iron

Introduction

By Jon Cooksey

Railway Wood on the Bellewaarde Ridge, near Ypres, September 2007. As the group of twenty or so travellers gathered around a small, white cross overlooking a peaceful, sun-drenched Belgian pasture, one of their number, Hugh Montagu Butterworth, pulled a sheet of paper from his pocket and began to read the following words, written almost exactly ninety-two years earlier by his half-brother also named Hugh Montagu Butterworth:

Belgium, September 1915.

(I am posting this myself just before leaving. Perhaps I shan't be killed!!)

I am leaving this in the hands of the transport officer, and if I get knocked out, he will send it on to you. We are going into a big thing. It will be my pleasant duty to leap lightly over the parapet and lead D Company over the delectable confusion of old trenches, crump holes and barbed wire, that lies between us and the Bosche, and take a portion of his front line. Quo facto I shall then proceed to bomb down various communication trenches and take his second line. In the very unlikely event of my being alive by then I shall dig in like blazes and if God is good, stop the Bosche counter-attack, which will come in an hour or two. If we stop that I shall then in broad daylight have to get out wire in front under machine-gun fire and probably stop at least one more counter attack and a bomb attack from the flank. If all that happens successfully and I'm still alive, I shall hang on till relief. Well, when one is faced with a programme like that, one touches up one's will, thanks heaven one has led a fairly amusing life, thanks God one is not married, and trusts in Providence. Unless we get more officers before the show, I am practically bound to be outed as I shall have to lead all these things myself. Anyway if I do go out I shall do so amidst such a scene of blood and iron as even this war has rarely witnessed.

Second Lieutenant Hugh Montagu Butterworth of the 9th Battalion, the Rifle Brigade, did not survive. He was killed in action, as he had foretold on the eve of battle, on 25 September 1915, during one of the three bloody diversions to the Battle of Loos, which opened the same morning 30 miles to the south. Did he die in vain?

1

That last letter is a stunning document – honest, realistic and resigned – and yet there is a final nod to the heroic and to an end that befits a temporary 'warrior' of his social standing who had sworn to do his duty for his King and Country.

Hugh's letters had been intended for his colleagues and pupils at his beloved Wanganui Collegiate School on the North Island of New Zealand, where he had taught and coached cricket for seven happy years before the war. He had written them to the school but his colleague and great friend John Allen, who had arrived at Wanganui just a year before Hugh and who would go on to become Headmaster during the 1930s, was the man Hugh had entrusted with opening the envelopes. It had been another colleague of Hugh's, H E Sturge, who had written Hugh's obituary in the school magazine, the Wanganui *Collegian*, in December 1915 and even as he had been writing that memorial tribute John Allen had decided to publish Hugh's letters as a lasting legacy in association with Mr Sturge. We can pinpoint exactly the moment when the seed of the idea to publish Hugh's letters was sown. In a letter to the editor of the Wanganui *Collegian* of December 1915, John Allen wrote:

Dear Sir,

I wish to take this opportunity of informing present and past members of the School that I intend, with the assistance of Mr Sturge, to publish in book form the series of letters which Mr Butterworth wrote to me from Flanders between May and September. They are intensely interesting: we feel that there are many who would value them very highly as a permanent possession. We hope that they will be ready next term. Applications for copies can be made to either Mr Sturge or myself.

Yours sincerely.

J. ALLEN.

The volume, which eventually bore the title, 'LETTERS, written in the trenches near Ypres between May and September 1915, by H M Butterworth, 9th Rifle Brigade, who fell in action on September 25, 1915', was printed by Whitcombe and Tombs Ltd, of Wellington, New Zealand, and appeared in early 1916. Copies were purchased by, or sent to, family and friends and the scope and importance of its contents have been largely forgotten ever since, save for the appearance of short extracts which found their way into other publications, undergraduate studies and discussions and debates on various Great War related web forums.[1]

In 1930 the illustrator, novelist and dramatist Laurence Housman, younger brother of A E Housman, edited and published abridged extracts from two of Hugh's letters, separated by several days, in the volume *War Letters of Fallen Englishmen*.[2] Adding to a torrent of books on the war – memoir, fiction, autobiography and collected letters – that were published between 1928 and 1934, Housman noted in his introduction that the letters that he had selected represented 'two voices'. On the one hand there was the voice of a large majority, which, although firmly convinced that their actions were right – or at least right in the sense that there was an inevitability about them – showed 'their 'detestation of war in its operation', yet at the same time some expressed 'the keen satisfaction it gives them as an individual experience – mainly as a test of themselves, of their power to conquer fear, to live at the full push of their energies, mental and physical. To them, individually, active warfare gives life a fuller expression: 'for it is a life lived daily in the power to face death'.[3]

On the other hand, Housman recognised that amongst the letters he had collected were those of a minority, equally worthy of respect and yet representative of other types of mind and character. These were of men who had not been,

> ... born fighters, men who have had a hard struggle to conquer their individual
> fears, temperaments and disgusts, and have not come through with elation or
> even conviction. In some of these letters there is a cry of a violated conscience
> or at least of poignant doubt. In many – in some of the best – is the record of a
> diminishing hope: of men who went into war with ideals, from which the reality
> (military and political combined) slowly crushed out the life.[4]

Reading the sweep of Hugh's letters from late May 1915 to the eve of his death in late September the same year, it is clear that his voice could be heard clearly as an advocate of both camps. In some letters we hear exuberant examples representing that 'majority voice' but, as the war progresses and his battalion become involved in some of the worst fighting of 1915 in the Ypres Salient, we listen intently and with mounting concern as he grapples with his internal fears, doubts and uncertainties.

Housman's work, and therefore the same extracts from Hugh's *Letters*, surfaced again in 2002 in a reprint by the University of Pennsylvania Press with a specially commissioned introduction by historian Jay Winter. The ambiguities evident in Hugh's *Letters* reflect a theme picked up by Jay Winter when studying Housman's collection. Winter contends that Housman's volume was, like many works of the time, party of the 'memory boom', an attempt to retrieve the voices of what has become termed the 'Lost Generation'; men and women who were the natural successors to positions of power, influence and creativity in British society. He views *War Letters of Fallen Englishmen* as fundamentally a pacifist document and yet argues that the very content of the letters selected by Housman highlights the 'limitations of pacifist appeals in the inter-war years', much as the term 'Lost Generation' – when applied to the post-war gaps in the ranks of the social classes that ran Britain and the Empire – became a self-serving argument and a 'demographic explanation for Britain's dismal economic and political record between the wars'.[5]

Most of the men who served came home to their families or settled down and started families and although many struggled to cope with the debilitating effects of wounds or gas, many more went back to their jobs and 'stuck it' during the lean and hungry years of the Depression, just as they had in the trenches and somehow hung on to contribute to Britain's economy as best they could.

There are valid arguments as to why the concept of the 'Lost Generation' may be flawed and whilst it is handy to regard it as a smokescreen for those who would not face up to the realities behind Britain's social, economic and political woes of the 1920s and 1930s, it is also an inescapable fact that when the war claimed the lives of its participants it also claimed their promise and their potential. One could look at the two Butterworth cousins, Hugh and George, as examples and muse on that thought. Hugh Butterworth had given so much to so many as a teacher in New Zealand by the time he joined the Army in 1915 and several of his pupils would indeed go on to achieve great things and very high office in public life. What more would he have given had he been spared? What of the promise and potential of his cousin George, already a talented and respected composer and a friend of Vaughan Williams before he joined up? What great works would have been produced if he had survived? Would he have been hailed in the same breath as Elgar and Vaughan Williams as one of Britain's greatest composers? What if, what if?

For Jay Winter at least, the republication of Housman's collected *War Letters of Fallen Englishmen* served a broader purpose in that at least it enabled its audience to appreciate the complexities and ambiguities in war literature as well as the frailties of the pacifist movement in the years 1900–1950.

A very short fragment of one of Hugh's letters initially selected by Housman in 1930 appeared in the late 1980s in a book entitled *British Butchers and Bunglers of World War One* by Australian author John Laffin. It is not the purpose of this intro-duction to enter into a detailed analysis of that work. Suffice to say that Laffin's chosen title conveys as much about his central thesis of the failure of leadership on the part of those in positions of high command in the British Army as one perhaps needs to know with regard to the present work.

All historians who commit their thoughts to paper make judgments regarding the selection and editing of their source material and in this regard Laffin is no different to any other. Where he has been criticised, however, it has been on the grounds of his biased selection of evidence or in the misrepresentation of his sources. What John Laffin was certainly not attempting to demonstrate was his appreciation of the 'complexities and ambiguities' in war literature, particularly when applied to Hugh's own words given those he chose to extract from Housman's earlier work.

The scrap of Hugh's letter used by Laffin appeared in a chapter entitled 'What the Soldiers Say', in which the author used various extracts from many soldiers to support his assertion that they amount to:

an exposé of what it was that the 'Great Captains' expected men to endure in the name of God, King and Country – and their own egotism. . . . In a few cases, the soldier writers of these letters are explicit in their indictment of senior leadership. In many cases the indictment is implicit. In all cases they reveal the truth about the reality of war and the futility of British tactics. The soldiers' testimony against their commanders is damning.[6]

In the light of the above it is worth reproducing here the extract exactly as it appears in *British Butchers and Bunglers*:

Early August 1915. We're out temporarily but shall probably be back tomorrow night. We had an awful time. The whole show lasted about 96 hours and is probably by no means over yet. We may quite easily be shoved into the attack almost at once. This letter fails hopelessly. I can't express what we felt or give you a real idea what Hell looks like. We lost two hundred and fifty men.

Laffin abridged the first six lines of the second of Hugh's letters to be published in Housman's *War Letters* and stitched them together with the first three lines of the last paragraph, missing out two paragraphs and several hundred words in between. Crucially, he did not set the letter in context. What Laffin did not reveal was that Hugh's letter dealt specifically with his impressions of his involvement in the German liquid fire attack at Hooge on 30 July 1915. The 'whole show' which, according to Hugh, lasted for ninety-six hours, was not a British attack cobbled together by those 'Great Captains' of which he was so dismissive but a dogged British defence in the teeth of a terrific German onslaught in which flamethrowers were used as terror weapons on a large scale for the first time.

The British at Hooge were fighting for their lives to hold on to a key position – militarily vital ground – which dominated the Ypres Salient. In such circumstances there was little wonder that casualties were very heavy, for this was trench warfare fought at a high tempo and a terrific intensity. That Hugh found it difficult to 'express' what he felt should not surprise readers – although he did a pretty good job when one is able to digest the whole piece.

John Laffin spoke of the letters in his selection as revealing the 'truth about the reality of war' and the 'futility of British tactics', but he excised from the same letter Hugh's references to his riflemen 'repelling the attack' which Hugh admits was hard to verify given the 'noise, dust and general tumult' and the confusion, chaos and fluidity of the situation given that stretches of trench changed hands several times.

Laffin argued that each of the extracts revealed 'something about the unpleasantness, at best, and the vile horror at worst, of the war' and indeed Hugh admits that the battalion had 'an awful time'. However, Laffin missed out a section Jay Winter would almost certainly classify as demonstrating the 'complexities and ambiguities' inherent in much war literature. With Hugh's men 'right over' the parapet and 'firing like blazes' he goes on to describe himself bestriding the trench:

half on the parapet and half on the parados with a revolver in one hand and a rifle near the other and a cigarette going well, using the most unquotable language. Do you know that really was a good moment. I can't pretend to like bombardments, nor war generally, but that really was a moment when one 'touched top' (as opposed to touching bottom) but you'll feel that it was an interesting moment in one's life.

Clearly Hugh's overwhelming emotion regarding the 'reality of war' in that split second was anything other than a feeling of futility.

Another short extract from Hugh's first letter in the Housman anthology was used as source material as recently as 2006 in an undergraduate study by a student at Rochester University in New York State to support the thesis that social class influenced the attitudes of other ranks.[7] Tantalising snippets had thus been read but the full story of Hugh's war as recounted in his own words in his *Letters* had not been heard for many decades.

In September 2007, up on the Bellewaarde Ridge, the group stood mute as the final few words of Hugh Butterworth's valedictory – given voice again by his brother after a silence of more than ninety years – drifted away over the very field upon which he had charged headlong towards the German front line on that fateful September dawn in 1915. The only sounds were the breeze softly brushing the trees behind and the gentle rustle of paper as the second Hugh Butterworth – head now bowed – folded his sheet and placed it back in his pocket. Here and there, around the group, tears were already beginning to fall. It was a while before we were able to move on. At that moment I realised the incredible foresight of Hugh's friend and Wanganui Collegiate School colleague John Allen in wishing to gather together his letters from Flanders and to publish them. I knew that the words of Hugh Montagu Butterworth contained in that single volume – at once hating war and yet conveying an intoxication borne of the sheer adrenalin of the action of it; alive, vibrant and powerful again after more than nine decades in obscurity – deserved a much wider audience than the few kindred spirits gathered around his half-brother on a sunny September morning in Belgium. Here they are. I hope that you feel the same.

Jon Cooksey
Snitterfield
Warwickshire
2011

Chapter One
Born into Sport

Cricket fans perusing the pages of the cricketing bible *Wisden* for the year 1916 will come across the following entry under the obituaries for 1915:

2nd Lieut. Hugh Montagu Butterworth (9th Rifle Brigade) was killed in Flanders on September 25, aged 29. He was educated at Marlborough, where he was in the Eleven in 1903 and 1904, being sixth in the averages in the former year with 13.36 and first in the latter with 34.13. In 1904 he played a first innings of 78 in the match with Rugby at Lord's. Proceeding to Oxford, he made many good scores for University College, but did not obtain his blue, although he was accorded a few trials in the Eleven in 1906 on the strength of an innings of 130 in the Seniors' Match, wherein he and C J Farmer scored 157 for the first wicket. In 1905 and 1906 he played Rackets (Doubles) for Oxford v Cambridge, in the former year having the Hon C N Bruce as a partner and in the latter G N Foster. Subsequently he settled in Wanganui, New Zealand, where he kept up the game, and in the early part of the 1914–15 season scored 296 and 311 in consecutive innings.[1]

The above and, by necessity, rather brief entry paints a picture of a cricketer and sportsman but Hugh Montagu Butterworth was so much more than a cricketer and racquets player. He sprang from the same mould that shaped so many middle and upper middle-class Edwardian gentlemen and through his family, educational and sporting connections mixed or came into contact with the great and good of society. Like so many of his ilk, including men like his own cousin, the composer George Butterworth, Ronald Poulton Palmer, the great England rugby international, philanthropist and heir to the Reading Huntley and Palmer biscuit empire or Noel Chavasse, gifted athlete, doctor and the recipient of the Victoria Cross and bar during the Great War, he epitomises the very qualities of those who belong to what has become termed the 'Lost Generation'.

Hugh was a much-loved son and brother, a fine sportsman, a gentle and caring teacher and a true friend and it is through his great friendship with John Allen, a fellow master at the Wanganui Collegiate School during the early years of the twentieth century, that we are able to gain an insight into the life of this particular

Edwardian gentleman at war in the trenches of the Ypres Salient during the dreadful summer and autumn of 1915.

Hugh Montagu Butterworth was born on 1 November 1885 at Saffron Walden, Essex. He was the son of George Montagu Butterworth, a young and relatively newly qualified (1884) solicitor whose father had been the vicar of the Priory Church of St Mary at Deerhurst near Tewkesbury in Gloucestershire – formerly the priory church and one of the largest and finest Saxon churches in the country. His mother Catherine Lucie Warde was the daughter of Captain Charles Arthur Madan Warde of the Bengal, later Royal, Artillery and Mary Warde, née Fisher, born on 12 July 1861 in Bengal, India.[2]

Returning from India after his retirement on a pension and his elevation to the honorary rank of lieutenant colonel by 19 July 1876, Charles Warde had initially moved his family to Bath, but by the time Hugh was born his maternal grandfather had returned to Kent to take up residence at Squerryes Court, the Warde family seat near Westerham. Almost exactly a year after Hugh's birth, Lieutenant Colonel Warde had been nominated for the position of Sherriff of the County of Kent in the Queen's Bench Division of the High Court of Justice and four months later, at the Court at Windsor on 7 March 1887, he was duly appointed 'by Her Majesty in Council for the year 1887'.[3] Like so many of his class and his time, there was a certain amount of 'military DNA' in Hugh's blood.

After Hugh's arrival in November 1885 came five younger sisters which completed Hugh's immediate family. Hugh was the nephew of Sir Alexander Kaye Butterworth – a solicitor like his father – who first represented and then became general manager of the North Eastern Railway. Hugh was thus a cousin of Uncle Alick's son George Butterworth, the gifted young composer who was awarded the Military Cross before being killed in action near Pozières during the Battle of the Somme on 5 August 1916.

Within a few years of his birth, Hugh's father moved the family from Saffron Walden to Swindon – which at that time was a booming hub of the Great Western Railway Company – when his father decided to branch out on his own and set up his own legal firm. The family first moved into a house on Brunswick Terrace and then, as the business grew and two partners were recruited, George Butterworth purchased two large Georgian houses – nos 8 and 10 on the High Street – no. 8 becoming the family home, whilst an architect was drafted in to work up plans for the conversion of no. 10 into offices for his legal practice. As his young family settled into life in Swindon, Hugh's father set to with a will in building up his practice but at the same time he devoted a good deal of his not inconsiderable energies into knocking the lawn into shape as a tennis court. Sport had always played a large part in George's life and indeed that of his wife Catherine. Both had had a good deal of success at lawn tennis; indeed the couple had the sport to thank for bringing them together, and the move to Swindon did not diminish George's desire to 'play on'. Hugh grew up in an environment in which active games and sports played a key role and where family life and the entertainment of guests, particularly during the summer months, seemed to centre on the grass tennis court at the rear of the house. The children were even employed as green keepers, lured by the promise of a shiny penny for every 100 plantains grubbed out from the surface of their father's beloved tennis court. Tennis had been, and whilst the family lived in Swindon, continued to be a passion for Hugh's father. In his youth and early adulthood he had enjoyed a good deal of success in wielding a tennis racquet and had even graced the hallowed lawns of what was then known as the All England Croquet and Lawn Tennis Club, at the time situated off Worple Road in Wimbledon.

What were eventually to become the world-famous Wimbledon Championships we know today had begun in 1877 and in 1880 Hugh's father entered the 'single-handed' competition in a sport that was then in its infancy. He was beaten in the 'fifth round', or the semi-finals, on Tuesday 13 July by Herbert Lawford in a relatively undemanding straight-sets victory: 'Mr Lawford's match with Mr Butterworth did not last long, as set after set was won by the former. The first set Mr Lawford won by six games to two; the second by six games to three; and the third by six games to one.'[4] As a beaten semi-finalist, George Butterworth received 6 guineas.

He entered again the following year but did not progress beyond the second round and in 1884 he took part in the inaugural 'four-handed', or Gentlemen's Doubles, event. After a convincing 6–4, 6–3, 6–2 victory in the first-round tie, he and his partner W Milne were beaten by the outstanding sibling partnership of Willie and Ernest Renshaw in the next round despite the 'capital play' of Mr Butterworth being 'very effective', according to All England referee Henry Jones, writing as 'Cavendish' in the magazine the *Field*.[5]

George Butterworth had not gone down without a fight. Out of the competition again, he had nevertheless written a footnote for himself in the annals of the All England Club in what was the historic year of 1884; the first year in which the All England Club had held a Ladies Singles Championship. Although Hugh's mother had not been one of the first thirteen women trailblazers to take part in that inaugural event, she had nevertheless been one of those active daughters of the comfortably off middle and upper middle classes before her marriage to his father. A keen devotee of the newfangled game of lawn tennis, she had entered the mixed doubles competition in the first West of England Championships held in Bristol in August 1884. The dashing George Butterworth had also entered but without a partner. The Committee duly paired him with Catherine and, if readers will forgive the rather blatant tennis puns, the couple hit it off immediately and the union proved to be a love match. After a very short engagement George Butterworth's tennis partner went on to became his partner in life in the New Year of 1885.

Having inherited his parents' 'active' genes, it was only natural the Hugh should develop into a first-class athlete in sports that required moving balls to be struck by a variety of implements. Hugh was the apple of his father's eye and, as soon as Hugh had been old enough to pick up a racquet and try to hit a ball, George would take him out on to the tennis court and coach him. As Hugh grew in strength and stature his father would never allow him to serve a double fault or fail to return the ball, quickly sending over another ball in its place and stressing that selfishness should be kept out of the game as much as possible because it was 'the rally that mattered not who won the game'. Indeed, Hugh went on to represent every one of the educational establishments of which he became a member – from prep school to university to Wanganui Collegiate School in New Zealand – at a variety of racquet, stick and contact sports and, judging from the writings of others after his death, obviously carried that ethos of 'sportsmanship' with him throughout his life, handing it down to others as he went on. For Hugh and for so many young men of his class and era, 'playing the game' was an essential element of a philosophy by which they lived their lives.

Chapter Two
'Fairly Useful' – School Days

Although now a resident of Wiltshire, Hugh was nevertheless packed off to Hazelwood Preparatory School in Limpsfield near Oxted in Surrey. As Lieutenant Colonel Charles Warde, his maternal grandfather, was by then in residence at Squerryes Court a little way along what is now the A25 to Westerham and just over the county boundary in Kent, it was not surprising that Hazelwood was entrusted with Hugh's formal primary education. He settled in well and got into the routine of writing long letters home at the weekend, the delivery of which his family always anticipated eagerly at breakfast on Monday mornings.

At Hazelwood, not unnaturally, he joined in and excelled at all manner of sports. Figures for the First XI cricket team published in the *Nutshell – The Hazelwood School Gazette* show Hugh as fourth in the batting averages, scoring a total of 149 runs in 11 innings for an average of 14.9. As a bowler he delivered 104.3 overs – 38 of those being maidens – taking 28 wickets for 185 runs for an average of 6.6, the average being the total number of runs divided by the total number of wickets taken. The accompanying report, however, hinted that, although he clearly had potential, there was, perhaps, more than a shade of youthful exuberance that needed to be channelled if progress was to be made. Hugh was, wrote the anonymous coach, 'a great disappointment as a bat; ought to have been far better, as he *can* hit hard and also play steadily, but he practically made no improvement. Came out as a very difficult bowler latterly. Never safe in the field but fairly useful'.[1] It is interesting to note that, judging by his averages, Hugh was clearly regarded as a bowler whilst at Hazelwood but gradually developed his technique to become recognised as a batsman at Marlborough College before moving on to Oxford. His performance in the field, however, never appeared to have been one of his strongest attributes.

On departing Hazelwood for pastures new in the summer of 1899, however, the *Nutshell* hinted that Hugh's energies and talents had not been restricted solely to activities on the playground or the games field. There had been so much more to the young Hugh Butterworth than mere athleticism. Under the heading 'FAREWELL', the *Nutshell* recorded that, following in the footsteps of both his father and Uncle Alick: 'H M Butterworth goes to Marlborough with a great reputation for every branch of athletics, a more than useful musician and quite at the top of the tree as an actor.'[2]

Hugh's name would appear in the *Nutshell* just once more, in January 1916, when a brief biography, including a short quote from his commanding officer that was later

11

reproduced in *Letters*, appeared in the 'Hazelwood Roll of Honour'.[3] Three of Hugh's contemporaries, who were also mentioned in the 'Farewell' section of the same edition of the *Nutshell* when Hugh left Hazelwood, were Harold Vernon Browne (Captain, Dorset Yeomanry, died of wounds in Gallipoli), Edward Estridge (Lieutenant, 12th Battalion, the East Yorkshire Regiment, killed on the Somme) and Cecil Twining (Captain, 1st Battalion, the Hampshire Regiment, killed at Ypres). They were also first, second and third respectively above Hugh in the First XI cricket batting averages for 1899 and, along with Hugh and Charles Robin (Captain, 2nd Battalion, the Royal Jersey Militia, attached 13th Battalion, the York and Lancaster Regiment, killed near Arras in 1917), made up the entire bowling attack for that particular Hazelwood team. Douglas Brandt, another First XI team mate of Hugh's, died of wounds at Ypres as a captain with the 1st Battalion, the Rifle Brigade, bringing the total of the 1899 Hazelwood First XI to lose their lives in the Great War to six.

Marlborough College

Hugh went up to Marlborough in September 1899. His entry in the Marlborough College Register for the years 1843–1933 reads:

> (C2) s. of G M Butterworth (OM), Westward Ho! b. Nov. 1., 1885; l. Mids. 1904. Hockey XI. 1903–4; XV. 1903; XI. 1903–4; Capt. R C 1903; Racquet Rep. 1904; Univ. Coll. Oxf; Univ Racquet Rep. 1905–6; asst. Master, Wanganui Sch., NZ. 'Letters from Flanders by HMB' printed by Wanganui Sch. *Great War*: 2nd Lieut., 9 Rifle Bde. 1915. Killed in action at Hooge, Sept. 25, 1915.[4]

Hugh's death did not go unremarked by his old school. His name, along with those of the 749 or so Old Boys who were killed in the Great War, is inscribed on the wall of the ambulatory at the rear of Marlborough College's Memorial Hall, a large assembly and concert hall opened in 1925 and dedicated to remembering the sacrifice of the 'Lost Generation' of Old Marlburians. In one of the entrance lobbies is a locked cupboard inside which are the Rolls of Honour – one book for each boarding house – bearing a photograph and short citation for each man who gave his life. Even for Old Marlburians of a far more recent vintage, including some who went on to choose the military as a career, the Memorial Hall and all that it represents is remembered as having a central role in the life of the College, being used for assemblies, occasional acts of worship, concerts and other important College gatherings. Those who gave their lives are truly remembered for evermore.

But Hugh's career at what has now become one of Britain's leading public schools conflated into just two lines in the College Register, began over a quarter of a century before the opening of the Memorial Hall inside which his name is inscribed.

It was a career that, according to his sister Irene, 'widened Hugh's character enormously . . . it opened his eyes more fully to the rounded joy of living and much else besides'.

Those few lines of potted history in the Register conceal the many joys, achievements, victories and defeats and, indeed, trials and tribulations that have been and continue to be enduring features of secondary school life for most people.

There was, perhaps, never any question that Hugh would not attend Marlborough. Hugh's Uncle Alick, as the eldest son of a clergyman, had been the first Butterworth to blaze the trail by entering the College – originally founded with the prime purpose of educating the sons of the clergy of the established Church of England – in 1868. Following a period under the tutelage of the Revd Francis Walsh MA, Headmaster of the Gentleman's School at 1 Waterloo Place, Leamington Spa, Hugh's father George duly followed his elder brother and hauled his school trunk to Marlborough in August 1872. Hugh's sister Irene, writing in 1975 about her father's school days, observed that the College had always played a huge part in the life of the Butterworth family: 'To my father there were three passionate devotions in his life – apart from his wife and in early days his family. The first was Deerhurst, the second was his school – the third was yet to be born.'[5] That third passion was, of course, Hugh.

The College Register reveals that Hugh's father had attended as a Foundation Scholar in Boarding House C1 for four and a half years. In his time at Marlborough, then a relatively young institution, having been founded as recently as 1843, but already with a turbulent history and a famous pupil 'rebellion' under its belt, George Butterworth had been a College prefect and had represented the College at racquets. He had partnered F M Lucas in the final of the Public Schools' Challenge Cup in 1877 when the Marlborough pair lost the final to the Eton pair of the Hon. Ivo Bligh, later the 8th Earl of Darnley, and C A C Ponsonby. Bligh later went down in history as the first English cricket captain to bring the small terracotta urn containing 'The Ashes' of English cricket, back from Australia in 1883 after the Australians' shock victory at the Oval the previous year had led to the publication of the mock obituary to and 'cremation' of the English game in the *Sporting Times*.

Much had improved at Marlborough since its early troubles but George Butterworth's time at Marlborough was nonetheless characterised by a somewhat spartan regime. L E Upcott, who joined Marlborough as a young master in 1875 and taught there during George Butterworth's time, set down his thoughts in the centenary publication *Marlborough College 1843–1943* and described the College thus:

> As I first knew Marlborough, it was unquestionably a rough school. I do not use the words in a bad sense. I mean that there was very little material comfort, nothing that could be called luxurious; much was primitive hard and uncomfortable. The school was intended to be, and was, a school for the sons of poor men.

When Hugh first set foot in College more than twenty years later as a nervous 13-year-old new boy at the start of the Michaelmas term in that autumn of 1899, he entered Junior Boarding House A2 under its housemaster F A Leslie-Jones, a man who would become Hugh's rugby coach when he turned out for the First XV a few years later. Placed in the Upper IV (1) under its master Mr Meyrick, his academic performance during that first term might best be described as 'middling', achieving a form position of eighteenth out of twenty-eight boys. Moving both forms and form masters for the Lent term of 1900, his position remained almost unchanged under Mr Preston in Shell B, but by the time he received his final report at the end of his first year at Marlborough he had achieved a quite respectable tenth place out of thirty boys. Returning to College after the summer break he was transferred to C2, one of the Senior Boarding Houses, under the watchful eye of housemaster P W Taylor, a dedicated teacher who evoked amusement and respect from the boys in equal measure. C2 was one of the wings of 'C House', the 188-year-old former seat of the 7th Duke of Somerset which, in 1750 on the death of the Duke, had been leased out as a coaching hostelry and was known as the Castle Inn. The inn had thrived to become a 'must visit' watering hole for the gentry and members of the fashionable society set as they plied their way in their droves between London and Bath at the height of the latter's fame as 'the' place to be seen. Over the next ninety years the Castle Inn was graced with visits from many famous personalities, ranging from prime ministers to none other than the 'Iron Duke' himself, the Duke of Wellington. The noisy clatter of the newfangled Great Western Railway, which drove into the region in the 1840s, however, was the death knell for horse-drawn coaching businesses and inevitably the Castle Inn's fortunes waned. It finally closed its doors in 1843 and the lease was snapped up by the founders of Marlborough College who seized their opportunity to inaugurate their school based on the nucleus of the old Castle Inn building which, with its large central portion and two wings, became the first three boarding houses. Although both Hugh's father and Uncle Alick had both boarded in C1, Hugh would remain in C2 for the rest of his Marlborough career.

The start of Michaelmas term 1900 also saw Hugh move forms again and for the next two terms he studied with Mr Taylor in Remove A. Something must have clicked for Hugh under the tutelage of Mr Taylor as he built on his improvements at the end of his first year and when College broke up for the Easter holiday of 1901 Hugh was able to go home with the heartening news that his form ranking had risen from ninth the previous Christmas to an outstanding third place out of twenty-seven boys. But a close analysis here of what modern educationists – obsessed with data crunching and league tables – would now term Hugh's 'academic profile' during his final four years at Marlborough reveals an erratic pattern of high attainment on the one hand, whilst on the other there are quite sudden and alarming slumps in performance during the summer terms.

Term	Form	Form Master	Final Form Position
Michaelmas 1899	Upper IV B	Mr Meyrick	18th of 28 boys
Lent 1900	Shell B	Mr Preston	19th of 29 boys
Summer 1900	Shell B	Mr Preston	10th of 30 boys
Michaelmas 1900	Remove A	Mr Taylor	9th of 27 boys
Lent 1901	Remove A	Mr Taylor	3rd of 27 boys
Summer 1901	Lower Vth (2a)	Mr Leaf	22nd of 28 boys
Michaelmas 1901	Lower Vth (2a)	Mr Leaf	4th of 27 boys
Lent 1902	Lower Vth (2a)	Mr Leaf	4th of 26 boys
Summer 1902	Lower Vth (1)	Mr Gould	22nd of 29 boys
Michaelmas 1902	Middle Vth	Mr Macdonald	15th equal of 25 boys
Lent 1903	Middle Vth	Mr Macdonald	No record survived
Summer 1903	Middle Vth	Mr Macdonald	12th of 27 boys
Michaelmas 1903	Upper Vth	Revd Wood	14th of 22 boys
Lent 1904	Upper Vth	Revd Wood	19th of 26 boys
Summer 1904	Upper Vth	Revd Wood	22nd of 23 boys[6]

On three occasions during his last four years at Marlborough, Hugh went home for the summer holidays placed a rather lowly twenty-second out of an average class size of twenty-six boys. The reasons for academic underachievement are many and varied; poor pupil–teacher relationships, illness, difficulties at home and emotional trauma are but a small selection, but there is no evidence to suggest that Hugh was suffering from any obvious impediment to his learning. In support of this thesis his sister claimed that being possessed of 'a fundamentally unselfish character . . . he did not create problems' and thus, she concluded, 'it may be argued that life went very well for him'. Logically, then there can have been only one reason for his rather poor showing in the form rankings during the long days of the summer months – an inordinate amount of time spent wielding the willow on the cricket field to the obvious detriment of his studies.

Not that Hugh neglected other sports and activities during his time at Marlborough. Contemporary issues of the College journal the *Marlburian* contain numerous references to Hugh's many and varied sporting exploits, as will become evident, but he also spent time on other more martial pastimes. The issue of 6 February 1903 recorded his promotion to the rank of cadet second lieutenant in the College Rifle Volunteer Corps. He was also elevated to the captaincy of the College Rifle Club and was thus no slouch as a shot. Thus by the year 1903 he had earned for himself a leadership role and was involved in weekly drill, basic military training and regular rifle shooting practice, all of which would stand him in good stead when he came to seek a commission in the New Army in early 1915.

But it was Hugh's terrific passion and appetite for the game of cricket – at least in the form the game was played at the turn of the century, with the more immediate cut and thrust of 'Twenty20' matches almost a hundred years in the future – that took up so much of his time in the summer.

Hugh broke into what was called 'The XI' by the summer of his fourth year. His pen portrait under the heading 'Characters of The XI 1903' described him as a 'good forcing bat, who, by learning to play straight, improved almost out of knowledge. Quite the best runner on the side. A fast field with a poor return and an uncertain catch'. The batting averages published in the next column recorded that he batted for 11 innings, scoring 147 runs for an average of 13.3 with a top score of 50. The opponents are not listed but a perusal of Hugh's own record of scores over 50, published along with his letters, shows that particular 'knock' to have been against Liverpool.[7] This is slightly at variance with Hugh's recollection of his highest score that season as he records a score of 55 made for the College against the Warwickshire Regiment, also in 1903.

Hugh's involvement in the First XI brought him into contact with other senior boys who went on to become firm friends. The proximity of Marlborough to Swindon – at 12 miles distant it was an hour and a half in the family's light, four-wheeled horse-drawn brougham or just half an hour by train – had terrific advantages as he could take home special friends for certain parts of the holidays. Two boys in particular, Noel Thirkell White and First XI cricket captain A P Scott, had parents living abroad and so 'N T' and 'Scottie', as they became known to the family, were soon seen as additional brothers to the Butterworth girls. Other visitors to 'No. 8' were Hugh's sporting friends Leslie Woodroffe and George Ireland, always referred to by the girls simply as 'Woodroffe' and 'Ireland'.[8] Irene Butterworth remembered those golden summers with affection:

I was only 11 when [Hugh] left Marlborough . . . As I was in the middle of the family I was allowed to join in all the various sports that marked our life both in the house and garden at No. 8. I was always put into his side or team in the position of a handicap because hard as I tried I could never take the boys' 'googlies' at the wicket, although they were always sporting enough to send down a few medium straight balls to begin with. But my innings tended, when I was young, to end in tears. In bicycle polo we played 3 to 1 with 'No. 1' firmly lodged as goalkeeper with cricket pads up to my waist, but when I saw Hugh charge the goal with bike, ball and stick in action, I fled in dismay through the gaps in the box hedge – also in tears. But through those perils I got to know him and that affection has never wavered.[9]

Despite a deep love of all things active, Hugh was certainly not without intellect. Although an operation for acute appendicitis clashed with the examinations for the VIth Form – thus preventing further study at Marlborough – he had every opportunity to read widely whilst at home on visits or during the holidays. Irene thought that:

> He had strong intellectual leanings. . . . I got used to all the banter that went on with the [older] girls, May and Margaret, and his friends . . . full of phrases snatched from the classics, the poets – particularly Browning, Shakespeare, the Bible (because of the compulsory attendance at daily Chapel) and above all the *Rubaiyat of Omar Khayyám*, the Fitzgerald translation which had just been published [5th edition, 1889] and most of them seemed to know it by heart. It was all over my head but I remember my surprise later on when I found that 'Ichabod whose glory has departed' was not a character in Shakespeare but figured in the Old Testament.[10]

Although cricket was undoubtedly Hugh's great love, he also represented the College at rugby, hockey and racquets during his five years at Marlborough, earning his place in the first teams at hockey and rugby and being one of the two 'Racquet Reps' in 1904.

The *Marlburian* attempted to shed some light on the 'Characters of the Hockey XI' in 1903, describing Hugh as 'a fast and useful outside; needs more judgment in passing'. This was followed by a match report of 'The School v G W Bartholomew's XI' played at Reading on the Berkshire County Ground. Marlborough conceded three goals before waking up in the second half and pulling two back; Hugh crossing the ball for G R J Round to score the second, but press as they might they ran out of time.

Rugby was yet another winter sport at which Hugh excelled. Both his father and uncle had been ardent players of the Union Code and had both joined Clifton RUFC in 1874. Hugh's Uncle Alick had been an England trialist in the 1875/1876 season and his father, working his way into the first team as a 19-year-old by the 1877/1878 season went on to captain Clifton in 1880/1881.[11] At 10 stone 5lb, lithe, yet strong and determined with a quick turn of speed, Hugh had the perfect physique for a three-quarter back. His entry in the reports on the members of the Rugby XV compiled in mid-December 1903 reads: 'Till he hurt his knee, he was a very dangerous wing three-quarter of great pace and possessed of a very difficult swerve inwards. He can take passes cleanly and at full speed; his saving and tackling are both fair. His injury to his knee put him quite off his game, and his loss has been severely felt'.[12]

The knee injury was to plague Hugh during his final year at Marlborough and would dog him throughout his sporting career at Oxford. Such was his complete commitment to every sport he played that he was bound to take a few knocks but his knee problems were a constant drain. In 1906 Hugh's knee broke down on the verge of his selection for Oxford in the Varsity match against Cambridge and, cruelly, he was injured again by the time the 1907 fixture came around. The perennial knee problems, coupled with injuries to his ankles, eventually robbed him of his rightful hockey blue and, perhaps, his cricket blue as well.

With such a sound grounding in racquet sports, Hugh's obvious skills were quickly recognised by Marlborough racquets coach A J Crosby. W G Pound and Hugh were selected to represent Marlborough, as Hugh's father had been almost thirty years before, as the College's 'Racquets Reps' for the Public Schools Championship of 1904 held at Queen's Club, West Kensington. Racquets, a game similar to squash but played on a larger court and with a small, hard white ball, is not widely played today beyond a select band of English public schools and private clubs in the UK and North America. In the early 1900s, however, the game was very popular in what are now seen as the first rank of English public schools and as such it attracted a good deal of attention.

Hugh's first and only appearance in the Public Schools Championship was in his final summer term of 1904. Gliding into the second round with an 'easy' 15–5, 15–7, 15–12, 15–18, 15-9 victory against Eton 'Reps' J J Astor and J Steel on 13 April, *The Times* correspondent nevertheless remained unconvinced about the standard of the Marlborough duo's game:

> Although they are certainly a strong pair, Marlborough were rather dis-appointing yesterday. In the rallies Mr Pound made many bad mistakes, and Mr Butterworth often threw away chances of finishing the rally by reckless hitting. They won the first two games easily, but Eton then showed consider-able improvement, and, after getting 12 points in the third game, they won the fourth at 18–15. The fifth, however, was won by Marlborough, who thus secured the rubber by four games to one.[13]

In the semi-finals played on 14 April, Winchester were drawn against Rugby whilst Hugh and his partner Pound were pitched against Malvern in the first game of the day. Play began at 2.00 pm and the standard of play in the two matches was the highest yet seen with the 'form in the first match . . . of a rather higher class than in the second'. Malvern had had a fairly easy journey into the semi-final stage, with their star player G N Foster exuding class, but in Marlborough they met 'a strong and evenly matched pair . . . The Marlborough pair played well early in the match and the service of both players was effective. In the rallies Mr Butterworth again showed that, as a school player, he is decidedly above the average, but perhaps he tried to do rather too much of the work, with the result that the pair did not work so well together as in their other matches'.[14] The first two games were thrilling affairs; the first, which reached 13–all at one stage, could have gone either way but Malvern pulled it out of the fire to win 18–16. Taking the second 15–9, Malvern's Foster then found his form; serving well, hitting the ball hard and low in the rallies and making few errors and the last two games were secured at 15–9 and 15–6. Beaten by 4 games to love, Hugh and his partner had done their coach Mr Crosby proud and coach and boys could at least return to return to Marlborough with their heads held high. Malvern went on to play the Winchester pair of the Hon. Clarence M Bruce and E L Wright in the final with the Hon. Clarence Bruce's Winchester emerging as eventual champions by four games to love.

Hugh would not play Championship racquets for Marlborough again but it would not be the last time he would step on to a racquets court dressed in competition whites, nor had he seen the last of his partner Pound or the Malvern and Winchester stars Foster and Bruce.

That final summer was a terrifically busy time for Hugh as, inevitably, his studies slipped as they gave way to sport, much to the consternation of his form master the Revd Wood. After the excitement of racquets at Queen's Club he immediately immersed himself in preparations for his final season in the cricket XI. The entry in the *Marlburian* after the conclusion of Hugh's final season for The XI notes his improved technique, particularly in the field: 'H M Butterworth (average 34.1). A very much improved cricketer. His batting was at times brilliant, though he is inclined to play too much at the pitch instead of at the ball, a dangerous fault if the ball turns at all. His aggressive confidence as a batsman may well be copied. A keen and sound fielder.'[15] By now Hugh had collected several awards and trophies in all manner of sporting events, including the athletics championship cup and sister Irene remembered Hugh's bedroom with affection during that last year with the main wall covered with 'individual small photographs of friends, school teams, seventeen cups and the brightly coloured caps with tassels that hung from the corners of the pictures. He took his success easily, as he took his disappointments. He loved living. He had every reason to.'[16]

That final cricket season, indeed Hugh's Marlborough career, culminated in the plum fixture on Marlborough's cricketing calendar – the two-day match against Rugby School held at Lord's in late July. Sports mad, the entire Butterworth family had regularly driven over to Marlborough to watch Hugh chase a ball around a field in 'rugger and hockey matches on freezingly cold days' but now, in high summer, George Butterworth trooped his wife and daughters up to London to watch Hugh in his final ever outing in whites for his Marlborough swansong. Hugh went up to London earlier with his teammates after attending their final prize-giving the day before. They travelled with the words of the relatively new master Frank Fletcher and the Bishop of London ringing in their ears. Fletcher had introduced 'enthusiastic Old Marlburian' the Bishop of London at the prize-giving, along with Mr W S Bennett, who claimed the distinction of being the first boy ever to attend Marlborough College. The Bishop had confided to the assembled boys that he had heard, at the universities, that 'Marlborough boys had no side about them' and told of a phrase he had learned from one of his Marlborough masters and which he felt was worth passing on to another generation as it moved on to greater things: 'Look straight at the light and you will always have the shadows behind'. Frank Fletcher remarked that, 'a long list of honours had fallen to the school during the past year' and doubtless Hugh and his First XI teammates had wondered whether they could add to the haul in this, their final 'innings' as Marlborough boys. Sister Irene recalled that: 'In his last year he played at Lord's against Rugby on 26 and 27 July. We went up and stayed two nights at the Langham Hotel . . . in Portland Place. It was glorious weather. Scottie [A P Scott] was captain and he and Hugh opened the batting.' Such was her perspective of the opening day of a fixture that had a long and distinguished history.

Marlborough had first played Rugby School at cricket in 1855 and had first beaten them in 1862. Up to and including the match in 1903, Marlborough had played Rugby forty-six times and had won on fourteen occasions.[17] *The Times* carried a full report on the game over two days:

> Marlborough came up with a reputation as a batting side, and this they sustained, for they went in first on a very soft wicket and between 11 o'clock and a quarter past 4 played an innings of 358 . . . Mr A P Scott, the Marlborough captain, carried off the batting honours with a very fine innings with a score of 155 . . . Mr Butterworth, who had a big share of the 153 made for the first wicket, played a fine forcing game and Mr Ireland too was very good.[18]

'Scottie' and Hugh made 153 between them until Hugh drove a ball to mid-off on 78 and was caught by Rugby Captain G C Tripp off the bowling of D C F Burton. Hugh's other great friend George Ireland made 67 until he too was caught down at third-man. Marlborough's final score for the first innings was 358. Rugby then went in and scored 127 by the close of play and so had to continue their first innings the next day. It was an auspicious start and Hugh's sisters were on the edge of their seats from the opening ball when they took them the following day.

> The excitement was immense. . . . Rugby scored 221 and then 203 in the follow on. During this innings Rugby became set. Wickets were not falling and at the change of the over the captain threw Hugh the ball, to everyone's surprise, as he was no bowler. Hugh sent down a fast one which took [J E Gordon's] middle stump [for 0] and after that Rugby crumpled. Hugh made a duck next innings [clean bowled by his first innings nemesis Tripp], but the necessary 67 was soon notched up. It was a wonderful way for Hugh to leave the school and in two days' time he and Ireland arrived home in time for breakfast wearing 'O M' ties – I wondered how the school would go on.[19]

For a young man not now recognised as a 'bowler', Hugh had, nonetheless, done remarkably well in his 5 overs, bowling 3 maidens and taking 1 wicket for just 11 runs.

With the conclusion of the game against Rugby, Hugh's time at Marlborough was at an end and all that remained was for the Committee of the Old Marlburian Club to confirm the election of Hugh and certain other 'gentlemen' as Members, which they duly did at a meeting on 11 August 1904. At the same meeting the Committee decided to 'present bats to H M Butterworth, G H Ireland, N W Milton and A P Scott for their scores in the Rugby match'. The Club's minutes record that Leslie Woodroffe (Marlborough 1898–1904) was also elected as a Member at the same time, as was a certain Siegfried Lorraine Sassoon, who had joined the College in 1902 and left at the end of the summer term of 1904 with Hugh.

For a pupil with such a distinctly average academic record, it might appear that getting into Oxford at the turn of the nineteenth century for someone with Hugh's family background was almost something of a formality. Hugh gained a place at University College, Oxford for the start of the autumn term of 1904, along with Leslie Woodroffe and George Ireland. Of his other close friends, N T White also secured a place at Oxford – bound for Trinity where he would lodge on the same staircase as Hugh's cousin George – and cricket skipper Scottie won a scholarship to Peterhouse in Cambridge.

Hugh could have eased himself back into family life for the rest of that post-Marlborough summer during which the Butterworths had planned to decamp to the West Country for their family holiday at the end of August 1904, staying first in Lynton in North Devon before moving on to Porlock in West Somerset. But for an 18-year-old cricket-addicted youth, having left secondary school and with time on his hands there was no question of Hugh 'easing' into anything. The cricket season was still in full swing and there were several weeks still to fill before the family vacation. For Hugh this meant applying himself to the very serious business of trying to cram in as many Minor Counties cricket matches for Wiltshire as he could manage.

Records show that Hugh turned out for Wiltshire a total of 21 times, 16 of which were in Minor Counties Championship matches during the 3 seasons from 1904–1906; 5 times in each of the first 2 of those seasons and 6 times during the 1906 campaign.[20] In all his matches for Wiltshire he scored a total of 697 runs; his highest score of 106 being recorded in his second innings against the MCC on Trowbridge Cricket Club's ground in July 1905.

Before the dizzying round of Minor Counties matches began, however, Hugh represented Wiltshire in their annual fixture against the MCC at Lord's on 8 and 9 August 1904. He managed to score 22 in the first innings and 12 in the second in a match that was eventually won by the home side by 90 runs. His first Minor Counties fixture, a two-day match against Buckinghamshire, which began the day after the last day of the match against the MCC on 10 August, took Hugh to Bletchley Park, a location that would achieve lasting fame almost four decades later during the Second World War for breaking code rather than breaking 'ducks'. Hugh went in at no. 3 and scored a useful 30 in Wiltshire's first innings total of 251 but, dropping down the order to no. 5 for the second innings, he did not bat and the match was eventually drawn.[21]

The day following the conclusion of the game against Buckinghamshire the Wiltshire team made the relatively short trip to Northampton to take on Northamptonshire at The County Ground. Wiltshire lost by an innings and 25 runs. Back home in Wiltshire less than a week later, the county side entertained Surrey Second XI at Hardenhuish Park in Chippenham on 19 and 20 August and then travelled up to London for the return fixture at the Kennington Oval two days later, winning the first encounter and drawing the latter. Hugh's final appearance for Wiltshire in the 1905 season was the return fixture against Northamptonshire at Trowbridge and again the visitors ran out eventual victors with a margin of 70 runs.

Hugh had played 6 matches for his county in the space of 20 days, scoring a total of 123 runs in 10 innings; a gruelling schedule by the standards of any period but obviously for the young Hugh, full of youthful energy and a deep love of the game, it appears to have been no trial at all.

A few days later the Butterworths travelled to Devon, yet even when on holiday, cricket was never far from Hugh's mind or indeed from that of his father and intriguingly Hugh's own list of cricket scores includes one of 92 made by Hugh for Lynton Visitors against Lynton Residents.

Hugh's own diary of that late summer break gives an interesting snapshot of family holidays in Edwardian England. There is no description of their outward journey from Swindon, but as the family returned via Minehead, it is reasonable to assume that they travelled to Minehead by train and then via horse-drawn coach to Lynton. The journey would have taken a great deal of organising as besides luggage for a family of eight, some of the family had taken their bicycles.

The match against Lynton took place on 1 September 1905 at that very attractive ground in the Valley of the Rocks. The 'Visitors' batted first. Hugh made 92 and his father 17 not out, out of a total of 155 but the 'Residents' proved far too strong and won by 8 wickets.

A very different match took place later after the Butterworths had moved on to Porlock. After lunch at the Ship Inn, Hugh and his father walked to the cricket ground. Hugh's description of the game revealed that his team 'won the Toss and promptly lost 6 wickets for 28 runs', after which Hugh was joined by his father at the crease. He goes on to tell us that: 'The pitch was truly terrible and the ball did the most remarkable things. I batted for nearly 1½ hours for 43'. Hugh's father made 27 and the innings closed for 104. The home side were duly dismissed for 56.

An Edwardian holiday was certainly energetic; a staggering itinerary of long walks punctuated by equally hard-fought games of tennis. One particular day was, by modern standards, certainly exceptional. Some of the party decided to visit Combe Martin, a small seaside village some 12½ miles away. Most of them went by coach but Hugh and his father George decided to cycle – using very primitive bicycles on non-metalled roads. Their route would have been along the Barnstaple road to Blackmoor Gate – a distance of 8 miles – and they would then have turned right onto the Combe Martin road. After a stiff climb out of Lynton they would have descended down a 1 in 4 (25 per cent) hill into Parracombe with a similar ascent the other side.

Hugh commented that, 'the wind was dead against us. This caused us much discomfort for the first few miles' until, at Blackmoor Gate, father and son turned towards the sea. 'Then we had a grand descent [into Combe Martin] of nearly four miles'. After lunch on the beach they climbed the Little Hangman – an ascent of over 700ft in 35 minutes – but did not have time to continue to the Great Hangman at over 1,000ft. After tea in the village they set off on their return journey, Hugh, even after all that exercise, still brimful of vim, vigour and vitality: 'We had to walk the first three miles but after Parracombe the ride was most enjoyable as it was nearly all down-hill and I came along at full speed.'

Chapter Three
'Univ' and New Zealand – A New Start

After that idyllic summer sojourn in North Devon and Somerset the family returned home to Swindon and Hugh began to prepare for the next stage of his educational career. In October 1904, a month short of his nineteenth birthday, he went up to Oxford to study law at University College.

Signing the Admissions Register as 'the only son of George Butterworth of Swindon', Hugh moved into ground-floor lodgings in New Buildings 1, which faced onto the 'High'. It was the ideal position for passionate, exuberant and idealistic young men of Hugh's acquaintance to gather for breakfast parties or sit up and talk into the early hours debating and propounding theories which might have addressed issues such as social inequality, political reform or religious controversy. Not that University College was renowned as a hotbed of academic rigour during the Edwardian period. Writing to the 'second' Hugh in January 2008, University College Archivist Dr Robin Darwall-Smith remarked that, 'in general [University College] was a very sporty place at this time – not at all intellectual – and someone as good at sports as Hugh would have fitted in very well'.

The institution of which Hugh was now a member could trace its origins back some 655 years to its foundation in 1249, as a result of a bequest from William of Durham. University College or, to give it its full title, The Master and Fellows of the College of the Great Hall of the University of Oxford, was, in 1904, a male-dominated institution which had then, and still has today, a legitimate claim to being the oldest College endowment in either Oxford or Cambridge. Beginning its life as a small college of just four fellows permitted only to study theology, it was not until the sixteenth century that it opened its doors to undergraduates. Eschewing the rather lengthy title of his chosen institution, Hugh, just as today's students do, would almost certainly have abbreviated the name to 'Univ'. Stepping out into the Main Quadrangle, the Radcliffe Quad or studying in the library, built just over forty years earlier, Hugh was following in the footsteps of some already famous Old Members such as Percy Bysshe Shelley – expelled in 1811 for, as the College Register put it, 'contumaciously refusing' to answer questions regarding the authorship of the anonymous pamphlet *The Necessity of Atheism* – and others who came later but who would also go on to find fame. Clement Attlee was one such 'Univ' man who graduated the summer before Hugh arrived and who also went on to serve in the trenches. Unlike Hugh, Attlee survived the war and entered politics and, after serving in Churchill's

War Cabinet throughout the Second World War, eventually succeeded him as prime minister in 1945.

It is interesting to note that the authors of several documents written after Hugh's death appear to link Hugh's career at 'Univ' with the word 'unlucky'. Whether 'luck' had any part to play or not is a moot point but there is no escaping the fact that circumstances well beyond Hugh's control conspired to rob him of high honours, both in the examination hall and on the sports field. A revealing entry in the University College Governing Body Minutes of 27 April 1907 records that 'H M Butterworth would be away' and that permission was granted for this. Something was clearly amiss, indeed Hugh was bound for New Zealand. Hugh was just weeks away from his final examinations and it might seem strange, for those looking in from the outside, that his extended family could not somehow contrive for Hugh to stay in Oxford for just a few more weeks so that he could sit his finals. His Uncle Alick would, after all, have probably been delighted to have been asked to help. But the Butterworth family's difficulties ran much, much deeper than simply a parental decision to move the family lock, stock and barrel to a new life half a world away on a whim. Were there 'tales of financial troubles in the family?' queried Dr Robin Darwall-Smith. There most certainly were, and the family's financial woes had begun even before Hugh had gone up to Oxford.

Hugh's sister Irene had sensed, as youngsters often do, that the equilibrium of the family home had been disturbed at some point in 1903–1904.

When I was about eleven I sensed a change of atmosphere in the home. My father often seemed to be very worried and preoccupied. I was very conscious of this when the older children were away at school. The shadow of insecurity had arisen of which I was totally unfamiliar. I could see that my mother gave him increasing support in every way. I did not know that a law suit had been filed against my father. My parents went up to London for a week and I was simply told that he had won the case. What case I had no idea. Then the following year, either the case was re-opened or a second one was brought. This was much more serious. I know very little about it but it appears that my father, in common with other solicitors of that day, had been speculating on the Stock Exchange with his own and clients' money . . . my father was a solicitor not a stockbroker, and I cannot feel that he knew enough about the Exchange to be a reliable adviser, also he was far too sanguine by nature. It appears that there was only one investment which went very wrong, but it involved a lot of people and sadly enough, not well-off people, whom my father was trying to help. Anyway the courts held him responsible.[1]

Irene remembers that her father became anxious; his moods unpredictable. Everything, it seemed, was sold or cashed in to try and pay everybody off in full. Hugh's Uncle Alick rallied round and helped in formulating the rescue plan which also involved him contributing a good deal of his own money to bolster his brother's reparation. When all was paid off there was very little left. It was, without question, a financial, business and personal catastrophe of enormous proportions for George Butterworth and it struck his family equally hard:

> Our house was sold and practically everything that was in it. The business went on as the other three partners were not involved. My father stayed in Swindon for six months to wind up his affairs. He joined us at the weekends. This great trouble did not destroy his capacity for happiness which was deeply embedded in his nature but it clouded his life. . . . One morning as in a dream I saw the family get into the brougham to drive down to the station and the handsome front door with the heavy brass knocker was shut on us for the last time.[2]

With Hugh already up at Oxford, his father decided to move the family there too – at least those children who were not at boarding school – as a temporary measure whilst he tried to salvage something – anything – from the wreck of his financial affairs. They rented an 'attractive Georgian house' called Grandport on a backwater of the Thames at Folly Bridge; its garden, complete with mulberry tree and, perhaps unsurprisingly, a 'rather inadequate' tennis court, running down to the towpath of the backwater where a punt, tied beneath the arches of the house, bobbed up and down on the water.

In Oxford, with Hugh's father appearing at the weekends, the Butterworths tried to put the past behind them. May, the eldest of Hugh's sisters, was able, through her brother, to join in the life of an Oxford undergraduate. Chaperoned, she attended several College 'Commons Balls' and took part in the gaiety of Eights Week; barges bedecked with flags and crowds cheering on their chosen crews in the 'bumping races'. For a brief and happy interlude there were dances most evenings, perhaps ending with breakfast in College at 4.00 am. Occasionally Hugh, his college friends and May would walk down the garden in full evening dress and sit talking in the punt under the arches of Grandport until the early hours when the small crowd dispersed to catch up on some sleep. May always claimed that those experiences gave her 'a splendid start in life'.

Hugh had been at Oxford for little more than a month before his name started to appear in the national press recording his successes in the sporting arena. Although it may appear strange to followers of modern athletics, used as they are to a season centred on the summer months with training and indoor meets taking place in the winter, in the early years of the twentieth century athletics events ran on into the winter. On a beautifully crisp but cold morning on Tuesday 8 November 1904, a gaggle of hopeful athletes – including two American Rhodes Scholars – gathered at the Oxford University track to compete in the 'Freshmen's Sports'. Signed up for the blue riband 100yd event, Hugh took his marks in the first heat alongside, amongst others, Christopher Maude Chavasse of Trinity College, twin brother of Noel Chavasse also a Freshman at Trinity and the man whose actions would earn him two VCs in the Great War, the second of which, for actions in August 1917, would be awarded posthumously. Hugh had turned 19 a week earlier and having had plenty of fresh air and exercise during the summer was in good physical condition. When the starter fired his pistol the field charged towards the finish. The race, which, according to *The Times* 'did not produce a fast sprinter', was nevertheless a close-run thing; Hugh just managing to breast the tape first in a time of 11.2 seconds, half a yard ahead of Christopher Chavasse in second place. Both men went through to the final to be held the following Thursday – the day after the latter's twentieth birthday. At another well-attended event Hugh improved his time, shaving off that 0.2 of a second and crossed the line first again in a time of 11 seconds dead, Christopher Chavasse pushing him all the way with just inches separating the first three runners. As close as it was, Hugh's victory and his accession to the title of 'Oxford Freshmen's 100yd Champion' may perhaps have soured the excitement of Christopher Chavasse's birthday celebrations the day before.[3]

Hugh, it appeared, seemed intent on filling every available moment of every season with some form of competitive sporting activity. Records show that in addition to competing with the very best sprinters at Oxford he represented the University both on the games field at hockey, rugby and cricket and on the racquets court. He was selected to represent Oxford University at hockey during his first winter at 'Univ' and went on to play in the 1905/1906 and 1906/1907 seasons.

In November 1905, Hugh was a member of the Oxford team that achieved a 'most noteworthy' result by beating Hampstead by 5 goals to 3. It was noteworthy in that this was Hampstead's first defeat of the season and although the score stood at 1–1 at half-time, Oxford 'showed much the better form' in the second half with H Church, E P Poulton and Hugh 'all playing brilliantly'.[4] Edward Palmer Poulton, then in his final year at Balliol College, was the elder brother of Ronald Poulton Palmer, the pre-war England Rugby Union captain and heir to the famous Reading biscuit empire of Huntley and Palmer. Ronald, a flamboyant three-quarter back, was killed by a sniper's bullet near Ploegsteert Wood in May 1915. Edward Palmer Poulton went on to become a noted physiologist with research interests in, amongst other things, diabetes and oxygen therapy.

Selected again the following season, the goal for Hugh in his second year must have been selection for the Varsity match against Cambridge, which was due to be played at Surbiton on 21 February 1906. As a student then in his second year, his appearance would have earned him a blue. Sadly, as has been noted above, that honour was to elude him.

On Wednesday 14 February, Oxford crushed Surbiton by 14 goals to 1, even though *The Times* reported that 'the usual outside forwards were absent'. This was a reference to Hugh and his fellow winger G R J Round, another ex-Marlborough hockey teammate who had gone up to Trinity, both of whom were sidelined through injury. With the Varsity match just a week away, the selectors were trying to delay naming the team for as long as possible. 'For the Oxford and Cambridge hockey match . . . some delay is being experienced in the selection of the Oxford team, owing to accidents to . . . H M Butterworth (University) and G R J Round (Trinity). It will not be definitely decided until Monday whether they will be able to play or not.'[5] Even with the delayed selection there would be no good news for Hugh.

> The 17th annual University hockey match will be decided today at Surbiton beginning at 3 o'clock. Owing to the accidents to H M Butterworth, G R J Round and J C B Drake, the Oxford captain [A M Horsfall, Marlborough and Oriel] deferred the selection of his side until yesterday, but the players mentioned are not sufficiently recovered to be able to play. Oxford have won the last four matches and seven in all. Cambridge have proved successful on six occasions, while three games have been drawn.[6]

Oxford's run of four consecutive victories was broken and at least one source hinted that Hugh's absence may have been a contributory factor: 'Oxford had to play without their two regular wing forwards, Round and H M Butterworth, and the large margin by which they were defeated (4–1) was partly due to their absence.'[7]

Scanning the newspaper columns for a mention of Hugh in the reports of the Varsity hockey match the following year, one could be forgiven for thinking that the commentators had simply dusted off their old copy and changed a few names, locations and numbers. Sadly, for Hugh, readers of *The Times* studying the published post-match report could have been forgiven for being stricken with an overwhelming sense of déjà vu:

> The 18th match between Oxford and Cambridge was decided yesterday at Bromley, and after a close game ended in victory for Cambridge by three goals to two. . . . Both sides had been unfortunate, Cambridge owing to the illness of R S Preston . . . and Oxford not only through the break-down of H M Butterworth some time ago, but also because Gamage, their centre-forward, had broken his collar bone the day before the match.[8]

The recurrent knee problem had struck again and Hugh would never get another opportunity to play in a Varsity hockey match.

In his 'In Memoriam' piece which appeared in the *Marlburian* after Hugh's death, his great friend Leslie Woodroffe recalled that Hugh was,

> a splendid athlete, and, whatever he played, he played hard; but he always recognised games in their proper proportion. He accepted his many dis-

appointments at Oxford with philosophic resignation; it was indeed hard that one, who was regarded as the best hockey forward in Oxford, and who made 130 in the Seniors' cricket match, should have been deprived by ill-luck of the crowning honour.[9]

Although Hugh's friends and relations were adamant that Hugh's injuries and life's twists and turns had somehow conspired to 'rob' him of a clutch of blues including one in hockey, he had more success in representing Oxford at racquets, to which sport he turned his attention in the spring of his first year at the close of the hockey season. In 1905, partnering his old Winchester racquets nemesis, the Hon. Clarence Bruce, who was then studying at New College, Hugh found himself pitted against the losing Cambridge pair of the previous year, E W Bury and his 'weak partner' R P Keigwin. There was every expectation that Hugh and Clarence Bruce would be victorious but it was not to be and the match was lost 4–2. The encounter is recorded in *Fifty Years of Sport at Oxford, Cambridge and the Great Public Schools*: 'It was a good performance by the beaten Cambridge pair of 1904 to win in 1905, for Mr Bruce and Mr Butterworth of Oxford were, though young, both good players. Mr Bury hit very finely and Mr Keigwin had improved, and in spite of his short-sightedness, which was a handicap, played a steady second string game.'[10]

Hugh was chosen to represent Oxford again the following year; his selection for the doubles pair a consolation perhaps for having been beaten at Queen's Club on 18 April 1906 by his eventual partner Godfrey Foster for the honour of representing Oxford in the singles. Hugh duly stepped on court at Queen's Club on Friday 20 April in the company of his old Marlborough racquets partner W G Pound, but this time they were on opposing sides. Once again the outcome of the match did not run true to form:

In 1906 there was a great surprise; Mr Pound, an ugly but determined player, and Mr St J F Wolton, who also had a few strokes, represented Cambridge. Mr G N Foster and Mr H M Butterworth were the Oxford pair, and it was long odds to them. But Cambridge played as they had never played before and snatched an exciting victory by the odd game [4–3].[11]

Two defeats in two years must have been something of a bitter pill to swallow but at least a coveted sporting blue was, by 1906, in Hugh's possession.

Already with 'form' as a Minor Counties player with Wiltshire, Hugh's cricketing career at Oxford began brightly with his selection to bat at no. 3 for 'Mr K M Carlisle's Side' in the Oxford Freshmen's match against 'Mr W S Bird's Side', which began at Oxford on 8 May 1905.[12] Further up the order, and opening the batting with another of Hugh's old Marlborough cricket XI team mates, D V Coote, was the Hon. Clarence

Bruce, whilst his 1906 racquets partner and old public-schools adversary, Malvern-educated Godfrey Foster, batted at no. 4 for the opposition.

Winning the toss, Mr Bird's Side elected to bat first and by the time their innings closed at 6.00 pm they had run up a total of 328. With 20 minutes of play left, Mr Carlisle's opening batsmen struggled with the pace of the wicket and when Coote was bowled out for 2 by the South African Hoskin, Hugh joined Clarence Bruce at the crease. Sadly this pairing with his Oxford v Cambridge racquets partner of 1905 did not last long as Hugh became the second of Hoskin's victims after scoring just 4 runs. Losing 2 wickets for 6 runs in 20 minutes was a disastrous start to the innings but Hugh's side recovered the next day to make a respectable 306. In the second innings the match was there for the taking as Mr Bird's Side were bowled out by mid-afternoon.

> This left Mr Carlisle's side with 180 to make to win, and after a good start by
> Mr Bruce and Mr Butterworth it looked an easy task. Mr Bruce, however, was
> out to a weak stroke on the leg side . . . Mr Butterworth made a few good strokes
> but no one except Mr Burdikin troubled the bowlers for long.[13]

Hugh managed a much more respectable 18 before being bowled by Hoskin a second time, but nonetheless his side were eventually defeated by 67 runs.

It was not until the following season – the late spring and summer of 1906 – that Hugh became involved in a hectic schedule of trial matches which led to his selection for Oxford University in the first of what would prove to be his final total of three 'first-class matches'.

By the time he had commenced the second year of his course at 'Univ' he had already notched up another five appearances during the summer vacation for Wiltshire in the Minor Counties Championship in addition to his first-year per-formances, so his skill as a batsmen was not in question. His performance in the Oxford Seniors match on 1 May 1906 – an innings that, as has been seen, Leslie Woodroffe felt compelled to mention when he recalled Hugh's cricketing feats after his death – was perhaps his finest hour. It certainly served to bring Hugh to the atten-tion of those seeking to select the best batsmen in Oxford.

> Mr Butterworth and Mr Farmer, the two overnight not outs, continued their
> innings for Mr Buxton's side yesterday [1 May], and 150 was on the board
> before Mr Farmer made a tame return to the bowler. . . . Mr Butterworth and
> Mr Farmer played delightful cricket. . . . Mr Butterworth, although he was
> lucky to make so many runs as he was missed five times, has a delightful style,
> and showed no compunction in hitting the loose balls. His best stroke was an
> off-drive between mid-off and extra cover.[14]

Hugh's mammoth haul of 130 runs was almost half of his team's first innings total of 271 and he showed he was no slouch in the field either, taking 2 catches and forcing a stumping in his opponents' first innings.

A few days later Hugh was involved in a trial match playing for 'Oxford University' against a side that went under the name of 'Oxford University Authentics'; a three-day match played on the Christ Church Ground beginning on 7 May 1906. Hugh went on to make 27 in the first innings out of an Oxford University total of 207. His second innings score of 6 out of 310 was not quite up to the standard of his first but nonetheless his Oxford University side won by 81 runs.

Hugh's own record of his cricket scores of 50 and above, which was included in *Letters from Flanders*, include two references to a University Trial match in 1906. These refer to his scores in his two innings in a match between The First Twelve and The Next Sixteen – and the team did actually consist of sixteen players – on 11 May 1906. Hugh made 63 not out, in the first innings – the highest score for his side – and 57 in the second, a consistent performance and one that perhaps assured him of his place in the Oxford University side for his 'first-class' debut in a three-day match against H D G Leveson-Gower's XI played at University Parks, Oxford beginning on 14 May 1906. Also making his first-class debut for Oxford alongside Hugh that day was John 'Jock' Herbert Bowes-Lyon (1886–1930), the brother of Elizabeth Bowes-Lyon, the future Queen of George VI and Queen Mother of Elizabeth II, and of Hon. Fergus Bowes Lyon, 8th Battalion, The Black Watch, killed in action two days after Hugh on 27 September 1915 at Loos. Oxford eventually emerged victorious by four wickets.[15]

Hugh's last two first-class matches were played within a week of each other towards the end of May 1906. Hosting Lancashire CCC on the Christ Church Ground over three days, Oxford were eventually beaten by 141 runs; Hugh scoring a duck and 6 respectively.

The last of the matches to count towards Hugh's first-class tally was played on the University Parks between 21 and 23 May 1906 when Oxford entertained the MCC. In a strange quirk that has, as yet, eluded any attempt at explanation, Hugh actually turned out for the MCC. Batting at no. 3, he scored 31 in the MCC's first innings, improving on his previous highest first-class score of 30 made against Leveson-Gower's XI the week before. Making 9 in the second innings his final first-class game was something of a success as his 'adopted' club eventually won by 134 runs.

Perusing Hugh's list of cricket scores above 50 in *Letters*, it would appear that just over a week later he took up the bat against his erstwhile 'club' when he turned out for Swindon against an MCC side at Swindon. Hugh's records reveal that he made a very healthy 80 runs but that was not the reason why this particular game would enter the annals of Butterworth family myths and legends. The reason, according to his sister Irene at any rate, was that the visitors to Swindon on that day, 2 June 1906, were captained by none other than English cricketing legend W G Grace and that her brother caught him out.

By June 1906 'W G' would have been in his forty-second season of playing first-class cricket during which time he had captained, amongst others, England, Gloucestershire CCC and the MCC. In her memoir dedicated to her father, mother and Hugh, Irene recorded that the 'highlight of the game was when the batting was opened by the great W G Grace'. The bearded, burly sage of the greensward had presumably strode to the crease to take his guard and by the second over of the match it is claimed that he had edged his score up to 4. Irene takes up the story:

> Hugh was fielding in the deep, W G hit what he intended to be a boundary, but Hugh ran like the proverbial hare and caught the ball in one out-stretched hand before it fell to the ground. The great man walked in rather lugubriously but saw two curly headed youngsters – my two sisters – clapping their hands off at the foot of the pavilion. Being a child lover, he stopped and asked them, 'Why are you so excited?' They replied, 'Hugh did it, Hugh did it'. This amused the gruff old celebrity and putting one up on his shoulders and holding the other's hand, he walked into the cheering crowd at the pavilion.[16]

Although Irene Butterworth writes a note to the effect that she had contacted the MCC in 1975 and that a Mr Stephen Green 'went to some trouble' to check her statement that Hugh had caught out the great W G Grace for 4 at Swindon on 2 June 1906, the author, despite strenuous efforts, has been unable to confirm this.[17] This leaves us with a puzzle. Hugh's own record of his cricket scores can be cross-referenced with other sources, so why does there appear to be this anomaly? Perhaps we will never know; perhaps it is one of those lovely, rose-tinted, 'hand-me-down' stories of which every family has a stock, the facts of which, with the telling and re-telling, become entwined with the happenings on other occasions. True or not, it is still a delightful tale and if one lets one's mind free for a moment it is possible to ponder the merits of such a catch, if indeed it was taken in the style Irene would have us believe. We might allow ourselves to muse on the fact that Hugh, then an energetic and invincible 20-year-old, should perhaps have had the presence of mind to 'drop' the ball; after all Grace would then have been 57 years old and the crowd would have undoubtedly gathered to see him bat rather than to watch a young upstart of an Oxford under-graduate field! Nevertheless, given W G Grace's position as the 'father' of the modern game, that one 'catch' – if it was ever made – must have been an historic and un-forgettable moment for Hugh and would have been replayed over and over again in his mind during the years that followed.

It is not clear whether Hugh had to grapple with some tough decisions regarding which teams he turned out for towards the end of June 1906, or whether those decisions were made for him by the Oxford selectors but what is clear is that Oxford began the first day of their fixture against the MCC and Ground at Lord's on the same day that Hugh turned out for Wiltshire against the touring West Indians. In 1906 the West Indian touring side was a quite different entity from the famous 'Windies' sides of the likes of Sir Gary Sobers, Clive Lloyd and Brian Lara but nevertheless there were several black players in the side whose batting and bowling skills could test the best of those gentlemen then playing in the English game. We will never know whether Hugh felt that taking on the men from exotic Caribbean islands such as Barbados, Trinidad and St Vincent by turning out for Wiltshire would challenge and extend his batting skills or that he simply knew in advance that he had not been chosen to represent Oxford and was therefore free to travel to the County Ground at Swindon on 29 June.

Hugh opened the batting for Wiltshire with John Elgar Stevens and was stumped on 19 by 26-year-old West Indian opening bat and fast bowler Richard Cordice Ollivierre of Kingstown, St Vincent, off the slow, left-arm bowling of Trinidadian Sydney Smith.[18] Making 3 in his second innings, Hugh helped Wiltshire to secure an 86-run victory.

Hugh's appearance for Wiltshire at the same time as an Oxford match may go some way to explaining why he did not play in the 1906 Varsity cricket match – won by Cambridge by 94 runs – which took place a little over a week later. The Oxford and Cambridge batting and bowling averages published the same month (July 1906) reveal that Oxford had played 9 first-class matches of which they had won 1 and lost 8. The tables record that Hugh batted for just 4 innings, scoring 38 runs with a top score of 30. There would be a little more cricket to be played that summer but the end of the 1906 season and the academic year 1905–1906 effectively marked the end of his cricketing career at Oxford.

Hugh embarked on his third, and what should have been his final, year at 'Univ' in the autumn of 1906 and he moved back into Room 2 on Staircase X of the Radcliffe Quadrangle into which he had moved for his second year. It was a fine room, recalled his sister Irene, boasting a sitting room with tall windows and a deep window seat which also overlooked the High and, according to Robin Darwall-Smith who has researched the records of students' accommodation, it was deemed a 'rather good' room. Indeed, Hugh's residence in such a room rather surprised the current University College Archivist in the light of the Butterworth family's financial collapse, as both the New Buildings and the Radcliffe Quad offered 'rather classy sets of rooms'. Until the 1930s, he explained, 'rooms were rented out in College on a sliding scale of fees according to their grandeur or lack thereof. There were at least half a dozen bands and yet the New Buildings set was in the third most expensive band and the Radcliffe Quad on the second most expensive one. The family was evidently not very good at retrenching!'[19] It is entirely possible, of course, that Uncle Alick, whose own son George – the celebrated musician, who was then studying at Trinity College Cambridge, was also subsidising Hugh's accommodation expenses.

As noted earlier, Hugh was, at that time, still in the running for representative honours at hockey until injury finally and irrevocably put paid to any lingering hopes of a hockey blue that he might have clung to. By late February 1907, however, it was clear that other important elements of the lives of the immediate circle that made up the Butterworth family were also 'breaking down', just as Hugh's knee had done.

New Zealand – A New Start

The Times of 2 February 1907, p. 14 featured a long list under the heading 'Partnerships Dissolved'. There, buried deep amongst the densely packed litany of the broken businesses of 'grocers', 'boot and shoe dealers' and 'oil and colourmen', was the following: 'G M Butterworth, H W Rose, T Kimber and C C Bradford, solicitors, Swindon, Wiltshire, under the style of Butterworth, Rose, Kimber and Bradford'. It must have been a sickening moment for George Butterworth; there in black and white, in the columns of the very newspaper that had trumpeted his youthful successes on the courts of the All England Club, was the final confirmation that his business had failed. His daughter Irene has gone on record as saying that the 'great trouble' of this experience 'clouded his life' and after what must have been very trying and perhaps tearful family discussions it was decided that there was nothing for it but for George to sweep away the 'clouds' and seek new horizons. Finally, after much soul-searching, it was agreed that he must make a fresh start by sailing for New Zealand to seek employment and begin to forge a new life before calling for his family to join him.

It was always intended that he travel alone but George Butterworth's decision had far reaching ramifications for his only son. After some thirty months of study and just weeks away from his final examinations, Hugh was obviously driven by a sense of filial duty and felt that he could not let his father travel half way around the world alone in the light of the climactic events of the previous few years. He duly wrote to the University College authorities to inform them that he wished to take leave of absence which, as was noted above, was granted by the governing body towards the end of April 1907. And so, just weeks shy of his final examinations, Hugh packed his trunk and left Oxford, never to return. Irene Butterworth recalled that:

> We had distant cousins in New Zealand and they suggested that [my father] should come out and visit them with the idea of us all settling there. Hugh saw that he couldn't possibly travel alone and he gave up his last year at Oxford, which meant having no degree and [ended] his chances of considerable athletic successes, and sailed with him. They were welcomed by our cousins the Archers, and Hugh soon got a small job [as a clerk] at Dalgetys – the huge wool exporters, and in six months time he was taken on as one of the masters at the

Wanganui Collegiate School in the North Island. He was there for his whole time in New Zealand and was extremely happy.[20]

Hugh's mother and sisters sailed to join them later. Irene continues, 'My sister Margaret, went out ahead of us with our late Aunt Fanny's husband and they found an eight-roomed house for us all to live in. We – Mother, May, myself, Molly and Dora – . . . were going to live in Christchurch in the South Island.'[21] It is interesting to note that Hugh's entry in the Wanganui Collegiate School Register more than forty years later, in 1948, even makes reference to the Butterworth family's circumstances at the time:

BUTTERWORTH, H M
1907/14
Owing to financial difficulties gave up what would have been a brilliant scholastic and cricket career at Oxford. First house tutor of Selwyn. Captain Rifle Brigade. Killed in Action 1915.

The December 1907 edition of the *Collegian*, the Wanganui Collegiate School journal, records that Hugh had joined the staff in the September of that year and it was at Wanganui, at least according to John Allen, a man who was to become one of his greatest friends, a future headmaster of the school and the driving force behind the publication of Hugh's *Letters from Flanders*, that his 'real life's work' began. 'For seven short years,' observed Allen in his *Times* obituary of Hugh in October 1915, 'he gave of his best to the service of the school'. Having sailed for New Zealand in the spring of 1907, it had thus not taken him long to make the transition from wool-exporting company clerk to serving schoolmaster but Hugh might never have found his vocation had it not been for the relationship he had struck up with a 'young Englishman' with whom he and his father had shared the passage to New Zealand in early 1907.

That young Englishman had, according to family stories, been appointed to teach at Wanganui but, according to Irene Butterworth, had not been able 'to hold the job' and in talking over the matter with the headmaster, 'the young man remembered Hugh and spoke up well on his behalf'.[22] That young man can now be revealed as E Walker, a brilliant classical scholar with an MA from St John's College, Oxford, who, according to the school's records, took up his position in August 1907 and 'left' by the end of the same year. Sadly, his short tenure was not due to incompetence or misconduct but to the onset of serious illness.

An entry in the December issue of the *Collegian* noted with regret that: 'Mr Walker was amongst the victims of the measles this term. His recovery has been long delayed owing to an attack of congestion of the lungs, but we hope that by the end of the term he will be well on the road to recovery'. That same issue also noted that Hugh had joined the staff just three months earlier. At some point during the early stages of

Mr Walker's illness, when one assumes it became clear to all parties that he was unlikely to fulfil his duties due to failing health, he must have discussed his future with the headmaster and, remembering Hugh from the voyage south, had put in a good word. At the time several masters at Wanganui had been educated in the English public-school system and Oxbridge and on the strength of Walker's recommendation Hugh was invited to travel to the town on the west coast of the North Island for an interview.

The headmaster at the time – Walter Empson BA (Oxford), who was at the helm from 1888–1909 – interviewed Hugh and despite the fact that he was, at 22 years old, not much older than some of the senior boys and had no letters after his name having left 'Univ' without completing his degree, he was nevertheless taken on the staff as an assistant master for the start of the academic year in September 1907. He had no qualifications and no teaching experience but, instead of being a hindrance, perhaps that fact rather went in his favour during his interview with Walter Empson. Hugh's first headmaster had also sailed from England more than twenty years earlier with no particular career in mind, had laboured on sheep stations and had even tried his hand at growing bananas in Fiji before joining the staff at Wanganui. Hugh, however, settled in quickly and again, very much like Empson, soon became intoxicated by teaching and the pace of life at a small but busy boarding school. He confided to his sister Irene that after taking his first lesson, he knew that he 'could do it' and, of course, he spent a great deal of his time out on the greensward or in the nets, coaching what he liked to call his 'young charges' at cricket; it was played over two terms in New Zealand rather than just the summer term, as was the tradition in England. Hugh quickly became known as 'Curly' by the boys on account of his full head of tight, curling, sandy hair. 'From that time – September 1907', wrote one of his teaching colleagues H E Sturge, 'till December 1914, when the call of the War came, he lived in and for the School, "a presence that was not to be put by".' Hugh was ecstatic at securing his new post but life was not all plain sailing. The school board, strapped for cash, pegged salaries at a pitifully low level and masters pestered its members with an endless stream of requests for a raise. Free board in return for duties in boarding houses ameliorated the situation somewhat and a year before Hugh joined the staff had been given their own lavatories, wash basins and had had their rooms papered, but making ends meet was clearly difficult. The headmaster badgered the board on his staff's behalf and some were rewarded but others still languished in penury. Hugh was one of them. In the November of the term he joined he had to go cap in hand and ask for an advance – he could not wait until the end of term when his salary would be paid.[23] Coming hot on the heels of his father's financial collapse, Hugh must have felt acutely embarrassed to have been in such a position.

Although budgets were tight, he nonetheless loved his new life but whilst Hugh's star rose and he flourished in his new role, the 'young Englishman' whose place he had filled in the autumn of 1907 was fading fast. In his speech to mark the end of the year 1907, Walter Empson announced to the school that Mr Walker's health was failing and that there was 'but faint hope of his recovery'. He died in 1908.

Like any community a school has it fair share of triumphs and tragedies and, like any community, change and development is a constant. Wanganui Collegiate School at the start of the twentieth century was no different. Hugh joined an institution that, although still sited close to the centre of Wanganui when he arrived, was about to undergo a period of radical change and development; it was in effect a school in transition. Originally founded in 1852 as a school to serve the local indigenous Maori population and the pioneering community of what was then the tiny settlement of Wanganui, the Collegiate School was built on land granted by Sir George Grey, the Governor of New Zealand, to the Anglican Church in the person of the Right Revd George Augustus Selwyn, Anglican Primate of New Zealand from 1841 to 1868. From its early beginnings as a simple country home, where a handful of students lived with the headmaster, the school population grew steadily and the institution eventually relocated; first to a collection of gabled, timbered buildings on Victoria Avenue which was filled by boarders from all over the country, and then, to accommodate an ever-increasing roll, the decision was taken by the Trustees to move the school to a virgin site at the very limits of the original land endowment during the first decade of the twentieth century. The core of the school that still stands today – the core that Hugh would have been part of shaping – was built during this period. It was a huge undertaking:

> Sand hills were levelled, lagoons drained and trees planted. Much of the hard and heavy work was undertaken by the students. In 1911, four years after Hugh had joined the staff, the 'new school' was officially opened with three brand new boarding houses, a classroom building ('Big School'), a dining hall and the Headmaster's residence. Funds for a new chapel were raised during the first Easter Weekend on the new site.[24]

When the 'new' school was officially opened on its present site in 1911, Hugh joined housemaster H B Watson (1911–1914) on the staff of the newly built Selwyn House, one of the three original boarding houses – along with Hadfield and Grey – named after Bishop George Augustus Selwyn (1809–1878). It was inevitable that Hugh should gravitate towards those of his own age and of similar passions. Of the thirteen staff of the 'Senior Common Room' who gathered for a photograph before the move to the new site, five, including Hugh, had been educated at either Oxford or Cambridge and had joined the year before or a year or two after Hugh. One of those men was John Allen. Allen, who had joined the staff in 1906, had seen active service in South Africa as a second lieutenant in the King's Own (Royal Lancaster Regiment) and had only been promoted to lieutenant in the 2nd Volunteer Battalion of the regiment in England less than five years earlier.[25] He had contracted a form of rheumatism

during the campaign which resulted in bone damage and the shortening of one leg –
hence his nickname 'Hoppy'. A gifted mathematician who would go on to become
senior maths master, John Allen later became acting housemaster of Hadfield House
in 1914 whilst the housemaster Mr Neame was away in England getting married, and
then took over the reins at Selwyn House from 1915–1931.

John Allen was, like Hugh, also passionate about cricket and so it was no great
surprise that these two got on famously when Hugh joined in 1907 and the two quickly
became great friends. 'Hoppy' and 'Curly' became almost inseparable; the open and
optimistic 'Curly' Butterworth being the perfect antidote to 'Hoppy' Allen's more
taciturn nature. Indeed, it had been John Allen's idea to collect together Hugh's open
letters sent back to Wanganui from the Ypres Salient and publish them as *Letters from
Flanders* in 1916. It was Allen too who was instrumental in plans to raise a new cricket
pavilion in 1917 in memory of Hugh and his own brother Charles, who was killed on
the Somme with the New Zealand Expeditionary Force on the opening day of the
Battle of Flers-Courcelette in September 1916.[26]

Hugh later became assistant housemaster of Selwyn House and John Allen, spared
the same fate as his brother due to his medical problems, went on to serve the
Wanganui Collegiate School community until 1935, the last four of those years as
headmaster. It was John Allen who remarked in Hugh's obituary that he had 'played
no small part in this difficult period' of the school's history, which included the
change from the old to the new buildings. Allen wrote that:

> His influence was great and always increasing; he was wonderfully popular but
> never courted popularity. Beneath a modest and somewhat careless exterior he
> had a strong and inspiring personality, the outstanding features of which were
> a large measure of human sympathy, his enthusiasm, his cheerfulness, his sense
> of humour, his unswerving loyalty to his friends and to what he conceived to
> be right. Such qualities could not fail to attract boys; he possessed their
> complete confidence and won their intense admiration.

The following appreciations of Hugh by several pupils of the time who went on to
become very famous and influential Old Boys, were published in the *Wanganui
Collegiate School Centenary Number* in April 1954, and speak more eloquently than
any narrative. The Hon. Kenneth Macfarlane Gresson, LLB. Student number: 1438
(1903–1911). Head prefect in 1911:[27]

> At Selwyn House was Mr Butterworth 'a fellow of most joyous mood and quaint
> contrivings', brimful of fun and humour, invigorating, gifted, altogether
> delightful – a joy to know. Later the war called and he went – never to return.
> Even trench warfare could not quench his irresistible wit, and when the final
> summons came he met it undismayed.

Sir Arthur Porritt KBE FRCS (Eng). Student number: 2177 (1914–1918):[28]

> In 1915 the event that somehow still comes first to one's mind was Mr Butterworth's death. He was essentially, such a 'youthful' master that he was almost automatically loved by every boy that knew him, and his death brought home to many of us, as probably nothing previously had done, the ghastly finality of war.

Arthur Ernest Roy Joblin Esq. Student number: 1887 (1910–1915):

> H M Butterworth's understanding of the boy must have amounted to genius. No words could adequately express our feelings for him. It had been my intention to write quite a deal about him; to describe his sportsmanship, his almost permanent good temper, his brilliant wit, his ever accessible sympathy and his love of all that was straight and clean. I find I cannot do it. One of his Old Boys took up the same profession and he told me once: 'Whenever I'm puzzled, I say, "Now what would Curly have done?" Then I do that'.

Joblin wrote his reminiscences of his teacher some eighteen years after Hugh's death. 'No school', claimed a much later edition of the *Collegian*, 'could afford to lose such a man'. It is a mark of how much the school meant to him that, amongst other belongings, Hugh left all his books to Selwyn House in his will.

As Greek was not Hugh's strong suit he taught English language and literature along with Latin. His sister told of 'strong intellectual leanings', although his colleague H E Sturge reflected later that 'Academic he was not', and yet even Sturge realised that his love of life led him to 'love its reflection in literature'. Sturge tells us that Hugh knew the works of Dickens, Thackeray and Kipling minutely and, in a tribute to what his sister termed 'his solid intellectual merit', was also known to have dipped into Tolstoy in French, Horace and Virgil in the original and Euripides and Aristophanes in translation. He even read the *Ring and the Book*, a 21,000-line, dramatic narrative poem by Robert Browning, in the intervals between matches of tennis and cricket one summer holiday. Away from books and the classroom, he continued to immerse himself in almost every sport and activity imaginable; playing rugby, football, hockey and racquets, as well as adding golf, dancing, riding and motor cycling to his repertoire. Above all, however, and as had been the case in England, when not actually teaching or engaged in house duties, Hugh could more often than not be found on and around the cricket pitches; either spending a great deal of his free time coaching the boys or practising and playing himself. 'Wanganui boys do not need to be reminded of his wonderful scores at cricket', wrote Sturge, 'and of his inspiring captaincy'. An anonymous member of Selwyn House recalled after his death that the boys 'remembered him best on the cricket field'. He was, according to John Allen:

a fine cricketer in the best sense of the word, he was able to inspire others with his own enthusiasm for the game. He devoted himself heart and soul to coaching and, above all, he strove hard to create an . . . atmosphere without which one's efforts are of little value. As a bat, he was in a class by himself here, he made prolific scores in all parts of the country but his greatest joy was to watch a good innings by one of his own boys or to see the School XI play good cricket.

As Wanganui was situated on the southwest coast of the North Island and the rest of his family were resident in the Cashmere Hills district of Christchurch on the South Island, there was little physical contact apart from time spent together during part of the annual holidays. Christmas came in the middle of the long southern hemisphere summer break whilst the autumn vacation included Easter. In the spring holidays – September to October – Hugh and several of the other English-born teachers often rented a house together either in the attractive region of the hot springs of Rotorua or on the Bay of Islands on the east coast of the North Island's outstretched arm. There, according to Irene Butterworth, 'they enjoyed boiling their billycans on the hot sands and becoming acquainted with the Maoris whose home territory it was'.[29] In addition, Hugh spent part of his holidays visiting the homes of some of his pupils, especially the Marshall clan whose houses were a second home to him. There was a very good reason for all this travelling and house hopping. Until 1911 Hugh had survived on a paltry £150 per year as a residential bachelor tutor. When Julian Llewellyn Dove had taken over as headmaster in 1909, far from being valued and paid for their seven-days-a-week pastoral care of the boys, the bachelor tutors had been charged £65 per year for board. At holiday times the school was closed and so Hugh was forced to find alternative accommodation which didn't eat into his bank balance. Lacking funds when he started, Hugh remained chronically hard up although all the boys seemed devoted to him and he had become an almost irreplaceable member of staff.[30]

In spite of his travels with his friends Hugh made it a rule that he would spend as much time at home with his family as he could manage in the holidays. Making the transition from a large house with servants in Swindon to rather cramped, rented accommodation in New Zealand via the comfortable Grandport house in Oxford meant that the Butterworth family did not entertain.

When he made the long southward journey to Christchurch to stay with his family – especially his younger sisters – he was showered with invitations for games of tennis and golf at the local clubs and, not unnaturally for an erudite, athletic and handsome young man, to many dances which were fashionable at the time. Hugh was a good dancer. By that time Irene Butterworth had observed that the young New Zealanders tended to talk rather condescendingly about young Englishmen and so she once challenged a girl, who was 'being very eloquent' on the subject of the lack of virility in the Englishmen. 'Do you include Hugh in this category?' asked Irene, at which the girl looked horrified and replied, 'Of course not. He is just like one of us.'

The holidays appeared to pass all too quickly for all concerned and in April 1913, Hugh invited Irene up to Wanganui for the school's annual sports and dances where she stayed with a married couple connected with the school. Irene remembered a wonderful week of activities and visits, the highlight of which was an invitation from a family to stay with them in their home which lay at the foot of Mount Taranaki or, as they would have known it, Mount Egmont. The scenery was glorious – the mountain resembling Fujiyama, Japan's sacred mountain, in the eyes of Hugh and his sister – and the hospitality warm and endearing. She cherished her memories of that week, all the more so because she was to see Hugh only once more in New Zealand, during the mid-winter holiday of 1913, for by then he had been involved in further momentous family discussions which once more rent the Butterworth family asunder.

It was clear by late 1913 that neither of Hugh's elder sisters, May and Margaret – known as Molly – were ever going to settle in New Zealand with its lack of opportunities for energetic girls with lively minds. Thus it was decided that May and Molly would return to England, there to set up a small girl's school – Barton Court – at New Milton on the south coast in Hampshire, taking a rather ill Irene with them to stay with the ever dependable Uncle Alick in the hope that she might recover. By the end of the year the sisters were rounding Cape Horn homeward bound for the 'old country'. Just eight months later, on 4 August 1914, Britain declared war on Germany and Hugh decided that it was his patriotic duty to give a term's notice in the hope that he could book a berth on a ship bound for Britain in order to enlist.[31]

The decision made, Hugh began to put his affairs in order. First, he asked John Allen if he would open any communication addressed to 'Butterworth, Collegiate School, Wanganui' during his absence and then, two days before Christmas 1914, he visited the Wanganui offices of the district manager representing the New Zealand Public Trust Office to draw up the paperwork to appoint the Public Trustee as his agent to pay life insurance premiums and other matters. More importantly, perhaps, Hugh finalised his will:

THIS IS THE LAST WILL AND TESTAMENT of me HUGH MONTAGU BUTTERWORTH of Wanganui in the provincial district of Wellington and Dominion of New Zealand, Schoolmaster.

    1. I REVOKE all prior wills and testamentary documents heretofore made by me and I APPOINT THE PUBLIC TRUSTEE of the said Dominion (hereinafter referred to as 'my trustee') to be the executor and trustee of this my will.

    2. I DIRECT my trustee to pay my just debts funeral and testamentary expenses.

3. I GIVE AND BEQUEATH the following legacies free of all duties and deductions whatsoever:-

(a) To WILLIAM DENNIS ALLEN son of John Allen of Whanganui [*sic*] Collegiate school, Schoolmaster, the sum of twenty pounds (£20).

(b) To PATRICK RHODES GODBY son of Michael Godby of Pendalton, Christchurch, the sum of twenty pounds (£20).

(c) To my godchild, the eldest daughter of J W Kimber [the child of one of Hugh's father's business partners when practising law in England] of Wokingham, England, the sum of twenty pounds (£20).

(d) To the housemaster, Selwyn House, Whanganui Collegiate School, the sum of twenty pounds (£20) to be expended by him in such manner as he thinks fit and I DIRECT that the receipt in writing of the housemaster for the time being of Selwyn House shall be a sufficient discharge to my trustee.

(e) To my sister MAY BUTTERWORTH of Barton Court School, New Milton, Hampshire, England, my Athletic Cups and Trophies.

(f) To the Library of Selwyn House, Whanganui Collegiate School, aforesaid all my books and I DIRECT that the receipt of the Housemaster for the time being of Selwyn House shall be a sufficient discharge unto my trustee.

(g) To JOHN ALLEN of the Whanganui Collegiate School all my pictures and the residue of my personal effects to be disposed of by him in such manner as he thinks fit PROVIDED that the receipt of the said John Allen for such pictures and effects shall be a sufficient discharge unto my trustee.

4. All the rest and residue of my estate both real and personal of whatsoever nature and wheresoever situate not hereinbefore disposed of I GIVE DEVISE AND BEQUEATH unto my mother KATHERINE [*sic*] BUTTERWORTH of Cashmere Hills, Christchurch, absolutely PROVIDED that if my said mother shall predecease me then I DIRECT that such residue shall go to my said sister MAY BUTTERWORTH.

5. I DECLARE that my trustee may at his discretion sell, call in or convert into money the whole or any part of my real or personal estate either by public auction or by private contract in such manner and subject to such terms and conditions in all respects as he thinks fit.

AS WITNESS my hand this 23rd day of December one thousand nine hundred and fourteen.

Hugh Montagu Butterworth

SIGNED AND ACKNOWLEDGED by the said HUGH MONTAGU BUTTERWORTH as and for his last will and testament in the presence of us together present at the same time who in his presence and at his request and in the presence of each other have hereunto inscribed our names as witnesses.

Hugh waved goodbye to Wanganui, to his beloved school, to his beloved close friends and pupils, for the last time in January 1915 and sailed for England – never to return. He went straight to his Uncle Alick's flat for a night immediately upon arrival and then travelled to Aldershot to sign up as a soldier of the King in a far 'Greater Game' than any he had been involved in before.

Not long after Hugh's departure, his then headmaster, Hugh Latter MA, who had taken over from the Revd Julian Llewellyn Dove in 1914, strolled into Hugh's old and empty classroom one day shortly before the annual prize-giving ceremony. Surveying the scene in silence, his eyes came to rest on the blackboard on which a boy had written, 'in loving memory of "Curly" Butterworth'. Hugh Latter later commented that: 'To many boys, he was the most attractive, the most powerful influence in their school life, and his influence was all for the good'. How tragically prophetic that scribbled comment in chalk was to prove.

Chapter Four

The Rifle Brigade

Reporting to Talavera Barracks in Aldershot on 6 March 1915, after staying the night with his Uncle Alick, Hugh duly began to fill in his application for a temporary commission in the Army 'for the duration of the war'. Answering all the questions on page 1 – confirming that he was ' British born' and answering 'yes' to the question as to whether he was 'of pure European descent', he gave 43 Colville Gardens, Bayswater as his address for correspondence. Turning to page 2 he was required to sign in order to confirm that the particulars given were correct and to request that he be appointed to a temporary commission. As his pen scratched away in the space provided, Hugh Butterworth effectively signed his life away, for in truth the 'duration' of Hugh's war would be a little more than six months.

Although candidates were given the opportunity to state a preference as to which branch of the Army or specific unit they wished to join, Hugh did not write anything down but the following succinct note, scrawled in a spidery hand on a single foolscap sheet which still exists in his service record file held in The National Archives, probably decided his future for him: 'Message from Col. Stuart & A.S.L.F, 2 more subalterns wanted'.

The note is unsigned and undated but it is significant in that Hugh's application for a temporary commission came at the very moment when the call of an outspoken and experienced officer of the Indian Army, recently appointed to command one of the first tranche of Service battalions of Kitchener's New Army, was united with that of an Oxford University philosopher, classicist and Officer Training Corps (OTC) stalwart in an urgent request for junior officers.

'Col. Stuart' was Lieutenant Colonel (later Brigadier General) William D Villiers-Stuart, known universally throughout the Indian Army as 'V–S', whilst 'A S L F' was Major Arthur Spencer Loat Farquharson (1871–1942) who taught at and was a Fellow of University College, Oxford – Hugh's alma mater – from 1899–1942. In March 1915, Villiers-Stuart, who had joined the Army in 1884, was in command of the 9th (Service) Battalion, the Rifle Brigade (9/RB) applying the finishing touches to his unit's training prior to its anticipated departure on active service. For his part, Hugh's referee, Arthur Farquharson – known simply as 'Farky' or 'the Fark' in Oxford circles, was so much more than a tutor, philosopher and classicist. Known to such later literary giants as C S Lewis, he was also keenly involved in the Oxford University OTC, teaching military science to those undergraduates intending to serve in the Army using Lieutenant Colonel G F R Henderson's *Stonewall Jackson and the American Civil War*, first published in 1898, as a set text. Farquharson's promotion to major in the Oxford University Contingent of the OTC had been confirmed as recently as 4 July 1914, and, by March 1915, his considerable intellect and talents had already been harnessed by the War Office.[1] When Hugh finally arrived in Britain and began to pursue a commission in the British Army as a 'temporary gentleman' it is hardly surprising that he should turn to an ex-tutor from his old college and fellow member of the OTC to assist in gaining a commission by asking him to vouch for both his academic record and 'good moral character'. Although not directly involved in teaching Hugh, who had studied law, Farky had nevertheless served as dean of 'Univ' throughout Hugh's time at Oxford and was well known and respected by generations of members of University College. He was just the sort of man who would have remembered Old Members and to have been glad to help by putting in a good word on their behalf. Farky duly completed and signed off two 'certificates' in Hugh's application forms on 8 March, confirming that he had known him 'for the last 10 years' and stating from personal knowledge that Hugh had been 'educated at Marlborough & University College Oxford'.[2] The confluence of circumstances that saw Farquharson – Hugh's personal and academic referee – working at the War Office at a time when its walls echoed to the vociferous and insistent urgings of a thrusting commanding officer like Villiers-Stuart for officers, officers and yet more officers for his New Army battalion of the Rifle Brigade were certainly in Hugh's favour. On the same day that Hugh filled in and submitted his application forms he was seen by Villiers-Stuart, who would have noted from page 1 that he could ride and that in 1903 he had attained the rank of captain in the Wiltshire Regiment, 'Marlboro' College Corps', only resigning his commission on leaving the college in 1904. After he had written 'Mr H M Butterworth' in the pre-printed paragraph, which certified that he had seen Hugh and recommended him 'as a suitable candidate for appointment to a temporary commission in the Regular Army for the period of the war', Villiers-Stuart added, 'I should be grateful if he might be appointed to this battalion' in his own hand. Hugh was then examined and passed 'fit' by a lieutenant colonel of the Royal Army Medical Corps after which the application was duly passed back to the War Office where Farquharson endorsed it two days later.

His path thus decided, Hugh was quickly granted a commission as a second lieutenant and, at the relatively advanced age of 29, became a junior officer in a unit that was, to use the words of its CO, 'a very different battalion' to the one which Villiers-Stuart had first encountered in August 1914. A little more than two months after Hugh had signed his application forms that battalion, with Hugh at the head of a platoon, would board a ship at Folkestone on 20 May 1915 bound for Boulogne, from where it would travel by train to Cassel before unloading, falling in and marching in the wake of its CO 'V-S' towards the sound of the guns in the Ypres Salient.

When Hugh first joined the battalion in March 1915, however, its embarkation date, travel plans and final destination were unknown to Villiers-Stuart or his brother officers. At that time Hugh's new CO was driving the men hard to fine tune his unit before its inevitable overseas posting. After a difficult period of initial training in various locations in the south of England and on the east coast, the battalion had only moved back into Talavera Barracks in Aldershot a month before Hugh had entered the fold. 9/RB was part of 42 Infantry Brigade of the 14th (Light) Division, one of six new divisions that had been raised in late August 1914 from the tens of thousands of volunteers who had responded to Lord Kitchener's appeal for men during the first few months of the war. Originally formed by Southern Command based at Aldershot and dubbed the 8th Division, it had been re-numbered the 14th when enough returning regular army units were eventually gathered together to create a regular division which then exercised precedence over New Army units. A little over eight months after its formation, the 14th Division would achieve the distinction of being one of the first three New Army divisions – along with the 9th (Scottish) and 12th (Eastern) – to arrive in France in May 1915 and to see action on the Western Front.

At Aldershot the order of the day was brigade or divisional manoeuvres across open ground with, to Villiers-Stuart's deepening chagrin, little more than lip service paid to practising for trench warfare. For his part Hugh began to get used to donning his khaki uniform in place of tweeds and a tie or cricket flannels and tried to get to grips with the mores of what must have been, for a rather laid back personality, a very alien existence. He also grew a moustache, that beloved adornment of British Army officers of the time.

The battalion Hugh joined for this final, frenzied spurt of military activity, consisted largely of men – Londoners, Mancunian cotton spinners and the men of West Midlands towns such as Smethwick – of the 'First Hundred Thousand' who had responded to Lord Kitchener's call for recruits in the blazing summer and balmy autumn of 1914. Although 9/RB was a New Army, Service Battalion, formed in the main of volunteer, citizen soldiers for the duration of the existing emergency, it was, nevertheless, part of a regiment with a long and distinguished history. It is interesting to note the tenor of Hugh's letters at this stage in his Army career. They often gave the impression of a civilian in uniform looking at the great institution that was the British Army in a slightly detached way. He wrote regularly to his mother Catherine, to John Allen in Wanganui and his sister May in Barton-on-Sea in Hampshire and the latter, writing daily in return, took it upon herself to keep the rest of the family abreast of his movements. In his second letter to the family he wrote:

The men seem a very nice lot indeed. We have quite a sprinkling of Colonial Englishmen. I share a room with a Rhodesian who has been fighting the Germans in British East Africa. The extraordinary thing is suddenly to be treated with such reverence by everyone one meets. The Colonel is a terror officially, as is my Company Captain but both are very efficient and won't get us unnecessarily cut up. In the Army, seniors apparently curse all juniors, and juniors curse those under them – it doesn't seem a good system. I think I'm getting on alright at any rate. I haven't had a row with anyone which is helpful.

That experience was yet to come.

Hugh's brief pen portrait of his CO would have been recognised as accurate by many under his command. It would not be unkind to record that 9/RB's commanding officer had not been an altogether willing convert to the Rifle Brigade fold. Described by a Rifle Brigade officer of a much more recent vintage as a 'crusty bachelor' of 42, Villiers-Stuart was a veteran of the North West Frontier (he ultimately earned seven campaign clasps) and something of a 'martinet with a low regard of all other officers – superior, contemporary and junior, but he loved his men and was dedicated to soldiering'.[3]

A seasoned Indian Army major serving with 1/5th Battalion, the Gurkha Rifles, William Villiers-Stuart just happened to be at home on leave in Kilkenny in Ireland as the political crisis in Europe lurched from bad to worse during the summer of 1914. Convinced that there would be a war with Germany and equally convinced that he would fight that war with his Gurkhas, on 26 July he had received orders to stand by for a return to India. Two days later he was ordered to report to London and was told by the India Office that his return passage to India would be repaid as all Indian Army officers would be sent out on troopships. After Britain's formal declaration of war on Germany on 4 August he was asked by an official in the India Office if he wished to be considered for home employment with the BEF, then busily preparing for departure for France; 'certainly not,' he replied, 'I wish to go to war with my own Regiment'.[4] With orders to embark aboard the SS *Dongola* at Southampton on 11 August, he moved into the Grosvenor Hotel in London on 10 August and determined to catch the 10.00 am boat train the next morning but in the early hours of the day of departure he received a phone call telling him to report to the War Office immediately. This he did only to be stung by the news that his return to India had been cancelled and that he had now come under War Office orders. 'For years I had been preparing my battalion for war', he grumbled to his diary 'and now I was prevented from joining it'.[5]

The War Office had effectively 'jumped' Villiers-Stuart and many experienced men like him. Faced with the prospect of shaping more than 100,000 raw recruits into effective Service battalions that could take the fight to the Germans on the Western Front, Kitchener and the War Office had seized the opportunity to 'hoover up' as many men on the Indian Army list of officers on home leave as they could, to assist in training the willing but largely untutored mass of citizen volunteers. The rate and scale of expansion of the Army at that time was staggering by any standards and willing or no, the fate of men like Villiers-Stuart was now to be inextricably linked with that of the men, like Hugh Butterworth, of Kitchener's New Army.

After several unsuitable postings, Villiers-Stuart had finally fetched up on Old Dean Common near Camberley in Surrey one morning in late August 1914 where 2,500 recruits had been ordered to report for training with 9/RB under their new commanding Officer, Lieutenant Colonel Arthur Grant – ex-4th Battalion, the Gurkha Rifles. When he had first entered the battalion Villiers-Stuart was absolutely appalled to learn that, including himself and his new CO, 9/RB mustered a grand total of just eight officers. Indeed, a chronic lack of officers appears to have bedevilled 9/RB from its inception and it was a state of affairs that was referred to again and again in the writings of both Hugh and Villiers-Stuart and is even referred to pointedly in the pages of the unit's official War Diary. Little wonder then that Villiers-Stuart, who, after all, had connections with those who could pull strings at the highest levels in the War Office, had sent a note asking for more subalterns at the time of Hugh's application for a commission.

It was not long after the battalion had been raised that 9/RB's already lean Officers' Mess was trimmed again and the casualty was none other than the CO himself. Lieutenant Colonel Arthur Grant had not lasted long in post. A whispering campaign, co-ordinated by a cabal of some of his senior officers during the month of September 1914, had fatally undermined his authority and had made his position untenable. After some discussion and further deliberation, Villiers-Stuart had been ordered to take command of the battalion by his superiors and his elevation was duly noted in the *London Gazette*:

Service Battalions
The undermentioned officers to command battalions of the New Army:-
Dated 1st October, 1914.
   The Rifle Brigade (The Prince Consort's Own), Major William D Villiers-Stuart, Indian Army, 9th (Service) Battalion, vice Lieutenant-Colonel A. Grant, and to be temporary Lieutenant-Colonel.

9/RB's difficulties during the initial months of its training had followed the now well-known template for many Kitchener battalions of its ilk, stuffed full of eager, mufti-clad civilians from all walks of life but with little or no military experience. Too many men, too few experienced officers and NCOs, a paucity of rifles, no blankets, bedding or eating utensils, no uniforms and perhaps worst of all for men keen to belong, no cap badges. After Villiers-Stuart's accession the situation had gradually improved; rifles, uniforms, boots and blankets had arrived along with the coveted caps and badges – sourced by the CO himself from a manufacturer in Birmingham – and the brighter, sharper recruits had been earmarked as future NCOs. The number of officers had also increased: Henry Howard – an ex-RB officer who had retired shortly before the declaration of war – had arrived and had been put in command of A Company and a clutch of bright, young public schoolboys – several of them from Eton

– had come onto the strength, of whom Villiers-Stuart felt that Neville Gladstone, Douglas Carmichael, Herbert Garton and E D Horsfall were the pick of the bunch. Carmichael, for example, was seen as a rising star in the eyes of his CO – 'a delightful man and the bravest person I ever knew' – and as 'an above average officer' was appointed as machine-gun officer. There was also 'a good Australian boy too called Hayward', Villiers-Stuart recalled, 'but the rest of my young officers were pretty useless. The latter were four or five years older than the others and had neither the mental nor the physical capacity of the Eton boys'.[6] Hugh's new commanding officer did not pull any punches when sitting down to gather his diary extracts of the Great War into what, many decades later, eventually saw the light of day as a second volume of his memoirs. His account is replete with caustic remarks and anecdotes regarding the shortcomings of both his subordinates and his superiors in the larger units such as 42 Infantry Brigade and the 14th Division, of which 9/RB was now a constituent part. The following sideswipe at one of the brigade staff may serve as a typical example of his strident views.

> The BM [Brigade Major] was Donald Wood, who I am sure was a really nice fellow at heart but he considered it necessary to play the arrogant staff officer – and there was no doubt about it, he despised people from India. Eventually he admitted he was wrong, but a more congenial and equally efficient man would have done much better.[7]

Equally, for those men whom, in Villiers-Stuart's eyes at least, had 'come up to the mark' he demonstrated an unfailing loyalty and respect. In the dedication to Book II his editor, Robert M Maxwell, noted that:

> V-S has not always been very complimentary about his officers, but it must be remembered that his diaries were private and he is therefore entitled to vent his wrath – to himself – at some of their shortcomings. He would however, be the first to admit that he made exceptional officers, fit to take over his battalion – his pride and joy – and to maintain it at his high standards.[8]

What, one wonders, did Villiers-Stuart think of Hugh – this active, 29-year-old, civilian ex-schoolmaster with an independent streak? Did he fall into the Villiers-Stuart category of 'pretty useless'? There is no direct reference to him in his CO's memoirs, only two tantalising snippets in which 'schoolmasters' are mentioned with not a little disdain. The first concerns an incident that occurred towards the end of 9/RB's time at Aldershot – crowding years of normal training into just two months – when Villiers-Stuart was ordered to attend a 14th Division conference at Witley in Surrey on the subject of officer strength. When asked what he was short of Villiers-Stuart replied, 'four majors and six captains'. Firmly rejecting the idea that officers be transferred to him from other units, he proposed that he be allowed to promote officers internally, an idea to which the divisional commander, Major General Victor Couper, agreed, to an audible sigh of relief from the other commanding officers present. This meant that some of Villiers-Stuart's brightest and best 20 and 21-year-olds – Neville Gladstone and Douglas Carmichael to name but two – would go to war as captains and majors, much to their delight. But, although the dates in the Villiers-Stuart memoirs are sketchy – a special file of all key dates that he intended to insert into the finished manuscript was accidentally burned – other officers were still being posted at around the same time that Hugh obtained his commission. 'At the last moment we had a great blow. Three schoolmasters were posted to us. Two I have forgotten, the other I will never forget. His name was Thomson [*sic*] and he came from Charterhouse – a poisonous person, conceited and a coward.'[9]

The second reference to 'schoolmasters' came on 22 May 1915 when the battalion had been in France for less than two days. Villiers-Stuart was keen to stamp out any 'slackness' regarding breaking out of camp and flouting the rules on the smoking of cigarettes which might result from his charges feeling that they could do as they wished on these matters as they were now on 'active service'. After publishing his orders and putting the men straight, the CO turned to his subordinates.

> I then had all the officers up and told them what I thought of them and that unless everything went on just as I had taught them I would consider they were not capable of doing their duty, and I would consider their replacement. I never had to speak to them again except in two cases – both of them schoolmasters who were thoroughly bad in every way. I had no opportunity to discover how bad they were or I would never have kept them so long.[10]

Hugh's letters written from the front line reveal that he did indeed experience one or two run-ins with Villiers-Stuart and certain of his brother officers, including his 25-year-old D Company commander, Captain the Hon. Francis George Willoughby, whilst 9/RB was serving in the Ypres Salient. He was honest enough to recognise when he was at fault but reading between the lines it is clear Hugh felt that Villiers-Stuart was something of a martinet, although one never gets the impression that there was any question of open hostility or feeling of loathing. On one occasion, on 23 June 1915, with the front still in a state of flux after a British attack on the Bellewaarde Ridge just a week earlier, 9/RB found itself on the receiving end of several ferocious German bombardments with sniping and machine-gun fire thrown in for good measure. Obviously intent on making the British pay for stealing some of their front-line trenches sited on a tactically useful stretch of elevated real estate, the Germans threw up a plethora of observation balloons whilst their aeroplanes continually buzzed over the newly captured trenches. On the night of the 23rd Hugh had just come off duty when Major Davis hustled down the trench and 'with the air of a man imparting cheery tidings' told him that a number of Germans had broken in between two lines of trenches and an attack was expected. D Company duly 'stood to' and peered into the darkness of no-man's-land. In his anxiety to 'give the Germans a cheery reception', Hugh told his platoon to, 'fix swords (you'd call them bayonets but I am an RB)' and the message duly crackled along the D Company line like a brush fire; unfortunately passing battalion headquarters on its way. A few days later Hugh wrote:

> It appears I was wrong and messages came hurtling down the line, 'Who gave the order to fix swords?' I put on my best countenance and waded up to Headquarters and told the commanding officer I was the culprit having contravened army order 3214 paragraph 14 9 (a) (i)!! However the commanding officer was very nice and explained the 'whys' and 'wherefores' and we parted on excellent terms.

Three days later, on 26 June, at the end of that particular nerve-wracking tour of duty, Hugh's platoon was the very last of the battalion to leave the trenches after a very difficult and dislocated night-time relief. With daylight already upon them, Hugh was resigned to his men – fully laden, with heavy greatcoats on and carrying shovels as well as rifles – being 'cut up' as they exited the safety of a communication trench somewhere along the Menin Road. Providentially a thick mist descended at just the right moment at which point Hugh ordered his sergeant to lead the men up and out of the trenches and to ' leg it as hard as he could go' across the open. They reached the relative safety of the suburbs of Ypres after galloping 'like race-horses' cross-country and then down the Menin Road, just in time to meet Villiers-Stuart who had 'popped up' from nowhere to greet them. He did not like what he saw. 'The Colonel told me we were marching like the Grenadiers,' wrote Hugh, 'which, he as a Ghurkha – regards as a horrid insult'. Hugh apologised profusely and told his CO that he had made the trip from the front line in record time, which seemed to mollify the grizzled Indian Army veteran. It is impossible to say of course but perhaps a steady accumulation of such incidents, including another breach of Regular Army etiquette almost a month later on 21 July 1915 when the battalion was 'at rest' in bivouacs near Linde Goed Farm between Busseboom and Brandhoek, struck a chord in Villiers-Stuart's mind when he came to set down his own story of the war and later recalled his relationships with his 'schoolmaster' officers.

Hugh did not have a good day on 21 July 1915. He had already spent two nights on working parties helping build a redoubt several kilometres west of Ypres. As orderly officer that day it was his job to move around the battalion and check that all was in order and he was just in the process of inspecting his own company's lines when the adjutant, Moore, 'came charging round to my bivouac to know why A Company lines were dirty'. As Hugh was still busy inspecting D Company he had not even reached A Company and so 'mutual recriminations followed' after which spat Hugh proceeded to mount the guard. What followed next must have bamboozled and slightly humiliated the independent-minded Wanganui man with his naturally 'slouching gait and lackadaisical manner':

> When I had finished the worst parts the commanding officer turned up and began to look on in his most crushing manner. When I told the guard to move to their post, the commanding officer recalled them three times. Each time I tried to find some new fault in what they had done. Finally the brigade sergeant-major, suggested that I had better ask the commanding officer's permission to move off the men. I did so and it was graciously granted. The sequel was a biting note to all officers (we get these three times a day) explaining that they had better learn squad drill, and they might also learn that it is not etiquette to move off troops without the commanding officer's leave, if he is present.

As a New Army officer Hugh had already been 'moving parties numbering from ten to a hundred about under shell fire for some weeks', so his final comment that the 'etiquette' of moving three men across a road 'leaves me a little cold' clearly demonstrated his irritation with what he obviously viewed as a tiresome layer of 'Old Army' pettiness.

Whether Hugh was, or was not, respected by Villiers-Stuart for his talents as an officer we shall never know now for sure. He was certainly elevated to command D Company when Captain Willoughby – a man whom Hugh described as 'a fine man and a very efficient soldier' – was killed instantly by a shell, which 'obliterated him entirely, leaving no trace', on 9 August 1915. Hugh felt his loss keenly and wondered whether he was up to the job of commanding a company as he knew he had 'a difficult place to fill'. Whether his promotion to company commander was due to his abilities as a leader of men or more simply a matter of being the next man in line due to a shortage of suitable candidates is now a matter of conjecture. Suffice to say that by mid-August 1915, of the four original company commanders three – Herbert Garton, Francis Willoughby and Captain Harold Thompson – had been killed or wounded and all their replacements, including Hugh of course, had been junior officers of D Company.

To his family, however, he certainly looked every inch the British officer in the photograph he had had taken of himself in uniform before he sailed for France, even though it unnerved his sister Irene. That photograph – a copy of which was sent by Hugh to John Allen, was very different from the ones in which he had appeared as a vibrant, fair-haired young man with a twinkle in his eye during his Wanganui years. Hugh himself did not think that John Allen would 'like it particularly' conceding that it made him look 'too much the sort of advertisement for the British Army'. For Irene, the image 'gave no impression' of the man she had known and loved. 'Here was the picture of almost a stranger, who like millions of others, was facing the fact that he was laying down something that was to him vitally important – the joy of actual living.'[11] It was an image that would stay with her, for she would see Hugh just once more prior to his departure on active service:

> It was an extraordinary experience to see Hugh again in March, 1915, for one brief weekend in London. He was in khaki and had grown a moustache. We went to a theatre I remember on Saturday night and the next day lunched with Uncle Alick and an old friend, who was to become his second wife. . . . It seemed a totally unreal and sad experience to me, and I so wished that I could have spent that 24 hours at Barton-on-Sea, where May and Margaret had opened a girls' school. . . . But in the light of what was going to happen, it seems now quite irrelevant.[12]

Irene was, of course, referring to the dreadful events of 25 September 1915, but it was clear for all to see, even in the final few weeks prior to Hugh's departure for the front, that a great swathe was being slashed through the young men of his class and acquaintance during the early part of 1915. The British Army had been heavily engaged for almost nine months and had fought its way along the route of the long retreat from Mons to the Marne and back up to Ypres again, where the best part of the old Regular Army had finally perished.

The year 1915 is often referred to as the 'forgotten year' on the Western Front with many of its battlefields dubbed 'forgotten fields'. They are not 'forgotten', of course; simply not as immediately evocative and therefore not as often visited as some of the more well-signposted sites of Ypres and the Somme. For the British Army, however, the Flanders Fields of 1915 had witnessed a series of 'firsts'. In March it had gone on the offensive for the first time in its own right when, four days after Hugh's application for a commission, it had launched an attack against the German trenches standing sentinel around the village of Neuve Chapelle, south of Armentières, in order to secure the vital ground of the Aubers Ridge beyond. Preceded by a bombardment, the ferocity of which had never before been witnessed on the Western Front, the German line was overrun by nightfall and during the course of another two days of heavy fighting the Germans had been driven back 1,000yd on a front of some 4,000yd and out of the village itself. But the final objectives had not been achieved.

A little over a month later, on 22 April, it was the turn of Germany to score a 'first' by 'perfuming' the pages of military history with the first use of poison gas – chlorine in this case – as a weapon of war, in their bid to break the British at Ypres and drive through to the Channel ports to secure an operational victory. With Hugh and the rest of Kitchener's New Army men still only half-trained and unable to take the field, the helter-skelter fight that followed sucked in those returned regulars, wounded at First Ypres, only for them to perish in the second round. Thus, what little remained of the 'Old' Army disappeared into the vortex of the

Salient which then began to suck in the men of the Territorial Force, Empire and Dominions.

Still heavily engaged at Ypres, the British Commander in Chief, Sir John French was nevertheless urged by his French counterpart, General Joffre, to press again at another point on the British front, this time by launching an attack, on 9 May 1915, in concert with a second French effort further south in Artois. Once again, the British objective was the capture of the high ground of the Aubers Ridge, thus denying its advantages of observation to the Germans and menacing Lille whilst simultaneously drawing German attention and manpower away from the struggle still raging in Belgium to the north. Fighting adjacent to some of the same ground as had been contested at Neuve Chapelle, the Battle of Aubers Ridge lasted for a day. No appreciable ground was taken and German reserves did not pour forth from other sectors to assist the defence. A total of 11,185 British soldiers became casualties. A week later and just a little further south, Sir John tried once more. This time the name of the battle, which began on 15/16 May and lasted for ten days, would become known to history as Festubert.

And what were the results of these various setbacks and Herculean efforts by the time the fighting had subsided at Ypres and Festubert on 25 May? Neuve Chapelle village captured and the British line edged forward and straightened just beyond it at a high price; the British and French forces around Ypres driven back to a tighter line to the east of the town with a terrific toll in dead and wounded – yet at least Ypres had been saved; a meagre amount of flat and shell-pitted ground taken at Festubert, again at heavy cost – but at least German reserves had been dispatched to counter a possible break in. At Aubers Ridge, however, there had been no such redeeming glimmers. Aubers Ridge had been an unmitigated disaster. There, on fields few visit today, the price in killed and wounded, for no gain whatsoever, was almost too dreadful for words.

It had been noted, by those who had eyes to see, that the length of the subsequent casualty lists that appeared in both the national and local press was increasing at an alarming rate and many names of Hugh's Marlborough and Oxford friends were amongst them; Kenneth Woodroffe being the first of the three Woodroffe brothers to lose his life. In April Hugh wrote to May: 'The last few lists have a lot of the names of my friends in', then, later, he informed his family that he had, 'just got the news of Anthony Wilding's death but I am afraid we have almost got resigned to it in the Army'.[13]

On 20 May Hugh and the rest of 9/RB finally crossed the Channel for France. He had had just nine weeks of training. Prior to embarkation he wrote to his family of the wonderful weather; day after day of sunshine which brought out the amazing beauty of the spring countryside. The fine weather held during their first few weeks in France and Hugh penned what would become the first of his printed *Letters from Flanders* on 25 May 1915 in what his friends called his trademark 'unadorned and colloquial style':

We pushed over here the other day via Blanktown and Censorville and finally bumped into a village to accompaniment of distant cannon . . . We are absolutely on clover . . . a ripping farm . . . a ripping pond. In fact the back of the front is a good spot. We live like lords with unlimited food and beer.

Hugh knew, however, that the good times could not last and that he and his battalion did well to make hay whilst the sun – literally – shone, for their induction into the dark arts of trench warfare was just days away. 'What a contradiction', his sister Irene later remarked, 'that times of wholesale massacre should be preceded with such a display of beauty on all sides'. Hugh's company, she added, would become involved in the 'real war' on 16 June 1915.

Hugh could not, in late May 1915, have been aware of the particular slice of the Ypres Salient to which his battalion would eventually be allotted but the simple comment with which he concluded that first letter to his friends and pupils in Wanganui was more to the point, heavily ironic and much less philosophical than that of his sister: 'Shall push on to Bloodville shortly I suppose.' For Hugh and the men of 9/RB, their 'Bloodville' would become known to posterity as the Bellewaarde Ridge.

Chapter Five

Into the Salient

By the end of May 1915, 9/RB had been well and truly welcomed into the Theatre of War by both General Sir Herbert Plumer, the recently anointed commander of the British Second Army in the Ypres Salient, and Lieutenant General Sir Charles Fergusson, commanding the British II Corps in whose area of operations 9/RB would first see action. Hugh had thus marched through Godewaersvelde under the gaze of General Plumer on 30 May and the following day had stood to attention in Zevencoten to listen to Lieutenant General Fergusson's address before marching off at 7.00 pm that evening with an enlarged platoon of fifty men armed with rifles, picks and shovels to begin his war rather unglamorously, digging 'entrenchments' in the vicinity of 'Belgian Battery Corner', a few kilometres southwest of Ypres.

Perhaps this was not quite the war he and the Kitchener men in the ranks had envisaged when they had signed on so eagerly the year before, for this was dirty, back-breaking hard labour at its worst without the faintest hope of seeing any German soldiers, let alone taking them on in hand-to-hand combat. After digging and sweating all that first night the battalion returned to billets over 8 hours later after covering a total distance of 11½ miles there and back; the only casualty being the deliciously named Sergeant Cakebread, who fell out injured.

The battalion's gradual immersion into service at the front followed a similar pattern of labouring duties for the next few days; always moving out towards dusk to confound German observers, digging all night in the same area then returning to billets in the early hours just before sunrise for a few hours of well-deserved sleep. Casualties were light for the sweat expended; two twisted knees and a twisted ankle, but there may have been a few tears and a little blood as well as it was reported that – rather unluckily for him – one man was 'driven over by motor lorry' in the dark. The casualty figures were soon set to rise, however, as 9/RB was, like every other raw battalion then being sent out to France, attached to a more seasoned unit for a period of formal induction into trench warfare on 6 June.

By the time Hugh wrote that he was 'in the trenches and having a thoroughly satisfactory time . . . we are all being instructed in trench fighting' on 10 June, his D Company had been in the front-line trench system for a day as guests of the 1/6 Battalion, the North Staffordshire Regiment of the 46th (North Midland) Division; one platoon attached to each of the four companies of the North Staffs in the trenches just north of the Franco–Belgian border opposite the German-held town of Messines.

This sector, in close proximity to the village of Ploegsteert – Plugstreet to the British – and its associated wood, had settled down after fierce fighting towards the end of 1914 and had even witnessed the famous Christmas Truce of that year. As such, it was deemed a relatively 'safe' sector to use as a 'nursery' in which to induct newly arrived battalions into front-line service and the trench routine. Lieutenant Colonel Villiers-Stuart, an experienced soldier, later remarked that the shelling was negligible and that moving at night through trenches and the trench routine was much as he had imagined it to be but it was the 'smell' – a mixture of human and animal-body decomposition and chloride of lime – that was novel. It was a smell that pervaded the Ypres Salient; a smell that Villiers-Stuart later admitted, 'one got used to . . . not to mind . . . and in the end to almost miss'.[1]

Hugh did not mention the odour but evidently did not find his introduction to war on this sector of the Western Front too taxing and he was keen to tell his friends and pupils at Wanganui all about it. Writing from a dug-out, 'made of sand-bags with a corrugated-iron roof and with a glass window facing the rear', he told them that he was a guest of the North Staffs officers and had been out and about with them, sloshing around in the mud visiting advanced listening posts 50 or 60yd yards from the German fire trench or crawling up and over the British parapet to discuss the merits of the wood and wire obstacles known as *chevaux de frises*. Back in the officers' dug-outs they were, he said, living 'like lords'. Hugh regaled his readers with tales of lunch which, on 10 June, included, 'pâté de foie gras, comabere (or however you spell it), cheese, stewed apricots, biscuits, almonds and raisins, white wine, coffee and benedictine'. It was a fine repast indeed, interrupted only occasionally by 'bullets pattering up against the wall!' Hugh concluded that it was, 'very gentlemanly warfare', apart from the fact that at the end of that particular letter he signed off with the breaking news that: 'My servant has just got one in the head – not badly – which is highly annoying to me'. Not half as annoying perhaps, as it was for No. 1941 Rifleman Collins, who was the only D Company man wounded out of a total of five in the battalion on that day![2]

The attachment to the North Staffs ended the following day and 9/RB marched back to a rest camp where Hugh built, 'a fine "whare", 2 water-proof sheets fixed on wire between trees and my Wolseley valise to lie on. Très bon.' Eventually the battalion reached sanctuary in huts near Ouderdom, south of Vlamertinghe on 14 June. There it remained whilst several of Hugh's brother officers, including Second-in-Command Major Davis, Captain Willoughby, Captain Howard and Lieutenants Scholey and Heycock, went out on reconnaissance in what the War Diary sweepingly refers to as the 'vicinity of Ypres'. In reality they were gathering information in preparation for the battalion's more active role in the imminent British offensive planned to sweep the Germans from their dominant positions on the Bellewaarde Ridge, some 3km east of Vauban's angular ramparts of Ypres and bounded north and south respectively by the clean, straight lines – on the map at least – of the Ypres–Roulers railway and the infamous Menin Road.

The ground over which the coming British offensive was to be fought was already soaked with the blood of British, Irish, Canadian and German soldiers who had lost their lives in several bitter struggles for control of the relatively low but nonetheless militarily significant heights of the Bellewaarde Ridge and adjacent Hooge sectors. The ferocity of these encounters, instigated by both German and Briton in equal measure, was testimony to the tactical importance of this particular plot which, at that time, was at the very apex of the Ypres Salient.

When the time came for Hugh's battalion to move forward in support of the coming attack, the opposing lines on the Bellewaarde Ridge had ebbed to and fro several times. On 25 May, the very day that Hugh had penned his first letter from that 'ripping farm' at 'the back of the front', the final scene of the final act of the Second Battle of Ypres had been played out in what later became known as the Battle of Bellewaarde Ridge – 24/25 May 1915. Just over two weeks earlier, however, in a previous scene of the Bellewaarde saga, the Canadians of Princess Patricia's Canadian Light Infantry had stood firm on the Bellewaarde Ridge directly in the path of the German juggernaut that had steamrollered its way southwest down the slope from Frezenberg after that village's earlier capture. The hammer blow had fallen on the 550-strong 'Pats' at 4.00 am on 8 May 1915 and they had fought for their lives; beating off a series of German attacks under an almost incessant rain of high explosive until finally relieved at 11.30 pm. Their losses had been staggering – over 350 men – but they had stood their ground and had helped save the Bellewaarde position.

The Germans, however, did not let matters rest there; the lure of the advantages of the ridge for observation and thus dominance of the British lines of communication west towards Ypres and beyond was just too strong. At 2.45 am in the early hours of 24 May, the Germans had reprised their use of chlorine gas, which they had used to raise the curtain on the Second Battle of Ypres a little over a month earlier. Although fought over a front of some 5 miles on ground north and south of the eponymous ridge, as well as on the ridge itself, the Battle of Bellewaarde Ridge opened in a swirling cloud of chlorine – the largest gas attack to date – punctuated by the thump of artillery and crackle of small arms fire as the German infantry came on behind; this time succeeding in their westward drive to secure the vital ground around Hooge and the crest of the ridge to the west of Bellewaarde Lake and Farm upon which stood Railway Wood. Exploiting a flimsy junction between units in this sector, the Germans penetrated the British defences in Railway Wood and Y Wood to the south and even drove across Cambridge Road – the track that ran north from the Menin Road and joined the two woods – to seize Witte Poort Farm. Several British counter attacks succeeded in forcing the Germans back across Cambridge Road to a line running south from just inside the easternmost tip of Railway Wood down to and along the eastern fringe of Y Wood. But as the British attacks ran out of steam – and crucially out of men – in the teeth of withering German fire, the fighting died down and when, during the night of 24/25 May, the Germans finally called time on any further offensive operations – and Second Ypres duly fizzled out – it was there that the line solidified to German advantage.

Fierce but bloody localised struggles on 2 and 3 June succeeded in heaving the British from Hooge Château and dumping them into the Château's stables some 50yd distant to finally secure the sector. This left the British garrison in the Château stables dangerously exposed as the rest of the British line swept back across the Menin Road in a deep southerly arc to skirt the northern edge of Zouave Wood only to emerge back on the Menin Road roughly at the junction with Cambridge Road before snaking north towards the line of the railway. Now the Germans could get to work and concentrate on building, deepening and strengthening their new front-line system, which tied in a portion of Railway Wood on the forward slopes of the Bellewaarde Ridge, with Y Wood and the entire Hooge Château position. Just behind they made good use of what was left of the walls, finger-like chimney breasts and splintered roofing of the battered but highly prized Bellewaarde Farm which, due to its commanding position on the summit of the Bellewaarde Ridge, became a fortified position in their second line; its ruins and cellars concealing many loopholes and at least one machine-gun post, angled to sweep the ground dropping away to the south and southwest. Everywhere in this sector the German line dominated the British position; puffing out its chest on the crest of the ridge to correspond with the backwards kink of the British line. From Bellewaarde Farm and their foremost fire trenches, German observers had unrivalled and sweeping vistas out over the British lines to the west – towards what remained of the once majestic spires and towers of Ypres – and to the south, dominating the British lines of communication along both the Menin Road and the line of the railway to their junction at Hellfire Corner. Scanning further south, the Germans could see down to Sanctuary and Zouave Woods towards Zillebeke and beyond these their eyes could rest on the mound of desolation that was Hill 60.

It was a key position and the British determined to straighten the line and recapture the Bellewaarde Ridge on 16 June 1915 in a 'minor operation', which was also planned to divert German minds from another, and in the view of the Commander-in-Chief, Sir John French, more important attack at Givenchy to be launched on the same day some 30 miles to the south. The bulk of the task was handed to the battalions of 9 and 7 Brigades of the 3rd Division with 9/RB and other inexperienced units of the 14th Division drafted in to act as the V Corps reserve.

Although the British had, it seemed, always been plagued by a chronic shortage of shells of every type, the bombardment that began at 2.50 am on 16 June and lasted for just under an hour and a half, proved sufficient in duration, power and intensity to shatter the German trenches, scatter their wire and unnerve the front-line troops.

Just 20 minutes after the opening of that bombardment, Hugh was sitting and whiling away the time writing a letter in a 'very narrow packed trench', somewhere near the railway embankment just east of the ramparts adjacent to the Lille Gate of Ypres. He had been there since midnight. After having set out at 10.00 pm on the night of 15 June, the battalion was to move forward only on the orders of the Corps Commander to either exploit an opportunity if the assault went well or help avert a disaster if the Germans turned defence into attack. Under a terrific bombardment Hugh observed that shells were 'fairly hurtling through the ether' and he was convinced that he was about to take part in 'one of the biggest battles in History. With luck the sun ought to be up in half an hour – at about which hour my watch ends. But what a life!'

The move forward in the dark had been 'cheerless' only ending 'by a double along a railway-track from sleeper to sleeper . . . have you ever seen a Company armed to the teeth and shovel doubling along a very much "Jack Johnsoned" railway line with splendid shell-holes all over the place? A delightful experience.' Not so for the men who, after arriving, had been set to 'digging latrines and making improvements' whilst their CO awaited further orders. Hugh was still there, still scribbling under the canopy of the British barrage at 6.15 am:

> A terrific bombardment has been going on for the last three hours. . . . I expect the main attack will develop (good word that) in an hour or so. I shall probably not be in the limelight until a good deal later. . . . Well, au revoir. This is June 16th, and we ought to get something done by Waterloo Centenary. Perhaps we are about to make history – perhaps not.

On this occasion Hugh's battalion would not be required to 'make history' but by 6.15 am several battalions of the 3rd Division – including Royal Fusiliers, Royal Scots Fusiliers and Northumberland Fusiliers, the Lincolns, the Liverpool Scottish – including Noel Chavasse, later VC and Bar, whose brother Christopher had been beaten into second place in the Oxford Freshmen's 100yd by Hugh in 1904 – and the Honourable Artillery Company, had certainly contributed much to the annals of their respective regimental histories.

The attack had gone in at dawn 2 hours earlier; the first wave overrunning the German front line that ran along the eastern edge of the long arm which made up the shape of the letter 'Y' of Y Wood with ease. They were followed quickly by the second wave but, flushed with excitement, the inexperienced and eager troops of 7 Brigade behind, intended only to move if required, could not contain themselves and dashed across no-man's-land into the smoke and fire towards the captured trenches and simply kept going, on up the slope towards the second and third German lines. Total chaos ensued. Men ran into their own barrage, officers were killed or wounded, units became mixed and no one knew who or where anyone was or was supposed to be. The Germans capitalised on this lack of command and control and mounted several determined counter attacks, particularly to the south, as their artillery pounded their old positions now held by the British. Just before 10.00 am, 9/RB along with the rest of 42 Brigade, received orders to move up to assembly trenches behind Witte Poort

Farm but they were seen as they made their way forward and 9/RB was subjected to a heavy counter bombardment as Villiers-Stuart ordered his companies to dump their packs and advance in two lines either side of the railway embankment with him directing operations from the track-bed above. Hugh never got to 'make history' for about 1,000yd east of the ramparts Villiers-Stuart received orders to halt. The assembly trenches up ahead were by now so crowded with many men of mixed units and streams of wounded and stragglers were beginning to come down communication trenches in the direction of Ypres that the leading battalions just could not get on, causing chronic delays and tailbacks. Further efforts by the British to push on and regain the second and third German lines in the afternoon were bloodily repulsed.

By 3.30 pm, although the two leading battalions of 42 Brigade had slogged as far as the firing line under fire, 9/RB was told it was no longer required as there was simply no more room in the trenches. Caught out in the open at 3.15 pm along the line of the railway under a terrific rain of German high explosive, the men of 9/RB could do little but find what scant cover they could for the best part of 3½ hours and hope for the best. A further 1,000yd ahead, up at the sharp end, the attackers were gradually being forced back, pocket by diminishing pocket, to the old German front line. The attack was eventually called off at around 6.00 pm that evening with what remained of the assault units digging and wiring furiously under a vengeful German bombardment to reverse their stretch of 'new' front line and throw up some protection just beyond the easterly edge of Y Wood. The attack had succeeded in ironing out part of the kink in the line as had been intended and had pushed the very apex of the horseshoe that was the Salient even further out to the east but the cost had been enormous. Some battalions – the Liverpool Scottish for example – had practically ceased to exist and in all, more than 3,500 men of the 3rd Division had become casualties.[3]

Even as Corps reserve and not being heavily engaged in the fighting, the battalions of 42 Brigade had nevertheless suffered; 9 officers and 194 other ranks became casualties with 9/RB contributing 2 dead and 17 wounded to that total.[4] But the ultimate prize of securing the entire Bellewaarde position – including Bellewaarde Farm, Railway Wood and all – had slipped away; the Germans had managed to hold the ridge and they controlled it still when Hugh and 9/RB finally received orders, at 7.45 pm, to withdraw, first to the line of the ramparts and then to march all the way back to huts south of Vlamertinghe, many men losing their precious packs in the appalling confusion of the withdrawal. They arrived, 'dead beat', more than 24 hours after setting out; the men having had no food for almost the entire period. Their divisional commander, Major General Victor Couper, later wrote; 'the conduct of the men, all raw troops under their first experience of shell fire, was very satisfactory'.[5]

The comments were most encouraging given that 9/RB had not then served in the front line in its own right but the time was fast approaching when Major General Couper's 14th Division would shoulder the burden that had hitherto been borne by the 3rd Division. Very soon now Couper's command would assume responsibility for the Bellwaarde Ridge and Hooge sectors, stretching from beyond Railway Wood down to Hooge itself and extending further still, across the Menin Road to Zouave Wood, as more and more British divisions landed in France to take up more and more of the Allied line in order to meet the demands of the French.

After the fighting of 16 June, Major General Haldane, commanding the 3rd Division, set out to tour the newly captured ground on the Bellewaarde Ridge. With him was his young aide-de-camp, William 'Billy' de la Touche Congreve – later to win the VC and to be killed at Longueval on the Somme in 1916 – who wrote vivid descriptions of the shattered woods and trenches in the immediate aftermath of battle in his diary. Making their way east from Ypres, out along the railway and then on towards Y Wood, Congreve and Haldane then turned north and headed for the crest of the ridge:

> Eventually we worked our way to Railway Wood. Here the mess was very bad. Also the Germans were very close, only about fifteen yards. A burial party of some sixty men arrived and got to work, so I hope that when the 14th Division takes over, things won't be quite so bad, for it's a shame to put new troops into so bad a place as that.[6]

Hugh went 'up the line' with 9/RB to man the battered trenches in that 'bad place' of the Y Wood sector for the first time on the evening of 19 June, just three days after the attack. Leaving camp at 7.00 pm, the battalion was met at the Menin Gate by guides of the 1st Battalion, the Gordon Highlanders at 9.45 pm. Passing just yards from the very spot where his name would later be inscribed for eternity along with the names of so many others who marched with him that night, Hugh was struck by the sheer magnitude of the devastation he had just witnessed: 'marched through Ypres, the most impressive sight I've ever seen, the whole place is absolutely gone. Every house is smashed to bits, absolutely a wonderful sight and very awesome.'

Within 2 hours they had completed the relief, accompanied by a welcoming deluge of gas shells from the German guns and Hugh, mixing 'profanity and jest in equal measure' to jolly along his 'panicky' charges, had got his platoon into their positions. Alas, the hope of Billy Congreve that the burial parties had done their jobs well had come to nought. At 3.15 am on 20 June, after being knocked 'clean over' by a shell and having had a sand bag whipped off the parapet just a whisker above his head 2 hours earlier, Hugh found a quiet moment or two to write: 'The chief objection to this trench is the fact that it is more or less littered with dead, and if you dig you invariably hit some corpse . . . It's a gruesome business but perhaps we get used to it'. On his rounds a little later, he negotiated one of the traverses only to come face to face with, 'a dead Englishman lying exactly as he fell with his sword fixed in front of him on the firing platform'.

His commanding officer was stumbling across much the same trench tableaux as Hugh. Moving along the edge of the westerly arm of the 'Y' of Y Wood, Lieutenant Colonel Villiers-Stuart came across a young German:

quite dead of course – lying on his back with a smile on his face. A good looking boy wearing a Pickelhaube . . . and the very good German brown leather equipment with the old 'Fornister' or pack made of cowskin. But the most interesting thing to me were his trews, made of corduroy with scarlet stripes – and his boots were interesting too . . . these were laced and came about halfway up the calf and the trews were pushed into them.

As he went on he came across another 'terrifying' scene: 'two German soldiers kneeling and actually aiming towards me. Of course they were both dead and it was horrible because as I brushed past them they fell to bits.'[7] Taking a message for Villiers-Stuart, one of his runners, Norman Wood, had also come across two men kneeling in a trench. This time, however, they had been British. As they hadn't moved when Wood had asked if he could pass by he had tried to push past them and as he touched them they had 'collapsed into pieces'. Wood had been very upset, so much so that he had knelt down immediately, said his prayers and had then gone on to deliver his message.

So ended the first night in the front-line trenches at the furthest extent of the Ypres Salient; manning the line on ground that had just been the scene of terrific fighting and, as Villiers-Stuart put it, 'shot at from the front, from the flanks and sometimes from the rear as well'. A more vile location could not have been chosen for the first tour of duty proper for a New Army battalion and yet the CO was pleased with the way his men performed on that first day: 'For a new lot the men had done very well.'[8]

Needless to say, there was much hard graft to be done in salvaging abandoned ammunition and equipment and reversing the old German trenches so that the firestep and the parapets faced east and the dug-outs were made as secure as possible; all this under a steady stream of shells from German batteries still smarting from the effrontery of the British in storming and holding their front line. 'We simply waded about among dead Englishmen and Germans, in fearfully decomposed state. Horrible!', wrote Hugh the following day in a continuation of the same letter he had started on 20 June; 'A burial party carried on in front and all but one (23 out of 24) were physically sick, but they stuck it out splendidly.'

Now in the front line and subjected to accurate German shelling, Hugh saw his first casualties when a dug-out was blown in and several men killed; one man lost an arm and died later but there was more to come during that first stint of duty. V Corps, it seemed, had received intelligence that the Germans, 'may have been withdrawing troops from north to south in the last two days' and General Plumer was keen to see if the trenches opposite 42 Brigade were still being held in strength. Orders had been handed down to Brigadier General Markham at 42 Brigade to send out officer patrols to test the veracity of the intelligence. Scathing in the extreme of Brigadier General Markham's planning for the operations, Villiers-Stuart's memoirs leave the reader in no doubt that he believed any patrols or unsupported raids were doomed to failure from the outset. He claims – and a note in the 14th Division War Diary to the effect that, 'the question of rushing an enemy redoubt at I 12 A 0.4 without previous bombardment was considered but rejected', appears to bear him out – that he succeeded in dissuading his superiors from mounting an unsupported assault on the redoubt on the night of 21 June. He could not prevent a larger scale affair, however, this time supported by artillery, going ahead the following night to coincide with an attack on another redoubt by the 3rd Division at Hooge. On 22 June – much against the better judgment of its CO – 9/RB was required to loan Captain Willoughby's C Company and all the battalion bombers – the best part of eighty trained men – to the 5th Battalion, the Oxfordshire and Buckinghamshire Light Infantry (5/OBLI) for a localised attack with the objective of capturing that same troublesome German redoubt located in their front line at trench map reference I 12 A 0.4, which had clung, limpet like, to the eastern tip of Railway Wood in spite of everything the British had thrown at it on 16 June. Hugh recorded the incident when he returned to his ever lengthening missive at 4.00 am the morning following the attack:

> At about six in the evening we were suddenly told that we were in for a stunt taking a redoubt. Our company was in 'support' (fortunately!). Affairs started at seven-thirty. We began an intensive bombardment and the Germans came at us with equal intensity. Believe anything you are told about concentrated artillery fire. To say I've never been in anything the hundredth part terrific is merely banal. How can I describe it? It was like every noise you have ever heard, crashing over your head . . . ten or twenty shells passed over or burst all around us per second – we were ordered simply to lie 'doggo' at the bottom of the trench. This lasted for two and a half hours. For the first half hour one was in imminent fear of death. Sand and earth fell on you in heaps. . . . For the next half hour you rather hoped you would be finished off. It would be easier you thought. After an hour the battalions on the left and the right moved. We supported with rapid fire and machine guns, and were receiving a terrific fire.

Indeed, when the British bombardment had opened up at 7.30 pm on 22 June, the Germans had responded with interest. C Company of 9/RB had been mauled by this shelling as it had moved to join up with the assaulting parties of 5/OBLI and when the attack finally went in at 8.00 pm, the failure of a British howitzer battery – newly arrived and having problems with its signalling wires – to register and neutralise the redoubt had proved fatal. The men of the Ox and Bucks and 9/RB ran into a murderous curtain of shells and were raked by the crossfire from several machine guns firing north from further down the line and a single machine gun sweeping south down no-man's-land from the very redoubt at the point of the tiny German salient which they were hoping to pinch out. They stood no chance.

Only five 9/RB bombers reached and entered the German front trench but five against hundreds was no contest and the attack buckled and finally disintegrated under the sheer volume of metal hurled against it; the survivors managed to scuttle back to their own front line. Hugh noted that the front had 'quietened down' by midnight but that sometime around 2.00 am on 23 June there entered,

> a very weary subaltern from C Company who had been having a terrible time. Owing to blunders two of their platoons had been caught by the bombardment in the wrong place and had been badly hit. He'd got a lot of wounded he said, and could not get them away. The genial task of getting off with ten men fell to me . . .

Hugh found trenches blown in or blocked with men and when he arrived at his destination the Sergeant Major had already moved all the wounded out and Hugh was not required. Hugh's short vignette of the scenes behind the British line in the immediate aftermath of a failed attack is permeated with a sense of complete and utter confusion and frustration and it was not surprising that on his return from his excursion, 'wet through and covered with mud', that he felt the situation 'warranted a neat whisky for myself and my corporal'.

By the standards of the big battles fought thus far and those yet to come, the cost in terms of casualties was relatively low. 5/OBLI lost 16 men and 1 officer killed with some 37 wounded, whilst 9/RB had 5 men killed or died of wounds with a further score wounded. Two C Company officers were killed – Lieutenant Hugh Cecil Benson and 23-year-old Second Lieutenant Bernard Rissik. The death of Hugh Benson, 'a very nice fellow and a promising officer' angered Lieutenant Colonel Villiers-Stuart considerably. Benson had been hauled back to the British line by the survivors where he had been placed in a dug-out. Villiers-Stuart had hoped that it would be possible to:

> bury him decently after dark – but we were to learn that nothing of that sort could be done in the apex of the Salient – it would offer too good a target for the Germans. In the end poor Hugh was buried quietly – only to be blown out of his grave by a shell later on. I was furious at losing such good officers and men for nothing. It taught the Brigadier and his staff a lesson which should not have been necessary for them to learn in that way.[9]

For the remainder of June and on into July the battalion took turn and turn about in the trenches of the Bellewaarde sector around Y Wood and Railway Wood or spent time in and around towns such as Poperinghe behind Ypres resting, refitting, training and providing working parties for construction or carrying duties. On 23 July the sector finally became the responsibility of the 14th Division as the 3rd Division side-slipped to the south to take responsibility for a sector that included Hill 60.

Casualties mounted as Hugh graphically recorded the gruesome details of the results of incessant shelling on what he called 'absolutely beastly' days in the front line towards mid-July. He also observed, with not a little satisfaction, that as the weeks progressed and 9/RB began to develop at least some of the habits of 'old sweats', that he and his right-hand-man Sergeant Dyer, 'the two most successful thieves in the trenches' and 'a thoroughly immoral pair', were 'knocking out a pretty useful platoon'. Hugh was in the line on the day that the Germans unveiled their latest terror weapon, the *flammenwerfer*, or flame projector, at Hooge on 30 July 1915 as a prelude to driving the British once and for all from the last vestiges of dominant ground which they still clung to around the large mine crater in the vicinity of Hooge Château.

> Saturday (I think) 2.50. We're in the middle of the most terrific battle, simply awful, attack, counter attack, liquid fire, trenches taken and retaken. If ever I live to finish this letter I shall be surprised and lucky.
>
> 4.45. Things are now comparatively quiet and I may be able to give a coherent account of what has occurred. The business started Friday morning at 3.20 (always supposing today is Saturday). Suddenly we saw flames about 500 or 600 yards to our right in what is known as 'the crater' a position we captured by mining a week or so ago. I didn't think of it as being liquid fire at first. But it was. In a second the whole world became a hell. I cannot possibly describe the noise, smoke, smell and all the rest of it.

Later, out of the line, he reflected on his experiences and Hugh's recollections say much about the confused texture of the fighting near Hooge in that summer of 1915. He admitted that he could not say for sure whether he had been subjected to a liquid fire attack or not, or indeed whether his part of the line had been attacked or not but he had, however, felt the exhilaration of taking part in a major battle for the first time and conveyed his emotions eloquently. He described his men 'firing like blazes' over the parapet as he stood, 'half on the parapet and half on the parados with a revolver in one hand and a rifle near the other and a cigarette going well, using the most unquotable language. . . . that was a really good moment. I can't pretend to like bombardments, nor war generally, but that really was a moment when one "touched top".'

But the battalion had paid a high price in officers and men in helping to stem the German tide. 'We lost two hundred and fifty men. I left Aldershot fifth officer in the company. I am now second in command of it. I am I think fairly certain of my second star but we haven't time to think about promotion just now.'[10]

The day before the British 6th Division launched its 'revenge' attack to regain Hooge village and crater on 9 August, Hugh was in 'hospital' in the monastery atop the Mont des Cats, recovering from a bout of vomiting and enjoying the fine weather and the views north, towards the coast at Dunkirk, and south to Lille. Rallying and shaking off his sickness, he was back with the battalion towards the end of August and appeared to be in fine voice.

On Wednesday 25 August Hugh wrote 'we are now in dug-outs in reserve . . . simply on a perfect wicket as we have two companies here and can run them how we wish'. His particular dug-out was deep under the ramparts of Ypres, somewhere just to the north of where the Menin Gate now stands. It is ironic to think, skilled cricketer that he was, that he could probably have thrown a 5½oz cricket ball from the top of the rampart above his sanctuary and reached the panel on which his name is now inscribed.

9/RB had come out of the line the previous night – Hugh had dawdled after seeing the last of his men away safely, then ducked into the HQ of the relieving battalion and had 'a good drink on their commanding officer – a great ally of mine who used to be our major'.[11] Suitably fortified and doubtless imbued with a little Dutch courage courtesy of the 'drink', he then 'lit a good cigarette, disdained communication trenches and rolled down the road' towards the ramparts of Ypres. His battalion was just about to spend a relatively extended period in reserve. But 'reserve' was not inter-changeable with 'rest'. By night the battalion provided several large working parties of between 100–200 men for various dug-out and trench-improvement duties on the Ypres–Roulers railway embankment and trenches 'Y' and 'S19' on the Bellewaarde Ridge sector, whilst by day there were parades, physical drill, musketry and bayonet fighting to be practised. Working within that schedule, a draft of eighty-seven men arrived who somehow had to be integrated into B and D Companies. By now acting as the Officer Commanding D Company due to a chronic shortage of officers, Hugh had to attend to this as well.

On 1 September 1915, Hugh was able to get off a letter whilst the battalion was at the 42 Brigade rest area.[12] 'All sorts of rumours are afloat', he recorded, 'The prevalent idea seems to be that there will be a terrific "go" before the winter. . . . Our division will no doubt be in it up to the neck.' These prescient observations appeared to follow a strand of thought begun in a letter written just a few days earlier in which Hugh heaped scorn on those 'writers and experts, and officials' responsible for the 'jingoism and ultra optimism' of the preceding twelve months. Obviously exhausted and tasked with a workload that was more than usually arduous for a junior officer in an infantry battalion due to the officer shortage, Hugh was nonetheless scathing in his views on those who thumped the tub at home:

I fancy they are getting awfully 'fed up' in England with the papers and the official communiqués generally. . . . It makes one sick to live in this sulphurous spot and read the blatant tosh in the English papers. They don't seem to realize that the English Army has made no advance this summer. We have merely won back part of what we lost in April in the first gas attack. Secondly they are deadlocked in Gallipoli, thirdly, the Russians are 'strategically' retreating like rabbits! But the old, old cry is that 'the war can only have one ultimate issue'.

If the fact that the 'English Army' had made no discernible progress during the summer was all too clear to intelligent men like Hugh Butterworth, it had also been noted at the very highest levels of command on the Allied side. Indeed, the question of 'progress' and the methods by which to effect it, particularly on the Western Front, had taxed the minds of Sir John French, Commander-in-Chief of the British Expeditionary Force, and General Joffre, the French commander of her Northern Armies since the end of 1914. As a consequence, by the time Hugh sat down to pen his letter on 1 September, several large-scale attempts – as discussed earlier – had been made by both commanders to rupture the German line in the west with little to show by way of success in exchange for tens of thousands of casualties.

Hugh's comments about the British Army's lack of success were written on the basis of his knowledge of what had happened in the first eight months or so of 1915 but they presaged those of the British official historian, whom, writing in his preface to the second volume of the history of the war relating to the whole year of 1915, remarked that, 'the year was one of disappointment'; the disappointment over the lack of success on the Western Front overshadowed and compounded by the failure of the campaign in Gallipoli to achieve its lofty objectives. He continued, 'the story of 1915 is but a commentary on the straits to which the British Empire was reduced by lack of preparedness for war, and the consequent heavy cost in life and material as a result'. He even went so far as to reprint a paragraph from his preface to Volume 1 of his history of 1915: 'Its very misfortunes and mistakes make 1915 particularly worthy of study. In the remembrance of the final victory, we are apt to forget the painful and weary stages by which it was reached and the heavy cost in our best lives during these stages.'[13] This was not simply laziness on the official historian's part; an early twentieth-century 'cut and paste' job for a second volume. No, what he intended, I believe, was to re-emphasise the enormous cost to Britain as it groped its way towards taking a greater and more active role on the Western Front at the constant urging of the French, whose own casualties had been staggering in their enormity:

> The awful slaughter and pitiably small results of the battles of 1915 were the inevitable consequences of using inexperienced and partly-trained officers and men to do the work of soldiers, and do it with wholly insufficient material and technical equipment. The British nation had failed to keep up an adequate force, and had neglected to make reasonable preparations for war, in particular to provide for rapid expansion.

'War', observed Brigadier General Sir James Edmonds, 'is not a thing that can be quickly grasped by any person of intelligence or waged by any one of spirit dressed in military uniform and armed'.[14]

As a schoolmaster who had only been in the army for two months before his battalion sailed for France and Flanders in mid-May 1915, Hugh Butterworth may have been one of the very men to whom the official historian was referring. Reading Hugh's letters it is hard to ignore the fact that he was acutely and honestly aware of his own shortcomings and that he too could be dismissive of the soldiers under his command with whom he had to work. It is hard, too, to ignore the fact that he had more than an inkling that he might become one of those 'best lives' lost, for the Battle of Loos was still to come.

After the termination of the Allied campaigns of the spring of 1915, General Joffre had continued to call for the BEF to take a greater share of the Allied front – a reasonable request perhaps since the French were responsible for some four-fifths of the trench line on the Western Front. By 8 June, after a little high-level wrangling between the two commanders, men of General Plumer's Second Army had been shoehorned into a space vacated by the French north of Ypres up to the point where the northern arm of the Salient looped back to the bank of the Yser Canal at Boesinghe. This coincided with the period when the first of Kitchener's New Army divisions had begun to arrive in France; one such being the 14th Division, which included 9/RB with one Hugh Montagu Butterworth in its ranks; undoubtedly a 'person of intelligence . . . dressed in military uniform and armed' as the official historian was apt to put it. Now the British were responsible for the entire Ypres Salient.

Although the British Commander-in-Chief was not altogether happy with some of General Joffre's proposals for the further deployment of his burgeoning command to other sectors, Sir John French was nevertheless aware that he would have to take the offensive again in co-operation with the French as soon as circumstances allowed and those circumstances, for the British at least, revolved around the need for more shells, more heavy guns and above all more men. Sir John believed that the battles of the spring and early summer of 1915 had proved that a breakthrough could be achieved but that the element of surprise, achieved by a relatively short but ferocious bombardment followed quickly by infantry infiltration as had happened at Neuve Chapelle, for example, had been quickly negated due to the lack of heavy guns and the consequent failure to destroy hostile gun batteries and well-sited, well-entrenched German machine-gun posts. The lack of 'heavies' and sufficient quantities of high quality, high-explosive ammunition had also bedevilled the operations at Aubers Ridge and Festubert. For the British Commander-in-Chief the blame for the failure at Aubers Ridge rested squarely on the paucity of large-calibre guns and shells and the quality and effectiveness of both.

The 'shells scandal' initiated in his article in *The Times* of 14 May by Lieutenant Colonel Tim Repington, one of Sir John French's old friends, was based on information supplied by Sir John himself and raged throughout that month, contributing to the resignation of Asquith's Liberal government and its replacement by a coalition government, albeit still led by Asquith as PM and with Lloyd George as Minister of Munitions.

Further heavy losses, with a little ground gained at Festubert, only served to harden Sir John's developing theory that with more heavy guns able to probe the deeper German positions, with more high-explosive shells of good quality, with more time allocated to a methodical and thorough artillery fireplan and, crucially, with enough men to drive home the attack, he could break the 'tremendous crust' of German defences and get the 'Devils on the run'.[15] Under such conditions success, he felt, might be within his grasp. The logical casualty of this line of thinking was the element of surprise. In future operations, therefore, 'surprise' would be sacrificed on the altar of sound artillery preparation.

As the months had worn on and more divisions had arrived in France, so the British Army had continued to slide southward, initially assuming responsibility for the line amongst the slag heaps and pit headstocks of the French coalfield from Cuinchy southward to opposite Lens and then a further 15 miles from Hebuterne down to Curlu on the rolling chalk landscape of the Somme. It was in the industrialised region of the French coalfield, however, that the British would fight its last and greatest battle of 1915, in the Artois region around the mining town of Loos. It would be a battlefield that was not of their choosing.

Even as the lines of opposing trenches had begun to stabilise on the line of the River Aisne and then to stretch north to the North Sea coast towards the end of 1914, General Joffre had begun to consider his future options. The German penetration deep into France in the summer and autumn of 1914 had taken them to within 50 miles of Paris but the failure of their grand strategic Schlieffen Plan had left them holding an enormous westward facing balloon of a salient between Verdun and the North Sea coast, the apex of which was located near the town of Noyon on the River Oise. With the Germans just one day's cavalry move from the French capital, for Joffre and for France there could really only be one course open to them: to attack and attack again.

> The reasons were obvious: *les sales Boches* invaders were on French soil and must be evicted, and quickly too – over seventy per cent of France's coal and steel industry lay under German control. The French war economy needed its industrial base back. Secondly the whole doctrine and training of the French Army had rested for years on the spirit of the attack, stressing the value of morale above everything. For the French, the operational ethos was that '*cran*' – guts – could conquer all in a decisive battle.[16]

As the French had begun their strategic appreciation of the situation in the west at the end of 1914 they had looked hard at the Noyon Salient and especially at the hinterland and the infrastructure beyond. From Germany three main rail lines ran west feeding men and supplies to the Western Front and these in turn linked with a north–south railway behind the German line which ran from Metz in the south via Sedan to Lille in the north. This vital artery enabled the Germans to switch reserves quickly to meet any attacks. If this could be severed, reasoned Joffre, particularly by seizing the vulnerable Hirson–Mézières link, just 40 miles behind the German line in front of Rheims, in a two-pronged attack against the western – in Artois – and southern – in Champagne – shoulders of the Noyon Salient, then the Germans would have little choice but to pull back or risk the encirclement and destruction of 300,000 men of 3 German armies at the hands of the converging Allies. Spearheaded by cavalry supported by infantry in motor buses riding and driving hard for distant objectives on a line drawn between Ath, Mons and Namur in Belgium, it was an ambitious plan. Indeed, it was a very similar plan to those that had been tried and had largely failed in the spring and early summer of 1915, and once more the British, admittedly now with more men, were being urged to attack, this time in Artois, north of Lens across some very 'unfavourable' bare and open ground against the western arm of the Noyon Salient. Neither Sir John French nor his First Army commander, General Sir Douglas Haig, relished the prospect but after several objections Sir John finally acceded to Joffre's wishes by the late summer of 1915. Postponed several times, the date for the great Franco-British offensive was finally fixed for 25 September 1915. At dawn on that day, six British infantry divisions would advance amongst the slag heaps and pit heads of the *Borinage* in and around the mining villages of Loos and Hulluch, after a four-day bombardment and with the first release of chlorine gas by the British to speed them on their way.

Fighting on the left flank of the French Tenth Army, the Battle of Loos was to be the British Army's first really large-scale offensive on the continent of Europe since the Battle of Waterloo almost exactly a century before. But by the time the first yellowish white vapours of chlorine were vented from their cylinders at 5.50 am that morning, and before a single British soldier had stepped over the parapet in Artois, many of their comrades, including Hugh Butterworth, had been fighting the 'Battle of Loos' for over an hour.

On Monday 27 September 1915, *The Times* trumpeted the following to its readers:

Two Victories In The West.
Allies' Attack.
British Advance On Lens.
Capture Of Men And Guns.
Battle At Hooge.
French Thrust In Champagne.
Our Successes Maintained.

On Saturday the long artillery activity of the Allies in the West gave place to infantry attacks on a large scale. The British south and north of La Bassée and at Hooge; the French in cooperation with us round Souchez, and also from Champagne to Argonne, went forward to the assault. Large gains were made. South of La Bassée, the western outskirts of Hulluch – east of Vermelles; the village of Loos – east of Grenay; and east of Loos again Hill 70, are in our hands. The advance in this quarter swept over the German trenches on a front of over five miles, piercing at some points to a depth of 4,000 yards.

Large enemy reserves were drawn by another British attack north of the La Bassée Canal. Near Hooge, the Farm and Ridge of Bellewaarde fell to our men, but were retaken by the enemy. A little south of this we took and hold about 600 yards of enemy trenches . . . The casualty lists published today contain the names of 103 officers and 3, 874 men.[17]

On the same page the paper ran Sir John French's report:

Captures At Hooge And La Bassée.
Trenches Carried On Five-Mile Front.
A Village Occupied.
    GENERAL HEADQUARTERS, Sept. 26, 9.50 a.m.
    Yesterday morning we attacked the enemy south of the La Bassée Canal to the east of Grenay and Vermelles. We captured his trenches on a front of over five miles, penetrating his lines in some places to a distance of 4,000 yards. We captured the western outskirts of Hulluch, the village of Loos, and the mining works around it, and Hill 70. Other attacks were made north of the La Bassée Canal which drew strong reserves of the enemy towards these points of the line, where hard fighting took place throughout the day with varying success. At nightfall the troops north of the canal occupied their positions of the morning. We made another attack near Hooge on either side of the Menin road. The attack north of the road succeeded in occupying the Bellewaarde Farm and Ridge, but this was subsequently re-taken by the enemy. The attack south of the road gained about 600 yards of the enemy's trench and we have consolidated the ground won.[18]

Two days of fighting, according to *The Times*, had yielded a casualty list of almost 4,000 men but the situation was still fluid and behind the positive spin of the headlines and the official communiqués the reality was worse, much worse, for the untested Kitchener men of two New Army divisions – the 21st and 24th in reserve on day one – had been fed into the fighting on the second day and both had been cut to ribbons. More than 8,000 officers and men had been lost in under 4 hours and on the very day Sir John French's report appeared in *The Times* he was writing home privately quoting a casualty return of 'over 900 officers and 35,000 men up to this morning'.[19]

Loos was the biggest battle the British Army had been involved in on the Western Front to date and as such it was inevitable that it would be the focus of much attention but the reports had alluded to fighting taking place elsewhere in support of the main thrust in Artois. Indeed Sir John French's orders, issued on 18 September in the form of 'General Instructions for the Commanders of Armies and GHQ Reserve' referred specifically to subsidiary attacks to be delivered by each of the remaining British Armies on the Western Front, 'in order to hold the enemy's infantry and reserves, and prevent their withdrawal from the fronts attacked'.[20] Thus, the Indian and III Corps of General Haig's First Army, holding the line north of the La Bassée Canal and not taking part in the main assault, were to attack at Pietre, north of Neuve Chapelle, and Bois Grenier, south of Armentières respectively to divert German attention from the main battle front, pin their reserves in place and gain what local advantages they could. The first of these two 'feints', later dubbed the 'Action of Bois Grenier', was launched at 4.30 am on 25 September by the 8th Division of III Corps and although the first line of German trenches was carried in the first rush, by 3.30 pm that afternoon the British were back in their own trenches after being subjected to several fierce German counter attacks. A little further south a similar story had unfolded as the Meerut Division of the Indian Corps had launched the 'Action of Pietre' at 6.00 am, an hour and a half after the 8th Division had gone in. Once more, although some units had driven through as far as the German support line, they had been unable to hold their gains and by 4.00 pm the last detachments had withdrawn from the German trenches to their original positions. The two divisions had, between them, lost more than 4,000 men for no appreciable gain.[21]

The third subsidiary attack planned for 25 September had gone in even earlier than either of the 'Actions' at Bois Grenier and Pietre and had been planned to be a much larger affair than both. In many ways the assault of Lieutenant General Allenby's V Corps of General Plumer's Second Army in the Ypres Salient, across a front of some 2,000yd against the German positions on the blood-soaked soil around Hooge and the Bellewaarde Ridge, can lay some claim to have been the real curtain raiser to the Battle of Loos.

Much has been made of Loos being a battle of many 'firsts'; the first use of poison gas by the British; the first opportunity for the gunners of the Royal Artillery to execute a sustained fireplan and the first test of the much-expanded Army's staff to plan, organise and co-ordinate a major offensive, for example, but above all Loos is remembered as being the first battle in which the volunteer soldiers of Kitchener's New Army were 'blooded' in any large numbers – the first real test of that citizen army's capabilities and the resultant squandering of its potential. The latter point may hold true in terms of the New Army's committal in a major offensive but New Army men of several Kitchener battalions had already seen action in a major attack involving two divisions more than 24 hours before the men of the 21st and 24th Divisions moved across the open slopes towards Loos and oblivion on 26 September. Those trailblazing

Kitchener volunteers were men of the 14th Division and Hugh's battalion had landed a leading role in the 'Second Attack on Bellewaarde'.

Hugh's letter of 1 September 1915, in which he spoke of the belief that there would be a terrific 'go' before the winter, proved beyond doubt that the back areas were awash with chatter regarding an imminent large-scale offensive. If Hugh felt sure that his battalion would be in it 'up to the neck', he also questioned whether it was quite ready to take on such a task particularly as it was so short of officers. Several had been killed and many more had been wounded; some, like the popular Neville Gladstone, had been returned to England with what the War Diary simply termed 'shock'. The pressure on those who were left was even then starting to tell:

> We have six officers doing duty here at present . . . it's getting rough on us relics. I ought to get my captaincy next week. No promotions have got through yet, chiefly because our adjutant usually fills in the wrong form, and of course if applications go in on pink paper instead of green, all the machinery is jammed at once. I think that also accounts for the dearth of officers. The general result is that the commanding officer is in a thoroughly bad temper and we all get well cursed.

Hugh did receive recognition of his promotion to the rank of temporary captain in command of D Company as of 6 September 1915, with the official notification appearing in the *London Gazette* of 14 April 1916 – over seven months after his death![22]

Although the battalion's time on the front line had been relatively brief, the swathe that had been cut through the ranks of Hugh's original tranche of brother officers in the three months since its arrival from England was testament to the intensity of operations on its sector of the Salient. Whilst Hugh could joke that he now looked every inch the 'complete soldier', with Government Service breeches, boots and greatcoat teamed with 'trench worn puttees, tunic with pockets all gouged about by worming along narrow trenches [and] cap in the most dilapidated condition', his letters nevertheless convey a stark honesty regarding his own 'nerve strain' and his very keen feelings of fear, which were anything but those of the heroic British Tommy so beloved of the journals of the day:

> Perhaps as you study English papers, you imagine us in the trenches with a continual smile on our faces. I assure you that is not always the case. I have seen fear in the faces of almost all a company and I have felt my own inside go wrong, and heard the voice of the Tempter saying 'Now Butterworth, old son, that's the spot for you; if you're rushed you will be near the exit door and able to fall back' . . . I know exactly what fear feels like at two am in the morning.

He confessed that he longed to exchange his now tatty uniform for an old Norfolk coat, a pair of flannel bags and a pair of old brogues and 'seize a brassy and have a dunch', or better still, turning to the sporting love of his life, 'don the flannels and take that one off the middle stump for four'. Rather wistfully he concluded, 'I wonder if I shall ever play cricket again. Solemn thought!' A solemn thought indeed.

Hugh was cheered, however, by passing on the rather 'swanky news' that:

> the two first DCMs given to Kitchener's Army, are both men in my company!! That is rather a performance and shows more than anything that we have passed through thunder and fire. These men on about ten occasions brought back wounded under very heavy fire – the sort of VC work in an ordinary war. But this is not an ordinary war.

One wonders, as he was running the company with the aid of his senior NCOs and appears from his letter to know exactly what acts these men had performed, whether it was Hugh who recommended them for the awards.[23]

It rained heavily for the first few days of September, which interfered with the battalion's usual routine and training. A large draft of 119 men came in on the 2nd and an inspection by General Plumer for the following day was cancelled, but as it continued to pour he duly turned up on 4 September and the battalion duly turned out for him. On the evening of 6 September Hugh wrote that he was getting ready for another tour of the line at Railway Wood with 'not one single officer under me' and mused that it did not fall to many men of less than six months' Army experience to take into a 'very tricky trench, a company of one hundred and seventy men, eighty of whom have never seen a trench before'. They went in the following day and there was much to do during what was to be the battalion's last tour of duty before they returned again just a few days before the attack.

Certain key German strong points and machine-gun posts had already been identified and although surveys of the German line could be made through trench periscopes, both the Brigade staff and Lieutenant Colonel Villiers-Stuart needed to gather as much last-minute information as possible about the German trench system his battalion was about to assault and the ground over which it was to move. They were to be relieved in the early hours of 12 September in order to go back to spend several days rehearsing the attack. There would be no time to gather such information when they entered the line again for the last time late on the night of 23 September.

To that end, and throughout the nights of 9–11 September, Villiers-Stuart ordered officer patrols to crawl out over the British parapets and creep silently across no-man's-land towards the German lines. Looking and listening as best they could, they were charged with bringing back information on the strength of the trenches and strongpoints opposite, the nature and depth of the German wire standing sentinel in front of them and, importantly, the lie of the land and the nature of the ground on which the battalion would assemble and over which it would move. Bearing in mind that the battalion was still short of officers – when noting the numbers of other ranks drafted in on various days earlier that month the war diarist had felt moved to add pointedly 'no officers' – such work must have weighed heavily on the shoulders of those few available.

Nevertheless, the work had to be done and it was done well. A notable contributor to piecing together the pieces of the jigsaw that made up the German defences in the key sector of their line opposite Railway Wood was Captain Douglas Carmichael. Carmichael, at the age of 21 and then in command of Villiers-Stuart's C Company, was perhaps the most loved and respected of his young 'boys'. Not only did the CO hold him in tremendous esteem but his contemporaries too, Hugh included, admired his cool efficiency.

Born in Wandsworth, southwest London in 1894, Douglas Carmichael was the eldest son of Sir James Carmichael KBE and Lady Annie Carmichael. Educated at the Leys School, Cambridge and Jesus College, Cambridge, where he had gained a BA degree, he had volunteered in August 1914 and had joined the Rifle Brigade as a second lieutenant in early September 1914. Promoted to temporary lieutenant with 9/RB on 1 October 1914, Carmichael had been elevated again on 4 March 1915, just a few days before Hugh joined, to the rank of temporary captain along with Neville Gladstone and ex-Charterhouse schoolmaster Harold Thompson.[24] Villiers-Stuart's admiration for Douglas Carmichael permeates the pages of his memoirs but there is evidence that he also wrote at least one glowing letter – dated 29 August 1915 – to Carmichael's family informing them how glad he was to have a young officer like Douglas in his battalion:

I am taking the liberty of writing to tell you about Douglas. From the very beginning he was quite exceptionally valuable, and his capacity and industry were amazing. But he has in the last month been compelled to show himself as he really is – no longer to hide his magnificent qualities under his modest demeanour. The battalion was very badly knocked about in the fighting at [Hooge]. Your son's first act was to collect men of another regiment, who, by his personality and fearlessness, he rallied and kept with him till long afterwards they were able to rejoin their unit. As time wore on, the incessant bombardment and continued drain in wounded officers began to affect the battalion, and so your son, who had already organized in the most excellent way everything within reach, was sent to steady two companies. Many of the NCOs and riflemen have told me that while your son was near they were perfectly happy. He carried out every kind of duty under incessant shell fire till we were relieved, and I don't think he can have slept at all for many days. Since then I have had more opportunity than before of seeing his work, and the more I see, the more extraordinarily capable I know (not think) him to be. I have recommended him for some mark of distinction, and he thoroughly deserves such a mark. . . . I would much like you to know that I, an old soldier of many years' service in wild and rough places, would give command of the battalion over to your son to-day, with the knowledge that he is a better and more capable soldier than any I have seen in twenty-five years' service. His capacity you would know; his coolness is phenomenal, and his bravery quite exceptional.[25]

This was praise indeed from a character as prickly and irascible as Villiers-Stuart could be and judging by Douglas Carmichael's legacy, which can still be seen in the form of handwritten notes and meticulous diagrams in the files of the battalion's War Diary in The National Archives, he was obviously a committed, capable and assiduous officer. It is Carmichael whom we have to thank for leaving detailed and annotated coloured sketch maps and accompanying notes of the German lines in the Railway Wood sector, an analysis of the better British trenches and the maximum number of men they could hold and an appreciation of the ground and suggestions for sally ports and assembly positions in no-man's-land prior to the attack. From these sources it is clear that Carmichael went roving deep into no-man's-land as far as the German wire – and possibly even penetrated it on several occasions – to examine the German defences in some depth on the sector allotted to 9/RB for the attack. The information was passed back to Brigade Major Donald Wood at 42 Brigade HQ, busily collating the reports from other officer patrols of the front down to the junction with the 3rd Division, who typed it up and circulated the findings to the 42 Brigade battalion COs on 11 September.

Scanning the report in the peace and quiet of the house late at night under a desk lamp today makes for depressing reading. That the German defences were formidable in the extreme there can be absolutely no doubt. What must the commanding officers have made of Wood's two closely typed foolscap pages with its references to strong points – nine of which appeared in the front line alone – protected by 'masses' of wire, consisting of 'knife rests, coils of plain French wire & coils of barbed wire', numerous loopholes, 'carefully hidden . . . large framework, heavily roofed with iron, timber and sandbags . . . wooden uprights, front covered with earth' and parapets, 'sandbags on top and with a great thickness of earth in front . . . one iron plate facing south west, one facing south . . . MG emplacement faces south . . . square sandbagged work with machine gun facing north west'? And whatever little intelligence the British officer patrols and observations through trench periscopes could have gleaned of the German second-line defences did not make for any more uplifting reading: '[Point] 6.4 . . . appears to be a very strong work . . . large sandbagged breastwork can be seen on the south side . . . large mound of earth can be seen with the ends of timber sticking out. This again may be strong dugouts'. Fixed periscopes had been noted in at least four places. By any standards and for any battalion, never mind a volunteer, Kitchener battalion with less than six months experience on the brink of its first major offensive action, the 'Second Action at Bellewaarde' was going to be a tough assignment.

Having contributed more than its fair share in accruing this vital intelligence, the battalion was relieved on 11 September and came out yet another officer down – Captain Hayward being wounded – with Hugh and the battalion trudging into huts west of Vlamertinghe in the early hours of the 12th. From there they moved, on 15 September, a short distance into tents and the reason for the relocation soon became obvious. In the fields nearby men of the Royal Engineers, later to be assisted by fatigue parties of 9/RB, were busy spitlocking out an exact replica of the German trench system around Railway Wood and Bellewaarde Farm. With the start of the offensive just ten days away, Hugh was in for a hectic five days consisting of a gruelling round of training, practice and rehearsals 'in formations for the attack'. As the men readied themselves for their toils, a blizzard of paperwork in the form of Operation Orders had already begun to fly into battalion HQ from the ultra-efficient Donald Wood at 42 Brigade HQ and it kept on coming:

Operation Order S/50/BM 9 September, 1915:
For the purpose of the secret instructions given to you by the BGC trenches will probably be allotted as follows:-
. . . 9th Rif Brig – H19–H21 both inclusive
On the above basis please inform me as soon as you have thoroughly reconnoitred these areas –
(1) How you propose to distribute your battalion
(a) before assembly to attack
(b) on assembly to attack
(2) for (1) do you require any new trenches dug, if so, where?
(3) How much SAA you require as reserve, where you wish it put, and what dugouts for this purpose you require made?
(4) How many bombs you require, where you wish them put, and what dugouts for this purpose you require made?
(5) How many sandbags you require as reserve, and where you wish them placed?
BM 9/301:
Herewith 4 copies of each of the following aerial photographs – Nos BB 253, 255, 256, 258 and 260. Please acknowledge.[26]

Operation Order S50/15 BM 17 September, 1915:
The following details for training with the RE will report to Captain CHESNEY at 9th K R Rif C at 9 am tomorrow and subsequently at times selected by Captain CHESNEY:-
1. Trench blocking parties.

9th Rif Brig – 27 NCOs and men
5th Ox and Bucks L I – 3 NCOs and men
5th Shrops L I – 6 NCOs and men
2. For dugouts.
5th Ox and Bucks L I – 10 NCOs and men
5th Shrops L I – 10 -do-
3. Wiring parties.
9th Rif Brig – 18 NCOs and men
5th Ox and Bucks L I – 18 -do-
5th Shrops L I – 18 -do-

Operation Order S50/19 BM 19 September, 1915:
The BGC will witness a complete rehearsal of the attack on Monday Sept. 20th, as follows:-
5th Ox and Bucks L I – 9.30 am
5th Shrops L I – 10.30 am
9th Rif Brig – 11.30 am
All ranks to be in the positions which they will occupy prior to the attack and will be as far as possible equipped in the manner in which they will actually carry out the attack. Please acknowledge.[27]

On 15 September Hugh began what was to be the first part of his penultimate letter to John Allen. Written with the express intention of letting his friend know that, as life was about to become 'somewhat strenuous', he was 'writing this a week or so before I shall post it'. He continued, 'I hear there is going to be a big racket here and I need hardly to say that HMB looks like being up to the neck in it. This letter won't be posted until after it's begun, so there is not much harm in giving full facts'. Hugh then went on to describe, with some accuracy, the broad overall plan for the coming attack in concert with the French and the part his battalion was to play.

Beginning on 17 September, Hugh and the men of 9/RB spent five hard days practising and rehearsing their part in the attack against the replica German trenches represented by white tapes stretched out on the ground over shallow trenches in the fields near Vlamertinghe, west of Ypres. On 20 September, not only did Brigadier General Dudgeon – who had taken over from Brigadier General Markham – watch the rehearsals but he was joined by both the Corps and Divisional Commanders. Two days later Lord Kitchener of Khartoum arrived to inspect the battalion and cast his eye over some of 'his men' before their first big battle. Villiers-Stuart was impressed by the entourage that eventually rolled up:

By and by an enormous fleet of cars arrived and Lord Kitchener and FitzGerald, Plumer the 2nd Army Commander, and the whole of the General

Staffs of Corps, Divisions and Brigades alighted. You never saw such a mass of brass hats and shiny boots – there would have been a real mess if a salvo of crumps had arrived – as it might well have done. . . . 'K' took me by the arm and said 'Take me around'. . . . As always 'K' was very kind and walked around slowly looking at the men [and] asked questions: were they a good stamp?'[28]

After 'K' and his entourage had departed the men were given the rest of the day off. There was little doubt that they had earned their rest. They had entered the war at a particular time and in a specific place which has become synonymous with the relentless ferocity and diabolic innovation of its fighting given the introduction of poison gas and liquid fire as battlefield weapons on a large scale for the first time. Time was short; the men had to make the most of it. Jokes were shared, blissful sleep was enjoyed; last letters were written. Was this the time when Hugh wrote the last letter of his life – 'I am posting this myself just before leaving. Perhaps I shan't be killed!!'?

That night all the commanding officers of the 42 Brigade were sent for by Brigadier General Dudgeon and the details of the forthcoming attack were explained in detail for the first time. The following evening officers and men packed up all their kit and the equipment they needed for the coming struggle and were crammed onto trains for the journey east; finally alighting to swing through the shattered town of Ypres, out via the Menin Gate towards the Menin Road before ducking into the trench system for the slow, steady climb up the slope of the Bellewaaarde Ridge and the British line south of Railway Wood. For many it was to be their final journey.

Chapter Six

'Such a Scene of Blood and Iron'
– The Attack

As the battalion slowly made it way forward, bisecting the easterly arc of the Salient, the men were at last funnelled down into the maze of communication trenches towards the front and support lines around Railway Wood. The entire sector had always been a target for German gun batteries but the battalion found that it had taken even more of a pummelling since their last tour in early September. To all intents and purposes the 'wood' of Railway Wood now appeared on the trench maps in name only for German shelling had stripped it bare of trunks, branches and boughs. Not only that, many of the support trenches that had been earmarked for the assembly were in such a bad condition that it was hard to find shelter for most of the men and to provide precious cover from the accurate German bombardments that invariably came at dawn and dusk. Whilst officers scurried to and fro organising their men as best they could, the men themselves were oblivious to the fact that they were on the brink of playing their part in the British Army's greatest and most complex offensive of the war so far.

The specific plan for the most northerly of the Loos diversions on 25 September 1915 called for the 14th Division to attack simultaneously with the 3rd Division on its right, with the object of seizing and holding the German first and second lines and then for the troops of 9/RB to dig furiously to connect the captured trenches with the existing British front-line trench at the northeastern end of Railway Wood. This would have the effect of ejecting the Germans from the crown of the Bellewaarde Ridge thereby reducing their dominance of the Salient and at the same time diverting their attention from the events in Artois and keeping men in the north to guard against the possibility of further British attacks.

The orders handed down to brigades by 14th Division were, however, quite specific as regards the strict limitations of the operation: 'It is not the intention to advance beyond the line indicated, and troops are to be restrained from doing so without orders from their officers.' For 42 Brigade, and particularly for 9/RB, however, there was a caveat built into the above which, if the situation warranted, would directly affect the operation and would also, if it went ahead, extend 9/RB's area of operations some 300yd further to the north:

81

If . . . after the capture of the position indicated, the BGC 42nd Infantry Bde. is able to do so, he will push forward his left so as to join the line from I 12 A 6.4 [a point in the German second line 300yd east of Railway Wood] to the [British front-line trench at the] railway barrier [on the Ypres–Roulers railway]. This must not be done without due warning to the supporting artillery.

Three of the four battalions of 42 Brigade, supported by the fourth battalion – 9/KRRC – acting as a reserve, the 27th, 29th and 39th Trench Mortar Batteries, a section of 8/Motor Machine Gun Battery and 62 Field Coy of the Royal Engineers – were to attack the German first and second-line positions around Bellewaarde Farm and Railway Wood. The combined frontage for the attack was roughly 750yd stretching from Railway Wood itself down to the Eclusette stream, which flowed from the lock of Bellewaarde Lake and acted as a natural boundary with the 3rd Division to the right. Beyond the stream, and attacking the German first and second-line systems over a much longer frontage of 1,700–1,800yd down to the southeast corner of Sanctuary Wood would be two assaulting brigades of the 3rd Division (7 and 8) and elements of 9 Brigade. Although there would be no frontal attack in the area immediately to the north of 42 Brigade and technically beyond the limit of 14th Division's area of responsibility, the Brigadier General of 18 Brigade of the 6th Division had, nevertheless, promised whatever support he could muster in the form of sustained rifle and machine-gun fire.

Each assaulting battalion of 42 Brigade – from left to right, 9/RB, 5/OBLI and the 5th Battalion, the King's Shropshire Light Infantry (5/KSLI) – would attack using three companies divided into two columns – left and right – leaving a company in reserve. Each battalion would be responsible for seizing and holding roughly a third of 42 Brigade's front, thus 9/RB's attack front was roughly 250yd given the extra yardage caused by an almost right-angled 'dog-leg' in the German front line east of Railway Wood. In support of the attack and commencing seven days prior to 'zero hour', there would be 'irregular' artillery preparation to keep the Germans guessing, with a final whirlwind bombardment on the morning of the assault from 3.50 am to 4.20 am. To augment that final artillery flourish and to assist in catapulting the assaulting columns – and particularly 9/RB – forward to their objectives, V Corps had decreed that a certain degree of 'shock and awe' would be built into the overall plan as a nasty surprise for the Germans. To that end the 'moles' – the tunnellers – of 175 and 177 Tunnelling Companies of the Royal Engineers had already been working for many days to bring their part of the plan to fruition.

The overall plan of attack called for several mines to be 'sprung' just before the infantry went over. Four charges had been laid under the German front line opposite the 3rd Division's front by 175 Tunnelling Company (175 TC) – actually two pairs of charges; one pair of which had been placed under exactly the same spot in the southeast corner of Sanctuary Wood and was timed to be blown at 1 minute before 'zero' followed by the second 'blow' just 30 seconds later. On the 14th Division's front north of the Eclusette stream, 177 Tunnelling Company (177 TC) had inherited the workings in Railway Wood from 175 TC when the former had assumed responsibility for tunnelling operations in that sector on 25 July 1915.

Their task had been to drive a gallery some 230ft long out beneath no-man's-land from the bottom of Shaft No. 4 in Railway Wood and lay a relatively large charge directly beneath the particularly troublesome German redoubt which dominated no-man's-land at the very western apex of their front-line trench 'triangle' beyond the eastern end of Railway Wood. The latter would be fired at 4.19 am precisely, 1 minute before the attack went in. It was hoped that such a spectacular 'blow' would 'lift' the German redoubt, its garrison of 80–100 or so men and at least 2 machine guns to 'Kingdom Come'; erasing all from the face of the earth forever, whilst at the same time removing a key stumbling block from the path of the assaulting columns of 9/RB.

Another gallery had been driven from Shaft No. 5 further north and a smaller charge had been laid under another enfilading German strong point roughly halfway down the shallow slope towards the line of the railway northeast of Railway Wood. This was not to be blown at the time of the assault but was there to be kept up Brigadier General Dudgeon's sleeve. If all went according to plan, if the left column of 9/RB took all its objectives and if Dudgeon, heeding the wishes of his superiors and acting on his initiative, decided to push the left of his line forward towards the railway he would be able to order the second 'blow' to 'assist the operation'. By the time 9/RB moved up into the line for the attack on the evening of 23 September 1915, 177 TC had been hard at it in Railway Wood for many days getting everything ready to fulfil their part of the plan. Lieutenant Colonel Villiers-Stuart recalled the final mining operations:

> Taking over [the trenches] was quickly done and the relieved people were got rid of early. I went around to get all the reports and then found out how far the 'mine' had progressed. It was not finished but soon would be – and so far the Germans had not discovered it. The miners seemed confident that they would be under the German redoubt 04-24 before our attack. . . . Meanwhile large parties of men were wanted to move the spoil from the mine – all blue clay now. From now on I spent my time arranging this work and seeing different officers about a thousand different matters.[1]

There was a flurry of last-minute details to attend to and questions to be answered; were the ammunition reserves – 160,000 rounds at 200 rounds per rifle – in the correct places? Had the 6,000 bombs plus bandoliers been made available to the bombers? Had the 16,000 sandbags at 4 per man been distributed? Had all the men been assigned with one of the 500 shovels or picks? Where were the 50 trench boards, the extra wire cutters, the 200 fixing pickets and tarred lashings for re-wiring the captured trenches? Were the notice boards, painted with the legends 'A Column' and 'B Column' to ease the process of assembly, erected in the correct places and had the extra 1,400 shell dressings been issued along with extra rations and water? The list was almost endless. On top of this the CO had to find time to maintain his liaison with the officers and men of 177 TC with regard to the mining operations.

Villiers-Stuart must have spoken with many of his own officers during these final hours but whether he spoke personally to Hugh as the officer commanding D Company regarding a few of those 'thousand different matters' we will never know. Neither will we know whether he spoke directly to Basil Sawers, one of 177 TC's newly recruited officers, who was working on the mines.

Sawers, a Canadian mining engineer who had been studying at McGill University in Montreal before the war, had been serving as a corporal in the Canadian Engineers at Messines in August 1915 when he had received a personal visit from Major John Norton-Griffiths, the founding father of the specialist mining units then being created under the aegis of the Royal Engineers. Norton-Griffiths, a larger-than-life pre-war adventurer, self-made millionaire and MP who revelled in the nickname 'Empire Jack', had obviously heard that Sawers had had mining experience and three days after their meeting Sawers learned that he was to receive a commission as a second lieutenant in 177 TC under its commanding officer Captain Bliss. After a few days' leave in London, ostensibly to visit Moss Bros. to be kitted out in a brand-new second lieutenant's uniform, he returned to Belgium keen to start work:

That was about 8 September 1915. I was now in the British Army, Royal Engineers as a tunnelling officer. . . . [177 TC] was divided into two half companies – one fighting up in Railway Wood, and the other half doing odd jobs like dug-outs. The half company in Railway Wood was there all the time. Our dump was called Hell Fire Corner . . . at the junction between the Roulers Railway and the Menin Road. Just after the railway crossed the road it went into a cutting and to the right was a bit of a bump – this was Railway Wood. It was one of the few high spots we held in the line, and had a look over the Boche line. We could look half left over Wieltje and St Julien. High Command decided we must keep the hill. When I got there, there was no green in the wood at all; just a few battered stumps. Just before, a mine had been blown on the Menin Road at Hooge so we were moved into Railway Wood to keep the Germans from blowing it. It was the worst part of the Western Front for our work – had to pump as soon as we got down to two feet. It was a clayey loam, full of water. We put down two shafts and then a cross cut to get the air through and then ran out listening galleries. One of the difficulties was that there was a very wet layer 25 feet down which neither side could get through.[2]

When Basil Sawers eventually made his way up to Railway Wood and began his induction into the dark, dank and dangerous subterranean war being waged by his fellow sappers of 177 TC, they were already busily engaged working on three mines which originated from Shaft No. 4.

The persistent and heavy rains of the first few days of September had slowed progress through the wet and 'rather treacherous clay' but, nevertheless, work had continued on the mines known as 4A, 4B and 4C. German miners were also active in the Railway Wood sector and mines 4A and 4B were being dug as purely defensive measures, designed to guard against and destroy any German galleries that might encroach on the British workings. Indeed, by 5 September two charges had been laid – one of 65lb of gun cotton in gallery 4A and another of 35lb laid at the end of 4B as a precautionary measure as the alarming sounds of German tunnelling had been reported on the night of 31August /1 September. After 'careful listening', however, the sounds were not deemed 'conclusive' – merely a false alarm – and although gallery B was left charged, the rest of the workings were cleared and progress on the most crucial of the three galleries – that known as 4C bound for the German redoubt – continued.

Shaft No. 4 had already been dug to a depth of 24ft and the main drive had got out as far as 87ft but it was very soggy and exhausting going and it still needed to go deeper. On 7 September it had been decided to sink a subsidiary shaft in the chamber at the end of the main tunnel. Initially 5ft x 5ft square, the shaft narrowed to just 3ft x 3ft – no war for claustrophobics this – and in three days the men of 177 TC had sunk another 13ft in atrocious conditions. On 11 September, with less water found below ground and the condition of the soil improving, they had begun to dig south-east towards the German trenches once more. After that first day of graft they had burrowed 6ft closer towards the German lines and then kinked the gallery northeast. By 19 September they had pushed it out to more than 100ft but there was a still a long way to go. With just four days until they would have to begin laying, tamping and fusing the charge they were still 47ft short of their target and those last few days must have seen a frenetic round of extremely specialised and awe-inspiring work as the miners set to with a will and completed the gallery, forging ahead at a rate of some 12ft per day with the help of the infantrymen of 9/RB for the final few hours.

Towards midday on 23 September all was ready save for the finishing touches. The 177 TC War Diary proudly proclaimed that: 'Charging commenced at noon on 23 Sept and was completed at 2 pm on 24th. Charge 2,500 lbs of black powder. One instantaneous and 3 sets electric fuzes. Fired at 4.19 am exactly on 25.9.15.'[3]

It was predicted that such a quantity of black powder would make a crater between 85ft and 110ft across and some 25ft deep; a not insubstantial 'hole' in the ground. Blowing such a tactically significant chunk out of the German front-line system was surely going to make 9/RB's task easier?

The second mine to be prepared by 177 TC, the firing of which would be left in the hands of Brigadier General Dudgeon on the day if he felt the attack was exceeding expectations, had been started on 13 September. It was a continuation of an existing listening post which ran for about 40ft east from the British barrier across the line of the railway. Here the depth was more shallow – just 11ft deeper than the listening post – and the going was easier, the soil being loam with much less water. By 24 September it had been run out to a distance of 158ft and by 2.00 pm that day, at the same time as the team working on the 'large' mine were laying their charge, the team working 'No. 5' began to drive three bore holes, each 17ft long. By 9.00pm all three had been primed with 55lb of gun cotton.[4]

At last all was ready. From 177 TC's point of view they had completed all their work on time and had done all that had been asked of them in the overall plan. The 'moles' would not go over in the attack; the only Royal Engineers involved being those of 62 Field Company who were to help in reversing the captured trenches. It was now up to the artillery to perform its final act of battering trenches and cutting wire and, ultimately, the infantry to take and hold the German trenches.

As the 'moles' toiled in the troglodyte gloom to finalise their preparations beneath the fields of the Bellewaarde Ridge, Major General Couper was also putting the finishing touches to a document designed to impress upon his subordinates in the 14th Division the gravity and sweep of their role in the imminent operation. The previous day, V Corps HQ had issued a document headed 'Special Instructions' regarding the coming attack as a final fillip to the divisional commanders involved, and Major General Couper simply recycled the great bulk of the wording of that document when he duly issued his own version on the eve of battle, adding his own personal touches of encouragement for good measure:

1. The GOC wishes all ranks to be informed <u>as late as possible tonight</u>, that the operation in which we are engaged is only a part of a very large offensive movement on the part of the Allied Armies in the West, the object of which is to break the enemy's front line, throw him back and defeat him.

This offensive is being taken by our First Army and a very large French Army.

This movement is to be pressed with the greatest vigour and the enemy followed up and engaged so as to prevent him from establishing a new line.

2. We are therefore helping in what cannot fail to be one of the largest and most decisive operations of the great war and there is every reason to hope for a decisive success.

This should stimulate all ranks to carry through the operation with cheerful courage and determination

3. Although, for the operation in which we are engaged, a definite line to be seized and held has been given we must be prepared for the effect which the operations further South may have on the enemy in our front.

4. Touch must therefore be kept with the enemy by constant reconnaissances, so that we may lose no time in following him up if he retires.

5. All troops engaged in the assault should be informed as regards the firing of the mines, so that it may not cause surprise.[5]

With regard to the final point, Lieutenant Colonel Villiers-Stuart had scribbled his own notes regarding the blowing of the mines during Brigadier General Dudgeon's orders group meeting on the evening of 22 September to take back and relay to his own company commanders:

> If mine goes alright it is 30 secs before assault.
>   If it doesn't go it won't.
>   If the Germans cut our wires or try to we will hear it go off sooner perhaps –
>   Mine is <u>not</u> signal for assault.
>   Falling pieces. Crater 80 ft. May go 300^x – but slow and can dodge –
>   Dig a trench round crater
>   Don't let men into crater.[6]

All troops were to be armed, equipped, provisioned and ready in their allotted assembly trenches by 1.00 am on 25 September but before that there was one final scare which shredded the nerves of the officers of 9/RB and placed the success of the entire 42 Brigade operation in jeopardy. Villiers-Stuart was in his HQ dug-out in Railway Wood when John Purvis, the young officer in command of B Company, asked to speak with him urgently:

> Purvis . . . reported that he had made a bad mistake and had repaired the forward face of his parapet with sandbags filled with blue clay from the mine! Only one question could be asked – could all of them be got in again? No that was impossible. It was still quite dark and the Germans were restive – and though it was most unlikely that they would not notice the blue clay when dawn came their attention would certainly be drawn to the place if they heard our men working there at night. If they noticed, then of course every gun they had would be brought to bear on our trenches in the hope of blowing up our mine shaft . . . All I could do was to hope that the Germans did not notice.[7]

With the coming of the dawn on 24 September Villiers-Stuart and John Purvis became more and more anxious. As the sun finally came up the CO admitted that he trembled: 'I don't think anyone minded about the shelling that would come, but to be the people who by that one act of carelessness might ruin the whole attack was bad.' Nothing happened. The sun shone gloriously, the day warmed up, the Germans were quiet. As the day wore on and the relative calm continued, so the men of 9/RB began to feel that they had got away with it and breathed a collective sigh of relief. 'The anxiety was very tiring on the men, Villiers-Stuart remarked, 'but in the end the Germans never found out'.[8]

For most there were a few final loose ends to tie up but eventually everything was ready. With little else to do, the waiting began to tell on a few of these New Army men on the eve of their first big battle. Negative thoughts – similar to those given voice by Hugh in one of his last letters – borne of self doubt, a fear of failure, a fear of not living up to the expectations of your mates and of your country must have crossed many minds. Very few felt like eating and many just sat and stared at nothing, deep in thought.

Dusk began to fall and at 7.30 pm – obviously felt to be 'as late as possible' – orders were finally sent around to companies informing them that their objective was the:

> Bellewarde (sic) Farm position . . . the task allotted the Bn being to seize and hold the enemy's trenches containe in [points] A42 A72 A64 A24 A04. The Oxford & Bucks LI and King's Shropshire LI were to attack on our right, the 9th Battalion KR Rif C to be in support in RLY WOOD. The 9th KR Rif C moved into RLY WOOD in the evening & Coys of the battalion took up their positions for the attack.[9]

At 11.30 pm the officers' watches were lined up on a table inside the huge steel tubing structure known as the 'French General's Dug Out' in Railway Wood, which Villiers-Stuart had chosen as his battle HQ, and synchronised at midnight with a signal from Brigade HQ. Douglas Carmichael then hurried off to help Hugh and the other assembled company commanders – Lieutenants Purvis, commanding B Company, and Scholey in command of A Company – synchronise their own watches. Halting on the stairs, he quickly returned to sit beside his CO and thanked him for all he had done before setting out again. Villiers-Stuart recalled Carmichael taking, 'one more look', as he went up and out of the dug-out: 'I knew then how much I would lose if he didn't come back. I never saw him again'.[10]

Out beyond the parapets some men at least had not had time to sit and brood. Silently and stealthily these men were, even now, occupied either in constructing gaps or sally ports in the British parapets to allow the men to exit more easily, or further out still, were employed in the tricky business of cutting lanes in the British barbed wire obstacles to allow the men through unhindered.

Despite the poor state of the assembly trenches due to the German retaliatory bombardments, towards 1.00 am on the morning of 25 September Villiers-Stuart's adjutant, Captain Humphrey Bateman Moore, received the three incoming messages battalion HQ was waiting for:

> 12.50 am – from Lieutenant Purvis commanding B Company: 'B Coy is in its position.'

12.50 am – from Captain Carmichael commanding C Company: 'C Coy is in its position.'

1.00 am – from Lieutenant Scholey commanding A Company: 'Coy is now in position preparatory to moving out.'

There were just three hours to go.

The narrative that follows is an attempt to piece together, from a variety of sources including both British and German battalion, regimental, brigade and divisional war diaries and personal accounts, a coherent account of the battle from the perspective of 9/RB's involvement. Readers should always bear in mind that the reality of combat on the Western Front rarely reflected the sequenced order of events committed at a later date to a unit war diary or personal memoir and that, more often than not, chaos and confusion were the order of the day with a few individuals heaving themselves above the foetid fog of war to make a significant impact on events. Nevertheless, the official documents, diaries, messages and signals – sent and received – do provide an immediacy that is invaluable in trying to piece together, and thus attempt to understand, what actually happened to 9/RB and Hugh Montagu Butterworth that day.

At 3.50 am in the early hours of 25 September, the final phases of the British bombardment began and hammered the German first and second-line trenches, known strong points and communication trenches, throwing up fountains of earth intermixed with trench materials. For *Leutnant der Reserve* Böhner and the men of the *Königlich Württembergisches Reserve-Infanterie-Regiment* Nr. 248 (RIR 248) this final and ferocious onslaught was proof positive that the attack they had expected for several days was now just minutes away.

Böhner's regiment, raised in September 1914 in the Kingdom of Württemberg, had recently moved back into the trenches around Bellewaarde on 17 September after a well-earned rest.[11] It had not taken them long to settle down to the daily round of trench routine. Many of the men were seasoned veterans who had served on the Western Front since October 1914. That they knew the Bellewaarde–Hooge sectors intimately and were familiar with local conditions certainly made life easier. Indeed, the 108 Reserve Infantry Brigade, of which they were a part, had fought hard for this sector during the Battle of Bellewaarde Ridge in late May 1915 and had faced the British attacks of 16 June and 9 August 1915. However, two days into their latest tour, *Leutnant* Böhner had noticed a 'significant change' in the activities of the British artillery, which, paying particular attention to the area south of the Ypres–Roulers railway to the left of his regiment's front had, 'increased from day to day; from the early morning until into the night, sometimes with long, sometimes with short pauses. . . . The projectiles rained down upon the positions from the light field shell to the heaviest calibre. In the shallow trenches and deficient dugouts which only offered protection from splinters, our men were placed in a serious state'.[12] Unknowingly,

Böhner's regiment had re-entered the trenches just as the British gun batteries had been fine-tuning their fireplans for their preparatory bombardment.

Böhner had every reason to feel apprehensive as the British artillery had begun to get into its groove and began working through its timetables and rates of fire. Although the frontage to be attacked ran for about 750yd, for artillery purposes that frontage was to be stretched by a further 300yd or so north of Railway Wood, up to the line of the railway itself on the day of the attack, to occupy the Germans on the left flank of 9/RB where no troops would be going over. Although the bombardment would be dwarfed by the sheer magnitude of later efforts in other battles, the weight of iron that was systematically brought to bear on the German trenches, or in trying to cut four lanes through some 400yd of their barbed wire entanglements, represented the combined firepower of an impressive number of guns.

The 14th Division could call on its own artillery, consisting of 48 18-pounder field guns and 12 4.5in howitzers, which were further augmented by the heavier guns of 2nd Group Heavy Artillery Reserve – 4 9.2in howitzers, 4 8in howitzers, 4 6in guns, 12 60-pounder and 24 4.7in guns – which had been brought in to help by pulverizing German strong points and dug-outs and important road and trench junctions in the rear during the five or six days prior to the attack. There were even roles for a number of 2.75in mountain guns and Boer War vintage 15-pounders and 5.5in howitzers – the latter two weapons primarily issued to Territorial Force divisions such as the 46th (North Midland), which was indeed party to the overall plan by attempting to fool the Germans into believing that gas was being used by firing smoke on the actual day of the attack. Also booming out that morning, to stiffen the bombardment further, would be six 4.5in howitzers promised by the artillery of the 6th Division. A hand-written estimate of ammunition expenditure, found in the files of the 14th Division, broken down by the type of shell fired – shrapnel and high-explosive howitzer – from eleven different types of weapon for the entire operation came to a grand total of 63,000 rounds.[13]

On 20 September the bombardment had appeared to be particularly violent when viewed from the German side; so much so that German batteries were called on to reply in kind the following day, in order to give some respite to its hard-pressed infantry in the trenches. Although the retaliation had made the British pause for thought, it was not long before their batteries were back on task and, it appeared, with an increased use of the 'heavies'. Beginning in earnest again on the afternoon of 22 September, the bombardment had gained in intensity hour by hour until, by the late afternoon of 22 September, *Leutnant* Böhner reasoned that 'it had reached a level never known before'. Fearing that such relentless artillery preparation was the prelude to an imminent attack, those companies of RIR 248 in reserve and at rest had been alerted and moved closer to the line whilst the 9th and 10th Companies of its III Battalion had raced down from their positions north of the railway and scurried across the old track-bed to bolster the garrison of their comrades to the south.

Now on full alert, the Germans had waited; girding themselves for battle under the undiminished anger of the British guns. By 5.30 pm, however, the fire had begun to slacken until it had finally died away an hour and a half later. 'The expected enemy attack did not follow', wrote *Leutnant* Böhner, 'the reinforcement companies moved back again to their old position in their quarters'. The lull had given the Germans a little time to reorganise by relieving some units and putting men to work on trench repairs but they had still been plagued by the British 18-pounder field batteries. 'During the night the III Battalion was relieved in the southern regimental sector by the I Battalion. The enemy spread shrapnel over the entire area and thereby severely impeded the repair work on the damaged trenches caused by the bombardment.'[14]

During 23 and 24 September the British had again treated the German infantrymen to what they termed *trommelfeur* – drumfire – and conditions in the trenches on the other side of no-man's-land began to test even the most hard-nosed of Swabian veterans. These were difficult days for the front-line German soldier:

It required every man we had to endure long days in the heaviest artillery fire, in trenches that had been badly damaged from the enemy bombardment and which offered almost no more cover. Furthermore there was uncertainty about when the enemy attack would come [an attack which] definitely had to come after such artillery preparation. Almost superhuman effort was demanded from everyone in these heavy days. Communication trenches and dugouts were for the most part buried. With great effort and activity, work was performed during the night and the destroyed trenches were placed in a defensible condition again as far as possible. What was accomplished in the night with untold effort was shattered in the day by the enemy shells often after only a short time.

In what Böhner terms was an act of 'vengeance' for the relentless pounding suffered by RIR 248, the German artillery had showered the British trenches with 'a steady iron hail' on the evening of 24 September and as soon as darkness fell the Germans had set to feverishly in an attempt to fix the damage. 'Rest could not be thought of; there was barely time to consider food in the short time remaining. The night [of the 24th] 25th passed slowly with difficult work, interrupted over and over by shrapnel, which the adversary spread over the entire area from time to time.'[15]

Frantically they had worked throughout the hours of darkness under a rain of shrapnel designed to disrupt the repairs but now, for *Leutnant* Böhner and his comrades, the hour had finally come, as it had for the men even now awaiting the signal to move out of their trenches not more than 220yd away across no-man's-land.

Dawn on 25 September would be around 5.40 am and although there had been almost a full moon which would not set fully until a little after 8.00 am, the weather conditions decreed a dull, damp and cloudy start to a typically autumnal day. A 14th Division report recorded that 'it was an unusually dark morning, the moon being altogether obscured by clouds. Light rain was falling'.[16] Even so, as the minutes ticked by, the palest wash of dawn could be sensed in the dark backdrop of the sky behind the German lines.

> In the east the glimmer of the coming day was still hardly visible, because already by 4.50 am in the morning [3.50 am British time] the most violent enemy fire from every calibre came down like a blow from a fist upon our position south of the railway line. The fire significantly surpassed that of previous days. The positions of the 1st and 4th Companies suffered especially heavily under the fire, as well as the communication trench along the railway up to the *Jägergraben*. After a short time the entire area was shrouded in impenetrable dust and smoke-clouds. Units of the regiment lying in the rear immediately became alerted and moved to their support line because no one doubted anymore that the attack had come.[17]

The artillery duel, which had continued until late the previous evening – primarily to the south of the Ypres–Roulers railway line – had also led the artillery of the German 54th Reserve Division to conclude that the expected attack would be directed against the Railway Wood or, as they called it the *Eier Wäldchen* (Egg Wood) sector. Infantry patrols had confirmed that the British had 'opened assault lanes in his wire entanglements' during the night and so the battery commanders had worked through the early hours of 25 September to make the necessary adjustments.

> The batteries standing to the right of the railway received orders to provide flanking fire, supporting the left Group of this sector. Seven artillery and three howitzer batteries were now available for the defence as well as a different section C/73 and French guns at the disposal of the commander of the Field Artillery. Only one battery (3/54) remained [registered] against the front on the sector to the right of the railway. Each battery had a specific sector to protect and engage, to a width of 200–300m. All batteries were registered, even individual guns given different ranges as a consequence of the numerous irregular courses of the enemy trenches. Each battery had an average of 1,100 shells in the fire position.[18]

Sensing too that the time had come, the German guns now retaliated and roared into life. Their historian recorded the moment:

> A few minutes before 5 o'clock [4.00 am] on 25 September the attack began. Without any signal the enemy artillery fire suddenly began with maniacal rapid

fire, the numerical superiority of the enemy artillery was obvious. The night lit up like day from the countless shell bursts and Very lights. Our defences did not wait a moment and similarly started suddenly with all of our strength. In the rapid fire of smashing shells and exploding shrapnel, the sectors of individual batteries . . . without refraining, shaped an uninterrupted *Sperrfeuer* [barrier or barrage fire] that the enemy must go through during his advance. The attack was actually only carried out on the [German] left of the railway line, the batteries standing on the right of the rail line immediately opened flanking fire on the [British] second [line] trench junctions and contributed not a little to the success of the day. This fire disrupted the assault columns and hindered his reserves.[19]

Cocooned in the relative safety of the French General's dug-out, Lieutenant Colonel Villiers-Stuart must have been well aware of the German response to the collective bark of the British field guns and the deeper growl of the heavier batteries when they opened up to thump the German front-line trenches and more distant targets. The British guns had cast their nets further, searching out key field works and dug-out systems like the *Hecken Stellung* on Hill 50 behind Bellewaarde Lake, in order to discourage any attempt by the Germans to concentrate reinforcements and move them forward to help the front-line companies. On the stroke of 4.00 am Villiers-Stuart remembered that, 'the sapper in charge of the mine [under Point 04] brought in the galvanometer – the thing to set the mine off – and he said it was in working order. He then went off to see that all his men were away from the mine'.[20] At the same time, the bulk of the field artillery lifted from the German first line to concentrate on the second to form what the 9/RB War Diary called a '*tire* [*sic*] *de barrage*' – literally a barricade of fire falling just behind the German position and on either flank, in the hope of sealing off the area to be attacked.

Already under the cosh of the German artillery, this was the signal the impatient assault columns had been waiting for. At no point more than 250yd away from the furthest point in the right angle of the German front-line trench opposite, at 4.05 am the whole of A Company and two platoons of B Company, which formed the 'right column', clambered up and out of their assembly trenches – H19, S19 and the support or 'patrol' trenches just in rear – filed through the sally ports in the positions identified by Captain Douglas Carmichael previously, and moved through the gaps cut in their own wire.

Protected from hostile rifle and machine-gun fire to a certain degree by the umbrella of screaming ordnance hurtling towards the German lines above their heads, the men shook out and lay down in six waves facing east – in the cover of dead ground formed by a shallow dip in no-man's-land following the rough track that ran in front of and parallel to the British wire. At last they lay facing towards their first objective; the stretch of the German front line running north–south from the angle of the 'dog

The Assault of the 9th (Service) Battalion the Rifle Brigade During the Second Attack on Bellewaarde, 25 September 1915.

leg' at Point 24 to Point 42 (see map on p. 94). The men of the leading platoon were now some 50yd out in no-man's-land and just a 70yd dash from the first German parapet. Remarkably, A Company completed this manoeuvre 'without loss', but there was time yet. B Company was not so lucky; losing most of its dedicated bombers and the machine-gun team either during the move forward or whilst lying out in no-man's-land.

At the same time as the 'right column' was moving into position, C Company – forming the 'left column' – began to move out. One platoon moved forward from trench H 20 South via another sally port with few casualties and again tried to make use of the same shallow declivity, edged with a line of low bushes, to lay out in the open facing the northern arm of the 'dog leg' running west–east along the line of the Sunken Road from the snout of the German salient at Point 04 to Point 24.

A second platoon of C Company crouched in the British front line north of the barricade across the Sunken Road in Railway Wood opposite Point 04 ready to pounce, rush forward and seize the mine crater as planned after the 'blow' at 4.19 am. Unable to move forward, this platoon suffered under a rain of high-explosive shrapnel from German guns pre-registered on, 'individual and particularly well-constructed enemy strong points like the *Sandsackburg* [literally 'Sandbag castle' – the barricade across the Sunken Road] at the English [end of the] *Roschmannsappe*.'[21]

As these units took up their assembly positions the remaining platoons of B and C Companies moved into the trenches so recently vacated by their comrades so that they could follow up and carry the fight forward beyond the first objectives.

In the support trenches further back, Hugh's D Company waited to file into trenches H 19 and H 20 South as soon as the remainder of B and C Companies had moved out, ready to provide whatever assistance and support might be necessary. Hugh's services would be required almost immediately.

Getting 7 platoons – some 350–400 men – out of their own trenches, over the parapet, through the lanes in their barbed wire entanglements and into some semblance of an assault formation 50yd out into no-man's-land under the very noses of the Germans hinted at a superb piece of organisation and commitment for a battalion operating with just 15 officers. More astonishing still is that just to the south of the right column of 9/RB, the entire strength of B Company and one platoon of A Company of 5/OBLI had also crawled out into a shallow trench in no-man's-land north of what was called the 'hedge sap', which ran towards Bellewaarde Farm, there to await their own signal to go.

When one stands today and surveys the size of the field in which all this took place, in daylight and solitude – save for the herd of unconcerned cows munching away on the grass – it is absolutely astounding to think that so many men could have squeezed into so tight a space in anything approaching a semblance of order, let alone doing so in the murky, damp, half-light of a September dawn and under a terrific counter bombardment to boot. That such a feat was achieved at all by the assaulting columns of 9/RB was, in the main, down to Hugh's CO and a hard core of his 'original' subalterns.

Hugh had been in his fair share of scrapes with Villiers-Stuart but he recognised efficiency in his CO and his brother officers when he saw it. In a line 'writ by the candle-light of my tent' at 8.30 pm on 6 September 1915, he had spoken in glowing terms of the 'bonhomous crowd' of 'relics' of which he had become a part:

> [We are] a quaint medley, three boys of nineteen, two Australians, three young-sters of twenty-three or twenty-four and me!! I am the hoary headed old sport. One of the stock jokes at my expense is to ask one if they played cricket in top hats in my time . . . However they are delightful children and we have been through such times together that we know each other pretty well. Also we can trust each other's nerves pretty well. The three youngsters are, I believe, the coolest of the lot. The commanding officer seems to trust us all implicitly. We get it in the neck now and then of course, but he gives us carte blanche in the trenches. His organisation is very good indeed. His fault in the trenches is that he worries too much about us. Now he is in a terror that one or more of us will be knocked out. He is a curious character.

If Villiers-Stuart had been in a 'terror' thinking that he might lose one or more of his young charges during the daily grind of trench routine up to that point, then he must have been almost apoplectic thinking of them lying out in the open in no-man's-land at the head of their men during a terrific artillery bombardment, and all at his bidding. He had agonised long and hard as to how to get 9/RB out of their trenches in time for the attack after receiving word from the division that his battalion would go into action before sunrise. The decision to assault so early had been taken by divisional commander Major General Couper in order to allow troops to assemble out in no-man's-land – in positions generally well defiladed from the German lines – as close to the German front line as possible without their knowledge to minimise the effect of machine-gun fire during the actual crossing of no-man's-land. The 'how', the 'where' and the 'when' of achieving this had been left to individual battalion com-manders. Villiers-Stuart reasoned that if the men waited until the 'start time' before making a move they would never get out. It seemed logical to him, therefore, that his men should get out well before the off and then lie there,

> silently and trust to the Germans not finding out. Against the advantage of this it would be disastrous if the Germans found out about it. Could one rely on everyone not to make a noise or move about . . . Then again what harm would be done by the flying debris of the mine when it was detonated – timber, stones, weapons, bodies, shells had to fall somewhere? It was all very difficult to make a decision'.[22]

As we have seen, one of Villiers-Stuart's 'youngsters' in particular, Douglas Carmichael, had already worked unceasingly in preparing for the attack; consulting other company commanders on their requirements for numbers of bombers, checking the siting and positioning of bomb and small-arms ammunition stores, organising the digging in of 20-gallon water tins, supervising the building or modification of trenches and the felling of trees in Railway Wood. Indeed, such had been Carmichael's industry that Villiers-Stuart later conceded that, 'any success we were to have would be due to him for he worked incessantly to help in getting everything ready'.

Now Carmichael and those other 'youngsters', the 'coolest of the lot' according to Hugh – Lieutenant and Temporary Captain Charles Scholey (22) leading A Company, Lieutenant and Temporary Captain John Purvis (21) – Rugby School and Trinity College, Oxford, commanding B Company and Freiburg University and Trinity College Cambridge educated Second Lieutenant Edward Henn (23) – were completely exposed save for their self-confidence and courage under fire.

Denuded of the cover of their trenches, one can only imagine what these young officers and their men must have felt as they pressed their bodies deeper into the long, damp grass of an unkempt Flanders meadow, cleaving ever closer to the earth and the splintered row of stunted bushes and tree trunks that marked the eastern edge of that shallow dip in no-man's-land. There they waited exposed; their human frailties, flesh, blood and bone, protected by little more than the layers of their clothes and uniforms, their Sam Browne belts, 1914 pattern leather equipment and stiff-crowned service caps as a steady stream of shells screamed overhead, Bellewaarde bound, for a full 20 minutes until 'zero'.

It was perhaps inevitable that during that time some men would be hit by shell splinters or shrapnel where they lay – the Battalion War Diary remarks upon it and a divisional report alludes to fifty such casualties in A Company of 9/RB – as the British artillery raked back to the German front line to catch those Germans who had surfaced to man their posts believing the shelling had moved on. With their men now being hit, every British officer, be they those who had been chosen to lead the attack or those, like Hugh, given the equally important task of supporting, reinforcing and holding any gains 'at all costs', must have felt their responsibilities as leaders keenly and they certainly needed to exude 'cool' at such a crucial moment as an example to their men. Hugh had certainly been aware of a deep sense of responsibility and indeed pride in the days prior to the attack, borne of the fact that his men would 'come along with him anywhere'. Perhaps those feelings of responsibility and pride were becoming crystallised in those final few moments before the onset of battle, whilst the words of Major General Couper, which he had wished issued to 'all ranks' by commanding officers 'as late as possible' on the night of 24/25 September, were still ringing in their ears, competing with the wailing cacophony swirling about them: 'We are . . . helping in what cannot fail to be one of the largest and most decisive operations of this great war, and there is every reason to hope for a decisive success'.

Since Major General Couper had also insisted that all the troops should be informed about the firing of the mines, 'so that it may not cause surprise', one wonders whether that particular nugget of information, coupled with the now obvious wounding of some of their comrades from German shrapnel shells bursting just yards above the ground, was not responsible for heightened anxiety, not least amongst those lying nearest to the seat of the forthcoming explosion – the redoubt at the snout of the German line nearest Railway Wood. After all, the mine was expected to blow a crater up to 30yd across, with the spoil being flung out in all directions to a radius of 150yd. It would, perhaps, have been no comfort to the men now lying motionless on the ground that their CO had earlier jotted that briefing note to the effect that the 'falling pieces' would be 'slow and can dodge'.

As the minutes ticked down on Douglas Carmichael's 'very small wristwatch', which, according to Villiers-Stuart, was 'quite useless for taking accurate time from', who knows what images, voices and sounds raced through the minds of the 350 or so prone, khaki-clad riflemen of London, Lancashire and the Midlands.

For the Germans, unaware that hundreds of the 'English' were in no-man's-land, pumped up and waiting for the signal to fly at them like banshees, the final minutes of the bombardment were traumatic.

> Between the detonations of the bursting shells the rhythmic tack! tack! tack! of the English machine guns was clearly audible, which fired blindly into the smoke clouds. Everyone sought cover from this eerie fire as much as possible. The most protection was offered by the sap off the *Ypern Weg* [the communication trench that ran just alongside the Sunken Road from Railway Wood towards the small wood at Dead Man's Bottom] which was only a few metres distant from the enemy trench and had not suffered much at all under the hostile fire. Or maybe the English had a different reason for not bombarding this sap? Nobody suspected it [but the reason] became evident barely a quarter of an hour after the commencement of the shelling.'[23]

Back in Railway Wood, Villiers-Stuart watched the second hand flick its way towards the stroke of 4.19 am. The question as to whether his company commanders had the accurate time or not was perhaps irrelevant now. After all, it was he who would know when the mine would be fired and that would, as he put it, 'give a very adequate signal – it would be heard miles away'. Even at that late stage, however, doubts crowded into the CO's mind:

> Suppose the mine did not explode? There were all sorts of reasons why it should not; electric circuit failure, bad detonators, some shell might cut the wires, the enemy might discover it and defuse it before detonating time. It was essential that the mine must destroy the German machine guns if we were to have any

hope of getting across the open ground. All these unpleasant possibilities went round and round in my head and in the end I saw that I must just trust to all going as arranged and if it did not there was not much I could do about it.[24]

If the mine did not go up as planned, the attack was still to go in at 4.20 am and most of Villiers-Stuart's battalion would be caught in enfilade by the German machine guns and rifles in that same untouched sap and redoubt at the very point of the German salient off the *Ypern Weg* in which so many Germans were even now seeking shelter. Wholesale slaughter could be the only result. Pushing such thoughts away, Villiers-Stuart checked his watch again as the final seconds ticked away and at 4.19 am precisely he states that he 'pressed the key'. Nothing. Then, a moment later: 'the whole dugout rocked about: then there was a roar – followed closely by the opening of German defensive [artillery] fire to prevent our men getting out of their trenches. Then there was only the confused sound of MG and rifle fire.'[25]

For the Germans in the sap and redoubt at Point 04, it was the end of the world.

Suddenly a powerful explosion occurred. The ground oscillated for some distance, as if during an earthquake, so that even animals and birds became scared out of their nests and started to cry out fearfully. The almost impenetrable smoke cloud hanging over the area suddenly lit up with a column of fire as high as a house, which caused everything to appear eerie in the illumination. Almost simultaneously one saw red light signals everywhere, therefore no more doubt existed that the English attack, expected for days, had now begun.[26]

It was 4.20 am – 'Zero Hour'. The moment that Hugh had attempted to foresee in his penultimate letter, written from a tented camp on 15 September prior to the week of intensive attack rehearsals, had arrived.

At the exact time the countryside immediately in front of me is blown up, (I believe Hill 60 is going clean up too) the 9th Rifle Brigade step nimbly over the parapet, struggle over the delightful country between ours and the Huns' lines and then take them at the point of the bayonet. This performance is carried out amid shrapnel and high explosive, likewise machine gun fire from everything. Can you see your old pal Butterworth doing this? Of course what I ought to do is to wave a sword in the air, call upon D Company to remember the land of their birth, etc., and foremost fighting fall. What I probably shall do is to mutter a few oaths and put my head down and get over with the greatest precipitation.

It will be a great stunt, what our senior captain (aged twenty-three) [Douglas Carmichael – actually aged 21] calls 'a proper joy morning'.

Just ten days before the attack Hugh had been less than enthusiastic about his unit's chances: 'we expect to lose about half the battalion and . . . practically all the officers', and had put the betting of his own survival at 'about three to one against, but it is all luck, and I've got a sort of habit of scrambling through things'. Now, signalled by the terrific roar of the mine and the great gushing column of debris that rose, froze for a split second at its zenith, then began to fall back to earth in a potentially lethal deluge of topsoil, cart-sized clods of heavy, blue Ypresian clay, sandbags, fractured timbers and trench revetting, wire, weaponry, equipment and body parts, came the very moment of the battalion's testing; its first big attack. At exactly 4.20 am the British field guns lifted their curtain of fire from the first German trench and let it fall in front of the second line. There it would play for a minute before moving on again until it settled just beyond the second line as a protective shield at 4.23 am.

Now or never.

Rising as one, the greater part of the battalion began 'scrambling' – to use Hugh's own choice of word – to its feet for all it was worth. The six platoons of A and B Companies of the right column, led by Lieutenants Charles Scholey and John Purvis, charged due east in near darkness, guided through the gloom and the swirling smoke and dust towards the shattered German parapets between Points 42 and 24 by the stabbing shards of light from the explosions of the British barrage. Simultaneously, the platoon of C Company, with Douglas Carmichael at its head, ran north, heading for the stretch of front line the Germans called the *Ypern Weg*. At the same time, the platoon of C Company waiting in the British front-line trench H 20 North pushed through the gaps in their own wire and dashed across the open towards the gaping, smouldering mouth of the mine crater. With the onrushing waves of A and B Companies running east and northeast and C Company going north towards the railway almost at right angles, the men diverged and a 'fan-shaped' assault profile began to develop.

It was now that the key disadvantage of such an early assault – deliberately planned to minimise the effectiveness of German machine-gun fire – became apparent, with some men understandably losing both their sense of direction and touch with each other during the crossing of no-man's-land; the darkness blotting out well-known landmarks and objects which might otherwise have acted as guides. Eating up the last few yards of ground in no-man's-land, most of them were, nevertheless, across in seconds; clambering through the debris of shattered trenches, heaving obstructions to one side and leaping over the parapets of the German front line to land unceremoniously on top of the dazed garrison. The German accounts record the speed of 9/RB's advance:

Immediately after the mine flew up the English penetrated into the parts of our position buried by the explosion and into the trenches near by. In the first moments after the explosion a slight bewilderment emerged in us, because none of us had taken part in something so dreadful until now. These circumstances were an advantage to the English, who attacked initially without any opposition worth mentioning and advanced comparatively quickly into our trenches. Through the *Ypern Weg*, which was completely destroyed and buried and contained only dead and wounded, the English succeeded in getting into the rear of the 1st Company unobstructed. With fixed bayonets, with hand grenades and armed with 'blackjacks' [trench clubs] the enemy penetrated the lingering remnants of the 1st Company which remained.[27]

Before opening fire the enemy had skilfully utilised the protection of the darkness and had pioneers and bombers advance until in front of our wire obstacles. The Other Ranks of Reserve Regiment 248 fell victim to this as well as a strong mine explosion on the eastern corner of the *Eier Wäldchen*, and this made it possible for the enemy to force their way into parts of our front line trench. But from now the heightened strength of [our] increased artillery activity only allowed relatively small additional forces of the English to penetrate our lines.[28]

These men of RIR 248 were under attack from 9/RB's left column – caught in a pincer between Douglas Carmichael's platoon of C Company, sprinting across no-man's-land, intent on making the German trench between Points 04 and 24 their own, and the platoon cutting east from Railway Wood to seize and dig into the newly upturned earth forming the raised lip of the freshly blown mine crater at Point 04. Before the Germans could regain their equilibrium a platoon of Hugh's D Company, in the British front line in Railway Wood, got to work immediately with pick and shovel to dig a communication trench to connect it with the crater, whilst further out Carmichael and his men were in and amongst the Germans even as the debris from the mine explosion was showering down around them. Beating off what unsteady challenges there were in the immediate aftermath of the eruption, Carmichael and his men kept fighting and moving towards what looked like the front-line fire trench ahead but already the plan had gone awry. Such had been the ferocity of the blast from the mine that it had thrown the debris up and out, completely obliterating a portion of the German front line along the *Ypern Weg* between Point 04 and Point 24. Charged with adrenalin, Carmichael's men overran their original objective and jumped into a German communication trench (CT) marked on British maps as '10' then began to fan out, fighting their way down other communication trenches – CT 8 and CT 9 – in an attempt to bomb their way east, build up the battered trench, seal the northern flank against German bombing parties and, hopefully, link up with B Company who were supposed to take control of Point 24 in the right angle of the German front line.

But as successful as they had been up to that point, the very fact that they had made such rapid progress at all simply added to their difficulties of orientation. Trying to negotiate an unfamiliar trench system – consisting of deep fire and communication trenches with many bends and angles, and all in poor visibility, made the task of maintaining direction even more difficult. It is hardly surprising then that it was later reported that some of Carmichael's men had gone beyond their objective, driving through crumbling German resistance in the first 15 minutes of the attack, taking prisoners as they went, with a few even penetrating as far as the railway.

For their part, the infantry of RIR 248 desperately tried to reorganise and put up a fight as their divisional artillery, which had already caused casualties in A and B Companies in no-man's-land during the assembly, increased their fire, joined now by batteries of heavier guns as far north as Pilckem and as far south as Hill 60, which enfiladed the British trenches and plastered no-man's-land up to their own parapets. The Germans, however, were not about to let the British rush their positions without a struggle.

A relentless, tough fight developed, because the Swabian would not allow himself to be displaced from his position so easily and many Englishmen had to lose his life here. However, the brave flock was badly thinned from the shelling and [mine] explosion and was too weak to oppose the superior enemy strength; those who had not fallen became overpowered and [were] taken prisoner after a heroic battle. Many succeeded in fleeing on the way to the English position and in this manner escaped captivity, so among others *Leutnant* Widmayer, who was pursued by the English was able to break through to our lines and arrived in our ranks almost breathless and completely exhausted.[29]

Stung into action, German bombers gathered in numbers near the railway line further north, galvanised themselves and rushed forward towards Railway Wood to help their beleaguered comrades. Here they bumped up against Carmichael's advance parties who engaged them, trying to buy time for the men behind who were digging for all they were worth trying to convert the old German front line into a fire trench they could defend. But the Germans were determined. As the men of C Company began to fall, with losses amongst the nine teams of seventy-two trained bombers at the sharp end being particularly heavy, the remainder, digging in frantically on the line of the *Ypern Weg*, were sucked towards CTs 8, 9 and 10 and into the fight.

Lieutenant C Thatcher, the Machine-Gun Officer with the 6th Battalion of the Somerset Light Infantry (6/SLI) in 43 Infantry Brigade, was peering through the gloom from his observation post behind the British front line north of the railway.

At 4.19 am the mine under 04 was fired and immediately afterwards our troops were observed advancing along ridge 04, 24, 64. As far as could be seen the crater and two front line trenches at the latter named points were occupied with very little opposition and very few casualties, and they were immediately seen to start work on the crater. The latter was meanwhile being fairly heavily shelled chiefly with heavy shrapnel. Towards 5 am our troops were seen to be moving down the trenches leading from 24 to 26 and from 04 to 17 and in order to follow their movements the observation post was moved to a point in [the British front line] on the railway barrier. Our troops apparently met with no opposition at all in this quarter as they advanced straight down the trench until they were eventually held up by our curtain of fire stretched approximately from Point 17 to 47. They remained in these trenches for about an hour and a half.[30]

'A relentless tough fight' it was certainly going to be.

Meanwhile, the four platoons of Lieutenant Scholey's A Company had reached the German front trench between Points 42 and 24 with relatively little loss and encountered few defenders. But their task was not complete; they had more work to do. Now, as ordered, they summoned their strength for a further effort. Climbing out of the German front line they advanced across the open ground 200yd or so north of the tumbledown walls of Bellewaarde Farm and through the remnants of the German wire towards the second line between Points 72 and 64. Jumping in, those men designated as specialist bombers began to work along the trench, tossing bombs into dug-outs whilst others fought a series of close-quarter duels with rifle and bayonet or got to work with pick and shovel, digging frantically to turn the parapets through 180 degrees to give themselves a fighting chance of warding off the inevitable counter attacks.

Terrific problems were encountered here in trying to reverse the parapets of the trenches – some of which were 7ft to 8ft deep. Riflemen and Royal Engineers shovelled earth feverishly in a bid to raise the floor level so that they could simply gain enough elevation to fire over what had been the parados of the German trench, but in spite of their Herculean efforts it was still a slow, difficult and dangerous operation as they were under fire the entire time. Leaving these men to dig, small eight-man parties of dedicated bombers and their protective bayonet men forged ahead, disappearing around numerous traverses to become separated from their comrades, whilst others began to dig for all they were worth in the direction they had just come, trying to clear battered communication trenches to link their newly conquered gains with the old German front line.[31] German accounts acknowledge that they had lost many good men.

The enemy that entered our trenches raged terribly there. All of our wounded left behind were killed with hand grenades. In some shelters were ten to twelve men, who found their deaths in such a manner. The observer of the 4/54 [battery] and his telephone operator remained at their post to the last – the infantry was already forced to withdraw, they only narrowly escaped this fate. All were more or less wounded.[32]

Behind the leading waves of A Company came Lieutenant Purvis with his two platoons of B Company. Their task, also with attached Royal Engineers of 62 Field Company, was to hold and dig in on the German front line as far as Point 24 near the Sunken Road to provide support for A Company, whilst at the same time digging out the old German communication trenches to the east to try and meet up with those men of A Company digging west from the German second line.

The stronghold at Point 24 was to be held at all costs. Situated almost exactly halfway along 9/RB's attacking frontage and nestling in the angle of the German front line, it was a key tactical position which dominated the junction of three communication trenches and concealed a machine gun which could enfilade no-man's-land as far as the track leading to Bellewaarde Farm. With enough riflemen, bombers, bombs, ammunition and reinforcements to take and hold it, 9/RB would be able to command the approach from three directions and would, perhaps, stand a good chance of hanging on to consolidate the line to either side. By the same token, Point 24 could be approached and attacked using three separate routes well known to the Germans and if lost then the gains to west and south would be rent asunder; a gap would develop between the British garrisons, flanks would be 'in the air' and ripe for attack and, if casualties were high, the trained bombers were killed and supplies of bombs and ammunition ran out, the line would eventually become untenable. The importance of Point 24 was not lost on the Germans and it did not take them long to recover: 'The enemy immediately attempted to prepare the trenches captured from us and they began construction. The moment the batteries standing on the left of the railway received orders they directed their fire on our former front line in order not to give the enemy any time to prepare.'[33]

Now John Purvis's B Company command was being systematically pulverized by the German guns. There was little doubt that there had been a good many casualties thus far but just a quarter of an hour unto the battle, it appeared as though 9/RB had achieved what it had set out to accomplish – the capture of the saucepan-shaped portion of the German first and second line and associated communication trenches north of Bellewaarde Farm. But even as the British began to dig in furiously to try and hold the captured ground, the German infantry began to organise counter attacks and to respond with more venom. The field artillery batteries of the 54th Reserve Division increased their tempo of fire and German machine-gun teams in the fortified cellars of Bellewaarde Farm to the south and in and around the ruins of Oskar Farm on slightly elevated ground to the north of the railway began to exact a terrible price for that initial success. The German garrison north of Railway Wood was not under frontal attack so the left flank of 9/RB was already somewhat exposed and, as the overarching plan of the 42 Brigade attack had made clear, much depended on whether the one and a half companies forming the left column of 5/OBLI under Captain Charles Carfrae, attacking to the immediate right of 9/RB, were successful in pushing on and taking Bellewaarde Farm. They were not.

Although the 'right column' of 5/OBLI penetrated the German front line, destroyed three machine guns, including one in the southern ruins of Bellwaarde Farm and managed to get to the second line, the 'left column', which had suffered heavily from artillery and sniper fire and had even had some of its men flipped onto their backs by the mine explosion under Point 04, was, to quote the battalion diarist, 'practically destroyed before the assault took place', wiped out by shell fire and machine guns firing from Bellewaarde Farm. Of the 6 officers of that column, 4 – including Captain Carfrae – were killed and 2 wounded. Only 2 NCOs and 20 men remained to make the charge and of these it was estimated that only 8 men from the first wave and 7 from the second got forward and were driven north by the merciless lashing from German machine guns, where they merged with men from Purvis and Scholey's commands.

The 9/RB War Diary tells of 'strenuous attempts' being made 'to connect with the 5th Battalion Oxford and Bucks Light Infantry on the right but these had evidently not come up in line' and later, Villiers-Stuart was quite scathing about the inability of other units to get forward and the subsequent lack of support for his battalion that this entailed. It is interesting then, but not surprising perhaps, to note that in the 5/OBLI War Diary it is made clear that one of the reasons for the failure of its left column to get forward was that A and B Companies of 9/RB lost their direction and did not enter the trench they had identified as their objective. This, it was suggested, exposed the left flank of the assaulting units of 5/OBLI.

Whatever the perspective and in spite of any recriminations that followed, the grim consequence for 9/RB was that the German trenches immediately north of Bellewaarde Farm, including machine guns untouched by the British artillery and infantry in the front line which should have been taken by 5/OBLI and in the northern flank of the Farm's defences, were not, and never would be, occupied and cleared.

Now both flanks of 9/RB were left unprotected and wide gaps began to open up between those parties that had managed to penetrate the German trenches. Far from being the conquering heroes, the advanced parties of A, B and C Companies of 9/RB were now effectively boxed into a tightly defined area of the German trench system; a zone registered for defensive fire by the German artillery and which could be enfiladed by machine guns from north, south and even from behind. Surrounded on three sides by trenches, any number of which could be used as an approach route by German bombing parties, there was only one way out – and that was back across no-man's-land.

Although the 9/RB riflemen and bombers tried to throw up barricades in some of the captured communication trenches in an attempt to prevent the Germans from advancing, it was clear that sooner or later, determined parties of German bombers supported by machine guns would exploit the gaps and attack the flanks of those columns which had, like 9/RB, succeeded in gaining all their objectives. Sure enough, within half an hour of the start of the assault, some of the German bombers began to use the cover of that same murky morning to advance from the north and south and to seep into the widening gaps between the various British parties that had broken into their positions. Some of the Germans – all of them it seemed armed with plentiful supplies of hand grenades – simply got up and out of their trenches and, hugging the ground, moved across the open, bypassing the knots of British bombers in the trenches below to get within throwing distance of their captured trenches without effective opposition. In the trenches north of Bellewaarde Farm, with his right flank open and unsure as to how far his men had got towards securing Point 24, John Purvis and his men could also see the Germans moving towards them across the open from the unoccupied ground around Bellewaarde Farm; counter attacking in line, in force, each man carrying a grenade. Contrast this to the experience of one small group of riflemen deep in the labyrinth of German trenches which, at that hour, still had large quantities of bombs available but, as all their trained bombers had become casualties, none of the men left knew how to use them! Gradually, with flanks exposed and under constant artillery, rifle and machine-gun fire and under a hail of grenades, it was only a matter of time before the numbers of bombers and riflemen were gradually whittled away until their supplies of bombs and ammunition ran out and their positions became untenable. The Germans were relentless in their determination to succeed:

> After overwhelming the 1st Company the enemy succeeded in penetrating the width of another section in the area of the 4th Company. However he did not come far because a man from the 4th Company, with great pluck, led a hand grenade attack making a further English advance impossible and then threw them out of the company area again. With an extremely powerful effort it was possible for the [4th] Company to hold the position, with support from parts of the 10th Company which had, meanwhile, hurried here as reinforcements, despite the desperate efforts by the English to place themselves in possession of the same. Bombing parties of the 2nd and 3rd Companies also hurried here from the northern regimental sector, in order to give the 4th Company some breathing space and to advance to the *Ypern Weg*.[34]

The fighting deep in the German trenches must have been fierce in the extreme and it certainly gave rise to extraordinary acts of gallantry on both sides. A little under two months later *The Times*, of 17 November, reported the award of 203 Distinguished Conduct Medals (DCM) for 'acts of gallantry and devotion to duty in

France and Flanders and the Mediterranean', claiming that the very heavy casualties amongst officers, particularly on the Western Front at the time of the 'big push' in September and October 1915, had thrown 'great responsibility upon the non-commissioned officers, and even privates, in many regiments'. Amongst that number were three men of 9/RB and their citations for their actions on 25 September, published in the *London Gazette* of 16 November 1915, speak for themselves:

B/2391 Serjeant H J Willey, 9th Battalion the Rifle Brigade.

For conspicuous gallantry and ability on the 25th September 1915, on Bellewaarde Ridge. During the action Serjeant Willey passed continually backwards and forwards trying to establish communication with the Battalion on his right, and later, when all his Officers had been killed, he rallied and organised the men of his own and other Companies, and captured a position in the German second line trenches, which he held against all counter attacks. During the day he was under incessant machine-gun and shell fire. He also took six prisoners, and made them carry back the wounded of his party. He exhibited the greatest bravery and devotion to duty.

B/1556 Private C G Roberts, 9th Battalion the Rifle Brigade.

After all his comrades had been killed, held a barricade alone on Bellewaarde Ridge for over two and a half hours against incessant German bomb attacks. When his own bombs were expended he defended the barricade by rifle fire and by throwing German bombs which he found, and bombs which had been thrown at him and had not exploded.

B/681 Private H Hill, 9th Battalion the Rifle Brigade.

For great bravery on the 25th September 1915 in the action on Bellewaarde Ridge. He held a trench by himself for over one and a half hours against constant bomb attacks, which he replied to by throwing bombs from a German store and by rifle fire. Private Hill also took five prisoners in the first advance, and throughout the action exhibited the greatest courage and resource.[35]

Despite the best efforts of men like Sergeant Willey and Privates Roberts and Hill, Lieutenant Purvis needed more help and said so. He sent a runner back through a blizzard of bombs, machine-gun bullets and shell fire with orders to get an urgent message back to HQ.

Hugh and three platoons of his D Company, in battalion reserve, were sheltering in the front line waiting for word to reinforce the assaulting companies. Cowed under the German bombardment of the British front line, they must have been champing at the bit to get moving and they didn't have to wait long. Hugh had asked for 6 8-man teams of trained bombers with a further team of 8 acting as a reserve – 56 bombers in total divided between his platoons. These men had found their own bayonet men to protect them. The rest would fight as riflemen.

Within half an hour of the start of the attack, Purvis's runner made it through to Major Henry Howard, Villiers Stuart's Second-in-Command, at Advanced Battalion HQ about 40yd behind the sandbagged barrier where the British front line crossed the Sunken Road skirting the southern edge of Railway Wood.[36] Howard scanned the message; already Purvis's line was 'thinly held' and he needed 'some of D to help build my trench'. With one platoon of D Company already hard at work digging the communication trench to connect the British front-line trench at H 20 North with the mine crater, sometime around 4.45 am Hugh's turn to 'step over the parapet' had finally arrived. Despatching Hugh at the head of two platoons with orders to reinforce B Company in the German front line, Major Howard sent a message back to Lieutenant Colonel Villiers-Stuart telling him of his actions. Howard now had only one more platoon of the battalion reserve in hand.

As Hugh and his men left their trenches they must have become exposed to the fury of the German guns now beating a remorseless tattoo on no-man's-land and their own front line to prevent just such reinforcement taking place. Doubling across no-man's-land through the maelstrom, they must have run into the crossfire of machine guns scything back and forth along the width of that narrow corridor of death from north and south. Many were lost even before they reached the German front line and those who did make it to fight on were absorbed into A and B Companies. Writing after Hugh's death to his sister May, Lieutenant Colonel Villiers-Stuart informed her that: 'He led his company most bravely . . . but the German counter attacks were very heavy and our men were forced back by bomb attacks in great force. It was in leading a few men to counter-attack one of these that your brother met his death'.

We will, perhaps, never know when or how Hugh was killed. Was it at the very moment he rose to lead his men from the British front line or during the crossing of no-man's-land, or did he go on, only to die fighting to the last in a hand-to-hand duel with a German infantryman almost 12 hours later when most of his battalion had already perished? One wonders whether he actually muttered 'a few oaths', whether he kept his 'head down' or whether 'foremost fighting' he fell? Whatever his fate, somewhere in that small patch of a now peaceful Belgian pasture Hugh Montagu Butterworth's prophecy, expressed so poignantly in his final 'valedictory' letter to his friends in Selwyn House in Wanganui, half a world away, came to pass. The scholar, sportsman, tutor, officer and gentleman simply disappeared. He was never seen again.

The course of the battle that ensued can, when combined with German accounts, be traced – almost in real time – by leafing through the original messages and signals that still lie in the War Diary of 9/RB in The National Archives. They are potent documents indeed and Hugh is mentioned by name in that one significant message from Lieutenant John Purvis. Written in grey or blue or violet indelible pencil, many of the messages are scribbled frantically; the quality of the handwriting collapsing under the sheer pressure of pausing to bend – using a thigh as a desk – in an attempt to communicate from the very crucible of battle. Some are folded or crumpled by being in the hands of the runners whose duty it was to get the message through. The immediacy of documents such as these serves to take us closer to the action. Enough of the original tranche of messages and signals survive to piece together the action but who knows how many were written and were lost as courageous runners, criss-crossing no-man's-land under fire, perished; their undelivered communications left to flutter away onto the dank battlefield. None remain in the hand of Lieutenant Scholey, for example, whose A Company got into the German second line northeast of Bellewaarde Farm, nor are there any from Hugh. Might this suggest that these two officers were killed at an early stage in the battle?

Yet it is that first urgent appeal from John Purvis in particular, calling for help from D Company – obviously from the beginning of the battle – which catches the eye as one scans the pages of the War Diary and that is as much to do with its colour as it is to do with its content. It exudes a special poignancy that no amount of reading of the official histories or battle narratives composed at a later date can ever begin to approach. We know from official reports that it was raining that dark September morning but that one message, written in indelible pencil on page '61' and torn from Purvis's 'blue-squared' officer's notebook, is smudged with florets of violet where the rain drops have struck the page and smeared the pencilled handwriting at the very moment of its creation in the heat of combat. The message is untimed but, when placed in the context of the other documents, one can deduce that it was probably written sometime around 4.30 am and was probably the first to reach Major Henry Howard. I make no apology for running the following sequence of messages as they were written, sent and received during the battle where this is known. They speak more eloquently than any narrative written at a distance of almost a hundred years from the safety of a desk surrounded by sheaves of notes, documents and maps ever could. They tell their own tale of youthful vigour, of hope, of courage and duty as the call for ever more men, ever more bombs and ever more bombers reaches a heart-rending crescendo. They also speak of urgency, of anxiety and even, perhaps, resig-nation as the battle rages on and, one by one, like the gradually dwindling band of officers and riflemen fighting in the German lines the messages appear to 'fade away'. They stand as a fitting testament to the courage and determination of all those Kitchener men, and particularly those of the 9th Battalion, the Rifle Brigade, who fought until they could fight no longer on the Bellewaarde Ridge during the Loos 'diversion' of 25 September 1915 and to their officers and 'temporary gentlemen' like Hugh Montagu Butterworth:

Message – not timed – 25 September 1915 – from Lieutenant John Purvis, Officer Commanding B Company 9/RB, to Lieutenant Colonel Villiers-Stuart via Major Howard at Advanced Battalion HQ.

To CO
My line [Points] 24–42 very thinly held – A/C + part of B holding Bosh [*sic*] 2nd line. I need some of D to help build my trench – J R Purvis.

Message written 5.05 am, 25 September 1915 – from Major Henry Howard at Advanced Battalion HQ to Lieutenant Colonel Villiers-Stuart.

Purvis reports 1st and 2nd lines taken also 04–24. Purvis asks for reinforcements. Have sent up Butterworth and two platoons.

Message – not timed – 25 September 1915 – from Captain Douglas Carmichael, Officer Commanding C Company 9/RB, to Lieutenant Colonel Villiers-Stuart.

Getting along alright but rather heavy casualties.
Want a platoon of D Coy to hold trench. Not in touch with A or B yet but pushing on.

Message – not timed – 25 September 1915 – from Captain Douglas Carmichael, Officer Commanding C Company 9/RB, to Lieutenant Colonel Villiers-Stuart.

RBC1 Copy.
Getting on alright but want a platoon to hold trench. Not in touch with D Coy yet but are pushing on.

Signal sent 5.15 am, 25 September 1915 – from Lieutenant Colonel Villiers-Stuart to Brigadier General F A Dudgeon at 42 Infantry Brigade HQ.

Have taken [Points] 04 to 24 also 24 to 42 and 64–72. Reinforcements asked for, have sent two platoons D Coy.

Message written 5.25 am, 25 September 1915 – from Captain Douglas Carmichael, Officer Commanding C Company 9/RB, to Lieutenant Colonel Villiers-Stuart.

A has taken 1st and 2nd lines – we are in touch. Must have at least 1 Coy more and lots of bombs and bombers.

Signal sent 5.25 am, 25 September 1915 – from Lieutenant Colonel Villiers-Stuart to Brigadier General F A Dudgeon at 42 Infantry Brigade HQ.

Companies in [trench between Points] 24–42 have asked for help AAA had to send my reserve company to reinforce and now have had to call on 9th K R Rif C. After this I have no power to call for more.

Hugh Montagu Butterworth photographed *c.* 1910/11 whilst on the teaching staff of Wanganui Collegiate School. This was the photograph chosen by his close friend John Allen as the frontispiece for Hugh's collected *Letters*.

Hazelwood Preparatory School First XI Association Football team, 1899. Hugh, back row, extreme left. Courtesy Roger McDuff, headmaster Hazelwood School.

Marlborough College First XV Rugby Union Team, 1903. *Back row (left to right)*: L M Robinson, J F Macgregor, L Woodroffe. *Middle row:* F A Leslie-Jones (coach), Hugh, T R C Clough, G C Shipster, P G W Diggle, R H Mylne. *Front row:* L Parker, N T White, R S Wix, G O Evans (Captain), C H Fair, L A N Slocock, N W Milton.

The Marlborough College Raquets pair of 1904, beaten in the semi-finals of the Public Schools Championship by Malvern. Hugh (left) poses with coach Mr A J Crosby and partner W G Pound.

Images above and left courtesy Mr Terry Rogers, Honorary Archivist Marlborough College.

Hugh's final season with Marlborough College Cricket First XI concluded with the annual fixture against Rugby School at Lord's in July 1904. *Back row (left to right)*: E L Goodman, C H Fair, L A N Slocock, L M Robinson. *Middle row:* N T White, Hugh, A P Scott (Captain), H J Goodwin, N W Milton. *Front row:* G L Phillips, G H Ireland. Courtesy Mr Terry Rogers, Honorary Archivist Marlborough College.

1914, a fateful decision. Hugh is pictured back row, fourth from the left during his final year at Wanganui. Close friend John Allen is on his left. By the time this photograph was taken Hugh had already made up his mind to leave his beloved Wanganui at Christmas in order to return to Britain, join the Army and 'do his bit'. Images on this page courtesy Richard Bourne, Wanganui Collegiate School Museum and Archives.

Wanganui Collegiate School, New Zealand, 1907. The entire school is seen here, photographed shortly after Hugh arrived in September 1907. Hugh is standing third from the left in the back row, next to the man in the straw boater hat.

Wanganui Collegiate School staff or 'Common Room' in Headmaster Walter Empson's last term, 1909. Empson appointed Hugh in autumn 1907 as a replacement for E Walker, a young English master who became ill and died in 1908. *Standing (left to right):* G F McGrath, J E Allen, Hugh, F L Peck, J A Neame, C H Stephens. *Seated (left to right):* C T Cox, E C Hardwicke, J E J Bannister, W Empson, H B Watson, Revd C Price, B D Ashcroft.

Staff and pupils of Selwyn House gather for their annual house photograph in 1913. Hugh (top right) became the Bachelor Tutor in the new boarding house, built in 1911, under housemaster H B Watson (bottom right). The School moved to the new buildings and site in 1911. All images on this page courtesy Richard Bourne, Wanganui Collegiate School Museum and Archives.

John Allen, Hugh's closest friend and confidante at Wanganui who published Hugh's letters from Flanders. He went on to become headmaster from 1932–1935.

Hugh, cricket whites beneath overcoat, as he would have appeared to his young charges at Wanganui Collegiate School in New Zealand, c. 1913/14.

Captain Douglas Carmichael, one of Villiers-Stuart's most trusted junior officers. He was to die leading 9/RB's left column into action on 25 September 1915.

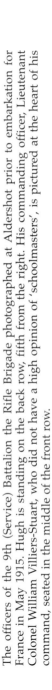

The officers of the 9th (Service) Battalion the Rifle Brigade photographed at Aldershot prior to embarkation for France in May 1915. Hugh is standing on the back row, fifth from the right. His commanding officer, Lieutenant Colonel William Villiers-Stuart, who did not have a high opinion of 'schoolmasters', is pictured at the heart of his command, seated in the middle of the front row.

'Too much the sort of advertisement for the British Army'. The photograph that Hugh had taken just before sailing for France in May 1915 and which so unnerved his sister Irene. She later remarked that it made him look 'almost a stranger'. Courtesy Richard Bourne, Wanganui Collegiate School Museum and Archives.

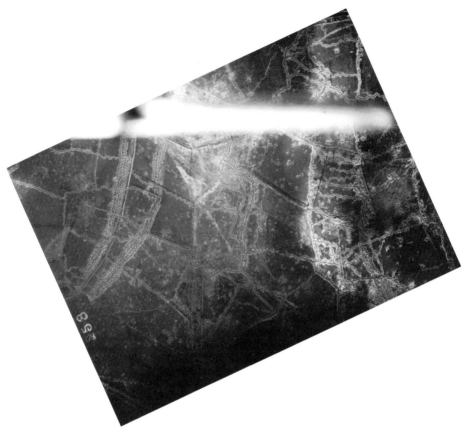

Aerial photograph taken a week prior to the attack to assist battalion commanding officers with their planning. The orientation of the photograph is north–south. The opposing trench systems are clearly visible – the German lines can be matched to the assault map on p. 94. Unfortunately light has leaked into the camera, the resulting damage to the negative cutting across Railway Wood and the German strong Point at 04. By permission of the Imperial War Museum.

German communication trench called the *Roschmann Weg* just behind the German third line on the Bellewaarde Ridge. The men of 9/RB fought in trenches such as this. Courtesy Ralph Whitehead.

Second Army Panorama 85 looking north to northeast from a position in the British front line opposite Bellewaarde Farm on 10 September 1915, just over two weeks before the battle. The pale sandbags which mark the breastworks of the German trenches running from the redoubt at the easterly end of Railway Wood (out of shot, extreme left) and along the line of the sunken road on the other side of no-man's-land can be seen clearly. No-man's-land is an unkempt patch of long coarse grass, weeds, old trenches and the stunted stumps of bushes along old hedge lines. Hugh disappeared somewhere in this area. By permission of the Imperial War Museum.

Line of Ypres-Roulers railway

Second Army Panorama 88 looking northeast from the British lines just inside Railway Wood on 11 September 1915. The striking feature of this image is the knot of sandbags centre left which make up the German redoubt at Point 04. The Germans called this the *Sandsackburg* – the 'sandbag castle'. An infantry marker banner is clearly visible above the German parapet on the left. The front lines here are relatively close and the British line is protected by coils of French concertina wire, barbed wire and stakes. The German parapet runs from the redoubt and away from the camera to the east and is built up with sandbags, earth and timber in places. By permission of the Imperial War Museum.

Above and below: Two views of the ruins of Bellewaarde Farm in autumn 1915; the lower image is taken from the German trenches. It is clear from these photographs how the Germans were able to conceal their machine guns in the ruins. Unaffected by the British preparatory bombardment these weapons cut the right column of 9/RB and the left column of 5/OBLI to pieces. Courtesy Ralph Whitehead (above), Malte Znaniecki (below).

Trichter vor Ypern (Weihnachten 1915).

The crater believed to have been created as a result of the mine explosion under the German strongpoint at Point 04 at the eastern end of Railway Wood on 25 September 1915. The German caption reads 'Crater before Ypres (Christmas Eve 1915)'. Courtesy Ralph Whitehead.

German officer casualties of Reserve Infantry Regiment 248 killed in the fighting of 25 September 1915. Courtesy Ralph Whitehead.

Harr
Leutn. d. R. im Ref.-Inf.-Regt. 248
gefallen bei Ypern am
25. September 1915

Kraft
Leutn. d. L. im Ref.-Inf.-Regt. 248,
gefallen bei Ypern am
25. September 1915

Schmid (Max Arnold)
Leutn. d. R. im Ref.-Inf.-Regt. 248,
gefallen bei Ypern am
25. September 1915

View east from the British front line towards the section of the German front line attacked by the right column of 9/RB under John Purvis and Charles Scholey. The German line ran left to right just over halfway between the fence line and Bellewaarde Farm on the right. Author.

The pasture in which Hugh lost his life. The German front line attacked by Douglas Carmichael's left column of 9/RB ran towards the camera from Railway Wood on the right up to the bend in the road. From there it ran south almost at a right angle. Author.

View north towards the site of Oskar Farm in the distance, centre right. The portion of the German front line attacked by 9/RB's left column ran from Railway Wood on the left and followed the line of the road indicated by the darker line running roughly horizontally across the image. Author.

Looking south from the site of Oskar Farm today. The fields of fire enjoyed by the German machine-gun teams as the men of 9/RB charged across the open in what is now the gap between Railway Wood (right) and the wood of Bellewaarde Farm can be appreciated. Courtesy Aurel Sercu.

Above and below: The cricket pavilion at Wanganui Collegiate School, erected by John Allen as a lasting memorial to Hugh and his brother Charles killed on the Somme in 1916, seen here during construction in 1916 and on its completion in 1917. Courtesy Richard Bourne and Wanganui Collegiate School Museum and Archives.

Inset: The memorial plaque inside the pavilion. Courtesy Rob van Dort.

ERECTED
IN MEMORY OF
A BROTHER
CHARLES
BRAMWELL ALLEN
AND
OF A FRIEND
HVGH MONTAGV
BVTTERWORTH
WHO GAVE
THEIR LIVES IN THE
SERVICE OF THEIR
KING AND COVNTRY
1917
VIVIT POST FVNERA VIRTVS

The cricket pavilion at Wanganui is still enjoyed by the pupils today. Courtesy Hugh Butterworth.

The memorial door at St Mary's Church in Deerhurst, Gloucestershire, commissioned by Hugh's Uncle Alick in memory of him and his cousin George. Courtesy Hugh Butterworth.

Hugh's name on the Menin Gate Memorial in Ypres, along with those of his fellow officers killed in the 25 September attack. Author.

THE RIFLE	BRIGADE
MAJOR	SERJEANT
KING A. M.	HEATH A. H.
	LANCASTER A.J.H.
CAPTAIN	LAVENU J.W.
BUTTERWORTH H.M.	LAWRENCE A.J.
CARMICHAEL D.	LIPSCOMBE H.
DIMSDALE E. C.	McLEAR J.
DRUMMOND S. H.	MANSELL A. C.
EDWARDS B. W.	MARSHALL A.J.
HARDY R. M.	MASON C.
IRVINE C. K.	MILLER A.
McAFEE L. A.	MOBERLY C. G. H.
MARTIN W.	MOWBRAY T. H.
PARKER W. M.	O'BRAN W.
PATEY E.	OFFEN G. W.
PAWLE B.	PATERSON A.
PURVIS J. R.	PERRIN A. J.
SCHOLEY C. H. N.	PERRY F. T.
TURNER B. A., D. S. O.	PLUMPTON F.
WILLOUGHBY	PORTT V. S.
HON. F. G. G.	RASMUSSEN J. F.

Above and below: Hugh's half-brother, also named Hugh Montagu Butterworth, reads Hugh's final letter to fellow travellers in September 2007, on a visit to the site of the attack in which Hugh was killed almost ninety-two years to the day. The spires and towers of Ypres are prominent in the background (top) and the view of no-man's-land behind the second Hugh in the lower image is that shown in Second Army panorama 85 on p. 9 of these plates. Courtesy Hugh Butterworth.

Message written 5.27 am, 25 September 1915 – from Major Henry Howard at Advanced Battalion HQ to Lieutenant Colonel Villiers-Stuart.

Urgent message from Purvis for bombs and bombers. I have sent up all bombs and bombers from the third platoon of D Company. Only one platoon here now complete with bombers and bombs.

Message written 5.30 am, 25 September 1915 – from Lieutenant John Purvis, Officer Commanding B Company 9/RB, to Lieutenant Colonel Villiers-Stuart.

To CO.
Oxfords are not up on our right as far as can make out.
O/C 24–42 [i.e. the trench between Points 24 and 42].

Signal sent 5.40 am, 25 September 1915 – from Lieutenant Colonel Villiers-Stuart to Major Henry Howard at Advanced Battalion HQ.

9th KRR have sent up two platoons to Purvis and two platoons to Carmichael all with bombers and bombs. Try send up more bombs with D Coy last platoon which you still apparently have in hand.

Message – not timed – 25 September 1915 – from Lieutenant John Purvis, Officer Commanding B Company 9/RB, to Lieutenant Colonel Villiers-Stuart.

To the CO.
We must have reinforcements for BOMBERS BOMBERS BOMBERS.

Message written 5.42 am, 25 September 1915 – from Major Henry Howard to Lieutenant Colonel Villiers-Stuart.

Herewith from Purvis. No more RB bombers left here they are all up in the firing line.

Signal sent 5.45 am from Lieutenant Colonel Villiers-Stuart to Captain Carmichael, Officer Commanding C Company, 9/RB.

Well done, have sent you 2 platoons 9th KRR.

Signal sent 5.40 am, 25 September received at 05.45 am 25 September 1915 – from Brigadier General F A Dudgeon at 42 Infantry Brigade HQ to Lieutenant Colonel Villiers-Stuart.

Inform me of possibility of taking [trench line between Points] 47 27 08 aaa
Congratulate you heartily on brilliant success. Hold on.

Signal sent 5.45 am, 25 September 1915 – from Brigadier General F A Dudgeon at 42 Infantry Brigade HQ to Lieutenant Colonel Villiers-Stuart.

Don't overcrowd your men aaa
What is situation that necessitates reinforcement from KRR

Signal sent 6.05 am, 25 September 1915 – from Lieutenant Colonel Villiers-Stuart to Brigadier General F A Dudgeon at 42 Infantry Brigade HQ.

Am careful not to overcrowd but incessant requests come for bombs and bombers AAA Enemy evidently not faint hearted and I think that Oxfords not having come up in line cause extra want of bombers.

Signal sent 6.30 am, 25 September 1915 – from Lieutenant Colonel Villiers-Stuart to Captain Douglas Carmichael, Officer Commanding C Company, 9/RB.

Can you say if you could possibly take the line in front of you [between Points] 47–27–08.

Signal – not timed – 25 September 1915 – from Lieutenant Colonel Villiers-Stuart to Brigadier General F A Dudgeon at 42 Infantry Brigade HQ.

Company in [trench between Points] 04–24 is in want of bombs and bombers as enemy are trying to bomb them out and they have some loss AAA Carmichael cannot get on to [line between Points] 47–27–08 AAA Companies holding [trenches between Points] 24–42 and 64–72 say they want bombers badly but are otherwise holding on AAA Oxfords are apparently not up on our right AAA If bombers are available I think Carmichael could try to get further.

Message – not timed – 25 September 1915 – from Second Lieutenant Robin d'Erlanger to Lieutenant Colonel Villiers-Stuart.

Continue hold at present.
If we had a lot of bombs we could do something?

Message – not timed – 25 September 1915 – from Second Lieutenant Robin d'Erlanger to Lieutenant Colonel Villiers-Stuart.

We must have bombs immediately, Germans in great force all round us. We are being bombed back and are being shot at by rifle fire and machine guns all round. Am just on right of crater. Carmichael on left but wounded.

Signal sent 6.40 am, 25 September 1915 – from Lieutenant Colonel Villiers-Stuart to Lieutenant John Purvis, Officer Commanding B Company, 9/RB.

You <u>must hold</u> the line [between Points] 64–72 ie the second German line – you have only eighteen men there and many in [the line between Points] 24–42 AAA Please put this right at once AAA You can make any use you like of 9th KRRC with you.

Message written 7.00 am, 25 September 1915 – from Major Henry Howard at Advanced Battalion HQ to Lieutenant Colonel Villiers-Stuart.

CSM Wood, A Coy reports that both German lines [between Points] 24 to 42 and 64 to 72 have been lost we having been bombed out. Practically no men left. Oxfords did not come up on our right. No men here for anything.

Message – not timed – 25 September 1915 – from Second Lieutenant Robin d'Erlanger to Lieutenant Colonel Villiers-Stuart.

Christie [Captain John, 9/KRRC] has taken his company with bombs to reinforce [trench between Points] 04–24 which I think can be held. I am staying at Cambridge Rd barrier trying to reorganize.

Signal sent 7.10 am, 25 September 1915 – from Lieutenant Colonel Villiers-Stuart to Second Lieutenant Robin d'Erlanger.

Please take your 20 men or so to dig a trench from [the British front-line trench] H20 to crater AAA This is urgent.

[NB This signal was initially marked as '6.10 am' but was overwritten with a '7' which makes it appear like an '8', but 8.00 am is surely too late in the light of a later communication from Second Lieutenant d'Erlanger which appears below.]

Signal sent 7.15 am, 25 September 1915 – from Lieutenant Colonel Villiers-Stuart to Brigadier General F A Dudgeon at 42 Infantry Brigade HQ.

Rifle Brigade driven right back into own trenches AAA Enemy attacking our front line AAA Davis [CO 9/KRRC and ex-Major 9/RB] has only one weak company left Rifle Brigade non existent AAA This is very critical indeed.

Message received 8.00 am, 25 September 1915 – from Second Lieutenant Robin d'Erlanger to Lieutenant Colonel Villiers-Stuart.

Communication trench to crater already dug. H20 North is quite untenable – there is no trench left at all hardly. I fear Major Howard has been hit as I can't find him anywhere. Nearly all the men I have with me are now wounded. Christie is still at crater but is being heavily shelled both by enemy and us.

Report timed at 8.00 am, 25 September 1915 – from Major Henry Howard to Lieutenant Colonel Villiers-Stuart.

I was acting as advanced Battn HQrs at Sunken Road barrier. I was first informed by OC Reserve Coy that [the trench between Points] 04–24 was captured and was being consolidated.
Subsequently OC A Coy [Lieutenant Charles Scholey] reported to me that he had carried both the German lines, but bombs and bombers were urgently needed.
I sent up the reserve Coy with all battalion bombs. Another message came for bombs and bombers saying that the Oxfords had not carried their lines.
Later on CSM Wood of the Coy holding the German 2nd line came in wounded and said we had been bombed out of both 1st and 2nd lines and that of A Coy he had brought back about 6 men.

Message written 8.05 am, 25 September 1915 – from Second Lieutenant Robin d'Erlanger to Lieutenant Colonel Villiers-Stuart.

Major Howard has returned to firing line and requests me to send message. Situation improving.
Sgt Major Goodey holding on with 20 men of C Coy right beyond the crater and Christie's Coy is advancing slowly. MMG [under Lieutenant Westropp, 8/Motor Machine Gun Company] has advanced also and is holding crater.
Bunting still seems to be going on at Bellewaarde.
I think anyhow that Railway Wood will easily be held and am organising H20, 21.[37]

Signal sent 9.20 am, 25 September 1915 – from Lieutenant Colonel Villiers-Stuart to Brigadier General F A Dudgeon at 42 Infantry Brigade HQ.

Including self and adjutant [Captain Moore] have three unwounded and three wounded officers left and 90–100 men only AAA I have searched everywhere for more men for a long time and have taken all evidence I could and am afraid

I can hope for no more unwounded men AAA The enemy killed a great number of our wounded AAA May I have orders.

Signal sent 10.00 am, 25 September 1915 from Brigadier General F A Dudgeon at 42 Infantry Brigade HQ to Lieutenant Colonel Villiers-Stuart.

Collect what you can and form support to KRR.

What can be gleaned from the above, when set in the context of messages and signals from other units, is that 9/RB's battle was all over bar the shouting in little more than 4 hours after the infantry assault began and, ravening beast that it was, had consumed all who had entered it at an alarming rate.

The 9/RB War Diary speaks of 'remnants' of C Company still holding out in the German communication trenches CTs 8, 9 and 10 east of Railway Wood until 4.00 pm when, realising that their situation was hopeless, they made their way back to the British front line. If any men really did survive for that long it was a remarkable feat, for they were without any effective artillery support for at least 2 hours. The 14th Division Artillery Diary reported that, 'by 2pm all fire had ceased except for occasional rounds by selected batteries'. But these men could only have been a handful and their fate was not representative of the battalion as a whole, if, indeed, one could speak of 'the battalion' by that stage. 9/RB had effectively been smashed to pieces by 8.30 am and those who had managed to survive had been driven back towards the area around the crater at Point 04 and the British front line.

It had all begun with so much promise but in the light of what followed, Brigadier General Dudgeon's signal of hearty congratulations on the battalion's 'brilliant success' despatched at 5.40 am seems, at this remove, to have been woefully premature.

Even after the committal of every single man of Hugh's D Company by 5.42 am the clarion calls for 'bombs' and 'bombers' had gone on unabated. Pressed on all sides by German bombing parties, the pleadings of Douglas Carmichael, John Purvis and latterly Robin d'Erlanger continued to fly back across no-man's-land to Villiers-Stuart who, in turn, pleaded with Major Davis, his erstwhile Second-in-Command, now commanding 9/KRRC – the reserve battalion – to send up some of his men to reinforce the forward units. Davis had acceded and at 5.25 am had committed two platoons to help in fighting the C Company battle raging in the German front line from Points 04 to 24 and north of the crater, then, 10 minutes later, after further entreaties from Villiers-Stuart, he had pushed another two forward to support A and B Companies in their attack north of Bellewaarde Farm.

But these had not been enough. A little after 6.00 am, with the Germans pressing their bombing attacks against both of A Company's flanks in the second German line and finally running out of bombs themselves, Scholey's command was obliged to retire back along the German communication trench CT 5 from where someone had given them an order to turn and stand their ground and open up with their Lee Enfields to check the German advance across the open with rifle fire. But even as the men of A Company had been raising their rifles to take aim and hold on in CT 5, the tenuous grip of the small parties of what remained of B Company in the German front line behind them had been broken. Purvis's men were in the process of being 'bombed out'.

B Company had taken the German front-line trench between Points 24 and 42 in the first rush, within 15 minutes of the attack, but it had cost it dear. All of the company's bombers and bombs had been lost and, as a result, it had been unable to resist German bomb attacks developing from the south. With B Company in such a precarious position, the Germans, having forced A Company out of their second line, had already called up their support companies to help. Then, using the unoccupied lateral routes of their communication trenches numbered 2, 3 and 4 to bypass the A Company garrison holding out in CT 5 to the north, they attempted to annihilate B Company behind them before turning to surround and snuff out what remained of the A Company threat. The German accounts reflect the urgency of their efforts to recapture their trenches and they too suffered casualties.

At the same time [as the bombing parties of the 2nd and 3rd Companies moved from the northern regimental sector] one platoon from the 9th Company received the order to attack the Englishmen lodged in the position of the 1st Company from the left flank and threw them back. Meanwhile Major von Flatow arrived at the *Jägergraben* and took command of the southern sector, together with the 11th and 12th Companies at the Battalion battle headquarters, from *Hauptmann* von Legl who was slightly wounded in the head. The 11th Company, under the leadership of *Hauptmann* Bauer, received the order to attack the enemy still found in our positions and to throw them out. [But] the sector commander was not permitted to experience the success of his orders. Wounded by a shrapnel ball in the neck, Major von Flatow was able to get to a medical dugout nearby where, however, he succumbed to his severe wound a short time later. With him gone the III Battalion lost its beloved commander, the regiment a capable leader and everyone an excellent chief and comrade. After the death of Major von Flatow, *Hauptmann* von Legl took further command over the sector. Sections of the 12th Company found in the *Jägergraben* received orders to proceed to the *Ausweichgraben*, in case they were needed to support the 11th Company in their advance.[38]

Under relentless pressure and with no bombs left, let alone trained bombers to use them, B Company had been forced to give ground and had made their way back across that deadly triangle of no-man's-land in front of Point 24 in the direction of Douglas

Carmichael's C Company holding the trench from Point 04 to 24 and the communication trenches beyond. Those who had got across unscathed came across small groups of C Company doggedly trying to hold off marauding German bombers around the vital strongpoint at Point 24. But even if every British rifleman had fought as hard as five, the Württembergers had not been content to let matters rest there. Set on claiming every last centimetre of lost ground it was not long before they had reclaimed Point 24, moving in behind a torrent of grenades.

Even then there had been no respite for the mixed band of B, C and D Companies and the 9/KRRC reinforcements. Having re-conquered Point 24, the Germans had begun to bomb their way west down the *Ypern Weg* running parallel to the Sunken Road, towards the gaping mouth of the mine crater at Railway Wood.

After [further supplies of] hand grenades and ammunition had arrived, the 4th Company succeeded, with support from parts of the 3rd and 10th Companies, to throw back the Englishmen in hard, close fighting in the direction of the *Ypern Weg* and the crater caused by the explosion. A machine gun here, that caused heavy losses to the [English], was the subject of an extremely bitter fight for a long time. Every attempt by the enemy to obtain possession of the machine gun failed because of the bravery of the crew, as well as the infantry that had hurried there to protect it.[39]

Still in his observation post, Lieutenant Thatcher of 6/SLI saw the tragic tableau played out along the German front line along the crest of the ridge as the light improved,

At about 6.15 am sounds of bombing were distinguished in direction of line 64 to 71 and shortly afterwards our troops were seen retiring along line 64–24, and then again from 24 to the crater. Heavy losses occurred during this move. The men who had advanced along trench 24 to 26 were thus forced to retire and immediately they gained the open they were also seen to lose heavily. Nearly all these casualties were brought about by two machine guns situated in the enemy's line near points 09 and 17 (opposite trench A1). Part of our men in 04–17 also withdrew to the crater but a small party held on to the top portion of the trench for some considerable time.[40]

The time for desperate action had arrived. There is no record of who organised what is reported to have happened next but someone – an officer, an NCO or simply a rifleman – succeeded in rallying the men of B Company who then heaved themselves out of the trench to charge east, across the open, towards their tormentors in an effort to try and retake Point 24. It was a brave but futile gesture. 'Skylined' along the crest of the ridge east of Railway Wood and spotted immediately by German machine-gun teams around Oskar Farm to the north, the brave attempt was cut to ribbons within a few strides.

Taking cover again the survivors had determined to try and hold on to the mine crater as best they could and to pass men back to the British front-line trenches running through and just north of Railway Wood and wait until more bombs and bombers could be sent up, although supplies of both were in critically short supply by that time. Almost every man in 9/RB, except HQ signallers, runners and 'a few men scattered around the trenches looking after kit and stores', had been drawn into the fight, but there were, nevertheless, still men available. Major Davis still had three of his companies of 9/KRRC in hand and, at around 7.00 am, responding to the ceaseless requests for men from his ex-CO and news that 'the 9th Rifle Brigade were giving ground', he had agreed to release another company under Captain John Christie to help in defending the mine crater and the trenches around it. Christie set off immediately and although 9/RB had suffered dreadful losses, those who could, continued to fight on.

Whilst it was true that B Company had been forced back from Point 24 by machine-gun fire, the battle for the German front line from the mine crater to the corner angle strongpoint at Point 24 had been far from over and Lieutenant Charles Scholey's A Company had still had a part to play. For almost an hour after the withdrawal of B Company, A Company had clung on to their precarious position in the German CT 5, which linked strongpoint 24 with the German second line north of Bellewaarde Farm. During that time A Company's numbers had reduced dramatically given that shell fire had also been brought to bear on them in addition to the merciless fusillade of grenades, rifle and machine-gun fire. A much-needed transfusion of twenty bombers from 9/KRRC, sent up to support the right flank with extra bombs at 6.45 am, had not been enough to stem the German tide and staunch the haemorrhaging of men. So exposed had their position become that there had been no other option but to withdraw, back towards the German front line around Point 24. Remarkably, although the Württembergers had already fought through that point and moved on towards the crater, it appears as though it had not been consolidated. After all, parties of Carmichael's C Company were still 'fighting like tigers', dotted about here and there in the German communication trenches towards the railway, and the British were still fighting to hold the mine crater.

Perhaps German attention was drawn by a desire to regain the lost ground ahead; perhaps they thought the British in their second line had been vanquished. Whatever the reason, as the remnants of A Company neared Point 24 they learned that B Company had been driven back and that the Germans had re-occupied their own front line. Sensing that the situation was critical, someone took yet another decision borne of desperation and a second helter-skelter dash across open ground was launched against the Germans holding the trench leading to the crater. Losses were again heavy but this time the charge worked and the Germans scurried for cover but some of the men of A Company did not stop there; catching sight of their comrades of C Company holding CT 10 and engaged in a slugging match against German bombers descending on them from the direction of the railway to the north, what was left of Charles Scholey's command ran on, across the open, to join them. The 9/RB War Diary notes that:

> They succeeded in doing this as at the time the enemy were busy with C Company in CT 10 [north of Point 24] They lost many men . . . This manoeuvre seems quite impossible but the enemy were taken quite by surprise and they were not quick enough to stop it. The Germans now heavily reinforced 04, 24, but still failed in driving us out of CT 9 and 8.[41]

By about 8.05 am the remnants of what, by now, must have been a composite force consisting of men from all four companies of 9/RB with a sprinkling of Royal Engineers and 9/KRRC men were either clinging to the far lip of the mine crater or fighting hard in and amongst the tight knot of German communication trenches 8, 9 and 10, some 80yd or so to the northeast. The crater now became the focal point of German artillery firing high explosive from the southwest, of trench mortar bombs and of unrelenting machine-gun fire from Oskar Farm. Any thoughts of digging in around its freshly raised far lip were soon dismissed as an impossibility and indeed the real fear, which had by now gripped those at 9/RB HQ, was that the Germans, flushed with the success of their counter attacks, would drive all the way up to the crater and maintain their momentum, pushing their advantage to go on and attack the British front line.

The battle had reached its tipping point.

> Leaving behind numerous dead and wounded the Englishmen finally gave up the fight, by [the end of] which we also unfortunately mourned many heavy losses. *Leutnant* Schmid of the 4th Company and *Vizefeldwebel* Herbert of the 1st Company found a hero's death here along with many brave comrades. A heavy bit of work had been done. It became clear that, so far, the entire position, with the exception of the mine crater and parts of the *Ypern Weg*, were back in our hands. Because the [Bellewaarde Ridge] dominated the positions and, in certain measure, formed the key to the position of the regiment, it was clear that if the English were successful in establishing a firm footing here, the entire position of the regiment would become untenable because from here the entire regimental sector could be seen. Therefore [the English] had gone to great lengths to make a lodgement.[42]

There was a real possibility that a catastrophe was in the making and that the British front line, wrested from the Germans at such huge cost on 16 June, would be lost. The injection of Captain Christie's company of 9/KRRC came just in the nick of time to prevent total disaster, allied as it was with the decision to call on the British artillery to hit the German front line to prevent a stout German defence from being transformed into a glorious victory.[43] Subsequently the British batteries brought their fire to bear along the entire length of the original German front line in 42 Brigade's area, except in the immediate vicinity of the mine crater around Points 04 and 14 as no one could be certain whether it was still in British hands or not.

Approaching from the trenches of Railway Wood, some of Captain Christie's men had fought their way forward and skirted the northern bulge of the crater – its newly raised lip still being lashed by at least three machine guns from the direction of Oskar Farm – whilst Christie ordered others to extend to the south and dig out a disused German trench running along the edge of the dip in the ground, running parallel to the British front trench in no-man's-land, as a block line. At the same time the battle weary remnants of 9/RB summoned their last reserves of strength and formed up just beyond the Sunken Road barrier opposite the mine crater. A machine gun was manhandled into position by Lieutenant Dansey of 9/KRRC and along with another of 8/Motor Machine Gun Battery under Lieutenant Westropp, engaged the German machine guns in the direction of Oskar's Farm at long last and succeeded in reducing their fire. The German infantry too was checked and they were finally brought to a halt just shy of the crater, a position that had been at the very tip of their front line at 4.20 am that morning.

The German artillery now started to drench the crater and the ground immediately around it with high explosive and shrapnel and by a little after 9.30 am what was left of 9/RB and the remaining platoons of 9/KRRC had withdrawn to the dubious safety of their own front line. German infantry followed up and, as their guns lifted, they percolated into the crater. Little by little, during the course of the next 4 hours or so, the Germans gradually began to reclaim it as their own, marking their progress with flags.

The enemy meanwhile had been collecting in small parties on the railway line in vicinity of point 42 but these suffered considerably from mg fire brought to bear by Motor MGs in Railway Wood and one gun of the Somersets in [the British front-line trench] A1. During the whole of this time no enemy had been visible along ridge 64, 24, 04 but his process of re-occupation of trenches was marked from time to time by his signalling back (apparently to his artillery) with flags; grey on the one side and white and black striped on the other. This was first seen as he moved up trench 10–04 and then again as he re-occupied line 64–24. No sooner had he re-occupied line 10, 08, 17 than he commenced sniping vigorously in direction of crater where there was no lack of targets and here again we lost a great many.[44]

A good many more were lost at the hands of their own countrymen as the British guns bludgeoned the German trenches too.

When the men of 9/RB and Captain Christie's company of 9/KRRC had begun to fall back towards Railway Wood some had remained in the 150yd-long stretch of the original German front line and an old disused trench running south from the crater, whilst others still were lost somewhere in the tangle of German trenches towards the railway. Major General Couper was under no illusions about the fate of these riflemen, essentially those trapped to the north of the battalion's 'objective': 'Some of these men were no doubt shelled by their own guns, but as the battalion commander had reported that the Germans were attacking his front trenches, it does not appear that any action other than that taken would have been advisable.'[45]

An urgent call was received by 41 Brigade, well back in bivouacs near Ypres, at about 10.00 am to hurry forward as insurance to guard against a German break-through. The 8th Battalion the Rifle Brigade (8/RB), itself badly mauled during the fighting at Hooge in the summer, was 'packed and off' within the hour, and rushed up into dug-outs behind Y Wood. A plan hatched by Brigadier General Dudgeon for 6/SLI of 43 Brigade to move up and launch another attack had been shelved at around the same time in order to try and gain further information as to the state of his own brigade. By 10.15 am, however, almost everybody, British and German – apart from the few doughty warriors of Douglas Carmichael's C Company, who hung on grimly to the crater and ground to the northeast until late afternoon – was back where they had started.

Now the Germans were ready to make one last gargantuan effort to erase the last vestiges of the British presence from their original lines once and for all:

With our united strength it was now necessary to snatch these important points from the enemy. After a thorough bombardment of the crater by our artillery, *Hauptmann* Bauer with the 11th Company and parts of the 3rd, 9th, 10th and 12th Companies, as well as the remnants of the 1st Company, were sent to take the hill. It was another hard task which faced the brave troops. The English knew this well; for he fought back with extreme obstinacy after the loss of the hill that had been the goal of his attack. A hard and bitter fight developed; step by step the ground was wrestled away from the enemy; every shell hole was contended. Many good Swabians found a hero's death here, amongst them *Leutnant* Harr of the 12th Coy also. The Swabian is not so easily discouraged from his goal and the English felt the crude Swabian blows here. At 3 o'clock in the afternoon [2.00 pm British time] *Hauptmann* Bauer could finally report that the mine crater was occupied by fifty men. Simultaneously they also succeeded in driving the adversary out of the *Ypern Weg* so that our overall position was again in our possession.[46]

As the men of II Battalion of RIR 248 made preparations to relieve their exhausted comrades of I and III Battalions during the night, recover the wounded and make a start on burying the dead and repairing the damage, the Württembergers reflected on the day's fighting:

> The enemy did everything to hold the [Bellewaarde] hill, as a result of which the numerous dead Englishmen, especially those laying around in heaps in the mine crater, were an eloquent testimonial. In the late evening the enemy trench was shelled by heavy artillery once more, in order to prevent the enemy from repairing his undoubtedly also very badly damaged position. With the onset of darkness the sound of fire heard on both sides died down. 25 September was a further day of fame for the regiment from early morning till late in the night, against a significantly superior adversary in the heaviest fighting [we] threw [him] back into his positions again after [his] initial successes without outside help.[47]

The Second Attack at Bellewaarde – indeed the entire diversionary attack in the north – was over. As would be the case when the subsidiary attacks at Bois Grenier and Pietre further down the line finally petered out that day, both sides were back in exactly the same place they had been at 4.18 am that morning – not one inch of ground had been taken or lost.

To paraphrase a comment that would be uttered two years later, however, by a British officer prior to the Battle of Messines in June 1917, the 'geography had been changed'. Where there had once been a German redoubt menacing Railway Wood, the gaping mouth of the newly blown mine crater now screamed at the sky. It would be joined by many others in that sector over the coming years – some of the men who would be involved in the mining operations are remembered with a memorial and lie beneath the soil to this day. Both the British and German trenches and the surrounding ground bore the brutal scars of the sustained and violent artillery duel fought by both sides.

And what of the cost? Well, the evidence of the enormity of the loss was there for all to see; heaped up in bundles of khaki rags strewn across no-man's-land or tangled together in grotesque khaki and field-grey poses; knotted in death around machine-gun positions and the entrances to dug-outs.

At noon the Corps Commander had had to concur with Brigadier General Dudgeon's proposal that 'holding the line' was the best that 9/RB, indeed the best that his entire brigade, could be expected to do. It was fit for nothing else. There was nothing for it but to relieve 42 Brigade with 43 Brigade at dusk and move it to the rear. As the leading men of the 10th Battalion of the Durham Light Infantry (10/DLI) of 43 Brigade began to make their way into the shattered trenches, Lieutenant Colonel Villiers-Stuart once more scoured the lines for any of his men and found another forty or fifty – visibly shaken – just sitting and waiting in an assembly trench under Second Lieutenant Robin d'Erlanger. These he added to the 6 wounded officers and about 100 men he had found earlier; they were all he had left out of the 15 officers and 1,150 men whom he had sent into battle at dawn:

> At last, being sure there was no hope of finding any more 9/RBs I started off for Ypres, taking the poor remnants of the battalion with me. All the way down the communication trenches were crowded with wounded, walking or being carried down . . . We had the greatest difficulty in getting down to Ypres where I picked up a few more ORs who were waiting at the Menin Gate barrier . . . They were so depressed that they could no longer do anything properly.[48]

Captain Humphrey Moore, 9/RB's adjutant, finally signalled, 'Relief complete' to 42 Brigade at 10.05 pm.

Once safely through Ypres the battalion marched to the Asylum where trains were waiting to transport all three battalions – 9/RB, 5/OBLI and 5/KSLI – back to Poperinghe, but where four trains had been required to take them forward to the attack two days earlier now just one sufficed – and there was room to spare on that.

At 2.00 am the train pulled out and on arrival at Poperinghe the small parties that now passed for once-proud Kitchener battalions got off and marched wearily towards their bivouacs; some of 9/RB even managing a song on the way. But a simple marching song was not enough to convince their CO that his battalion had been anything other than practically destroyed and the sight of the pitifully small band that finally reached its destination, to be greeted by those in the rear echelon who had been left behind and the eleven new officers who had arrived too late to go into battle, was enough to make grown men weep – literally. There were gaping holes in the ranks and almost every last one of the 'bonhomous' crowd of officers which Hugh had referred to as the 'relics' was gone; the industrious and indefatigable Douglas Carmichael, the brave beyond their years John Purvis and Charles Scholey and the self-styled 'hoary headed old sport' himself, Hugh Montagu Butterworth, who had foretold in his final letter that he was 'practically bound to be outed'.

For Villiers-Stuart the song that the men sang as they marched into camp signalled the death knell of the old 9/RB:

> From that time on it was an entirely new battalion: new officers, new NCOs largely and new riflemen. . . . As we reached our bivouac Old Chester, our QM,

came out and his first words to me were, 'Wherever is the regiment, Sir?' I told him this party was all that was left of it – and he burst into tears. I never thought that he cared so much'.[49]

The scenario so vividly sketched in Hugh's final few words to John Allen at Wanganui had come to pass. He, along with many of his battalion, had indeed gone 'out', amidst 'such a scene of blood and iron as even this war has rarely witnessed'.

Chapter Seven

In Memoriam

The *Oxford University Roll of Service* includes the following entry under the heading 'University College':

> 1904 Butterworth, H. M. (Mar. 11, 1915). 2nd Lt. Rifle Brigade. France, Belgium. Killed in action in the Battle of Loos on Sept. 25, 1915.[1]

We now know, of course, that Hugh was killed in action on the Bellewaarde Ridge, near Ypres and although factually incorrect, the *Oxford University Roll of Service* entry taps into the spirit of the truth for one could argue that Hugh did indeed die fighting the Battle of Loos. Certainly his commanding officer thought so. For anyone cursorily scanning the pages of the memoirs of Lieutenant Colonel Villiers-Stuart in order to seek a time and place as to when and where Hugh Butterworth was killed, a glance at the headings for Chapters Eighteen and Nineteen – 'The Battle of Loos – Preparation' and 'The Battle of Loos – We Attack' – only seems to compound the error made in the Oxford Roll, although 'V-S' knew full well which sector his battalion was fighting on.

The fighting in which Hugh died eventually became known as the 'Second Attack on Bellewaarde' thanks to the deliberations of the Battles Nomenclature Committee, formed after the war to decide on the names to assign to the many struggles involving the British Army from 1914–1918. That attack was part of the large subsidiary effort to distract German attention from the main thrust around Loos and to lock German reserves into positions north of the La Bassée Canal so that they could not be thrown into the fighting on the coalfields. Thus Hugh, and many of his comrades, lost their lives in attempting to secure the strategic success of the entire Loos operation.

In the light of the above we should not be too hard on the two learned compilers of the Oxford memorial volume who, when presented with the date '25 September 1915' made the erroneous entry, for it was then, and indeed is now, an easy mistake to make. The 25 September 1915 was, and still is, a key date in the history the Great War for the British, marking, as it does, the opening day of that great and controversial Battle of Loos; the largest British offensive of the war at that time. By midnight of that first day, after some 18 hours of fighting, more than 6,300 men had lost their lives. Offer the date '25 September 1915' to anyone with an interest in the Great War and ask them to name a battle in which a man may have been killed on that day and it would be short odds that the reply would be 'Loos'.

Why wouldn't it? The opening day of Loos, with its many 'firsts' and associated controversies, is almost always viewed as a day of missed opportunities. At almost every point along the battle front the six British divisions engaged on 25 September had broken through the 'crust' – as their Commander-in-Chief, Sir John French, had put it – of the German front line, had taken key redoubts and strong points and in a few cases had even broken into the German second-line positions. These divisions had, as the British *Official History* records, gone 'all out' in the first rush and had become exhausted and, without reserves of their own, their losses had been substantial indeed. Fresh men had been required urgently to consolidate their gains and capitalise on their initial success but they did not arrive. The initial thrust, which had opened with such a promise of momentous things, could not be maintained and the offensive had gradually ground to a standstill almost everywhere. As night fell and the opening day drew to a close, the greater part of the British infantry at Loos lay exhausted where they had been obliged to dig-in, still short of the strong German second-line trench system. Casualties had been 'very heavy' amounting to 470 officers and 15,000 other ranks – nearly a sixth of the total force engaged.[2]

Such a 'butcher's bill' is truly staggering but when allied with the controversies and recriminations surrounding the control, release, handling and subsequent destruction of the divisions in general reserve on and after the first day, the higher direction of the later fighting – and the further heavy losses – which followed, ultimately leading to the removal of Sir John French as Commander-in-Chief of the BEF and his replacement by Sir Douglas Haig, it is understandable that other actions of 25 September 1915 have been all but forgotten. The *Official History* devotes just 6 pages to the 3 British/Indian subsidiary attacks of 25 September and yet, in terms of raw casualty figures, the 4 divisions engaged in those 'diversionary' attacks suffered losses amounting to 291 officers and 7,935 other ranks killed, wounded, missing or taken prisoner that same day. This scale of loss represented more than half again the total of the first-day casualties at Loos itself.

In the Bellewaarde battle alone, the largest of the three 'Loos diversions', 132 officers and 3,742 other ranks of the 3rd and 14th Divisions became casualties. Of those, 54 officers and 1,767 other ranks losses were sustained by the 14th Division, the vast majority – 41 officers and 1,548 other ranks – being borne by the assaulting units of 42 Infantry Brigade and remarkably, of that total, 21 officers and 560 Other Ranks – more than a third – had been killed or had died of wounds.[3] In his second and more comprehensive report on the operations, the 14th Division's commanding officer, Major General Victor Couper, wrote: 'I much regret the heavy losses sustained. . . . In spite, however, of these . . . the men came out of action in high spirits and their morale is improved.'[4]

It was a moot point whether the loss of so many men and well-respected officers in 9/RB, for example, with not one single inch of ground gained to show for it, had lifted the spirits and improved the morale of those who survived but they might, just might perhaps, have been able to stomach such a sacrifice if they felt their comrades had died for the higher cause of securing a resounding victory in Artois. After all, Major General Couper was of the opinion that the attack had been, 'very well and carefully thought out beforehand, and it appears to me to have been within an ace of succeeding'.[5]

There is no doubt that Hugh's battalion, attacking in the gloom of a dull and damp late September morning, had succeeded in its objective of taking the first two lines of German trenches north of Bellewaarde Farm and in doing so had committed the Germans to do everything in their power to defend them. The same was true in several places along the rest of 42 Brigade's line but, and this proved to be crucial, some of the attacking columns of the other two battalions had either lost direction in the dark or had been virtually wiped out, leaving gaps in the line which the Germans, fighting on familiar ground, exploited to the full. Proud, determined, protected from the British shells by substantial, well-constructed dug-outs, armed with a seemingly limitless supply of bombs which every man had been trained to use and backed by well-sited machine guns which the preliminary bombardment had failed to destroy, the German soldiers hounded the British interlopers relentlessly. Fighting in unfamiliar trenches at the far limits of a tenuous supply line with dwindling supplies of ammunition, bombs and trained bombers to use them, the British capacity to resist was finite. As almost all of the officers of the three battalions of 42 Brigade involved became casualties early on in the fight – only one officer from the whole of the assaulting columns returned unscathed – communications between the headquarters and the assaulting companies of individual battalions became extremely difficult and those between the adjacent columns of different battalions virtually non-existent. It became almost impossible for commanding officers to find out what was happening deep in the labyrinth of German fire and communication trenches and to exert any influence on the battle's progress. Command and control effectively collapsed.

It hadn't helped that the British Army of autumn 1915 was using such a bewildering array of hand grenades or bombs – a state of affairs that made a mockery of any attempts at standardised bombing training. Consequently, only certain men – the dedicated teams of 'bombers' – had been trained in their use and when these men were killed or wounded there were very few who had knowledge of how to use the bombs to replace them, even if extra supplies had been got forward. Major General Couper was of the opinion that: 'The variety of grenades issued is a great drawback to adequate training – of the different classes issued to the Division, Nos. 6 and 7 were the best and Bethune's with Brock Lighters were fairly satisfactory. The Newton Pippins were not altogether reliable'.[6]

V Corps Headquarters had already gathered and digested earlier reports from its subordinate headquarters and four days after the battle had sent a memorandum off to General Plumer at Second Army:

> The time seems to have come when every infantry man should be trained as a grenadier, and carry grenades in the assault. In one case, when all the grenadiers were put out of action, there was an abundance of grenades but no man who knew how to use them. Although careful arrangements were made for keeping up the supply of grenades there were times when they ran short in the front line, owing to men carrying them losing their way in the maze of trenches or becoming casualties. The risk of this would be minimised if every man in an assault carried grenades.[7]

There has been much discussion during the past few years regarding the performance of the British Army from 1914 to 1918 as being akin to a 'learning curve'; analysing its shortcomings and mistakes, coming to conclusions and adapting its techniques and tactics in order to improve. With the days of plentiful supplies of the Mills bomb – which could be used by all ranks – still in the future, this perhaps serves as an early example from the gently sloping foothills on that ascending slope which was the 'learning' graph.

No matter what the men of 9/RB had achieved, however, no matter that Hugh Butterworth, Douglas Carmichael, John Purvis, Charles Scholey and Edward Henn had penetrated and taken the German trenches, no matter that they had fought so hard and for so long to hold them, the fact remained that the battalion had ended up back where it had started and all 5 of those officers and more than 150 of their men had perished in the attempt. Locally, tactically, and in spite of their almost superhuman efforts, they and their counterparts in the other battalions involved in the diversionary attacks had failed. But had they helped in the achievement of the higher goal; that of locking German reserves into positions north of the La Bassée Canal? It takes the British *Official History* just seven pithy lines to deal with both the tactical and strategic results of the diversions:

> All three subsidiary attacks had thus ended with the assaulting troops back in their original trenches, mainly because the British hand grenades were inferior both in quality and number to those of the enemy. No German reinforcements other than local supports had been required to meet them and they therefore had not the desired influence on the main battle south of the La Bassée Canal.[8]

If that was the official and rather brisk British conclusion regarding the results of the diversionary attacks, what of the German perspective? If it is taken as a given that no 'local advantages' whatever were gained on any sector where the subsidiary attacks took place, do the various official German accounts and unit histories at least provide any clues as to whether those diversions succeeded in preventing German reserves being shuffled south to bolster units facing the British offensive at Loos, or even being sent further afield to support the German armies facing the French onslaught in Champagne?

According to the official German account, *Der Weltkrieg*, by mid-September 1915, *Generaloberst* Albrecht von Württemberg, commanding the German Fourth Army and responsible for the front in Flanders from the North Sea coast to the Ypres–Comines Canal, had reported increasing British activity on his army's front. At that time the German 53rd Reserve Division, based around Roulers, was the reserve unit of the *Oberste Heeresleitung* (OHL) behind the German Fourth Army. It is significant that there is no specific mention of the Bellewaarde/Hooge attack in *Der Weltkrieg*, simply the following observation with regard to actions on 25 September: 'early in the morning, British forces had attacked against sectors of the 4th Army's positions in Flanders, but the army had been able to repel such attacks without the support of the OHL'.[9] This view appears to be supported by the standard work on the Saxon Army in the Great War, albeit a work published in 1919 and thus perhaps flawed somewhat by its proximity to the events it describes. Nevertheless, it is interesting to note that the involvement of both the 54th Reserve Division, providing the front-line units at Bellewaarde/Hooge on 25 September, and the 53rd Reserve Division does not warrant a mention. It would appear that the complete and utter suppression of the British diversion in Flanders was not worthy of note, at least in this particular standard work using an admittedly more 'broad brush' approach to events at the time and on a much larger canvas.[10]

One would expect a more detailed picture to emerge from the accounts in individual German unit histories. Although not part of the brigade to which RIR 248 – the unit facing 9/RB on the day – belonged, *Reserve Jäger Battalion* 26 (RJB 26) was also part of the 54th Reserve Division and had spent the whole day in reserve in the main German second position near *Eksternest*, north of Bellewaarde Lake. The battalion had not been called upon to go forward and had therefore not seen combat, although it had suffered casualties from the British shelling. The unit's regimental history is therefore fulsome in its praise of both RIR 248 and RIR 246, the two regiments of the 54th Reserve Division that bore the brunt of the British attack. These units are given full credit for the successful defence of their trenches; the RJB 26 account even going so far as to trumpet the counter attacks of the 'line regiments, over open fields' accompanied by *'Pfeifen, Trommeln und Signalhörner'* – pipes, drums and signal horns – as 'especially successful' without any need of support from the reserve units.[11]

Leafing through the pages of the official unit histories of the infantry regiments that made up the Saxon 53rd Reserve Division – Reserve Infantry Regiments 241, 242, 243 and 244 along with *Reserve Jäger Battalion* 25 (RJB 25) – positioned centrally behind the German Fourth Army's front, only one, RIR 241, was put on alert and sent forward towards Zonnebeke from its quarters around Iseghem and Rumbeke in the suburbs of Roulers, but it was stood down the same night without seeing any action.[12] Of the other units of the division, RIR 243 had been moved into rest at Woumen, south of Dixmude on 14 September and, despite the British attack, was not recalled until 30 September.[13]

So the official British summary of the results of the diversionary attacks, with respect to the Bellewaarde Ridge battle specifically, appears to have been vindicated; no 'local advantages' gained, no 'distraction' of German forces from the main battle front and no need of reinforcements other than that from 'local supports' to meet them.

But although reinforcements were not required to deal directly with the British assault, what of the other, more strategic objective; that of pegging German reserves to the north of the La Bassée Canal? Surely, if merely local supports had been sufficient to quash the British effort, then those units in reserve should at least have been available to German commanders faced with a much larger attack developing elsewhere? *Der Weltkrieg* observes that it was 'remarkable' that after 25 September 1915, OHL left the 53rd Reserve Division behind the Fourth Army's front near Roulers, although it could easily have been shifted to the Sixth Army, heavily engaged in Artois. Its conclusion was that: 'Obviously [Falkenhayn, the German Commander-in-Chief] counted on the possibility of serious English attacks in the vicinity of Ypres or landings in the [coastal] *Marinekorps* area. He had given orders to 4th Army in mid-August to hold the coastline at any cost.'[14]

Whilst there is no mention of any movement of large German units northward from other sectors specifically to assist in the fighting in Flanders and whilst the 53rd Reserve Division might be viewed more as 'local' support, as the British *Official History* puts it, the fact that the official German history states that this division was not moved south immediately towards Artois or further afield might indicate that the British losses of 25 September had not been entirely in vain, particularly when the movements of individual German units are analysed.

The picture painted in the pages of *Der Weltkrieg*, however, of the 53rd Reserve Division being held back in Flanders after 25 September in order to counter possible further assaults in Flanders or along the coast, does not tell the whole story. The regimental history of RJB 26, the reserve unit of the 54th Division on 25 September, contradicts the *Reichsarchiv* account by stating that the 53rd Reserve Division was sent from its rear quarters to Champagne in support of the German Third Army after the opening of the Bellewaarde/Hooge offensive.[15] A more detailed study of the movements of the infantry units of 53rd Reserve Division from 26–30 September/1 October 1915, however, reveals that of the five units concerned, only two – RIR 242 and RIR 244 – remained in positions north of the La Bassée Canal. These two regiments were not held in the immediate vicinity of Ypres but instead made a short hop south to take up positions with the German 40th Division on the right flank of the

German Sixth Army between the Rivers Douve and Lys in the Messines/Ploegsteert sector. They remained there until 15 November 1915. The remaining three regiments – RIR 241, RIR 243 and RJB 25, along with the 53rd Divisional Staff, Divisional *Pioniere* and medical orderlies – boarded trains between 1 and 3 October bound for the Champagne front, there to fight under the aegis of the German Third Army until November 1915. That was an odyssey that warranted an entire chapter in the official account of the Saxon Army, unlike the Bellewaarde battle, which had not been deemed worthy of even a passing mention.[16]

Thus the greater part of the German 53rd Reserve Division was very definitely moved south from Flanders and beyond the La Bassée Canal – more than 100 miles south of the canal line in fact – within a week of the short yet fierce struggle for the Bellewaarde Ridge and perhaps, in coming to a judgment regarding the strategic value of the Second Attack on Bellewaarde, it is all a question of timing. The movement of units to the Champagne front came five long days after the opening of the major offensives in Artois and Champagne, dubbed *Doppelschlacht im Artois und der Champagne* by the Germans. There was little doubt that the German command felt that the French offensives – involving 17 infantry and 2 cavalry divisions in Artois and 28 infantry and 6 cavalry divisions in Champagne – posed a far deadlier threat than the British nine infantry division 'diversion' at Loos. On the Champagne front the German Third Army under *Generaloberst* von Einem suffered grievously during those five crucial days following 25 September and cried out for any help it could get. Von Einem had constantly cautioned OHL against an imminent French breakthrough and later revealed in his memoirs that 25 September and the days that followed were the most critical of the entire war. Of course the situation in Artois was crucial as well, but after the first few days it became clear to OHL that at least the fighting in Artois could be contained. At some point on or around 28/29 September it also became clear to OHL that neither Flanders nor Artois were to be the crucial fronts and that Champagne was.

It would be cheering then to record that Hugh's death and the killing and maiming of many of his comrades in Flanders had had some tangible result and indeed there is some evidence to support that view. Perhaps at best it could be argued that because some units of the 53rd Reserve Division were kept in the north to counter the possibility of further British attacks between Ypres and Armentières, then German attention had been distracted 'from the main battle front' and since there was no movement of units from north of the La Bassée Canal before 30 September then the diversion had succeeded in its aim. Such a stance could be justified given the available evidence. On the other hand and at worst, with no ground gained, no extra reinforcements used up in countering the British break in and with two regiments and one battalion of a German division commencing their transfer to the Champagne region six days after the northern feint at Bellewaarde to help counter the French offensive there, the results of that action could be viewed as a grim and ghastly failure.

Taking the broader view, however, with regard to the restrictions on the freedom of action of the German OHL in the immediate aftermath of the Bellewaarde fighting, the sacrifice of Hugh Butterworth and his brothers-in-arms should be seen to have counted for something.

For the more hardened and cynical of observers, however, scanning once again the brief quote in the British *Official History* regarding the end results of the diversions and the note to the effect that the British hand grenades were 'inferior both in quality and number to those of the enemy', some might conclude that the loss of more than 8,000 men in total was a terrifically high price to pay in exchange for the knowledge that the Germans had better quality and more plentiful supplies of hand grenades!

Up on the Bellewaarde Ridge the day after the battle, the war went on. The forward battalions of RIR 248 had been relieved during the night of 25 September by their reserve battalion and *Hauptmann der Reserve* Schnitzer set down his thoughts as the sun rose on the battlefield on 26 September:

> A different day, a Sunday! Deathly silence! Friend and foe bury their numerous dead. We bury ours – provisionally – beside the railway line to Zonnebeke. Later they will be dug up, carefully wrapped and interred in the beautiful regimental cemetery at Polygon Wood. Two severely wounded English officers lay out in front of the 8th Company [under] Hauptmann Willich, who wail with heart rending moans and groans: 'Oh! Help us, help us!' The English are too cowardly to climb up out of the trench and get their wounded; self evident to us Germans. Suddenly a white handkerchief appears over the edge of the English trench and is waved. We answer in the same way. The commander of the 8th Company prohibits the sentries from shooting in case an Englishman should show himself above the trench. Indeed one does show himself there and asks for permission to be allowed to get both of the wounded men. Permission is granted. Four Tommies drag both officers into their trench, then take up a position on the trench parapet, wave their caps and shout: 'The Germans; Hurrah! Hurrah!' and vanish sinking into their trench again.[17]

A similar incident is described in the history of RJB 26 which relieved RIR 246 in the front line to the south of RIR 248's sector 'under constant heavy rain' during the night of 26/27 September. Their history notes that:

> Heavy rain began to fall during the day and drowned any desire on the part of friend and foe to carry on the fight. . . . On the 27th the enemy was in need of rest and there was almost no activity on both sides. The English noticed a wounded comrade between the lines and arranged a short truce to bring him in, thanking the Germans afterwards with a 'Hip, Hip Hooray!'. During the truce

the Saxon *Jägers* recorded that they had recovered an English machine gun which they had located in no man's land.[18]

On 27 September, two days after the battle, the funerals for the German dead of RIR 248 took place at the newly constructed regimental burial ground north of Polygon Wood and the task of repairing and rebuilding of the trench system got under way with the support of the German *Pioniere*. Again there is an admission in the regimental history of RIR 248 that makes it very clear that the British attack had had a significant effect on the integrity of the German positions, an effect that would be felt for weeks to come as reconstruction took place. There was hardly a single trench that had not been affected by the shell fire and the complete rebuilding of the front line took more than a month of strenuous labour:

> (Autumn 1915): Large portions of our position had been completely destroyed during the days of battle in September due to the mine explosion and hostile artillery. The damage had been repaired through hard, relentless work by the garrison, with the support of only a few *Pioniere* and *Arbeitskommandos* [which took] until the end of October. In the front line, splinter-proof shelters and loopholes, completely destroyed during the combat, had been reconstructed. At the same time one had begun to build bomb-proof concrete shelters; only a few – designed for men and as machine gun positions – had been ready for use during the first half of November. As necessary as the expansion was, it meant exhausting labour, especially when it came to the concrete constructions.[19]

It is interesting to ponder – given the amount of sheer hard graft that the Germans put in – as to whether the attack of 25 September actually had the effect of strengthening the German defences to a far greater extent than may have been the case had it not taken place at all. Certainly the Germans had thought that they had built a solid system on the Bellewaarde Ridge over the winter of 1914/15 but after being ejected from their front lines on 16 June 1915, they had toiled hard to improve their trenches further, constructing splinter-proof dug-outs and observation posts with the use of sand bags, timber and cement blocks to ensure that it did not happen again. In this they had been successful but the final sentence in the above quote is significant for it marks the start of a deliberate German policy of placing their faith in ferro-concrete defences in the Ypres Salient. Concrete pill-boxes – infantry shelters and machine-gun posts – would have been developed in any case but the attack in September 1915, coming just three months after the major effort to dislodge the Germans from the Bellewaarde Ridge in mid-June 1915, hardened German resolve to get the job of pouring concrete done and done well and quickly. The resulting structures would be the very concrete pill-boxes the British Army would have to take – one by one and at great cost – as it slogged its way up towards Passchendaele during the Third Battle of Ypres from the end of July until November 1917.

On the battlefield it had been sheer slaughter. Two officers and fifty men of the 14th Division Cyclist Company had been engaged to form a burial party for the period of the battle and its immediate aftermath, but such were the difficulties of recovering the dead from the battlefield that the bodies of British soldiers were still lying out in no-man's-land several days later when 8/RB moved up to relieve 10/DLI in the trenches opposite Bellewaarde Farm on the evening of 28 September. 8/RB had been one of the battalions that had borne the brunt of that summer's fighting at Hooge and the men who had been through it and had survived knew only too well the high cost of fighting determined German opponents on that sector.

Completed during the hours of darkness, the relief was carried out in dry weather, although it had by now turned colder, but with the dawn came torrential rain. It seeped into the already battered British trenches and they quickly became water-logged. As daylight struggled to break through the lowering sheets of cloud that smothered the Bellewaarde Ridge and lashed it with a merciless rain, the scene beyond the British parapets that greeted the 8/RB sentries was as grim and squalid a tableau of catastrophe as one could imagine: 'Remnants of the recent fighting seen every-where. Our own dead lying in scores in front of the parapet. The parapets and communication trenches much blown about . . . our own front very weak from lack of wire which had all been cleared preparatory to the attack.' [20]

Such was the carnage between the lines, with body parts scattered amongst the shell holes, abandoned trenches and mutilated hedgerows, that one 8/RB officer later wrote that it was as if a homicidal axeman had been let loose in no-man's-land. Those 'scores' of dead must have been a constant reminder for the men of 8/RB of the heavy losses suffered by their sister battalion and a grim preview, perhaps, of what might yet be in store for them. A few days later, on 6 October, under an almost constant and accurate deluge of German shells and suffering an increased level of sniping, the 8/RB diarist blurted out that there was 'a general feeling throughout the battalion that the 14th Division has had more than its share of this unpleasant salient. Men have lost confidence and do not show themselves at their best'. Later there were dark hints that the strain was becoming too much for some; 'the problem has arisen as how to deal with the many men whose nerves become broken in the trenches'. [21]

With the Germans still dominating the ground and bringing effective artillery and sniper fire to bear on the British lines it was nigh on impossible to clear the battlefield of its grisly contents, especially as many men had died in what had once been old German communication trenches running across no-man's-land. Unable to be brought in, the bodies remained where they fell in great numbers, open to the elements and the other non-human 'inhabitants' of no-man's-land.

This might explain why so many of those 9/RB men killed on 25 September have no known grave today. Of the 5 officers and 153 men killed or died of wounds up to 12 October 1915 – the day before the battalion went back into the line again at Potijze on 13 October – all 5 officers, Hugh, Douglas Carmichael, Edward Henn, John Purvis and Charles Scholey, along with a staggering 140 other ranks – a total of 92 per cent of those who died – have no known grave and are commemorated on the Menin Gate in Ypres. Only thirteen other ranks have recognised places of burial and all but three of those died of wounds. These men are buried in cemeteries ranging from those situated close to Casualty Clearing Stations behind the Salient such as Lijssenthoek near Poperinghe, to those on the coast that were near the large Base Hospitals at Wimereux, Etaples and Le Touquet and even in England, where one man was conveyed before he finally succumbed to his wounds on 8 October to be buried in Welford Road Cemetery in Leicester. Of those who have no known grave we know for a fact that some of the officers named above penetrated the German second trench and even threatened the third as far as Point 84 with a handful of their men and many perished there. Some would have been recovered by the Germans after the battle and buried individually, either in battlefield graves just behind the lines or in German cemeteries like that at Polygon Wood a little further back. With the ebb and flow of the titanic battles in the Salient still to come in 1917 and 1918 many of these graves would simply have been lost; smashed by shell fire or swallowed by the sucking swamp that characterised the latter stages of Third Ypres.

As far as can be ascertained only 1 man of the 158 of 9/RB who were killed on the day is buried close to the battlefield on which he fell – B/2747 Rifleman Charles Henry Campbell who lies in Hooge Crater Cemetery, whilst another who went missing – B/3051 Rifleman William Davis – is buried at Harlebeke Cemetery, 32km east of Ypres. This cemetery was formed after the Armistice in November 1918 and in 1924–1925 men were brought in from various German burial sites and smaller British plots. It is entirely possible that Davis was buried by the Germans initially and his body brought to Harlebeke in the mid-1920s.

Of Hugh Butterworth, however, there was no trace and after an interval of almost ninety-five years we know nothing more of his fate at the time of writing. We do know, however, that as the Battalion War Diary lists all the 9/RB officers involved as being 'killed' immediately after the action, as opposed to 'missing', one might assume that someone had witnessed Hugh's death. With no further news of Hugh in the days that followed and with no hope of him turning up alive, the following cable was sent 'OHMS' from the War Office to New Zealand on 30 September:

To Butterworth – Collegiate School Wanganui NZ
    Deeply REGRET TO INFORM YOU THAT Lt H M Butterworth KRRC [*sic*] killed in action Sept 25th – 26th.
    Lord Kitchener expresses his sympathy.[22]

Why Hugh chose to give his own name and address in New Zealand as the address for his next of kin we will never know but give it he did and as his great friend John Allen had been charged, according to Hugh's will, with opening any letters addressed to him it must have been John Allen who was the first to receive the news of Hugh's death before any of his close family.

In September 1915, *The Times* had encouraged relatives of fallen officers to forward, 'with the intimation of death, biographical details in their possession'. The following duly appeared on 5 October 1915:

Fallen Officers
"The Times" List of Casualties.

The death of a large number of officers, whose names have not up to the present appeared in the official casualty lists, is announced in our obituary columns today.

SECOND LIEUTENANT HUGH MONTAGU BUTTERWORTH, 9th Rifle Brigade, who was killed in Flanders on September 25, was the only son of Mr. and Mrs. G. M. Butterworth of Christchurch, New Zealand, and was 29 years old. He played rackets (Doubles) for Oxford against Cambridge in 1905 and 1906. In the former year he had the Hon. C. N. Bruce as a partner and in the latter year Mr G. N. Foster. He was on the losing side both years.[23]

This was followed up by a more detailed notice in *The Times* just under a week later:

LIEUTENANT HUGH MONTAGUE [sic] BUTTERWORTH . . . who was killed in Flanders on September 25, was the only son of Mr. and Mrs. G. M. Butterworth, of Christchurch, New Zealand, formerly of High Street, Swindon, brother of the Misses Butterworth, Barton Court School, New Milton, and nephew of Sir A. Kaye Butterworth. He was educated at Hazelwood, Limpsfield, at Marlborough, and at University College, Oxford. At Marlborough he was captain of the cadet corps, a member of the cricket, football and hockey teams, racket representative and winner of the athletic championship cup. At Oxford, where he went in 1904, he was a very good but unlucky all-round athlete. At different times he represented his university at cricket, football and hockey, and he won the Freshman's 100yards, but a bad knee and ankle only permitted him to obtain his Blue at Rackets. He played in the doubles with Mr. Clarence Bruce as partner in 1905 and Mr. Godfrey Foster in 1906. In 1907 he went to New Zealand and became assistant Master at the Collegiate School, Wanganui. Returning in March last, he at once received a commission in the 9th Battalion Rifle Brigade, and went to the front in May. He had been in command of his company since July 30. His colonel writes:- 'He showed, throughout the most conspicuous courage and coolness, and can never be replaced as an officer. His name had long been sent in for captain's rank'.[24]

By that time the news – doubtless revealed by John Allen – had travelled to the other side of the world. On 7 October 1915, two day after the first *Times* obituary, the *Auckland Weekly News* followed suit and published the following:

BUTTERWORTH, Lieutenant H. M., 9th Battalion, Rifle Brigade, killed in action near Ypres on September 28 [*sic*], was the only son of Mr. G. M. Butterworth, a well known Christchurch resident and was 30 yrs of age. He was a master at Wanganui Collegiate School and left there in January last and went Home to offer his services to the War Office, obtaining a commission in the Rifle Brigade almost immediately. Lt. Butterworth was a prominent North Island cricketer.[25]

Hugh's death, as recorded earlier, was a crushing blow for his old school. In December 1915, three months after he was killed, the Wanganui *Collegian* listed 349 Old Boys who were known to be serving in the forces. A year later the number had risen to over 500, amongst which were included 10 masters. Of these, sixty-seven were known to have been killed. In terms of the impact it had on the Wanganui Collegiate School community, one name on that list 'led all the rest' – and that was the name of 'Curly' Butterworth.[26]

During the months that followed further obituaries appeared in the magazines of the schools that Hugh had attended. In early November the *Marlburian* devoted what amounted to almost an entire page to a loving and emotional tribute written by Leslie Woodroffe, one of Hugh's closest friends during his Marlborough days.

In Memoriam
HUGH MONTAGU BUTTERWORTH
AT M.C. 1899–1904. C 2.

From *The Times*.—Lieutenant Hugh Montagu Butterworth, 9th Rifle Brigade, who was killed in Flanders on September 25th , was the only son of Mr. and Mrs. G. M. Butterworth, of Christchurch, New Zealand, formerly of High-street, Swindon, brother of the Misses Butterworth, Barton Court School, New Milton, and nephew of Sir A. Kaye Butterworth. He was educated at Hazelwood, Limpsfield, at Marlborough, and at University College, Oxford. At Marlborough he was captain of the cadet corps, a member of the cricket, football, and hockey teams, racket representative, and winner of the athletic championship cup. At Oxford, where he went in 1904, he was a very good, but unlucky all-round athlete. At different times he represented his university at cricket, football, and hockey, and he won the Freshmen's 100 yards, but a bad knee and ankle only permitted him to obtain his Blue at rackets. He played in the doubles with Mr. Clarence Bruce as partner in 1905, and Mr. Geoffrey [*sic*] Foster in 1906. In 1907 he went to New Zealand and became assistant master at the Collegiate School, Wanganui. Returning in March last, he at once received a commission in the 9th Battalion Rifle Brigade, and went to the front in May. He had been in command of his company since July 30th. His colonel writes:- 'He shewed throughout the most conspicuous courage and coolness, and can never be replaced as an officer. His name had long been sent in for captain's rank.'

The short biography of Hugh Butterworth, reproduced above, mentions the achievements by which he came into public prominence, and the events and changes which marked his life; but it says nothing of his high sense of honour, of his affectionate nature, of his straight-forward manliness of character, of his strong common-sense and clear-headedness, of his cheerfulness, of his humour; it says nothing of the willing sacrifice, on which he insisted, when, in spite of their unselfish wishes, he decided to accompany his people to New Zealand, and to give up his honour degree, an assured position in the legal profession, for which he was intended, and his excellent chance of a cricket 'Blue'; it says nothing of his second great sacrifice, when, having by sheer merit won himself a happy and comfortable position with good prospects at Wanganui, with congenial work, immense popularity and every opportunity for the athletics which he loved, he resolved to leave all and to offer his services and his life to his country.

He was a splendid athlete, and, whatever he played, he played hard; but he always recognised games in their proper proportion. He accepted his many disappointments at Oxford with philosophic resignation; it was indeed hard that one, who was regarded as the best hockey-forward in Oxford, and who made 130 in the Seniors' cricket match, should have been deprived by ill-luck of the crowning honour.

In New Zealand he devoted himself heart and soul to coaching the school teams, and he met with marked success; nor was he less successful in his other teaching. He had inherited a strong love for English literature, and he taught his pupils to love and appreciate all that was best in it. His influence was great and always for good; at school, at college, at Wanganui, and in his regiment everyone who knew him loved, trusted, admired and respected him; and it can safely be said that he never made an enemy. Marlborough never produced a more worthy son.

L.W.[27]

In January 1916, Hugh's prep school, Hazelwood, included, under the heading 'HAZELWOOD ROLL OF HONOUR', a short notice on the front page of its school magazine which also borrowed heavily from *The Times* obituary, along with obituaries for sixteen other Old Boys who had been killed, '*Pro Rege et Patria*'.

HUGH MONTAGUE [*sic*] BUTTERWORTH,
Lieutenant, 9th Rifle Brigade; killed in action in Flanders, September 25th, aged 29. His Colonel writes, 'He showed throughout the most conspicuous coolness and courage, and can never be replaced as an officer; his name had been long sent in for Captain's rank.'[28]

Even whilst the obituaries and memorial notices were being published, back in New Zealand, the question of probate of Hugh's will and the administration of his estate was grinding its way through the bureaucratic systems in both the courts of Wellington and the War Office in London. After receiving the official telegram announcing Hugh's death, John Allen had alerted the office of the Public Trustee of New Zealand and acting in his capacity of executor of Hugh's will, Mr T S Ronaldson began the process by writing to the War Office on 11 November 1915 to request a death certificate. Mr Ronaldson recorded that Hugh's estate in New Zealand was worth 'approximately £560' and enquired of the War Office as to whom Hugh had 'allotted his deferred pay, or, if no allotment was made, where such deferred pay can now be obtained, and also the amount owing to date of death'.[29] The death certificate was duly signed and dispatched after Christmas 1915:

105651/2 (C.3.A.L.)
CERTIFICATE OF DEATH
Certified that it appears from the records of this Office that Temporary Second Lieutenant HUGH MONTAGU BUTTERWORTH 9th (Service) Battalion, Rifle Brigade, has been reported as killed in action on the 25th day of September 1915, either in France or in Belgium.

(Sgd.) H. H. Fawcett
For the Secretary, War Office

Dated at the War Office, London,
this 31st day of December, 1915.[30]

In the event the official death certificate issued by the War Office was superfluous to requirements. After securing affidavits from John Allen and solicitor Frederick Fitchett, the Public Trustee in Wellington, in which a copy of the original War Office telegram of 30 September was taken as proof of Hugh's death, Hugh's will was proved on 25 November, 1915:

Public Trust No. 27
PROBATE
IN THE
Supreme Court of New Zealand
Wellington District

Be it known to all men that on this 25th day of November in the year one thousand nine hundred and fifteen the last Will and Testament of Hugh Montagu Butterworth, lately a Lieutenant in the 9th Rifle Brigade of His Majesty's Expeditionary Forces operating in Flanders, formerly of Wanganui, in the Provincial District of Wellington, Schoolmaster, deceased a copy of which is hereunto annexed hath been exhibited read and proved before the Honourable Frederick Revans Chapman, a judge in the Supreme Court of New Zealand and administration of the real and personal estate effects and credits of the deceased hath been and is hereby granted to the PUBLIC TRUSTEE the Executor in the said Will and Testament named being first sworn faithfully to execute the said Will by paying the debts and legacies of the deceased as far as the property will extend and the law binds.[31]

On 6 January 1916 the Assistant Financial Secretary at the War Office wrote to the State Treasurer of New Zealand informing them that they held a sum of 'fifty seven pounds, sixteen shillings and ten pence' (£57 16s 10d) due to Hugh's estate from Army Funds and asking that the Treasurer pay the executor on proof of the grant of probate. On the same day a letter was written to the Public Trustee acting as Hugh's executor, informing them that the State Treasurer had been instructed to pay the same sum on receipt of proof of probate. This sum of £57 16s 10d was in addition to Hugh's arrears of pay which amounted to £46 10s 0d representing 124 days at 7s 6d per day. Thus more than £100 was due to Hugh's estate from British Army funds and when this was added to Hugh's existing estate in New Zealand the executor could begin to fulfil Hugh's wishes by paying out the various monetary sums totalling £80 to the beneficiaries named in Hugh's will.

All of Hugh's books found a place on the shelves of Selwyn House library and John Allen received all Hugh's pictures and personal effects in Wanganui. The residue of Hugh's estate was to be handed over to his mother Catherine but as she had been struck down with 'consumption' – tuberculosis – just a few weeks after her only son had sailed for England in early 1915 and her condition was deteriorating his sister May was handed the responsibility. Although Hugh's mother was still in New Zealand when Hugh was killed and had spent six months in a sanatorium in the Cashmere Hills near Christchurch, it seemed only natural that the Public Trustee should entrust his sister May, running her school at Barton Court in New Milton, Hampshire with sister Margaret, with the 'disposal' of Hugh's non-personal effects. Hugh had, in any case, wished her to have all of his athletic cups and trophies, the whereabouts of which are unknown at the time of writing.

Hugh's tremendous and continuing impact on the Wanganui Collegiate School community has been alluded to and cannot be overemphasised; indeed his story is such an integral part of the warp and weft of Wanganui life that his war service was recounted during the ANZAC Service as recently as April 2008.

Hugh had, in his seven years as a master, made an indelible impression on Wanganui and loved the life he had made for himself there. Wanganui – the boys, his friends and the surroundings – had in its turn made a huge impression upon him. In the last paragraph of his last letter he had observed that: 'We are not a sentimental crowd at the Collegiate School . . . but I think in a letter of this sort, one can say how frightfully attached one is to the old brigade. Also I am very, very much attached to the School and to Selwyn [House] in particular. There are two thousand things I should like to say about what I feel, but they can't be put down, I find. Live long and prosper, all of you'. It was almost as if he was saying 'goodbye'.

His obituary in the Wanganui *Collegian* of December 1915 ran over three pages. An abridged version of the main text, written by another of his friends and school-master colleagues H E Sturge, who taught at the school from 1910 to 1918, found its way into *Letters* early the following year, but the sections that were edited out are worth printing as they provide additional insights into how Hugh Butterworth the man was viewed by his colleagues:

To write of Hugh Butterworth is no easy task. One feels something of the diffi-culty which faced Pericles when called upon to pay a tribute to those Athenians who had fallen in battle. 'Adequate words,' he says. 'are hard to find; for the friends of the dead will think that less than justice has been done to their virtues, while strangers will suspect exaggeration.' There is, of course, no need for us to consider the stranger's standpoint, as this will in the main be read by friends; but that they will feel that the very things for which they most valued his friendship have been left unsaid, is more than likely. Indeed, it can hardly be otherwise . . .

The cutting short of a man's life before he has done what it lay in him to do is one of war's darkest and saddest sides. Many have been swept away on these battlefields of Europe, crowned with honour, but still mere boys, robbed of all the pleasures and achievements of manhood. To Butterworth fate was kinder; war did not claim him till he had in some measure served his generation. We in this School had the privilege of knowing and loving him, and realising something of his many-sided powers during such years of manhood as it was his lot to enjoy. Out here, in his new surroundings and under the stimulus of change, he grew from a boy into a man. His sympathies, never narrow, were enlarged, and he found friends amongst the most diverse types. Thoroughly imbued with what was best and soundest in English ideas, he saw with a sure instinct exactly how far they were applicable to a different sphere. But indeed the secret of that influ-ence which he had over all with whom he came into contact lay neither in his up-bringing nor education, but in himself – in what Whitman calls 'a fluid and attaching character.' This it was that gave him that power over both men and boys which must have won him a distinguished position had he lived. . . . Thus all who knew him felt that so well-balanced a nature, at once wide in its sympathies and sensitive to impressions, would mature into a character rich with gifts for future generations of boys in the School that was so near to his heart . . .

When the war came he allowed his sense of duty to conquer his strong love of life. He was quite unmilitary in temperament; and military formalities and solemnities (although he had been captain of the corps at Marlborough – a fact which he usually concealed) always provoked his sense of fun. In common with most normal people, the wickedness and nightmare horror of a European war had always seemed to him incredible, a monstrous figment emanating from the brains of the less responsible members of the human race. But when it became a reality he was not long in making up his mind. . . . Hugh Butterworth was a leader and inspirer of boys who became a leader and inspirer of men fighting in a great cause – *Felix opportunitate mortis.*[32]

Below the main text by Sturge one of Hugh's boys from Selwyn House wrote:

Mr Butterworth joined this School in the third term of 1907, after a distinguished athletic career at Marlborough and Oxford. It was chiefly through his fine sportsmanship that he found so great a place in the affections of the School. We remember Mr. Butterworth best as he appeared on the cricket field, but we do not for that reason forget his perpetual kindness in the Selwyn day-room and in his classroom. Everywhere he showed the same generosity, the same keen interest in everybody's welfare, from nervous new-boy to his older school-fellow. We can well imagine how he must have endeared himself to his men in the trenches in Flanders; we have seen from his letters what good humour he was always in, and he could not have failed to inspire those under him with the same spirit of cheerfulness.

Hugh would surely have included the names of such boys, fellow master H E Sturge and perhaps, above all, his closest friend and colleague John 'Hoppy' Allen in any list of the 'old brigade' at Wanganui. At the time of Hugh's death, so stricken was the future headmaster of the school at the loss of his dearest friend that apart from deciding to gather together and publish Hugh's letters in a single volume he also decided to erect a meaningful and lasting memorial to the 'young golden master'. As he and Hugh had spent so many happy hours on the Wanganui cricket fields, both coaching and nurturing the talent in their youngsters and with Hugh providing spectators with some spectacular performances of his own, what better way to celebrate and remember his life and his service to the school than to build a cricket pavilion in his memory and that of Allen's brother Charles, killed on the Somme in 1916? Allen's vision was that this would be a structure that, day in, day out during the cricket season, would be a tangible and practical place of remembrance and constant reminder of a much-loved and respected teacher and colleague. It was completed in December

1917, incorporating a brass memorial plaque inside, and stands proudly on the cricket fields of Wanganui to this day.

Hugh is also remembered amongst the names of the fallen of Wanganui that are engraved with gold lettering into oak panels on the pillars on either side of the memorial arch just inside the main entrance to the chapel in addition to a separate memorial, in the form of a large brass plaque, to the seven masters who died which is on the Reredos and Sanctuary panelling.

Of the other educational institutions to which he belonged he is also remembered on the Hazelwood and Marlborough College War memorials and, as noted above, appears on the Oxford University Roll of Service.

But if the effect of Hugh's death had been a traumatic loss for his old school, it must have been catastrophic for his immediate family, particularly as he was a very popular only son and older brother to all his sisters. For his mother in particular, as ill as she was, the news of his death must have come as a hammer blow. The family had been torn asunder when four of Hugh's sisters had returned to England in late 1913 leaving his mother Catherine, father George and youngest sister Dora behind. During his mother's stay in the sanatorium near Christchurch his youngest sister Dora had been farmed out to various relatives and friends and she only rejoined her mother when she left the sanatorium and, in early September 1915, moved into a small house close by where someone looked after her. Hugh's father was away from home a good deal travelling as a representative for Little's Sheep Dip but the loss of Hugh so crushed his mother's already fragile state that Catherine Butterworth's condition worsened and it was decided that she should risk the long voyage to England with Dora to be reunited with her four older daughters. 'They left New Zealand in April 1916 in the ancient *Rimutaka* in which we had sailed out. It was her last voyage. . . . May and Margaret had prepared a small house in which to receive them. It was called 'Lane End' which seemed an appropriate name. Mother was very ill.'[33] Irene Butterworth recalled travelling down to Barton-on-Sea from her first job in Stratford-upon-Avon to see her mother, who, in spite of her grief at losing Hugh and her own suffering, never complained, or 'was ever angry or spoke sharply'. Catherine Butterworth lingered for several more months and finally died on 25 September 1916; exactly a year to the day after Hugh had laid down his life in Flanders.

On his wife's death Hugh's father returned to Europe and moved in with May and Margaret, as had the three younger sisters. George Montagu Butterworth determined to do something, anything, in order to serve and in so doing honour the sacrifice of his only son in some tangible way. Too old for combat at the age of 57, he enlisted and served with the Church Army behind the lines on the Western Front.

The trauma of the loss, first of Hugh and then their mother, affected other family members quite differently and in some cases dramatically; one of his younger sisters, Molly, flatly refused to speak either about Hugh or the war ever again.

A little over ten months after Hugh's death the Butterworth clan was rocked by another tragedy; the death in action of Hugh's cousin, George Sainton Kaye Butterworth. A few years older than Hugh, George – the son of Hugh's Uncle Alick who had done so much to bail Hugh's father out of his financial troubles – was a gifted composer who had first enlisted in the Duke of Cornwall's Light Infantry to do his bit on the outbreak of war. He later secured a commission in the Durham Light Infantry and was posted to its 13th Battalion. He was killed during the fierce fighting for a German trench named Munster Alley east of Pozières on the Somme on 5 August 1916 and as in Hugh's case, his body was never found.[34]

Sir Alexander Kaye Butterworth had, like his brother and Hugh's father George, already lost his first wife – George Butterworth's mother – and now, also like his brother, he had lost his beloved, golden son. Uncle Alick had always been ready to step in and support his brother in times of crisis and whether there were any discussions as to his brother's inability to afford a permanent memorial to Hugh or not is unclear but Uncle Alick decided that he would create a lasting tribute to both his own son and his nephew. He duly commissioned and funded a grand memorial door – complete with the regimental crests of both the Durham Light Infantry and the Rifle Brigade – which still graces the west entrance to the Priory Church of St Mary at Deerhurst. The choice of location for the memorial was no whim. Both Uncle Alick and Hugh's father had both grown up in the vicarage at Deerhurst from where their father, the Revd George Butterworth – Hugh and George's grandfather – had served the parish with distinction from 1856 to 1893.

Hugh's father may not have been able to erect a physical memorial to the son he lost on the battlefields of Ypres but he would leave a memorial nonetheless. In 1919 the Wanganui Old Boys' Association compiled and published a special memorial volume in memory of those who had died in the service of King, Country, Empire and Dominions between 1914 and 1918. Hugh's contribution to Wanganui and his subsequent service was recorded thus:

> For rather more than seven years a master here, [he] joined the staff in September, 1907, and immediately endeared himself to everybody with whom he became associated. In the face of what is now so well known of his life and work among us, it would be superfluous to add further expressions of the honour in which he was held. Leaving for England in January 1915, he was given a commission in the 9th Battalion Rifle Brigade, and left for 'Bulletville,' as he humorously described it, towards the end of May. During the few weeks of training he received at Aldershot, and indeed up to the actual date of his death, he wrote almost without interruption, and described in detail his experiences of military life in an altogether delightful style. Cheerful under all conditions, and full of enthusiasm for everything he undertook, he faced the war in a true spirit of self-sacrifice, his personality winning for him an affection

that can never be adequately described. He saw but four months of active service, and this in the neighbourhood of Ypres, being killed in action on September 25th, 1915. The news of his death caused universal sorrow, but his life of unselfish devotion to duty will serve as a pattern for many years to those who had the good fortune to know him.

It is fitting perhaps that the final words on Hugh should be those of his father, George 'Monty' Butterworth, which were written in a letter to Wanganui and included in the *In Memoriam* volume. These few words, from a man who had lost his only son to the 'Great War for Civilisation', seem peculiarly appropriate and perhaps deserve to stand as Hugh's epitaph: 'If he died as we believe he did, charging at the trenches, do you pity him? I cannot. Fancy trying to keep up with him! At that supreme moment as he glanced at his men whom we know loved him and would follow him anywhere, he tasted of life's elixir, and what mattered it whether it lasted only for seconds. It was the rapture of a lifetime!'[35]

LETTERS

Written in the trenches near Ypres between May and September 1915,
by H M Butterworth, 9th Rifle Brigade,
who fell in action on 25 September 1915

MEMOIR
Extract from the London Times, *October, 1915:*

LIEUT HUGH MONTAGU BUTTERWORTH, 9th Rifle Brigade, who was killed in action in Flanders on September 25th, was the only son of Mr. and Mrs. G. M. Butterworth, of Christchurch, New Zealand, formerly of Swindon, England. He was educated at Hazelwood, at Marlborough and at University College, Oxford.

At Marlborough he was captain of the cadet corps, a member of the cricket, football and hockey teams, racquet representative and winner of the athletic championship cup at Oxford, where he went in 1904. He was a very good, but unlucky, all-round athlete. At different times he represented his University at cricket, football and hockey, and he won the Freshmen's 100 yards, but a bad knee only permitted him to obtain his Blue at racquets. He played in the doubles with Mr. Clarence Bruce as partner in 1905 and Mr. Geoffrey Foster in 1906. In 1907 he went to New Zealand and became assistant master at the Collegiate School, Wanganui.

The above reproduction gives the facts of the early life of Hugh Butterworth up to the time when he came to New Zealand. Apart from his achievements as an all-round athlete, his school and university careers were much the same as those of hundreds of gallant Englishmen who have fallen in the war.

His real life's work began in 1907 when he joined the staff at Wanganui: for seven short years he gave of his best to the service of the school. He played no small part in this difficult period of its history, which included the change from the old to the new buildings. His influence was great and always increasing: he was wonderfully popular and yet never courted popularity. Beneath a modest and somewhat careless exterior he had a strong and inspiring personality, the outstanding features of which were a large measure of human sympathy, his enthusiasm, his cheerfulness, his sense of humour, his unswerving loyalty to his friends and to what he conceived to be right.

146

Such qualities could not fail to attract boys; he possessed their complete confidence and won their intense admiration. One could write at length of his many acts of supererogation and the innumerable occasions when he gave a helping hand to the younger members of the community. Nowhere was his influence for good used more effectively than in his House Dayroom, Selwyn has reason to be deeply grateful to its first House Tutor. When he went to England early in 1915 he received a commission in a battalion which had been in training for some time. To a man of his temperament the routine and environment of Aldershot were by no means congenial, but he worked hard to make himself efficient, and when the battalion left England in May it is clear that those in authority regarded him with considerable favour.

He spent his four months of active service in the neighbourhood of Ypres: when he went into action for the last time he was in command of his company. In the intervals of duty and sleep in the trenches he found relaxation in writing letters: to quote his own words:— 'It's a great joy when one gets a moment's quiet to sit down and retail one's moderate experiences.' His letters to me, written in a style with which many of us are so familiar, give a complete and intensely interesting picture of his life in the trenches. When the suggestion was made that they should be preserved in print I readily agreed, because I feel sure that there are many people, both here and in other parts of the world, who would welcome the opportunity of possessing them in a permanent form.

In the last number of the Collegian, a member of Selwyn House wrote:— 'We remember him best on the cricket field.' A fine cricketer in the best sense of the word, he was able to inspire others with his own enthusiasm for the game. He devoted himself heart and soul to coaching and, above all, he strove hard to create a cricket atmosphere without which one's efforts are of little value. As a bat, he was in a class by himself here, he made prolific scores in all parts of the country but his greatest joy was to watch a good innings by one of his own boys or to see the School XI play good cricket against Wellington. Before he went to England he made a complete list of all his scores of 50 and over, it is probably a unique record of its kind.

More eloquent than any words was the universal sorrow and the sense of irreparable loss which the news of his death in action called forth.

The chaplain of his brigade has written:— 'He was loved at University (University College, Oxford) and he was loved in the Rifle Brigade.'

We can fill in the gap and say with all sincerity – he was loved at Wanganui; we shall sorely miss him.

Wanganui,   J. A.
January, 1916.

Externally Hugh Butterworth's life calls for little comment. He went to the conventional English public school, shone at the conventional games, did the conventional minimum of work, and went on, conventionally, to the university. Then came a break in the smooth course of things. With his family he migrated to New

Zealand before he had finished his time at Oxford, – without the many 'blues' that were within his reach and without a degree. He came to Wanganui in September 1907, and till he left for the war in December 1914 lived in and for the School, 'a presence that was not to be put by.'

Butterworth's great merit as a school master was that he was entirely unprofessional – and completely human. He was a man of parts, not of knowledge. Energy was the keynote of his character, though partly disguised under a slouching gait and a lackadaisical manner which deceived the unwary. His physical energy expressed itself in the number of games which he played with exceptional skill. Wanganui boys do not need to be reminded of his wonderful scores at cricket, and of his inspiring captaincy. In Rugby football, hockey, racquets, tennis and running he held his own in the best company; while golf, dancing, riding, swimming and motor-cycling claimed his powers, each in due season. But if any thought he was a mere athlete whose bolt would be shot when his muscles began to stiffen, they made a great mistake. Behind the body lay a mind equally instinct with energy that expressed itself in racy prose and light verse and black-and-white sketches of no little merit. Academic he was not, but his love of life led him to love its reflection in literature. He knew Dickens, Thackeray, Kipling and Bernard Shaw minutely; he read the 'Ring and the Book' in the intervals of tennis and cricket one summer holidays. In order to explore unfamiliar regions of thought he would study works on socialism or evolution or religion. In the same way he would read Euripides and Aristophanes (in translations), Tolstoy (in French), and occasionally, in their original tongue, Horace and Vergil. We had all hoped to see the School enriched for many years with these many gifts and wide sympathies, deepening and maturing with the flight of time.

As to his private friendships nothing can be said; they are their own record. A man as cheerful, as sincere, and as loyal as he, could not only attract friends, but keep them; and there was no bitterness or cynicism to repel or hurt. One of his Oxford friends has written since his death that he was 'one of the most loved and lovable of men.' We who knew him in later years will not wish to alter those words.

When the war came, he allowed his sense of duty to conquer his strong love of life. He was not long in making up his mind. He left New Zealand in January, was gazetted in March to the 9th Battalion of the Rifle Brigade, and was in Flanders by the end of May. Until he fell on the 25th September he plied his friends with letters, written in an unadorned, colloquial style that mirrored both himself and his surroundings. As the months went by, though he never lost his light touch, the shadow of his approaching death seemed to add a seriousness to his letters which was absent at first, and now and then he lifts the veil from his inner thoughts and feelings. The programme allotted to him for the great offensive in September convinced him that the end was near, and his last letters, written just before going into battle, strike the note of farewell. In the last sentence of his last letter he wrote, 'I don't doubt my power to stick it out, and I think my men will follow me.' His friends are sure that his men followed him, and in those words he has penned his own best praise. Hugh Butterworth was a leader and inspirer of boys who became a leader and inspirer of men fighting in a great cause; – Felix opportunitate mortis.

Wanganui,   H. E. S.

January, 1916.

Copied from "The Marlburian," November, 1915.

The short biography of Hugh Butterworth which appears in the Marlburian, mentions the achievements by which he came into public prominence, and the events and changes which marked his life: but it says nothing of his high sense of honour, of his affectionate nature, of his straight forward manliness of character, of his strong common sense and clear-headedness, of his cheerfulness, of his humour: it says nothing of the willing sacrifice on which he insisted, when, in spite of their unselfish wishes he decided to accompany his people to New Zealand, and to give up his honour degree, an assured position in the legal profession for which he was intended, and an excellent chance of a cricket 'Blue': it says nothing of his second great sacrifice, when, having by sheer merit won himself a happy and comfortable position with good prospects at Wanganui, with congenial work, immense popularity and every opportunity for the athletics which he loved, he resolved to leave all and to offer his services and his life to his country.

He was a splendid athlete, and, whatever he played, he played hard: but he always recognised games in their proper proportion. He accepted his many disappointments at Oxford with philosophic resignation: it was indeed hard that one who was regarded as the best hockey forward in Oxford and who made 130 in the Seniors' cricket match should have been deprived by ill-luck of the crowning honours. In New Zealand he devoted himself to coaching the school teams, and he met with marked success: nor was he less successful in his other teaching. He had inherited a strong love of English literature and he taught his pupils to appreciate all that was best in it. At school, at college, at Wanganui and in his regiment everyone who knew him loved, trusted, admired and respected him: and it can safely be said that he never made an enemy. Marlborough never produced a more worthy son.

L. W.

Extract from a letter written by Colonel Villiers-Stuart, commanding the 9th battalion of the Rifle Brigade, to Miss Butterworth:

Dear Madam,

I cannot express my sadness at having to tell you of the death of your gallant brother, in the action on September 25th. He led his company most bravely, and for a time all went well, but the German counter-attacks were very heavy and our men were forced back by bomb attacks in great force. It was in leading a few men to counterattack one of these that your brother met his death. With him I lost all my officers but three. All his time with me your brother showed the most conspicuous coolness and courage, and he can never be replaced as an officer. I have no words to express my regret for you at his loss. Your brother's name had long been sent in for Captain's rank.

Yours sincerely,
W. VILLIERS-STUART

LETTERS

May 25th, 1915.

Cheer Ho! We pushed over here the other day *via* Blanktown and Censorville. Spent a day at latter place and then marched to Xburg where we entrained. To our surprise we meandered on, and were finally shot out into the murky night at about midnight. We heard the guns booming away on the starboard bow. At 2 we slipped off on what we were told was a 5 mile hop. It turned out to be 16 kilometres, and the men having had no food for 12 hours we had a rough time. However we finally bumped into a village to accompaniment of distant cannon. Sank into billets. We are absolutely on clover. Our Company is billeted in a ripping farm, the men in barns and we in the farm. We've got a ripping pond. In fact the back of the front is a good spot. We live like lords with unlimited food and beer. We are about half a mile from the village, and one can get into comfortable garbage. We've had some Company sports this afternoon. Great success. I figured in a Platoon Relay race, and ran like a hare, and almost collapsed at the finish. We've dug splendid baths, and put a waterproof sheet in to splash about. One trips over there in the dewy morn, dodging the cows. We are a great push at this farm, including one of the funniest of men, and we spend the day laughing chiefly and strenuous work on occasion. Shall push on to Bloodville shortly I suppose.

June 4th.

I've written two letters during last week, only they've been blown away or melted or got into the butter or something. I forget when I wrote last; somewhere when I was in the North of France. Well, of course, I can't say where I am, but we're in a mighty interesting spot – a place you've heard of several times. We're out every night these times within a mile of the Germans, but our battalion has had no casualties so far. It's very strange. There are guns all over the place wonderfully hidden. Flares go up all night continually, and then suddenly from some spot comes terrific rapid fire and the – – – of machine-guns. It lasts about 5 minutes, then silence there. The trench is either taken or not. We shall be in the front trenches next week. You would have liked to see But: doubling through a dangerous and shelled-out village reeking of badly buried corpses and horses. Doubling for men carrying rifles, ammunition, spades, etc., is a good game. Baths are impossible, one sort of puts in a wash of sorts in the morning.

We're in camp at present – of sorts. Up to lately we were in very good billets, but the time for good billets has now departed. However things are quite entertaining. Thank boys for letters. Will write when I can, but we're never in bed till 4 a.m., and one has things to do by day. We're usually out from 5 p.m. to 4 a.m. If I don't get into too grim a place I think I'll enjoy things pretty much. The officers in our Company are splendid lads, and we shall extract humour out of most things. Love to all. Give Wanganui my best wishes.

June 10th, 1915.

We are in the trenches and having a thoroughly satisfactory time. My platoon is in with a Company of the —s, and we are all being instructed in trench-fighting. We came in last night, passed through various shattered villages and then came up an immense communication trench with the bullets singing over our heads. We are about 90 yards from the Germans, and I have been out to the listening post in front which can't be more than 50 or 60 yards from them. Being so near them is really rather an advantage as they are very chary about shelling us. They are magnificent trenches with splendid dug-outs. My dug-out is made of sand-bags, with a corrugated-iron roof and with a glass window facing the rear! I am the guest of the —— officers, and we live like lords. At lunch to-day we partook of beef and tongue, pâté de foie gras, comabere (or however you spell it) cheese, stewed apricots, biscuits, almonds and raisins, white wine, coffee and benedictine, and this with bullets pattering up against the wall! Very gentlemanly warfare! The only objections are (1) lice (2) bad water – the Germans have a habit of dropping in arsenic (3) the fact that the ground has been twice passed over in the early days of the war, and the corpses are a bit lively. When one digs, (which one does 5 hours a day and most of the night) one usually rakes in a souvenir of sorts!

I'm glad to say we haven't yet been gassed, but we are provided with respirators, gas-helmets, and sprayers, so should be all right. We're just expecting what we call 'a little frightfulness,' as the artillery have just rung up to say that they intend to do a bit to it. When our new batteries open up we take to our burrows like rabbits!

I was out in front this morning for a bit with one of the subs. Men who have been out some months usually stroll about full in view of snipers with telescopic sights without caring a straw. We also selected quite the worst possible spot to stop and discuss the merits of chevaux-de-frise. However a festive Bosche got busy, and we hooked it hurriedly.

My men are very pleased with themselves. They averaged about 20 rounds during the night – without I suspect hitting anything, – and were full of joy. Also, I was pleased to note, they put their heads well over the parapet and took a proper sight before shooting. Many men their first night, I'm told, hold their rifles well above their heads and loose off anyhow. Men look fearsome ruffians in the trenches. The water is bad for shaving, as if you cut yourself you may get a bit poisoned, so they mostly grow beards. Personally I take a tot out of my water-bottle, but I haven't washed yet to-day (2.30 p.m.). 'We're in for four days and can't have our boots, putties or equipment off all that time. We've had rain, so I'm slopping about in gumboots fairly covered in mud owing to crawling operations this morning. Shall get a wash before dinner to-night. However officers don't get much sleep – about 4 in the 24. Also rifles and ammunition get filthy dirty and have to be continually inspected.

I am going out with the Captain soon to some spot where we can see the German lines very well. Of course I have looked at them through periscopes, and when flares are shot up at night. Shall probably work off a big mail before I go out, as there's plenty to talk about, and one can dart into one's dug-out when things are quiet. Best wishes to all. The only thing I object to is censoring my platoon's letters!

My servant has just got one in the head – not badly – which is highly annoying to me!

> *Rest Camp,*
> *June 13th or somewhere near.*

Back for a snooze. Got relieved night before last. We had rather a rotten time getting back, as our relief was very late, and the platoon ahead of us went the wrong way; we didn't get back till 3.30 and had to be up and off at 6. But we are now in camp. I have built a fine 'whare,' 2 water-proof sheets fixed on wire between trees, and my Wolseley valise to lie on. Très bon.

Last night 6 of us burst into — and had a splendid dinner. Also I had a historic bath. I don't seem to have amassed any lice. I slept yesterday from 2 to 6 and from 9 to 8.15!! The worst of trench work for officers is the sleeplessness. The men get a good deal of rest, and of course as officers get scuppered the work gets harder for the remnant.

I've just re-read letter and see that I haven't told about last day. We had a fair amount of frightfulness. Our artillery opened and we got plenty in return; 120 shells at trench to our left. No one killed! We got to it with rifle grenades. They replied with trench mortars and grenades. I went out with a cove very much ventre à terre in the literal sense, and we crawled up to about 20 yards from their trench. Grass high and remains of old French trench. We decided on a bombing base, and we were going out in the evening to have a go. Unfortunately we were relieved earlier than expected, so it fell through.

I suppose we shall be in again in a day or so, but at this game you are never given orders long before, and they're always washed out and altered at least twice the next hour.

Au revoir, mes amis. Best wishes.

> *June 16th,*
> *3.10 a.m.*

I, H. M. Butterworth, a man of peace, possessed of few virtues, but rather a good off-drive, am sitting in a very narrow packed trench, about to take part in one of the biggest battles in History. Shells are fairly hurtling through the ether. With luck the sun ought to be up in half an hour, – at about which hour my watch ends. But what a life! I went out yesterday morning to sort of 'reconnaisce' the ground, as it was my duty to lead the Company to its appointed support trench. We spun along on bikes without disaster though a few Jack Johnstons buzzed around. Past through Historic City, (d— the Censor), and found the way. To-night we stepped forth at about 10. Had a desperately slow march; (most of the British Army was coming along, I fancy), and ended a cheerless walk by a double along a railway-track from sleeper to sleeper. You have seen life in your time – have you every seen a Company armed to the teeth and shovel doubling along a very much 'Jack Johnsoned' railway-line with splendid shell-holes all over the place? A delightful experience made more so by the fact that telephone wires would trip you up every now and then.

6.15. A terrific bombardment has been going on for the last 3 hours. We must have hundreds and hundreds of batteries at work with whips of ammunition. Aeroplanes flutter round and have a look at us and get well shelled, but they go on rejoicing. I expect the main attack will develop (good word that) in an hour or so. I shall probably not be in the limelight till a good deal later. It will very likely be my pleasant task to stop a German counter-attack or something genial of that sort.

On the whole I'm rather disappointed with the noise of the bombardment from our end. We are very near about 100 guns I should say, and one can talk in quite a low voice.

We've got no washing or shaving kit with us, just 2 days' rations and a waterbottle of water. We shall be a quaint collection when we've finished – what's left of us.

The German's aren't replying to our artillery fire much just at present; I expect they are meditating something very unpleasant. Well, au revoir. This is June 16th, and we ought to get something done by Waterloo Centenary. Perhaps we are about to make history – perhaps not. Anyway best wishes to all. Curiously enough I feel as if I was playing bridge with you all – quite normal.

6.28 a.m. News through Canadians taken first line of trenches. Au revoir.

Trenches,
Sunday, June 20th, 1915.
3.15 a.m.

What a night! We left camp at 7, marched through Ypres, the most impressive sight I've ever seen, the whole place is absolutely gone. Every house is smashed to bits, absolutely a wonderful sight and very awesome. Well – at about 9 or so I picked up a couple of guides, (we were marching by platoons), Scotchmen, and they brought us up to these trenches. We got gassed just as we came up. We were entering the most complicated trenches imaginable and we got the gas good and proper. My men were distinctly panicy and I had to mix profanity and jest in even quantities, slight preference given to profanity. Every platoon in the British Army seemed to be mixed up. Fortunately we had respirators and good smoke helmets so we got through. It's rotten though. After a bit I collected my platoon, (I reached my position the first time with one corporal and one rifleman,) and got them told off in their places and then things started. We had continual shell-fire, shrapnel and gas-bombs and some very heavy rifle and machine-gun work away to the left and right. So far my platoon is unhurt, but we've had some close calls. I had a sand-bag whipped off just above my head at about 1.15 this morning. Bullets of course whizz the whole time. The chief objection to this trench is the fact that it is more or less littered with dead, and if you dig you invariably hit some corpse. It's quiet at last now and I'm penning this. It's a gruesome business, but perhaps we get used to it. One doesn't seem to have a dog's chance when things are moving. Oh! inter alia, I was knocked clean over by a shell coming in this morning but was unhurt – a quaint sensation it was too. Why it didn't slay me I know not. I will continue anon if I am still cumbering the planet. Au revoir. I must take a turn round the trench and see that all is serene.

8.45 (Can't find out whether day or night). Have you ever gone round the corner of a traverse and found a very dead Englishman lying exactly as he fell with his sword fixed in front of him on the firing platform? Don't do it as an experience. It almost put me off my 'brekker.' We've been working like niggers since five getting the trench a little safer. By to-night I think we'll have eliminated the more serious danger. I already have quite a decent dug-out. This trench has been held by various people X + Y times. We've found everything in the Army and Navy catalogue except a grand piano. We have garnered in 15,000 rounds already, and all sorts of tunics and lots of bodies and things. We have just been bringing in a man killed last night. One of my platoon produced a prayer book and all was well. By the way – do you ever read 'Watch Dogs' in Punch? That is the very trench I was in a fortnight or so ago for instruction. A quiet soft place, very different from the present gay spot! Do you remember the incident of the 'Verrey Pistol' he tells. A 'Verrey Pistol' is a pistol one shoots flares up with. It does no one any harm. Eh bien! The Germans had been a frightful nuisance one afternoon and these coves wanted a sleep, and so a fellow in a rage seized a 'Verrey Pistol' and fired it off. The Germans obviously thought it a new form of frightfulness and at once ceased fire and went to bed likewise. I can vouch for this yarn because I was there! Continue later. My sergeant is taking over for two hours, so I'll get some shut eye as I've been up all night and shall be until relieved. Incidentally I see Gresson has been wounded.

Monday. Another very fairly sultry evening. On the whole Sunday was quiet. Towards evening there was a certain amount of shelling. Just about 10.30 our Ration Party went out and didn't get back till 2 and had a pretty gay time. However I wasn't there. At about 10.15 p.m. I was sent for by the Commanding Officer and told to take a note to a cove in another trench. I was given a guide but he lost his way in a woolly maze of blown up trenches with dead all over the place. Fortunately we dropped into the right trench. You see this part is recently captured and there are very bad communication trenches as yet. We thought we were dished as star shells went up and though we lay as still as mice they flung some shells near us. Well – I had to stay in this trench all night on some duty and a very nice night we had! A dug-out was blown in and several men killed. We got about three shells and trench mortars plumb in the trench and lost some men and one poor fellow had an arm blown off and I think died. The stretchers couldn't be got through properly and I had to go back once and bring the bearers up. Personally I prefer open ground at night to bad communication trenches. They know the latter and can shell them. But in the open you can put your ears back and run, tripping over barbed wire and corpses. Well – finally I had to bring a man back to our trench and I told him I was running for it. We picked up two stray men who wanted to get back, and we ran like sin and jumped into a bit of communication trench plumb on the top of a ration party coming up! Horrid struggle. I forgot to say that earlier on I flung myself down to avoid a star-shell and landed on a corpse. Mon dieu! We've been losing men pretty consistently the last 36 hours – mostly shell-fire but a few sniped. I managed to snatch an hour's sleep towards morning. I shall probably have to take out a ration party to-night – a rotten job as the Germans shell all the roads and trenches on chance. The men are very cheerful. I hope they relieve us in four days as its very messy work. Continue later.

8.45 p.m. (probably Monday). A pretty moderate day. I got a certain amount of rest till 9 and then had to reconnoitre with the Major (one of God's good men) to find the best place to get a communication trench through to the company somewhere in front. The present trench is very bad. We simply waded about among dead Englishmen and Germans, in fearfully decomposed state. Horrible! We then went back and turned out the whole company to get to work on the trench. It was in dead ground mostly and we escaped notice for 2½ hours. A burial party carried on in front and all but one, (23 out of 24) were physically sick, but they stuck it out splendidly. I had just given the burying party orders to come in when the Germans spotted us from a balloon they sent up, and they got our range about the second shot. I got the men back along the trench in about five minutes – none hit – under fairly severe shelling. You can have no idea of the awful state of a captured trench. It has probably had three hours heavy bombardment to start with and been knocked to bits, and of course there are dead men in all sorts of conditions without legs, arms, etc. One man I found naked. Then of course there's equipment, rifles etc. of all sorts. The men get used to horrors after a bit and collect souvenirs as they call them. I'm afraid I have by no means done with horrors for the day as I believe I'm going out with some Scotchmen to go on burying.

Later (date unknown). Such is the extraordinary effect of this work and the want of sleep that I have been trying to decide whether it was yesterday or the day before that I finished the lines above. After mature consideration I've come to the conclusion that it was last night. Well – I went out with the Scotchmen and we dug in a lot of corpses. So much for that! Incidentally we had a pretty lively bombardment in the evening. I got an hour's sleep before we 'Stood to' and after that function I dashed off to my sergeant and a corporal to try and find some badly needed sand-bags that had been dumped down somewhere by a party last night. There are few couples in the British Army that move quicker or more doubled-up than my sergeant and I when in shallow trench under fire from snipers. After a bit we ran into gas but had not time for respirators and our eyes streamed. We picked up connection with a youthful subaltern, fixed up a carrying party back to the accompaniment of sniping and then had to get them passed on to A and B Companies in front. I took forty men laden with food and sand-bags and we dumped the things down and then had to stand by for a bit wedged in a narrow trench. We got back fit and well. We are getting this place in great order. When we came in, it was hopelessly unsafe and full of dead. Now we have cut communication trenches all over the place, but we lost a good few men. However the work had to be done. The men have worked splendidly – to-day for instance having gone a little wrong, we've had no water, but no one is growling. I'm awfully pleased with my bunch. I've come to the conclusion that I never lived till I breakfasted, (as I did this morning) after forty-eight hours of almost continuous work in a crazy dug-out, on a hard-boiled egg, some bread and neat whisky. Continue later.

Wednesday, 4 a.m. At about six in the evening we were suddenly told that we were in for a stunt taking a redoubt. Our company was in 'support,' (fortunately!) Affairs started at seven-thirty. We began an intensive bombardment and the Germans came at us with equal intensity. Believe anything you are told about concentrated artillery fire. To say I've never been in anything the hundredth part so terrific is merely banal. How can I describe it? It was like every noise you ever heard, crashing over your head. I suppose, – this is true talk, ten or twenty shells passed over or burst all round us per second – we were ordered simply to lie 'doggo' at, the bottom, of the trench. This lasted for two and a half hours. For the first half hour one was in imminent fear of death. Sand and earth fell on you in heaps. The air and earth trembled and shook withal. For the next half hour you rather hoped you would be finished off. It would be easier you thought. Mind you, one's nerves are a bit on edge after four practically sleepless nights – or is it five? I forget. Then you thought 'well hang it, if I haven't been "scuppered" yet, I may as well carry on.' I was in a traverse with a corporal of mine – a great nut, a most independent cove, who in times of excitement becomes delightfully familiar and says 'This is a bit of 'orl right, eh?' and so on. He also possesses 'guts.' After an hour the battalions on the left and the right moved. We supported with rapid fire and machine guns, and were receiving a terrific fire. By midnight things quietened down though the most mysterious things were happening. We were getting quite a brisk fire from a quarter where no Germans should have been and a subaltern in the left reports much the same – but we call him a liar! I may say that in the midst of all these things we had a ration party half a mile away, more or less concealed, dumping rations. At about two o'clock there enters a very weary subaltern from C. Company who had been having a terrible time. Owing to blunders, two of their platoons had been caught by the bombardment in the wrong place and had been badly hit. He'd got a lot of wounded, he said, and could not get them away. The genial task of getting off with ten men fell to me. I started off in the dark and could not pick up the right communication trench. Flares were going up and we were lying on our stomachs when a jovial fellow came out of the mirk and said he would get me down. Off we went, lying down in pools and bending double. When we got down to the road – this is quite unintelligible geography, but it can't be helped – I met our Sergeant Major – a splendid man – who apologized to me in the sort of tone he would use on Barrack Square and said he had got all the wounded away and I wasn't wanted. So we started back and finally reached the communication trench. We found it was blocked by C. Company. I tried to get a message up, but couldn't, so we darted back and tried for another. We found it had been knocked right in by shell fire. I collected my party in the safest place I could find and sent out a man to move on the men in the communication trench. Later I went myself and as I couldn't get them on and it was getting light I brought my men up over them and got them in. Mind you, all this time we had only to be seen to be shelled off the earth and flares were going up all the time. On getting back I thought the situation warranted a neat whisky for myself and my corporal. Incidentally I'm covered with mud and wet through.

8.30 p.m. (date unstated). Well, we're not being relieved to-night and have to stick together twenty-four hours. We've had a good deal of shelling but nothing continuous. I have got three hours' sleep, but otherwise we've worked sans cesse building up where we were hit last night and so on. The ration question is very difficult in a trench like this, our position is such that we are further from the base than any other trench on this line. We work it like this – our transport bring up the stuff nightly to about one and a half miles away. We send down a whole company under two officers, they are always shelled, and they bring it up to us. We then divide it up and parties have to take up rations to two companies somewhere in the front. That's over the explored bit where I spent my early hours burying and digging. We've had rain and the trenches are filthy. We're all sitting down in the trench at present as the shells are coming fairly regularly. I am coated with mud, feet soaking of course, but that ceases to worry, and bound about the waist with a waterproof sheet. We lost two officers killed and one wounded, and a good few men, last night.

Thursday, 7.30 a.m. We seem unable to avoid thrills these days. We expected trouble all yesterday. Bosche aeroplanes were looking at us all day and they were taking our range systematically by single shots from machine guns and occasionally trying a ranger and getting terribly near, bursting our parapet again in one place. Well, in the morning we heard we were not going to be relieved, so we waited on as it got dark for their bombardment to start. We had a good many shells but no real bombardment. We could hardly believe our luck. I was on duty till midnight and I had just came off when our delightful little major hustled down and with the air of a man imparting cheery tidings told us that a message had come through that a number of Germans had got through between two of our trenches, and we might expect an attack. This sort of thing sounds incredible but the trenches do not run on parallel lines. Then there are lines of trenches unoccupied (except by the dead) and altogether you wouldn't be surprised at anything happening. Anyhow, there it was, so we all 'stood to' and looked out. In my anxiety to give the Germans a cheery reception I told my platoon to fix swords (you'd call them bayonets but I am an R.B.) and the message went right along the company past headquarters. It appears I was wrong, and messages came hurtling down the line 'Who gave order to fix swords?' I put on my best countenance and waded up to Headquarters and told the commanding officer I was the culprit, having contravened army order 3241 paragraph 14 (a) (i)!! However the commanding officer was very nice and explained the 'whys' and 'wherefores' and we parted on excellent terms. News, soon came that the report of the Germans was false, so we stood down. The awful part of the work is the ghastly weariness. Imagine five whole days – each lasting twenty-four hours to a minute – when you are on the stretch the whole time. Add to that, that you are very dirty – probably wet. Add to that the fact that water doesn't get up perhaps in proper quantities. Add to that that in a small rough trench like this you eat anyhow in a small cavern in the earth, lying flat when shells arrive. Add to that that the men are so tired sometimes that you have to pull them up when they fall asleep at 'stand to.' Do we earn 7/6 a day?

Later, (time not stated). The worst has happened, I've broken both available pipes. Later. Out of trenches. To conclude, we've been out two days now. Our getting out was an absolute miracle. We were to be relieved at eleven p.m. At twelve o'clock there was no sign – my watch ended, so I turned in. At twelve fifteen we had a gas alarm. I was pulled out by the boots by an enthusiastic rifleman. It turned out to be very mild, so I slept again. At two o'clock I was again led out and told that A. and B. were being relieved, then C. and we were to leave after them. Of course it was almost daylight. Well, I was the last platoon to leave, so I sat in a mud wall at the head of my platoon and waited. I was so certain that we were bound to be cut up that I didn't mind a button about anything. So much so that I had my one and only breeze with my company commander. The fault was entirely mine and I must have been extremely irritating. Well, at three o'clock we got away. By the most terrific luck a thick mist came down, of course it was broad daylight otherwise, and we waded off. We had coats on, fullish packs and a shovel. I had a shovel and a rifleman. My sergeant led and I brought up the rear. My orders to the sergeant were to leg it as hard as he could go. We disdained trenches. Trusting to the mist we moved across the open on to the road and moved down it like race-horses. When we reached —— we knew the worst was over. No shells were particularly near one and we lost no men at all. After that I had rather a nasty knock. I jested the men through the town – or what once was a town – and on passing safely through issued the historic order – 'thank God, and go easy.' I then got hold of a military policeman to find out the way. At that unfortunate moment up popped the Colonel who told me we were marching like the Grenadiers – which, he as a Ghurkha – regards as a horrid insult. I apologized and told him we had made the trip in record time and mollified him somewhat. All was plain sailing after that.

We marched six or seven miles more and here we are in a delightful town awfully comfortable. We are fairly leading the life, hot baths and beer are the chief attractions. I hope this is fairly intelligible. We ought to get a week off. On re-reading this I think I exaggerate my importance in the scheme of things. This letter merely tells my own jobs. Every other officer has other jobs all the time, so don't delude yourself into thinking that I do anything more than attempt to run a platoon.

July 2nd, 1915.

I hope you don't get over-deluged with my letters, but it's a great joy when one gets a moment's quiet, to sit down and retail one's moderate adventures. Yesterday I had a noteworthy day. I was awakened at midnight by our sergeant-major with a note from Headquarters to say I had to start off at seven o'clock with fifty men in motor lorries to —— (that dear old famous spot I'm always going through, you must have guessed it by now.) We turned out at the said hour and at seven o'clock we were tooling off down the road, the men in lorries, Butterworth in a 'Sunbeam' belonging to the A.S.C. We reached the spot and waited a bit on the railway station and was joined by a signalling subaltern, who like all the casual men and children I drop upon here, was a ripper. We strolled off. A certain amount of shelling was going on in other parts of the town – I'm not putting on side – one really does not mind now provided it's a street or two, away. We had to dig a trench for the telephone wires linking up batteries, a most necessary thing as they get blown to bits and communication is lost. We had to take this line through the heart of the town or ruin, as it is now. After some time a Major man came up and looked on and opined that we were digging a trench. According to orders I merely stood at attention and said 'Yes, Sir.' He waited a bit and passed on. Enter in one minute two artillery officers – both with eye glasses – and two sergeants. 'Did I know the man?' 'No,' well, they thought he was a spy, no one knew his face. So I gathered in my revolver and off we sprang. We failed to find him. About two hours after I saw the man coming through again. So I approached him with drawn revolver (isn't this a good yarn?) told him that I was sorry but I must stop him and take him back to be identified. I called but two riflemen as a guard. Of course they fairly loved it – so did I. I then marched him off to a captain of engineers and he questioned him. Finally he seemed satisfied and let him go. I wasn't satisfied at all and followed him up on the quiet, I struck some artillery men and asked them if they knew him. 'Oh! yes,' they said, 'he's our Major!!' So I've arrested a full-blown Major: However when I reported the matter, I was told I'd done absolutely right. In this war anyone can arrest anyone on suspicion and nothing is said. In fact it is the only way with spies in uniform all over the country. Rather funny though, wasn't it? We had a smoke for dinner and a swim in the moat, ripping. There must be a lot of corpses therein but that didn't worry me at all. Every now and then I darted off and examined the town and had a good look at the cathedral and . . . . in ruins, of course. The place is more or less looted by now but you can pick up more or less what you want for the asking. We went back to our lorries and I went out to play bridge with some men in another regiment. So ended a good day. We're having a fine rest. I suppose we go to the trenches again at the end of the week.

July 5th, 1915.

Still sleeping! One begins to wonder what has happened to the war. True they shell the town occasionally and we see wounded coming through, but we ourselves still lead delectable lives. Yesterday – being Sunday – we went forth on nags to the Oxford and Bucks. Having lunched – we played cricket! A wonderful pitch of course but great fun. We made ninety-six, the Wanganui willow-welder taking a scratching quintette. It was terrifically hot. They then journeyed to the wickets and Butterworth (not captain I may say) bowled unchanged and snaffled seven wickets. They beat us by two wickets. We then returned 'au galop' to our billets. I had a delightful pony that pulled like the very mischief. On the whole a great day. At present I'm riddled with mosquito bites, the brutes. The only stuff I can get for it is Eau-de-Cologne which isn't very effective. We had a genial evening last night sub luna. Divers genial sports rolled into our bivouac and we ran through every comic opera from San Toy to Rag-time. We always sing at our meals and during bombardments. I've got a wonderful rifleman in my platoon. My priceless sergeant said to me one day 'You know Sir, I don't think Quick is right in the head, very religious man Sir.' The aforesaid Quick uses the biggest words known. He always says 'declivity' instead of 'slope' and when in the trenches the other day, I asked him what the — he was doing – this being the military form of interrogation, he confided to me that he was making an 'aperture.' I wish we could get some more officers sent over. We started with thirty-one, and have lost six one way and another, and two are off on special jobs. There remain twenty-three including the Commanding Officer, Second in Command and the Adjutant. Result – that we are continually out for trouble in the trenches. However, I expect officers are not too easy to come by these days. Not much news but I daresay a regular budget will turn up this mail from me.

Friday, July 10th [9th],
aux Trenches, 9.30 a.m.

There is a so-called bombardment going on. I don't think much of it at present, but as we have to be more or less umbraging, I can scratch a line. I just dash up and down the line now and then between frightfulness to see that parapets remain standing and that the men are awake.

We 'came in' last night in the true military style. Everything was mapped out to the square inch and we came cheerily up. I came with some of the men on G.S. waggons. We had to drive about ten miles, and then detached and had a hasty meal. Then we toddled off, Butterworth rather taking it in the neck as he was leading and moved off at 8 p.m. as per orders, but omitted to send orderly to adjutant to report departure.

However he wasn't unduly moved. On reaching —— (our old friend) we were met by our Company Commanders who had gone ahead, with the news that all arrangements were washed out, and everything had to be done differently. That was a jolly situation when you're in Shellville and companies are marching at fifteen minutes interval. Followed a scene of unparalleled profanity. Tandem we got re-sorted. Fortunately it was a particularly quiet night, off we got. We then tooled off over the open – dead ground – and then went through about two miles of communication trench – a wearisome performance as they're so narrow. However we got in safely and 'took over' in approved style. About ten minutes later we got a parapet blown in, but no one was hurt. I rather objected to its being the parapet I was behind at the moment.

We are in the front trench and in a tricky place, as is usually the case with the R.B. The Germans are about one hundred and fifty yards off, and we've got a listening post going half-way out. It's eerie out there at night. Also we're not wired yet, which is bad. I expect I shall have to do some of the wiring, – a rotten business – at night of course, and if you're spotted, what ho! for the machine guns. Sed faciendum est. The night passed away quietly and we hoped for a good day's work – spoilt by our confounded gunners wanting to bombard; it's a sort of obsession of theirs. Oh, incidentally, according to the Daily Mail and other experts, they're just due for another go at Calais. If they do it while we're here, we shall probably be scuppered, the front line always is. I've got a ripping map of all the trenches round here taken from an aeroplane photo; I wish I could send it you. It's an extraordinary thing. You never imagined such networks of trenches.

We had a ripping rest before coming in. I finished with a momentous dinner – the sort of dinner that makes you very nervous when you have to halt and be identified by a sentry on the way home. But I think we'd earned a little dinner, don't you? We get dashed little water (observe the train of thought) in this front trench and it's very hot; otherwise it isn't bad – for a trench. I must tool off and look round.

Friday, 4.30 p.m.

They've started the bombarding again. Our people must have too many shells or something. They hit it up for an hour and a half at nine, then started again at three, and I believe are going to have another go at 5.30. We haven't had many very near us so far. However it's a dashed nuisance as one can't get any thing done. The artillery aren't a bit popular with the infantry in this trench war except in emergencies. On a good quiet day the artillery tee off behind, and of course the Germans retaliate on our trenches. We can't do anything except sit still and hope for the finish. I've had rather a good day really though, as there wasn't much doing, and so I have snatched five hours' sleep altogether since we got in. That's the best I've ever had in the twenty-four hours of trenches. We've got a rum selection in my bit of trench, a machine gun section, and six bombers up the listening-post in front. If only we had wire out I'd be easy, but as it is one may so easily be rushed at night.

Saturday, 7 a.m. [July 10].

A very nasty time since I wrote last. The third bombardment proved one of the intense variety. In the middle of it one of my parapets was blown in and all the men buried, and one man horribly hurt. It was a ghastly business. His eye was taken clean out, his nose broken, and several of his teeth driven down into his throat. Of course he was smothered in blood. He was wonderfully plucky. We patched him up as well as we could, and after things quietened down managed to get him away. He may live. Later when night came on we started wiring, but didn't get a lot of work done as the Germans got wind of it, I fancy. One man drilled plumb through the leg – I should say by an explosive bullet. We got him in over the parapet and dressed him and tied the leg to a rifle and got four men to take him down. This is a hopeless trench to get wounded away from. It is impossible by day, and frightfully difficult by night. One of our men went right out to the German lines last night and got to their papapet, and tried to find out what they were doing. He was nearly nabbed, but got back.

It's comparatively calm now, but we shan't get much peace, I fear. It's an awful thing to see your men knocked out in this way. Thank the Lord, the wind is still blowing the right way, so we are spared the additional joy of gas. I hear rumours of more bombarding today. –! Must stop for a bit.

Saturday, 2.30 p.m.

An absolutely beastly day, so far. Bombarding has gone on more or less incessantly. Considering, our casualties have not been large. Three men were killed and one badly concussioned by one shell. A gruesome business. They were all completely buried, and three of them hit by high explosive. When I got up to them they were being dug out. The first man was on his face almost in half. The next had his arm taken clean off and was dying, and the third was dead; (we never found the legs of the third man). The fourth was dug out more or less unconscious. He is at my side now, sleeping, and still pretty bad, waiting to be taken down to-night. One dead man is three yards to my right waiting for a lull for burial. The others are buried, I think. Shells are whizzing all over the place as I write. I am writing as much to keep my mind clear as anything else. The man next me is an Australian-American, – the coolest man I've seen – a rifleman. He is at present studying the Daily Mail, the next man is asleep! the next two are cooking! My Australian-American friend and I passed a portion of the time before dinner in trying to put together Omar Khayyam; perhaps a curious pastime between an officer and a rifleman in a trench, but one strikes curious anomalies in Kitchener's First Army. (——these shells!)

About three quarters of an hour ago our shrapnel began to burst over us. As it synchronized with the appearance and disappearance of a soi-disant artillery officer in a trench near, one may conclude he was a spy. Every so-called observing officer that turns up should be arrested.

Well, I'll write again later. I got a letter from A . . . . H . . . . . during bombardment. Posts and rations turn up regardless. It's awfully cheering to read the Daily Mail in a trench and see that the Germans are supposed to be preparing a terrific move in the exact spot you happen to be holding. However!

Saturday, 7.20 p.m.

The day goes on. Things have quietened considerably, tho' shells still hurtle; in fact they've done nothing else since dewy morn. But the foe have devoted their energies more to other trenches. I must say our artillery have been in some form on the whole. From my periscopic views and occasional peeps over the parapet I have observed German sandbags and redoubts leaping heavenwards a good deal. Whether we have slain any enemy I don't know. Perhaps what cheers one most is that the wind remains honestly in the west. In previous existences I have watched the wind at Wanganui, to see how it would effect me biking to the links, but never have I viewed a good sharp breeze with such joy as I do at present.

I wonder what we shall all be like after the war – those of us who happen to scrape through – I suppose a few will. If anyone drops a bucket or anything noisy we shall all with one accord drop behind an invisible parapet. If the word 'gas' is whispered we shall all finger our pockets and necks for respirators and smoke helmets, uttering weird and deadly oaths. We shall always expect to find a town in ruins, and the first thing we shall do will be to dig in in case of shelling. At moment of writing a taube is up and is being shrapnelled and high-explosived, but it isn't hit. Aeroplanes are hardly ever hit – an aeroplaner's life is the safest job here except perhaps the A.S.C. Funny, isn't it? Then come cavalry, but they have to go to trenches sometimes. Then artillery, they have their purple patches: – lastly (easily) infantry who dwell on intimate terms with death for twenty four hours a day. This afternoon I went to bury two of the poor fellows killed this morning, and get their equipment and identity discs, and pay-book, etc. A month ago I couldn't have faced men in that condition. One man had lost both his legs and most of one side. The other was horribly mutilated too. Our stretcher-bearers are fine fellows. They have to do the grimmest things, but do them willingly.

Goodnight; it's just 'stand to,' and I must prepare for my third examination of rifles to-day.

I hope the Germans don't attack to-night!! [Shrieks of 'No, No,' and 'Coward.']

Sunday, 10 a.m. [July 12].

Quite a good night after the alarms and discursions of the day. Things had quietened down by 'stand to' in the evening, and so we decided to do some work. I took out two men to wire in front. It's most entertaining work; I really enjoyed it like anything. First we threw the wire over the parapet, – French concertina wire – then scrambled over landing on all fours. Then the two men came over and we dragged it forward about two yards; then opened it out and pegged it in. The first bit took us some time, as I got it too close and had to alter position. Every time flares go up you hide your face in the earth; the grass is fairly long. We got a little mild sniping in two places, but they were shots aimed at our parapet, not at us, I think, and when we got the idea of them we could keep out of line all right. Having got it pegged down we crept back and swarmed over. Was in considerable danger of extinction from one of my own sentries, as it being darkish I came back to the wrong bay. The sentry I'm glad to say stood the men to on catching sight of us, and I narrowly escaped man-handling from one of my corporals. Quite a good night in fact. There's fun in that sort of thing, and the excitement to keep you going, whereas this shell-fire is simply rotten and you can't do anything at all. I got to bed at three and slept like a top till eight, the best sleep I've had in a trench. We're expecting more bombarding this morning, and then peace for a bit, I believe, is the programme. There was very heavy firing away to the north last night, Belgian, or French it was, I should think. We shall hear of the result I suppose from the papers later. Such is war.

Cheer Ho! I'm just going for another wander. It's rather monotonous work. Every sentry you pass has to say as you pass; 'No: – post, no: – platoon, all correct,' or what-ever it is. You say 'Right,' or 'Thanks' or 'Carry On,' or some other genial remark, have a look yourself by periscope or over the top, and carry on to the next bay. – Au revoir.

Sunday, 2.30 p.m.

A delightful day so far. We are doing great work too. We have got all our men ranged on certain points of their line, and a very sharp watch is kept, and when anything moves, or a spade shows, or a sandbag heaves we let them have it. In fact we're brewing all the frightfulness we can for them. It makes all the difference with the men. A fort-night ago in these particular trenches the German was top dog. If we hove over a shell they threw back three, their snipers simply dominated the line. The brigade before us did excellent work, and I think we're carrying on. Now we fling shells at him regardless of expense, and really we've stopped his sniping tremendously. It improves the morale of all concerned to feel they're on the offensive. Shelling to-day is mild; the only shell that has been nastily near us was one of our own high explosives, which caused us to warble down the 'phone to some tune. However it doesn't often happen. There's a lot of work to be done to-night. I expect I shall have to be in front most of the night, wiring and building up the parapet a bit.

Monday, 7.30 a.m. [July 12].

A night with the wind up? That is the army expression for an evening when everyone suspects everybody else of sinister designs. Towards evening my captain, became convinced that we were going to be attacked. His only reason seemed to be that things had been quiet for some time previously; so we stood to with some zeal. Things began to buzz when I noticed that flare lights were being shot up from some way in front of the German trenches. Immediately afterwards listening-post reported same thing, and that there were Germans in a sap place running out to our lines. This was endorsed by a man I sent out to reconnoitre. Mind you, it's very easy for men to get a bit rattled on a dark night with shrapnel about, and with a general feeling of suspicion around. The officer's rôle, is to patrol the trench in a supercilious and easy manner, as if he was absolutely happy. I tried to do this. At about this stage we had several shrapnel casualties. One not very bad case was sent down the communication with one of our men. The latter soon came darting back with news that C.T. was blown in. I consigned him to blazes, and told him that if it was blown in he must walk round the bad places over the open; then detailed three men with spades to put things right. These men darted off and returned later to say they'd walked all through the trench and out the other end, and couldn't find any place blown in. Apparently our friend had met a few sandbags on the floor and was rattled so jumped to conclusions.

At about this time the following messages came down the battalion. (1) 'Stand to and prepare to fire.' (2) 'Fix swords.' (3) I forget the third. (4) 'Stand down and continue working parties.' These messages nearly drove us mad. We refused to take them as their source was not stated. Apparently a company had spotted some Germans, and orders had been given, and the message came all round. At the time it was confusing and not very funny. I felt like a man in the maddest of plays, for a bit. So things ambled on. I had 'Germans in front' reported to me several times, but I think they were imaginary. After midnight we got some wiring done. Owing to reduced number of officers I always get duty till 3.30 a.m., and get a bit of a rest then. We are relieved to-night and go to a support trench, fairly comfortable, I believe.

Wednesday, [July 14].

Why not go on writing? The night before last we were relieved from front trenches. What a night it was! The battalion relieving had never taken over a trench before, and they didn't half mess it up. Any way it's an intricate business, and our trench was difficult to relieve. Any way everything went wrong, and for half an hour my trench was held by five sentries and Butterworth. I was preparing to fire the last cartridge and die laughing, when some cheery lads turned up. True, they walked through and round and disappeared again, but I gathered them in. I then proceeded to place the men. They were absolute fools, and I did it entirely by profanity and man-handling. The child-sub, relieving was a good boy and did what I told him. I then gave him all the necessary tips, handed over stores, and tooled off with my faithful five. Later on we ran into a lot of sappers who were doing the wrong thing chiefly, whom also I cursed with such fluency that their officer (whom I hadn't seen and who wore whiskers) said, 'What d'you mean by talking to my men like that, Sir?' Further on the whole trench was choc-o-bloc with some of these relieving coves. We cursed them and got them more or less right, and I got out by climbing over the parapet and running for it. We got away finally and down about two miles of trench to our present place in Brigade Reserve. We live beneath the earth here in dug-outs and have to dive if an aeroplane arrives. We spend the night rationing ourselves and the men in the trenches. Rationing consists of 1. Carrying food. 2. Carrying water. 3. Carrying stores, wire, etc. 4. Falling over wire. 5. Falling into holes. 6. Swearing heavily and heartily. 7. Being shelled all the time. But to me shelling doesn't have half the same terrors if one's out in the open. I'd much rather move over an open field and put up with indirect shell fire than have direct fire in the safest trench in Belgium.

The officers of two of our companies (including ours) were called up before the Commanding Officer this morning and praised for our work in the trenches. It is about the first time on record that he has praised anyone. My chest assumed unusual proportions. It *is* nice though when you come out of trenches tired and feeling you've worked your eyes out, to have a few kind things said about one.

I think as far as our battalion goes we're at just the worst point now. At first everything is fresh and even shelling has its points. Then you get nervy and are afraid of death, then one gets callous. My nerves are surprisingly steady, I find. Several of the officers are awfully jumpy. My turn will come, no doubt, but I am pleasantly surprised that I am not more terrorized. But it's fairly rotten really.

I dare say you'd like to know how the trenches are worked. A division has a certain front, half a mile to one mile. A brigade takes up the front trenches, half in firing trench, half in support. Behind the support – about two miles – are the brigade reserve, either in dug-outs or trenches (where we are now). Then there is a brigade about three miles back again, and the third about three miles further back again. It is the depth formation, and effective, I should say.

Wednesday, 6.30 p.m.

The day drags on, deadly dull. We have nothing to do by day except keep hidden from aircraft. The atmosphere in this dug-out is awful. It is eight feet by six, and we've got three in here at present – singing. Also it's raining, and we have to be out all night rationing. Of course we've got no sort of change of clothes with us, and it's beastly cold at night. Like an ass I brought up a Burberry instead of a great coat this time, and it's frightfully chilly. Also and beside which, lying in a dugout all day is very demoralizing. I didn't bring a book up this time, but shall in future. We've actually had no shelling for over an hour. Long may it continue! In fact things are a little boring at present, as I have indicated.

Oh, by the way, get the Sphere each week, Matania's pictures of life on the English line are jolly good. He's been over here and knows something about it. He's had a lot about our particular bit of Hades.

The Huns have opened up the shelling again. As a matter of fact it always starts about now; we call it 'The Evening Hate.' Let me discourse to you about shells and their habits. Firstly there is Jack Johnson. He is simply terrific, of course, and makes a hole big enough for a motor-bus to get in; this is true talk. Then there's a fellow we call 'Rubber-Heels,' I call him Alfonso sometimes. He's a long distance bloke, and creeps over very slowly, well up. We like him, 'cos he doesn't come near us. Then there's the high explosive sport. I think he's what they call the Coal-box. We call him 'Crump,' 'cos he sounds like that. He's a nasty fellow and makes a beastly mess. He is fairly local, I'm glad to say. Then there's shrapnel of course. I don't think we've got a nom-de-guerre for him. My hat! he goes off with a crack, and the bits go whizzing over one's head – if one is lucky. Then there is the 'Whizz-bang.' I fancy he's a howitzer, frightfully fast. He's used on the front trench chiefly. He comes so fast that it's almost impossible to get down to him; rather a beast. Then we have the trench mortar shot from near to. He goes well up and then owing to law of gravitation comes down again; a powerful bloke. There are also rifle grenades and bombs, all hostile folk. Then the gas shell. I think he doesn't hurt much on explosion unless a bit hits you. I've had 'em burst pretty near too in the open and have only been knocked over. But the fumes are nasty; I think I swear at them more than at anything. However I can usually worry through them without a helmet. It touches the eyes up. Lastly we have gas proper squirted at you out of a tube. If ever I catch a man suspected of squirting gas, I'll slay him in a peculiarly painful manner. I think we're all a bit afraid of it. That's more or less the complete set. One hardly counts rifles and machine guns except in an actual attack. Snipers snipe all day, of course, but one doesn't mind that hiss of a bullet after shells; also if they hit you they do it decently, and don't cut you in half or tear your inside out. I found some dum-dums in an old German dug-out the other day – the bullet turned. One finds all sorts of things in German trenches.

This letter is assuming alarming proportions. Awful thought! We've got at least two more days in the underground. In future days I shall build me a sky-scraper and live on the roof. Au revoir.

Thursday, 10 a.m., July 15th.

More experiences, but this time not necessarily of a warlike kind. I left here at 8.45 with 100 men to carry up 4000 sand-bags to the trenches. Never having been along that particular bit before I was a bit nervous, but I managed it all right. It's very trying work leading 100 fairly heavily laden men. One is sniped at intervals, and shells appear now and then. But you must not go more than just over a mile an hour; you long to hustle, but you can't, As we tooled along it began to rain. Later, on the return journey it was pouring. By the time we got home we were fairly dripping. We turned in and the rain got worse. My dug-out leaked a little, but nearly all the men's leaked a lot, and some were inches deep in water by morning. So we all turned out at 4, and got to work making fresh dug-outs and draining and so on. It took us till 9. Rain however has two points. It prevents gas, and it seems to drive the artillery indoors. Result, a wonderful quiet reigns over the land. I expect we shall have a lot of frightfulness this afternoon to make up for it. With luck we get out to-morrow evening, but of course anything may happen. No news at present.

Thursday, 4.35.

We've just had a very unpleasant hour. Our gunners behind started whanging away like lunatics. I should say they flung 100 shells over. So of course the Germans replied a little later. We had a fiendish time, 2 men killed and one wounded. One shell pitched 10 yards from my dug-out, and another 3 yards. Fortunately they weren't big shells and the explosion was forward. They fired wonderfully well, got our range in a minute. No doubt we shall get it again to-morrow. On the whole I think it was the crispest hour we've had yet. Both the men died instantaneously, I am glad to say. We're very sick with the gunners, though. They're going away to-night and being relieved, and I believe they were simply shooting away to amuse themselves – The artillery get all the fun out of this war, and the infantry get slain for it.

Friday, 1 p.m., July 16.

I fancy the worst has happened, and we're not going out to-night, but have to wait till Sunday. It's a nasty blow as we're sick to death of the place. Six days in dugouts under constant shell-fire is quite suffish. We have been shelled this morning practically all the time. I suppose it's the battery hard by they're aiming at, but we get a good percentage of it. The firing trench is bliss as compared with this.

The rumour is going round this morning that the Turks are suing for peace.

10 p.m. On the whole I think the most depressing day I've ever spent. There are at least two batteries just by us – one about 40 yards behind us, and they fired without ceasing from 10 to 6. Apparently they took over last night and had several days allowance of ammunition in stock, and so loosed it off. The Germans didn't reply with the venom we expected, but we had it quite enough, thank you! Imagine us cooped up all day in dug-outs that are barely splinter-proof, let alone shrapnel or shell-proof, while these infernal shells whizzed and whizzed and burst. Heavens! we were sick, of it. Swear? I don't think! Give me fire-trenches every time. However as we shall be in reserve again from time to time, we are importing a gramophone and numerous records, so that when these gunners start off on their morning's hate or their after-noon's frightfulness we shall turn on ragtime.

Also it's raining, and my roof leaks. Everyone else is out with ration parties. It's my turn at home. They'll have a jolly time, roads, trenches and paths swimming in mud, men falling down, every one at his profanest.

I have now had my clothes on without change for eight days. I slip off my socks and boots and wash my feet in the morning, also shave, wash face and hands, and, if lucky, neck, and give my teeth a scrub. But apart from that I go unwashen. Nice, isn't it? However, I find one gets used to dirt in time. Anyway, I'm feeling better now. I've had a good tot on it, and the shelling has stopped (incidentally that confounded gunner loosed off again as I wrote 'shelling.')

It is quaint in reserve at night. Here I am in my dug out with a candle and the door blocked to keep in the light. On the floor my waterproof sheet and a few sandbags. My pillow is my haversack, my knapsack thing and an inflated pillow affair that is punctured and dis-inflates in about half an hour. All round is the incessant rumble of rifle-fire, with now and then guns and machine-guns. Rifle-fire one regards now as a mere incident, but I must confess to a respect for high explosive. They make such an awful mess of one, and I hate lying about with my inside hanging out and my body in Belgium and legs in France. But no doubt that's mere prejudice on my part.

Have you ever studied the great theory of re-action? e.g. I have been horribly hipped all day, lying doggo to accompaniment of shells, and now quiet (relative) reigns, I have fed and had a good drink, I feel as happy as a king – reaction. When we 'touch bottom,' the orsifers of 'D' Troop gather in this dug-out and we sing. It does us good, but we are not encouraged to foregather during shelling, for they say, 'We don't want the whole lot of you scuppered together.'

The great point of this war is that everyone is expected to be going to be killed some time, unless he has the luck to be wounded instead; that is quite the understood point of view. No doubt sound. I'm not particularly afraid of death, but I dislike the thought of dying because I enjoy life so much and want to enjoy it such a lot more.

This dug-out life gives one plenty of time to think, I tell you, and the danger is one gets down to a minor key and stays there. There's no doubt you want to be a man like —— with absolute faith in the universe, and then you'd sit and listen to the crumps and bless them all. Anyway I feel that I've expiated every crime I ever committed. I fancy that when we warriors fetch up at the Final Enquiry, They'll say 'Where did you perform?' We shall reply, 'Ypres salient.' They'll answer, 'Pass, friend,' and we shall stroll along to the sound of trumpets and sackbuts. If anyone ever puts me on a salient in private life I shall hate him. Consider a salient. In ordinary war they shoot at you from in front, but in a salient they also enfilade you from both sides, and if they can make the ball turn at all they get you in the back. But now our artillery does that, so that doesn't matter.

If only we'd brought up a pack of cards! Never again shall we omit to do so. Well, I've perpetrated a lot of drivel to-night. I think I'll gather my Burberry about me and snatch a bit of sleep. Unfortunately my dug-out pard will turn up at midnight (unless he's dead) very wet, very profane, and very thirsty, so I shall be awakened and we shall discuss the iniquities of gunners and snipers once again. – I'd give a lot for a snug rubber at Wanganui to-night. I'd compromise on Upokongaro! Salute the Brethren, and tell them that despite several things I remain cheerful. Good-night. God bless the man who invented tobacco. It is a very present help in trouble.

Saturday, 2.30 p.m., July 17.

Quite a good morning. Wet, I admit, but our gunner-sport has lost his ammunition or wanted sleep, or gone to London or something, and we've been quite peaceful. The first item of interest this morning was the fact that my roof dripped. I got out all my match-boxes and tobacco-lids and cups and so on, and placed a fairly clever field, but I soon found I wanted three slips, an extra cover, and a short leg. However as I am certain to be wet now until I get out, it doesn't worry me a lot.

Later we found a pack of cards belonging to an acting-corporal and borrowed same, and fixed up a quartette in a ruined barn. Our table was a shutter blown off the chateau near by, covered with sand-bags, our seats water-cans. We had three rather good rubbers, and hope to continue shortly, only it's raining, – also the Huns are flinging a few over at us in the direction of the barn. We hope to re-incipiate shortly. I think that barring accidents we shall be relieved to-morrow. Of course there's always the chance of an offensive starting in, and then we shall trot up like good little boys and act as living targets.

My word! this will be some life in the winter. It's chilly and damp enough on a wet day in summer. I tremble to think what winter will be like. Of course one wears goat-skins and gum-boots, but even so I shall take very few tickets on it. But it's a long time till then. I can't really realize it's summer, as summer without cricket and tennis seems meaningless.

They've just served us out with motor-goggles to keep the gas fumes out of our eyes. We *do* look knuts, I tell you.

The modern warrior is not a picturesque sight. He wears a noisome cap with ear-flaps now-a-days and motor-goggles. And of course we all get frightfully untidy, except a few men who always manage to look as if they were in Piccadilly. I fear that is not my forte. But never mind!

Saturday, 7 p.m.

Such, a peaceful day. Raining – which accounts for it. At 9.15 I bone off with fifty men to meet a guide. They select as our rendezvous the worst shelled spot in Belgium. I don't know what we're going to do; carry stores, I expect. Cheer Ho! Going out to-morrow!!!!!!

Sunday, 10.30 a.m., July 18.

Had a night of considerable moistitude. Bumped off from here with fifty men, and met a guide, and all sorts of strange things we had to carry. We strolled off, and after going some way along an unspeakable road fell into the correct communication trench. Words can hardly describe the state of said trench. It was over ankle-deep all the way in water, and often over the knees. We waded about, fell in, cursed, climbed over and under telephone wires, and reached the spot at about mid-night. We got a few whizz-bangs over at that stage, but no damage done. As we started down we ran into a party of two hundred men carrying rations up. Fortunately it was a very wide trench and we could swim past each other. I tried to cheer up my down north-country guide by asking (1) if many people had been drowned yet, and (2) if they allowed mixed bathing there, but nothing altered the severity of his outlook. Lancashire probably! The other party apparently thought we moved too slowly. It is part, of the Rifle Brigade religion never to let parties lose connection. So they came past us in what I was pleased to tell them looked like 'Column of Rabble.' However it didn't worry us a lot. Later when we got on to the road, they had to form up and call the roll, and swear themselves faint, and we moved past in that particularly quiet and offensive Rifle Brigade manner which is ours when we consider ourselves superior to the rest of the British Army. Got back finally at one fairly soaked up to the knee. I then took off boots and puttees, put on dry socks, (I always carry six pairs), wrapped my legs in dry sand-bags, ate two hard-boiled eggs and some apricot jam, drank a good whisky and water, smoked two cigarettes, and then slumbered. I slept so successfully that I was not awakened by quite a bombardment around us. Fortunately the sun has eventuated this morning, and I've dried puttees partially. In the army we dry boots by burning paper inside them. It seems to work all right.

One has very funny conversations in the dark with unknown men. One's platoon gets blocked by some other party perhaps, and while we disentangle ourselves one chats to some genial subaltern. One picks up some quite amusing bits of gossip and perhaps hears a good story and then passes on into the night. There is 'a certain liveliness' this morning. They tell me our artillery knocked spots out of the German front trench opposite us two days ago, so much so that a lot of Huns (Saxons probably) got up and legged it back to their supports, what time our lads browned them. Perhaps true, perhaps not. Our artillery is good, I think, and now that it is getting munitions makes a fearful nuisance of itself (to us among others).

This letter is becoming so immense that I shall shortly have to ring down the curtain, or it will never pass the censor. I fear we are in for a complete day of 'Hate.' The gunners are in immense form, but somehow I don't mind it to-day. I expect it's the fact that we're going out to-night that makes the difference. Also if you've been in a dug-out for five days and they haven't dropped a high explosive on you, you hope they won't be rude enough to do it on the sixth. Deuce of a lot of aeroplanes up this morning. They haven't been able to do much last thirty-six hours owing to wind and rain, so they're making up for it to-day, I suppose. But it means we have to remain, hidden all the time, and our sentries are such fools that if the 'plane goes into a cloud they always signal 'all clear,' and out swarm the men and have to be chased back again. The men really are appalling fools. They take it as a fearful affront if you stop their building enormous furnaces to cook on. They don't seem to realize that if spotted by a 'plane we should be shelled to blazes. The only thing to do is to put man after man under arrest. When we have our first Orderly Room after our return, I shall spend about an hour stepping smartly forward, saluting, and saying 'Sir, on the night of the twenty-third instant the accused, etc. – ,' you know the jargon. Incidentally I've got a corporal I want broken. When we went out at nine-thirty last night our party was one short. It's very difficult to trace a missing man on a dirty night, when you have to move punctually. I think I've got the brute though.

I don't like Orderly Room at the best of times as the Commanding Officer has a way of proving that the thing is much more your fault than the prisoner's! I'll end this letter. Only about nine hours to go before relief. Bless all Selwyn and salute the staff. Cheer Ho.

July 22nd, 1915.

I got a letter from you to-day and was very cheered to get a certain amount of gossip. The general opinion is that the war will be over by Christmas, but no one can say why. At the moment of writing Warsaw is tottering, and if it falls I suppose we shall have an odd million or two flung at us hereabouts. Anyway there is such a crush on this salient that we shall all fall over each other. If there is a real big scrap on this front there will be the most fearful mess on record. The whole place is full, full, full of guns and men, and both sides will spend a day or two passing through 'curtains of fire.' However let me dismiss that for a day or two more. The chief news from my own point of view is that my particular bit of trench is being mined. We suspected it a fort-night ago. I reported and had up mine experts and even offered to make a bomb attack! However things hung fire and I understand the mine has gone too far to be stopped. So I'm expecting a good 'tour' next time. Nasty things these mines. I saw one go up the other evening. It is pouring with rain at the present moment and I shall most certainly be orderly officer to-morrow. Result – things very moderate. I have been building a redoubt these last two days. The subaltern-in-charge – a sapper fellow, had lived for five years in Auckland and we had a splendid chat. It was great sitting on a parapet next a great 9.2 howitzer, talking about Takapuna and the 'Masonic' and so on. Yesterday was a typical rest-day. Having been out for two days running, digging a redoubt, we were promised a rest. I also was orderly officer. The adjutant came charging round to my bivouac to know why A company lines were dirty. I was at the moment inspecting D lines and had not reached A company, so mutual recrimina-tions followed. I then proceeded to mount the guard. When I had finished the worst parts the commanding officer turned up and began to look on in his most crushing manner. When I told the guard to move to their post, the commanding officer recalled them three times. Each time I tried to find some new fault in what they had done. Finally the brigade sergeant-major, suggested that I had better ask the commanding officer's permission to move off the men. I did so and it was graciously granted. The sequel was a biting note to all officers (we get these three times a day) explaining that they had better learn squad drill, and they might also learn that it is not etiquette to move off troops without the commanding officer's leave, if he is present. Personally as I have been moving parties numbering from ten to a hundred about under shell fire for some weeks, the etiquette of moving three men across a road, leaves me a little cold. Well – at three-thirty (this being a rest camp) I departed on a horse with ten men and a government service waggon, to a place where we loaded five thousand sandbags. We then departed to Ypres and laid them out neatly packed in bunches of twenty-five. We then sat down and expected a hundred men at seven-thirty. I need hardly say they arrived at nine-thirty. By that time I was asleep in the middle of a square on six sandbags. On arrival we loaded up and strolled to our working place. Some sappers met us and told me we were making a 'high command.' I thanked them for the information and asked how they did it. Our men, who have an uncanny way of doing the right thing, seemed to know by instinct and we got great work done on the said 'high command,' which is a sort of trench that goes up instead of down. Very dangerous I should say. Owing to that strange providence that watches over us, shells had been all over the place before we arrived. But none came over while we were there. At one o'clock we began to sneak home. A fussy major of the 60th, who was in charge of the whole party of four hundred men, got the horrors that we should be slain by our own guns. I tried to persuade him that it didn't matter whether we were or not – that being my state of mind always at two a.m. – and he rushed about and worried us a lot. At length, we struck some motor-buses and after putting various drivers and people under arrest, we returned home and sank into bed at 4.15 a.m. No doubt we shall be turned out for another job to-night. As a matter of fact, I rather enjoy these stunts, especially when I am given a few men and move off on my lonesome. I will write before we entrench again.

Considerably later,
Day unknown.

After messing about for sometime we get out of our trenches and dashed about under a very heavy shell fire, and finally settled down, packed like sardines, under a railway embankment. We had two of our guns – enormous great beasts – just behind us, and of course the Germans were dropping shells all round us. The first thing I knew was that a shell had exploded in the midst of my platoon and had more or less removed the head of one of my men. We had to lie quiet under this for three hours. My platoon was lucky and lost no more men. The stretcher bearer and doctor were hard at it all the time. Then things became hotter and hotter. The Germans began a fierce counter-attack, with terrific artillery fire. At about seven o'clock we got the genial news, 'The——'s will advance.' So up we get. The men were splendid. I don't think a man in our battalion flinched or wasn't cheerful. Well, off we whipped down this railway line, and over it, where we were all spotted by the Germans, and hit a field where we had orders to dig in. The Germans got our range in exactly two and a half minutes and we got shrapnel and all manner of nastiness. A sapper-fellow, – a major I fancy, – loafed up to me and asked if they could help us dig in and I graciously gave permission. So we dug in. During this genial performance the ——'s were legging it back to some tune. Well – while at this job, to a continual shout of 'Stretcher Bearers' – we suddenly got orders to retire. We did so in excellent order and collected our kits which we had stacked under the ramparts of ——. Quo facto we were off to some other gay spot but to our joy someone else had mopped up all the available trenches and we turned back to a shelter camp. Some other parts of our division had a much worse time. The —— who were in barracks with us at Aldershot were in the thick of it, and came through, with flying colours. We only saw the severe rear-end, and that was quite cheery going for peace-living citizens. However we saw a few German prisoners which cheered us up. I hear the Canadians did excellently again. Rumour says that the Dardanelles are forced. I wonder if it is true. If so, good for New Zealand, Australia and the British Navy. Well, given fine weather I may still be alive when you get this. I was tired last night, I haven't shaved for three days. All our kit is some-where to blazes, but I got a wash this morning. If I get through this racket, I'll never move out of a slow walk again and shall probably develop into a hopeless slacker! I wonder! We are very bucked about the men though, they stood it all easy. I was pleased to note also that I didn't feel the terror-stricken rabbit I expected to. I'm not very clean and I've got a grisly beard, but I am quite cheery!

Trenches,
July 27th, 2 p.m.

Here we are again. We left camp yesterday at four, marched to near Wipers, had a meal, and off we got at eight. We were cheered by the news that by information received from agents, spies and others, a German attack was due to eventuate that night; we were to relieve if we could. If we ran suddenly into our old friend the 'Tir de Barage' or curtain of fire we had to do various and diverse things, as seemed fit unto us. We therefore departed in a fairly military state of mind, trusting that we should behave in a fitting manner. About half way up an attack began away to our right, the old familiar rapid fire, machine gun and guns. One had time to speculate, as one wallowed along, on whether it would develop into a general attack or whether it was local. It proved to be local, I know not with what result.

We then effected a beautiful relief, I took over from a sergeant with a shrapnelled nose and was all in and posted by eleven-thirty, a good performance. I am now absolutely in the fore-front of the battle. Our company is honoured by being right up against them twice running, the same two being in support again and the same two in front trench. I found that the trench had not been wired and the grass is very long in front. I have indented for wire and sickles and shall take out an agriculturist rifleman and get to work, if possible to-night.

Unfortunately there is a full moon to-night. The chief fly in the ointment is the fact that we are undoubtedly being mined. We are also counter-mining, but there is always the chance of a sudden leap to glory. However, personally, I believe one is right except with an east wind. I'm certain the Germans won't attack in strength unless they have a 'gas' wind and of course blowing up a mine is followed by an attack always. I may be wrong, very likely am, but while the wind is south west it is cheering creed. So far to-day as I noted in the trench log, the situation has been, quiet. They fire a lot of rifle grenades at us, and the whizz bangs are very enfilading, but so far we've had nothing serious to growl about. I've got a palatial dug-out, which is good.

Am glad to say I've picked up some very sound men out of our last two drafts, older men than most.

4.15 p.m. Life continues its placid course, which probably means we shall have a 'windy night' – that means in civilian parlance that everyone expects immediate attack from all sides. I don't think myself that a quiet day means an attack, as to my mind the batteries would be doing a little bit of ranging and so on, and 'experience teaches' that a quiet night usually results.

We are getting sniped a good deal but without disaster so far. Ours is such an extraordinary position that if you drew a circle round my dug-out and had the correct value for R and π = and so on, and then divide the circumference up into ten equal parts, you would find that you could be sniped from eight of them. We're quite used to having the enemy on three sides of us by now. It's a wonderful sight at night. One sees flares going up absolutely all round. What I chiefly object to in a salient is the getting in and out.

Of course one's camp has to be some miles from the beginning of the wretched thing: so you have to walk out of the dashed horse shoe and then off again for four or five miles.

One is becoming distinctly more military though. One takes pot shots over the parapet by day quite genially now. This trench is by now well placarded with names. Most bays have a special name 'Whizz Bang Corner,' 'Hell's Gate' or more homely 'The Commercial Hotel,' 'Holly Bush Tavern' and so on. Then one strolls along and sees helpful notices, such as 'Please keep down here, dangerous.'

Of course we've renamed Belgium and put the new names on maps. For instance we have 'Clapham Junction' here, another place is Hell Fire Corner and so on. I hope when things end – always provided that I haven't ended before – that I shall be able to bring back a trench map or two. Most interesting things, I tell you.

Cheer Ho! They started shelling, I must trip out and see that all is well.

Wednesday, 1 p.m. Had a thoroughly strenuous night. We were again warned to be very much on the qui vive, as there was the chance of an attack. However it didn't eventuate. When it got dark I teed off with about twenty men to dig (as usual!) We had to make another trench behind our present lines about one hundred yards behind I suppose it is. It had only just been begun in fact the traverses were only spitted out, of course our old pal the moon was very much in evidence and there was a lot of flare firing and suspicion around. However we weren't spotted; got a good few bullets about us, but those only chance shots, I fancy. Anyway we dug (Butterworth included) for four hours. I slipped off for half an hour in the middle to put out some wire in front, that was also accomplished without disaster, we 'stood to' with our customary zeal from two fifteen to three forty-five. I then handed over to my sergeant, had a snack, turned in and slept like a bird.

Was on duty again at 8. We've got a good deal of work in hand and I've been superintending that of course inter alia and très diversa. The Commanding Officer rocked in about 10.30. At present minute, our company is very much in his good books. I'll tell you about that later: He said that authorities (Brigade I suppose) didn't seem to know where the trench I was digging last night ran out. So I had to perform my well known crawling act. I had only been through as far as we had dug and from there on it was crisp, stomach work to avoid the genial sniper. As a matter of fact it came out in the most obvious way possible and I think the Brigade came up with red hats to look at a place: they begin to do so and probably a whizz bang or two comes over and they find they've got very important business elsewhere. That of course is only the mere trench dweller's view. As a matter of fact they do their job jolly well, and after all it isn't necessary that they should be shot more than necessary, only in our muddy dug-outs we rather jeer at the red hats safe behind with beds and plates and chairs and things.

We know our sector very well now. By jove, it makes a difference! The result is we can run it about ten times better than we could at first. I think if the Germans had rushed us when we first came in, they'd have eaten us. It was a wild place to send a new regiment to; only all regiments are new now-a-days. Now the men have got down to the position, their sentry work is excellent and our sniping is quite fair, they work splendidly. We work them very hard, but no digging or wiring party ever goes without an officer, that is the way to get the men along. If one takes out a party of men somewhere they don't know – in the open probably – to dig, they'll go like lambs as long as they've got an officer with them. The curious thing is that in civilian life they've probably cursed us as plutocrats, out here they fairly look to us. The other night some time ago, I had some men and had to get somewhere I'd never been to before in —— as a matter of fact it wasn't difficult and we had ample directions, so before we started I was told to send the men with a sergeant. Said the sergeant to me 'I wish you were coming, sir, I don't know the way' I said 'my dear man, nor do I.' To which he made this astounding reply 'Very likely not, sir, but the men will think you do and they know I don't'! He got there all right. My own sergeant is different from most of ours. He's a tip top A1 regular, and we work in wondrous harmony: Whenever I forget things – as I often do strangely enough – he always remembers and gets them done without rushing to me for orders. He has an uncanny knack of knowing all the stores, etc., one has in the trench. One has to keep a log and so on and you have to know to a round what ammunition you've got and every other dashed thing.

Probably at two I get a message to report at 1.30 (usually a message comes after the time at which you have to report) how much S.A.A. and so on I have. I dart up to

Sergeant Dyer, who consults his note-book and gives me the thing cut and dried correct to the nearest round. We also are probably the two most successful thieves in the trenches. And he has taught me this splendid habit – if wild messages arrive inquiring whether this or that is done and why the deuce isn't it, we always report it is done and do it instanter. In fact we're a thoroughly immoral pair, but I believe we're knocking out a pretty useful platoon.

My instructions in case of attack are simple, my trench must be held at all costs, and I must say it is a very important position; if they got into it they could bomb up and down to the adjoining trenches. It's difficult to explain, depends on contours and slopes and things a good deal. Any way them's my orders. Cheer Ho! I think I'll turn over and have a nap. This is always the quietest part of the day.

Thursday, mid-day. A much less pleasant time, we had a very strenuous evening to begin with. The General came up in the afternoon – as I before stated I think – forget if I did or not – anyway he observed the bit of triangle where my line runs to, saw we were constructing a base to it. He ordered that the base trench, we call it Charing Cross – should be finished during the night. The result was pure hell. After standing down, the whole company had to be turned on in some way or other leaving only one sentry per bay. We thought it fairly criminal as we couldn't possibly have stopped a rush. I thought that anyway I'd do the best I could and get the rest of the front wired as fast as we could. So I collected all available wire and also my company wirer – splendid chap, ex-sailor and very handy – and we spent about one and a half hours in front. It wasn't a bit nice. We are very near the Germans, there was an absolutely full moon and their snipers were horrid active. One could hardly avoid being spotted from time to time, but they kindly didn't turn a machine gun on. The sport with me had two very close calls, bullets hitting the ground just by him. I had nothing more to talk about than the dear old Zepp. round one's head. I turned in at four and out at 7.30 – having apparently slept through some very nasty heavy trench mortar stuff they sent at us. I fancy they spotted a machine gun emplacement in our trench, we've now moved the gun. However we had a bad time during my four hours from eight to twelve – a steady bombardment all the time. Whizz bangs at first killing one and wounding two. And then they lengthened out a bit with shrapnel and high explosives. They have now come back to the old trench mortars, which are shaking the earth around me. It's a noisome weapon – throws a fifty pound shell and you can see it coming. I believe the German trench mortar has a range up to one thousand yards. It and the whizz bangs are easy first for nastiness. On the whole we two companies up in the fire trench have lost a good few men, C company a good many more than us. Let's hope they'll give us a quiet afternoon.

Friday, 1 a.m. What an hour! However I 'came off' at twelve and have got nothing particular on till two, so having had a neat meal of bread, potted meat and honey, I may as well scribble to keep myself awake.

Well, yesterday went on being pretty nasty. Shelling was very continuous. Our company was lucky. An officer who joined us three days ago was knocked out. He's not dead, but bad concussion, I expect he'll get all right. Since dark, it's been pretty quiet. Every now and then they send over one of their infernal trench mortars. They are the most grisly things. They come very very slowly and you can see them, also, they make the noise of three motor buses, and when they hit mother earth, they kick up the most awful explosion and smell in a particularly revolting manner. They really are the limit. Much more cheery news has arrived for us to-day. We were to be going back to those beastly dug outs we were in before. But now we are going to Ypres ramparts, which are fairly safe and distinctly comfortable – a vast improvement.

We're performing prodigies of valour in the digging line up here. New trenches are springing up in all directions, communications chiefly. Between the writing of 'directions' and 'communications' in previous line, two trench mortars went off. It isn't right at this hour of the morning (another!) What a life! However we're all expiating our many and various sins, I hope. Perhaps we're banking up a stock of expiation on the credit side – and we shall need it when we get home I fancy!

Cheer Ho! Au revoir! I shall go out to the fire trench and see if the sentries are awake and watching.

Friday, 4 a.m. Battle still proceeding. I'm taking short rest, have had one hour in last 36. But can't manage to sleep much. It's fair to middling hell.

Saturday (I think), 2.50. We're in the middle of the most terrific battle, simply awful, attack, counter attack, liquid fire, trenches taken and retaken. If ever I live to finish this letter I shall be surprised and lucky. However I thought you'd like Captain Coe's latest and probably last. Cheer Ho! Best love to all.

4.45. Things are now comparatively quiet and I may be able to give a coherent account of what has occurred. The business started Friday morning at 3.20 (always supposing to-day is Saturday.) Suddenly we saw flames about 500 or 600 yards to our right in what is known as 'the crater,' a position we captured by mining a week or so ago. I didn't think of it's being liquid fire at first. But it was. In a second the whole world became a hell. I cannot possibly describe the noise, smoke, smell and all the rest of it. This went on for some time, one and a half hours I dare-say. I had kept my men from firing as our trench wasn't being attacked. Suddenly I got the report that a party of Germans was coming over? I shall never know now whether there were Germans there – bombing party say – or not. The smoke and so on was terrific. Any way I opened 'Rapid' on what we took to be Germans. Nobody reached us, so we either drove them off or they weren't there. The intensive bombardment lasted three and a half hours and continued off and on to mid-day. Result – Germans captured part of a trench. At two we started the counter attack, three quarters of an hour artillery preparation, then the 41st Brigade – part of ours but not our battalion – went forward. We supported with fire. That lasted all told for four hours. The 41st got in and bombed back most of the trench. Our brigade captured another new bit. Our brigade lost heavily, we lost six officers and I believe two hundred men (a minimum), another battalion lost twelve officers. Night came eventually, all of us fairly done in. My men were so done that I allowed every third man to sleep. If I ever sat down myself, I went straight off. I went off standing two or three times. Suddenly at 2.30 a.m. the Germans came again, liquid fire all over the place and the deuce of a counter attack. It was finally stopped by our 'rapid' gun fire and things were quiet by about 6 or 7 a.m.

Since, the Bosches have been very quiet. Our artillery have been firing all day and they have replied very little. We all expect another attack to-night or to-morrow morning, probably the latter.

I believe forty thousand troops have been massed behind us, in case we let them through. God grant we don't. I will try and describe what it all feels and looks like later, but now I think I'll sleep for an hour. I got four hours this morning and am feeling fit. They are relieving us as soon as they can, but I don't think they'll do it to-night. Somehow they got some rations up to us last night, I know not how.

Wednesday. We're out temporarily but shall probably be back to-morrow night. We had an awful time! I haven't read through the previous pages of this letter so I don't know what I said, anyway the whole show lasted about ninety-six hours and is probably by no means over yet. We may quite easily be shoved into the attack almost at once. When the show is over the whole division will undoubtedly go away somewhere to refit and recover.

Now we are out of trenches and can sort out impressions. I think that there is very little doubt that the liquid fire attack was also attempted on us, but the fire turned to smoke before it reached us. I was otherwise engaged when the blaze broke out, as I had to rush up my trench to persuade the men that that wasn't the exact moment to watch a fire on one's flank. So I've had a curious experience. Everyone in neighbouring trenches wants to know about the liquid fire in my trench and I can't say if I had it or not. Secondly I can't say for certain whether I was attacked by Bosche or not!! No one who hasn't been here could understand, but the noise, dust and general tumult is such that anything might be happening. I wish you could have seen my men during that three or five minutes (or hours, I don't know how long it was) when we were actually 'repelling the attack' (if there was one). They all were right over the parapet firing like blazes, my sergeant bucking about persuading them to fire low, my humble self standing half on the parapet and half on the parados with a revolver in one hand and rifle near the other and a cigarette going well, using the most unquotable language. Do you know that really was a good moment, I can't pretend to like bombardments, nor war generally, but that really was a moment when one 'touched top' (as opposed to 'touching bottom') but you'll feel that it was an interesting moment in one's life.

I felt absolutely as cool as ice during that part, one was so worked up that one felt that one could stick anything out. However when one has spent four sleepless days and nights with all sorts of alarms and bombardments and attacks and counter attacks going on – that, was fair Hell. At the end of it, our relief went hopelessly wrong, and we walked out in broad daylight. When we got half way to Ypres, our big guns opened up bombarding. I was too tired to worry much, but I just mentally noted that the whole company must infallibly be wiped out. But our star was there again and we got out and went home in a Willesden bus. This letter fails hopelessly. I can't express what we felt or give you a real idea what Hell looks like. We lost two hundred and fifty men. I left Aldershot fifth officer in the company. I am now second in command of it. I am I think fairly certain of my second star but we haven't time to think about promotion just now. I'll post this and perhaps I'll catch a mail. If we attack to-morrow night, I've got just a one in three chance, I suppose. But there's always the chance of being wounded and getting Home. Any way if it isn't to-morrow, it'll be another day.

Blessings and love to all.

Mont des Cats,
August 8th, 1915.

I am at present in a hospital place for a short time, I got poisoned in some way or other, either the water or tinned food or something I expect. Anyway, when we got out of the trenches I was pretty rotten, sick and so on, and was sent to the field ambulance and from there up here for a few days. I have quite got over the poisoning now and merely want a bit of strengthening. This is a Trappist Monastery standing right up on a hill with a wonderful view of the British line. One can see Dunkirk and the sea, and away south to Lille. We had a grim time in the trenches this last time. Our division got the liquid fire attack, the first of its sort made on the British. We had been in four days when it began and were to have gone into support that night, but as it was, we had to hang on for another four days. The bombardments were simply terrific, and there was a series of counter-attacks. I can't actually say whether the fire was spurted at my trench or not: certainly if it was, it turned into smoke before it reached us. But the hubbub and rapid firing and artillery and smoke and dust and so on was so terrific that one found it pretty difficult to know what was going on. As a spectacle a German attack must be a wonderful sight – to the angels out of range. They used all sorts of coloured lights (this was just before day break) and it is a wonderful scene. However I had not much spare time to admire the view. Our division was terribly cut about. Our battalion was luckier than most, as although we lost over two hundred men and six officers, all the officers and most of the men got off with wounds. It is almost impossible to describe the four days as they were pretty well confused and one was so much on the go all the time. I feel a bit of a brute, being up here in comfort. The battalion may be still out of the trenches or they may have pushed them back. We can get no news at all up here. I should think when this present racket is over, they would send the division back and get them straight again.

August 17th, 1915.

Life has been very strenuous. We have finished the Hooge fighting anyhow pro tem. It was a grim and grisly business and we were pretty well all through it. We lost heavily, but slew an immense quantity of Huns. I think a lot of lives were needlessly flung away, but I suppose we ought not to criticise. Incidentally I spent five days in hospital, my inside went astray, water or tinned food or something. Anyhow I am fit and well again now. I forget if I've told you I have now got a company and hope to be gazetted as captain shortly – which will be a double step. Authorities seem to think I have done well, though without false modesty I don't think I have done anything out of the ordinary. The test in the trenches is, will a man's nerves stand the strain? For some reason mine seem to, although the strain is pretty considerable, especially in the firing trench, where I had eight consecutive days during the worst of it. We lost our company commander and the remaining officer, and about half the trench was blown in. The sergeant was killed, second sergeant wounded, and most of the platoon lost. Things were fairly moderate. Now I believe they are going to send us to a quieter place, and I hope we will get some more officers. We have got about ten out of thirty we started with, but of our officer casualties only three have been killed. My company commanding officer is a great loss. He was a fine man and a very efficient soldier. I have got a difficult place to fill. However I feel much more capable of doing it than I did a week ago. It is a most quaint thing but the four company commanders now were all in D company, when we came over. We are all great pals, and I am fully six years older than any of the others. Two of them are absolutely efficient and splendid, and the other is not half so clever, but he is absolutely plucky and very sound in the trenches, so that is our quartette. Add a major aged thirty-two, and a few children as subalterns, and you have the 9th Battalion Rifle Brigade. – I have just been taking my first Orderly Room. There were fourteen prisoners, mostly small offences, such as not getting up in time – but it is rather an ordeal the first time. Unfortunately our company sergeant-major was knocked out last time, so I have got a new man I have never seen before. He talks too much at present but I'll get him out of that I hope. No doubt you have read all about Hooge in the Daily Mail and so I won't go into harrowing details. I don't think I added to the slaughter personally, though I did a little mild sniping pour encourager les autres. We only talk of two things (1) the war, (2) How we shall spend our leave. The popular idea at present is grouse shooting; (except in my case!) plus a sufficiency of champagne.

The Trenches,
August 23rd, 1915.

I fancy I haven't written for a long time, but I've been very busy: While we were in camp I had a bit of work to do running the company, and we were trying to get it into shape after our hammering of the past weeks. We have now been up here for three days, in a slightly different bit of line, but only half a mile or so from the old delectable spot. We have only ten officers up here, in fact, nine, as one was wounded yesterday and so we are very short handed, and so desperately overworked. For instance, an officer has to be in the fire trench all day and all officers must be in at night. Night is now officially from seven-thirty p.m. to four-thirty a.m., nine hours and this leaves fifteen of which we must be in seven and a half, as I have only one subaltern. So one is actually in the trench sixteen and a half hours out of the twenty-four. Add to that – I have an immense amount of work, eight different reports have to go in at various times throughout the day, one has to arrange returns and working parties and so on. Altogether the life of the Company commander in the trenches is not altogether a happy one. I am at very close quarters here, seventy-five yards or less at one place and I hold a pretty important post. It all means a lot of responsibility. However there it is! We shall be relieved to-morrow if all goes well, but 'one never knows.' To-day has been so desperately quiet that we are all a bit suspicious. Incidentally the wind which has been behind us for weeks, has shown signs of veering round; and so we have to be very much on the 'qui vive' for gas. We all hope they will take the whole division right away soon, as we are very much under-officered and naturally still feel the effects of weeks of almost continual bombardments. Some divisions have all the luck, they go to a soft spot and stay there for months, whereas others strike a rough spot like this, and also stay on for months. However all this is rather a growl, caused I think, because I am tired and have been trying to sleep and can't. We heard to-day of a big German naval loss in the Baltic, in an attempt to land at Riga. Perhaps it's true, but rumours have a way of being incorrect. Here we have quite a pastoral view. In our last trenches we saw nothing but desolation and rain, but here, looking at the rear, it is rather a pretty view, with a fine red poppy field almost half a mile back. When I become a civilian again (if ever), the sight of a sand-bag will make me scream.

Tuesday, August 24th, 7 a.m. Well, we had a night of absolute calm, a most unnerving thing. You see we veterans don't regard a day as normal unless there is at least six hour's bombardment. Really I almost prayed for a few whizz-bangs last night. The Germans have all sorts of queer night-stunts, which may mean something or may be merely intended to worry the opposition. For instance the following things may occur. I've known them all happen within forty-eight hours, but never all in one night. They'll suddenly shoot up one or two red flares – but as the liquid fire attack was ushered in by red flares, that gets one craning over the parapet. Then they will flick up a green one. Then they will fire a flare from away back in their support trench, within their own fire trench. They will blow two blasts on a whistle, or will suddenly sound a bugle. All these things are duly reported to me as I take my steady way round. – But the most trying thing happened two nights ago. Suddenly they sent up a shell which burst almost noiselessly and became a great black mass of smoke. It was a perfectly still night and the smoke hung up there for minutes before it dissolved. – Personally, I think it was a wind-test for gas. They did it twice that night. The wind is doing it's best for us. There has barely been a breeze for three days, absolute still-ness, but at critical times such as dusk and dawn, the west wind usually manages to get up a few puffs. It is now seven a.m. I have been on duty for over twelve hours continuously and I am distinctly tired. It is at almost dawn, one feels so dead to the world. If I sit down I go to sleep. Rather an interesting duty of a company commander is the working out the directon of the enemy's fire. You see in this warfare each side knows roughly where the other side's batteries are. The whole country swarms with them. They are well concealed of course, but each side has the other batteries roughly registered. So when a gun opens up on us, I leap off to a big scale map and try to find the direction of the fire on it. The map has lots of points numbered on it, and if the gun is annoying us, blowing in our parapets and so on, I ring up and say that a whizz-bang from direction fifty-seven (say) wants dealing with. Whereupon some battery major behind puts down his novel, gets out of his arm chair in his bomb-proof dug-out, and gets his battery to work. The next few minutes are usually fraught with considerable interest and some danger. When our battery opens up, the enemy gun usually puts in some pretty brisk business on us. Perhaps a third party chips in in the game, in the shape of a big Hun gun which fires at our battery. Eventually one imposes it's will on the enemy, and quiet perhaps reigns again. We have got a very enterprising gunner behind who would fire all day if required to do so. I'm going to knock off now as my subaltern (who is incidentally senior to me) has had his ration of sleep and it's my turn to-get down. So, good morning!

Wednesday, 2 p.m. We were relieved last night. Quite a reasonable and early relief. It's wonderful how one feels as soon as one has got one's men out. During relief one sees one's men out and then one lurks about with the new comers and shows them in and around. Finally one slopes off with one's orderly. Personally I dropped in at head quarters of the relieving battalion and had a good drink on their commanding officer – a great ally of mine who used to be our major. I then lit up a good cigarette, disdained communication trenches and rolled down the road. We are now in dug-outs in reserve. We were simply on a perfect wicket as we have two companies here and we can run them as we wish. But we have just had a telephone message from the commanding officer, and he is apparently coming up with Head quarters, which prob-ably means unending trouble. We shall be here four days I suppose, unless trouble arises. If they do, of course we trail up for a counter attack, previously making our wills! But we hope for peace, though personally I suspect the Hun at present. I had a good ration of slumber last night and hope to do likewise to-day.

Saturday. I fancy they are getting awfully 'fed up' in England with the papers and official communiques generally, and all the jingoism and ultra-optimism of the last twelve months. Personally, I think the man to whom the nation owes a debt of grat-itude is Northcliffe, though I don't suppose that is your view out in New Zealand. But it makes one sick to live in this sulphurous spot and read that blatant tosh in the English papers. They don't seem to realize that the English Army has made no advance this summer. We have merely won back part of what we lost in April in the first gas attack. Secondly, they are dead locked in Gallipoli, thirdly, the Russians are 'strategically' retreating like rabbits! But the old, old, cry is that 'the war can only have one ultimate issue.' I would take all these writers, and experts, and officials, and put them facing Hooge chateau for one calendar week. I should then open intense bombardment, and see what they reckoned about it all. Later I should erect a suitable number of crosses and bid them a tender farewell. The country round here literally swarms with bodies most of them buried now. One buries them as best one can, and I expect it does not matter whether they have a burial service or not. My own men I try to bury with some little form, but there isn't time for much. I've seen some grisly sights. I was prospecting for a trench the other day, and I suddenly saw an arm and hand sticking out of the earth. Lots of other sights also, that three months ago would have finished me off. I had nearly forgotten some rather 'swanky' news. The two first D.C.M.'s given to Kitchener's Army, are both men in my company!! That is rather a performance, and perhaps shows more than anything that we have passed through thunder and fire. These men on about ten occasions brought back wounded under very heavy fire – the sort of V.C. work in an ordinary war. But this is not an ordinary war. You can be certain that any man who has been at this long, has had to do a good many things of which he is secretly rather proud. And the nerve strain! In one's trench one must be ready for gas and liquid fire, one is probably being mined, the night is one long period of suspense. One has to hide from aeroplanes, one has to suspect everyone one does not know as a potential spy. Add to that the fact that one has to struggle with the infantile minds of riflemen who are the biggest fools in existence I should think. Mind you, they have got some redeeming features. Perhaps as you study English papers, you imagine us in the trenches with a continual smile on our faces. I assure you that is not always the case. I have seen fear in the faces of almost all a company and I have felt my own inside go wrong, and heard the voice of the Tempter saying 'Now Butterworth, old son, that's the spot for you; if you're rushed you will be near the exit door and be able to fall back.' At those times, the only thing to do, is to take oneself by the neck and get right into the heart of things, swarm about and cheer up the men, and generally restore your own confidence in yourself. I know exactly what fear feels like at two a.m. in the morning. I had to knock off writing here I forget why. I was out all last night working. I am to-day officer commanding 'Detachment,' two companies, as the other company commander has left on leave. Lucky fellow! I am rather busy, I must stop. I hope we get relieved to-night.

September 1st, 1915.

There is no news, but you may like to know that I'm still alive. We had a very quiet time in the trenches this tour, the first quiet we have ever had. And we are now resting. All sorts of rumours are afloat. The prevalent idea seems to be that there will be a terrific 'go' before the winter. All I hope is that I get my leave first. If not one's chances of ever getting leave again will be only moderate. Our division will no doubt be in it up to the neck. Our battalion is more or less impossible at present. We have six officers doing duty here at present; every other battalion seems to get new officers and we don't get one. It's getting rough on us relics. I ought to get my captaincy next week. No promotions have got through yet, chiefly because our adjutant usually fills in the wrong form, and of course if applications go in on pink paper instead of green, all the machinery is jammed at once. I think that also accounts for the dearth of officers. The general result is that the commanding officer is in a thoroughly bad temper and we all get well cursed – I seem to dodge a good deal of the cursing. Why, I don't know, as I usually stroll about in my ordinary manner and alter times for parades (contrary to standing orders, paragraph 54c, a22, etc.!) and do the most unutterable things. However when the commanding officer approaches and wants to know why, etc., I seem to mollify him by standing strictly to attention and saying, 'Yes, Sir' and 'No, Sir,' like a good little boy. It's a quaint life.

September 2nd, 3 a.m. A sudden change in life. We are all out on a spy-hunt. A great go! I am in command of a 'Road Section' with various posts and patrols under me, and I am at present at my headquarters in an Estaminet or Public House. I have commandeered most of the bar and am at the receipt of custom, with my interpreter, waiting for spies to be brought up in large quantities. I shall probably stay here for about thirty-six hours, smoke a bit, consume a certain amount of execrable 'vin rouge' and finally return home. However it is a variety, and one can do worse things in rainy weather than sit in a bar and read! My interpreter is a singularly useful person seeing that he talks no Flemish and the people here talk little else. Now-a-days one thinks nothing of turning in fully dressed for an hour or so, and then rising at two and boning off somewhere. But the men are the slowest things imaginable in the early morning. They were all late this morning and in the murky gloom I used some terrific language. Another man got leave to-day in our battalion. I think if I can survive the next trench-stunt, I ought to hit London. Imagine me dropping in on London after four months of this — with a good balance at Cox's. It will make up for a good deal of whizz-banging and trench mortaring won't it? It will be the rottenest luck to get the neck shot in the eleventh hour.

September 2nd, 1915.

I still remain seated in this Public House, terribly bored. I arrested a soi-disant Belgian soldier some time since, but I have not heard what became of him. Picture me therefore in the bar tête-à-tête with an aged and homely landlady, who is knitting stockings. She talks Flemish and French un petit peu. I talk English (more or less) and French un très petit peu. Our conversation is therefore amusing to the gods but not enlightening to each other. At the present moment she has just taken off her stockings and is trying on the ones she has knitted. I know not whether to be shy or not. She isn't. I can't make out about my photograph, most of them seem to have arrived. I expect yours will fetch up or has fetched up by now. I don't think you will like it particularly. I look too much the sort of advertisement for the British Army. Now I feel that I look more like a warrior with Government Service breeches, Government Service boots, Government Service great coat, trench-worn puttees, tunic with pockets all gouged about by worming along narrow trenches, cap in the most dilapidated condition; and generally the complete soldier! How I should love to get into an old Norfolk coat, a pair of flannel bags, and a pair of old brogues and seize a brassy and have a dunch, or better still don the flannels and take that one off the middle stump for four. I wonder if I shall ever play cricket again. Solemn, thought! A pal of mine came along just now and put his head in at the window and said that he leaves for England by the one-thirty to-morrow. I threw all I had at him. I wish this army life did not bore me so desperately. All the routine out of the trenches simply tires me to death. The trenches would be rather fun if there was not such a good chance of being killed. But I don't think I could stick the army after-wards. I haven't any ideas about the future. But that's not worth worrying about. There is a sort of feeling about again that the war is going to end in the winter. Personally I can't see it. Russia is right in the mud. Gallipoli does not progress. We can't get on here. One wonders what Germany's next move will be. I hope they won't fling Hindenburg, Mackensen, etc., at us. I am rather inclined to think they won't. They seem to have their eyes more on the East. Anyway this will be a nasty enough spot in the winter without jolly old Hindenburg. I imagine the Hun hates it just as much as we do, and wants to get back to his frau and his lager. The Hun is occasionally a sport. We lost an aviator-man in the Hooge straafe and the Hun airmen flying over us a day or two after, dropped a note saying that they had buried this man behind Hooge chateau 'with all honours due to a brave man.' In fact, if these Prussians were mopped up, they would be a decent crowd. There is not much quarter given now-a-days. At the end of the Hooge contest we rushed a redoubt (called now the Rifle Brigade redoubt). The Huns had all crawled into dug-outs and the festive Tommy rushed along, lit the fuse of a bomb and then flung the thing clean into the dug-out, shouting – 'Souvenir, Fritz.' This went on till they were tired more or less. It is rather nasty but really these brutes had been liquid firing, and so on, and deserved all they got. But imagine a bomb being hurled into and exploding in a crowded dug-out. It is very quaint how regiments differ. I went up digging the other night and heard a great straafe going on on the right. I met a subaltern loafing about and asked him the cause of the frightfulness. Apparently some Jocks (Gordons, I fancy) had just taken over and were signifying their disapproval of the Huns by flinging grenades at a terrific speed. In the same way the Canadians when they take over, always open with fifteen rounds rapid. Of course their reputation is such that if the Huns know the Canadians are opposite, they sit pretty doggo until said Canadians go out. The Canadians have the best repute as scrapsters here and they won it at the second battle of Ypres, the great gas attack. They were simply magnificent I believe. I forget if I told you the yarn of the Canadian who was asked what his officers were like, and who answered, 'That they didn't reckon much about them, but he guessed they carried them about as mascots.' However they are regarded as 'Pucka.' You will excuse the campaign slang that creeps into my conversation. But words like straafe, morning hate, frightfulness, have become part of the army vocabulary. An amusing stunt eventuated unpleasantly near me the other evening. I was in support in a dug-out. We brought up a great gun and got to work on one of their observation balloons, known as a Gas-Bag. They got some shrapnel on to it, and it went down very quick, and then they flicked over all they had got at where they reckoned it would land. So far, so good – In a short time the Huns began to search for that gun, and my word, they did search, with every conceivable thing. By some chance the gun was not hit, and they got it out safely at night. But they put some poisonous big stuff on to it. I am a man of peace and I object to seventeen inchers landing in the next field. They are nasty people. They come very, very slowly, sort of slip along, then crash, boom, and there is a hole in the ground. C = $2\pi r$, r = 25 yards! (formula wrong – never mind.) It is on these occasions that I wish that I had the wings of a dove. I told you perhaps that I had no company casualties last tour. Well, when we got to the supports we had three of the best. 1. A new draft man shot himself cleaning his rifle, (for which he gets a Court Martial.) 2. One of my best corporals was hit by a stray bullet, over fifteen hundred yards from the firing line! 3. An excellent sergeant was flung from a waggon and properly messed up.

By the way, the first two D.C.M.s given to Kitchener's Army came to my company, did I tell you? One of them is still in hospital but the other is magnifique. The salute he throws me makes me feel a Field Marshal. They have not been presented yet, and I suppose a red hat will drop round, and I shall stand properly at ease and do all the jolly old stunts. When Red Hats see me at the head of a company with one star and a delapidated hat I find they regard me with a bit of suspicion! Best wishes to all of you. I am thinking and dreaming of London, I shall be livid if I am hit before leave arrives.

September 6th, 1915,
8.30 p.m.

Just a line writ by the candle-light of my tent. We have had a good instance of brigade chop and changing to-day. We had fixed to go up to-morrow night. We company commanders were to go up to-day to arrange relief. This morning this was all washed out. We were not to go up for an indefinite time, but were to be kept back and dig, much joy! To-night at about six-thirty, they suddenly send round an orderly to say that we go in. So now we have got to dart off to-morrow early to make arrangements. I have not one single officer under me and it is a business to run a trench like mine single-handed. However I suppose I shall carry on, but it does not fall to the lot of many men of less than six months army experience to take into a very tricky trench, a company of one hundred and seventy men, eighty of whom have never seen a trench before. We are being abominably treated in the way of officers, but I suppose they can't help it. Of course the thing will be ludicrous if two or three of us are scuppered. It is a wonderful thing, but these men are no good without officers, and they know it. I gave my sergeants a good telling-off this morning to keep them up to the knocker. They are good sergeants but will skimp work if they can. I have got a proper new sergeant – a Regular – and he is going right up to the top if I get a chance. I am gradually civilizing my sergeant-major, but what a quaint life for Butterworth!

The relieving feature of it all is the extraordinary good terms all we 'relics' are on. We are a 'bonhomous' crowd. A quaint medley, three boys of nineteen, two Australians, three youngsters of twenty-three or twenty-four and me!! I am the hoary-headed old sport. One of the stock jokes at my expense is to ask one if they played cricket in top hats in my time. But I assure you I get my own back in the way of subtle jokes. However they are delightful children and we have been through such times together that we know each other pretty well. Also we can trust each other's nerves pretty well. The three youngsters are, I believe, the coolest of the lot. The commanding officer seems to trust us all implicitly. We get it in the neck now and then of course, but he gives us carte blanche in the trenches. His organisation is very good indeed. His fault in the trenches is that he worries too much about us. Now he is in terror that one or more of us will be knocked out. He is a curious character.

September 15th, 1915.

As life is about to be somewhat strenuous, I am writing this a week or so before I shall post it, and perhaps I'll add a line before going up. I hear there is going to be a great racket here and I need hardly say that H.M.B. looks like being up to the neck in it. This letter won't be posted till after it's begun, so there is not much harm in giving full facts. Well, as you know, the Belgians hold a bit of line to the north, where they are well protected by floods. Then come the French down to two or three miles north-east of Ypres, and then we come. There is a division between the French and the 14th — —. Then we carry on of course for a long way to the main French line. Well, there is going to be a combined attack. The French, I fancy, are actually going to try to get through. Anyway they hope to get a long way and have lots of men and shells to do it with. The division between us and the French is not moving. Then we are stepping forward from our left to Hill 60, and probably further south, I don't know. Operations start in two or three days from now with a week's artillery bombardment. The French have already bombarded for over a fortnight! We, who are detailed for the charge – and our battalion is for it – go up thirty-six hours before the end of that and get into assembly trenches and so on, about two hours before charging time. The bombardment is concentrated on their first line. At the exact time the country immediately in front of me is blown up, (I believe Hill 60 is going clean up too) the 9th Rifle Brigade step nimbly over the parapet, struggle over the delightful country between ours and the Huns' lines and then take the giddy trench at the point of the bayonet. This performance is carried out amidst shrapnel and high explosive, likewise machine gun fire from everything. Can you see your old pal Butterworth doing this? Of course what I ought to do is to wave a sword in the air, call upon D company to remember the land of their birth, etc., and foremost fighting fall. What I probably shall do is to mutter a few oaths and put my head down and get over with the greatest precipitation. It will be a great stunt, what our senior captain (aged twenty-three) calls 'a proper joy-morning.' We expect to lose about half the battalion and (unless we get a new consignment) practically all the officers. The consolation is we go into it together (and probably out) and it is a real 'pucka' show. No one particularly objects to taking the neck shot in a real show, but one does hate being sniped in a trench when you are having lunch or something silly like that. I suppose it will be the biggest thing done this summer. I believe we have got every possible thing, gas, liquid fire, the whole bag of tricks, and I expect worse than anything the Germans ever used, (three cheers for Pecksniff), but I don't know if we shall want them. I hope I slip through; simply to have done it will last me for life. I think the men will come alright, provided a certain number of officers get through the first rush. Isn't it incredible that these fellows will follow an officer anywhere and won't go with an N.C.O.? I had a heart-to-heart chat to my sergeant-major on the point, last evening. I said to him 'Here am I, I could not possibly drill a company and am pretty vague on arm drill; half of the men have only seen me for a fortnight, why should they come along with me anywhere and refuse to follow some of these sergeants with three or four medals?' He could not give a reason, nor could I. But it gives me a considerable sense of responsibility, and one feels a little proud too. I am not the slightest brave, but I don't for a moment doubt my ability to do the needful in this case. So cheer Ho! I put the betting at about three to one against, but it is all luck, and I've got a sort of knack of scrambling through things. Anyway it is of no importance – as Mr. Toots said; I'll add a few words of valedictory before I gird on my kit.

Later. September 20th I think.

I have been so very busy that I have started odd letters to people and never finished them. I am writing a sort of valedictory to you and may leave it behind, or may post the thing myself. Things are moving. We find we are a part of a real proper show which we hope is going to mess up the Bosche a whole lot. Also we have been lent five officers and my lad is quite a tiger and I think will step in cheerily. However I have had to take the really bad job myself, partly out of shame, (one can't with decency give it to anyone else) and partly to assist the company's morale, as I think they will come after me if they see one jumping off into the dust and din.

I should not be surprised if there was a naval battle at the same time, but we know nothing really. We were inspected by X + Y Generals, Brigadiers and Corps Commanders this morning, a wonderful collection of red and gold. I can hear the guns hard at it at this moment. I hope they are worrying the Huns somewhat, of course we depend absolutely on the artillery. If they don't knock out the wire and so on it's goodbye to us. However they are pretty good, although ours can't be as good as a regular division's. The wind has gone to the east, I don't think we shall attack until we get a gas wind, as I am certain we shall use it. Our hypocrites at Home will probably deny it. But when you have had gas flicked at you once, as I have, you lose most scruples about it.

Belgium,
September, 1915.

(I am posting this myself just before leaving. Perhaps I shan't be killed!!)

I am leaving this in the hands of the transport officer, and if I get knocked out, he will send it on to you. We are going into a big thing. It will be my pleasant duty to leap lightly over the parapet and lead D company over the delectable confusion of old trenches, crump holes, barbed wire, that lies between us and the Bosche, and take a portion of his front line. Quo facto I shall then proceed to bomb down various communication trenches and take his second line. In the very unlikely event of my being alive by then I shall dig in like blazes and if God is good, stop the Bosche counter-attack, which will come in an hour or two. If we stop that I shall then in broad daylight have to get out wire in front under machine gun fire and probably stop at least one more counter-attack and a bomb attack from the flank. If all that happens successfully, and I'm still alive, I shall hang on till relief. Well, when one is faced with a programme like that, one touches up one's will, thanks heaven one has led a fairly amusing life, thanks God one is not married, and trusts in Providence. Unless we get more officers before the show, I am practically bound to be outed as I shall have to lead all these things myself. Anyway if I do go out I shall do so amidst such a scene of blood and iron as even this war has rarely witnessed. We are going to bombard for a week, explode a mine and then charge. One does see life doesn't one? Of course there is always a chance of only being wounded and the off-chance of pulling through. Of course one has been facing death pretty intimately for months now, but with this ahead, one must realize that, in the vernacular of New Zealand, one's numbers are probably up. We are not a sentimental crowd at the Collegiate School, Wanganui, but I think in a letter of this sort, one can say how frightfully attached one is to the old brigade. Also I am very, very much attached to the School, and to Selwyn in particular. There are two thousand things I should like to say about what I feel, but they can't be put down, I find. Live long and prosper, all of you. Curiously enough, I don't doubt my power to stick it out, and I think my men will follow me.

Hugh Montagu Butterworth's Cricket Scores of 50 and Over

Year	Score	Ground	For	Against
1914	311	Wanganui	School B.	Wanganui A.
1914	296	Wanganui	School B.	Victoria
1913	253	Wanganui	School B.	Wanganui B.
1910	241	Wanganui	Wanganui	Cosmopolitan Club
1912	216	Wanganui	Wanganui	Aramoho
1914	194	Wanganui	School B.	Wanganui B.
1914	184	Wanganui	School B.	Aramoho
1908	167	Christchurch	Nomads	United Club
1906	156	Oxford	University College	Trinity College
1914	156	Wanganui	Nomads	School
1913	155	Wanganui	School B.	Wanganui A.
1910	149	Christchurch	Nomads	A Christchurch XI
1905	140	Carsham P'k, Eng.	Lord Methuen's XI	Free Foresters
1914	135	Auckland	Nomads	Eden
1906	131	Trowbridge, Eng.	Wiltshire Wanderers	Wiltshire Regim't
1910	131	Wanganui	Masters	School
1906	130	Oxford	Seniors' Match	
1913	129	Auckland	Nomads	Ponsonby
1904	125	Trowbridge, Eng.	Wiltshire Wanderers	Pembroke Lodge
1904	125	Clevedon, Eng.	Wiltshire Wanderers	Clevedon
1905	122	Swindon, Eng.	Wiltshire	Dorsetshire
1912	122	Wanganui	School B.	Aramoho
1913	121	Masterton	Nomads	Wairarapa
1905	120	Oxford	University College	B.N.C.
1904	118	Trowbridge, Eng.	Wiltshire Juniors	Somerset Juniors
1910	117	Wanganui	Wanganui	St. Pauls
1913	116	Wanganui	School B.	St. Pauls
1908	113	Wanganui	Wanganui Present	Wanganui Past
1913	110	Wanganui	School B.	Aramoho
1905	109	Oxford	University College	Queen's College
1906	108	Basingstoke	'Unicorns'	Basingstoke
1900	107	Marlborough	'A' House	S.O.B.
1905	106	Trowbridge, Eng.	Wiltshire	M.C.C.
1909	106	Wanganui	Wanganui Single	Wanganui Married
1913	104	Wanganui	Nomads	School
1908	103	Wanganui	Wanganui	St. Pauls
1905	102	Oxford	University College	Keble College
1912	102	Geraldine	Nomads	Geraldine
1905	100	E. Grinstead, Eng.	J. L. Birley's XI.	Lancing Old Boys
1900	99	Marlborough	House Match	
1914	98	Wanganui	H. F. Arkwright's XI	School
1914	94	Wanganui	School B.	Wanganui A.
1910	93	Wanganui	Wanganui	School
1904	92	Lynton, Eng.	Lynton Visitors	Lynton Residents
1906	89	Marlborough	Marlborough Blues	Marlborough Col.
1910	88	Wanganui	Wanganui Trial Match	

Year	Score	Ground	For	Against
1913	86	Wanganui	School B.	Aramoho
1906	84	Marlborough	Marlborough Blues	Marlborough Col.
1908	83	Wanganui	Wanganui	Aramoho
1906	82	Magdalen College	University College	Magdalen College
1913	81	Palmerston, N.	'Teachers' XI'	N.S.W. Teachers
1906	80	Swindon, Eng.	Swindon	M.C.C.
1913	80	Wanganui	School B.	Wanganui A.
1907	79	Wanganui	Wanganui	Aramoho
1908	79	Wanganui	Wanganui	School
1908	79	Wanganui	Masters	Clifton Club
1904	78	Marlborough	Marlborough College	School
1904	78	Lord's	Marlborough College	Rugby
1904	77	Marlborough	Marlborough College	Free Foresters
1910	76	Christchurch	Nomads	Riccarton
1905	76	Marlborough	Marlborough Blues	Marlborough Col.
1911	76	Wanganui	'Great Unknown'	School
1906	74	Marlow, Eng.	'Unicorns'	Marlow
1909	72	Wanganui	Wanganui	St. Pauls
1914	72	Wanganui	School B.	Aramoho
1912	71	Wanganui	School B.	School
1914	71	Wanganui	School B.	Wanganui B.
1910	70	Wanganui	Wanganui	School
1904	70	Marlborough	Big Game	
1900	70	Marlborough	'A' House	Cotton House
1905	68	Oxford	University College	Corpus College
1905	68	Wallingford, Eng.	'University Bees'	Wallingford
1902	66	Marlborough	House Match	
1901	66	Tewkesbury	Tewkesbury	Cirencester
1905	66	Winchester, Eng.	University College	Winchester
1913	65	Hamilton	Wanganui	S. Auckland
1909	65	Wanganui	Wanganui A.	Wanganui B.
1902	65	Marlborough	House Match	
1913	65	Wanganui	Wanganui 1st XI	Wanganui 2nd XI
1906	64	Oxford	University College	Hertford College
1906	64	Cheltenham	University College	E. Gloucestershire
1913	63	Napier	Nomads	Hawkes Bay
1910	63	Wanganui	Wanganui	St. Pauls
1906	63	Oxford	University Trial Match	
1904	62	Marlborough	House Match	
1912	63	Wanganui	Nomads	School
1903	61	Bath	Wiltshire Juniors	Somerset Juniors
1905	60	Oxford	University College	Hertford College
1906	60	Bath	Wiltshire	Somerset
1906	60	Maidenhead	'Unicorns'	Maidenhead
1908	60	Wanganui	Masters	School
1908	59	Wanganui	Wanganui	Taranaki
1913	59	Auckland	Nomads	Auckland University

Year	Score	Ground	For	Against
1914	59	Wanganui	School B.	School
1908	58	Wanganui	Wanganui	Taranaki
1906	57	Oxford	University Trial Match	
1909	56	Wanganui	Wanganui	Aramoho
1914	56	Wanganui	H. M. Butterworth's XI	Williamson's Coy
1903	55	Marlborough	Marlborough College	Warwickshire Regiment
1905	55	Oxford	Old Marlburians	Exeter College
1914	55	Wanganui	H. M. Butterworth's XI	School
1909	55	Wanganui	Wanganui A.	Wanganui B.
1906	53	Westonbirt, Eng.	Free Foresters	Westonbirt College
1905	53	Marlborough	Marlborough Blues	Marlborough
1906	52	Swindon, Eng.	Wiltshire	Buckinghamshire
1914	52	Wanganui	Masters	School
1907	51	Bletchley P., Eng.	Wiltshire	Buckinghamshire
1908	51	Waimate	Nomads	Waimate
1913	51	Wanganui	Nomads	School
1909	50	Wanganui	Wanganui	Aramoho
1903	50	Marlborough	Marlborough College	Liverpool
1908	50	Timaru	Nomads	Timaru
1905	50	Shaw Hill	Shaw Hill	Lansdown
1913	50	Wanganui	School B.	Aramoho
1914	50	Wanganui	Wanganui	S. Taranaki

Appendix 1

9th (Service) Battalion the Rifle Brigade Killed in Action or Died of Wounds, 25 September–12 October 1915

Surname	Initials	Forenames (Where Known)	Rank	Service Number	Date of Death	Age (Where Known)
ADAMS	J E	JOHN EDWARD	Rifleman	S/6987	25-Sep-15	–
AIKENHEAD	W		Corporal	B/1109	25-Sep-15	–
AKROYD	J W	JOHN WILLIAM	Rifleman	S/6363	25-Sep-15	–
ALLISON	W	WILLIAM	Rifleman	S/9830	25-Sep-15	–
ARDREY	E	ELLIS	Rifleman	Z/2055	25-Sep-15	–
ATFIELD	A R	ARTHUR RICHARD	Lance Corporal	S/12047	25-Sep-15	–
BAILEY	W T	WILLIAM THOMAS	Rifleman	S/5310	25-Sep-15	–
BALFOUR	J J	JOHN	Rifleman	S/11208	25-Sep-15	–
BARNETT	T H	THOMAS HENRY	Rifleman	S/8205	08-Oct-15	36
BARNETT	T W	THOMAS WILLIAM	Rifleman	S/9740	25-Sep-15	–
BARRETT	H W	HENRY WILLIAM	Rifleman	B/1861	25-Sep-15	35
BARTLETT	W E	WILLIAM EDWARD	Corporal	B/1715	25-Sep-15	24
BEECH	A	ALBERT	Lance Corporal	B/2542	25-Sep-15	–
BELL	R R	ROBERT RALPH	Rifleman	B/3368	25-Sep-15	–
BELLAMY	C H	CHARLES HENRY	Rifleman	S/6531	25-Sep-15	–
BENNETT	F	FREDERICK	Rifleman	S/11822	25-Sep-15	–
BESSANT	W F	WALTER FREDERICK	Rifleman	S/13026	25-Sep-15	21
BRITTON	G W	GEORGE WILLIAM	Rifleman	Z/1979	25-Sep-15	–
BROWN	J	JOHN	Rifleman	B/1313	25-Sep-15	–
BURGAR	J W	JOSEPH WALTER	Rifleman	S/245	25-Sep-15	–
BURGE	E E	ERNEST EDWARD	Rifleman	5772	25-Sep-15	–
BUTLER	H	HARRY	Lance Corporal	B/2568	25-Sep-15	24
BUTTERWORTH	H M	HUGH MONTAGU	Captain		25-Sep-15	29
CAMPBELL	C H		Rifleman	B/2474	25-Sep-15	–
CAMPBELL	E	EDWIN	Rifleman	B/2392	25-Sep-15	26
CARMICHAEL	D	DOUGLAS	Captain		25-Sep-15	21
CHAPMAN	E	EDMUND	Corporal	B/1792	25-Sep-15	22
CHATTEN	C H	CHARLES HIGH	Corporal	B/2988	25-Sep-15	22
CLARSON	B		Rifleman	Z/995	01-Oct-15	–
CLENCH	J G	JOHN GEORGE	Rifleman	S/8600	25-Sep-15	18
COLLINS	A		Rifleman	S/8121	04-Oct-15	–
COUSINS	F L	FRANK LEONARD	Rifleman	B/1068	25-Sep-15	21
CROOME	A E	ALBERT EDWARD	Rifleman	S/9970	25-Sep-15	22
CROWE	E F	EDWARD FREDERICK	Rifleman	S/10637	25-Sep-15	19
DALE	H J	HENRY JOSEPH	Rifleman	S/10509	25-Sep-15	22
DAVIES	F R	FREDERICK ROBERT	Rifleman	B/1401	25-Sep-15	–
DAVIES	W		Rifleman	B/3051	25-Sep-15	–
DEIGHTON	S R	SIDNEY ROBERT	Rifleman	5730	25-Sep-15	–
DICKENSON	T	THOMAS	Rifleman	Z/2313	25-Sep-15	–
DOBBY	W A	WILLIAM ARTHUR	Rifleman	S/8816	25-Sep-15	–
EDEN	H A	HERBERT ALEXANDER	Rifleman	S/8692	25-Sep-15	–
EDWARDS	E	EWART	Rifleman	B/944	25-Sep-15	–
EVANS	T	THOMAS	Rifleman	B/2654	25-Sep-15	–
FALL	W G	WILLIAM GEORGE	Serjeant	5/349	25-Sep-15	–
FARRELL	W H	WILLIAM HENRY	Rifleman	3732	25-Sep-15	25
FIELD	W E	WILLIAM EDWARD	Rifleman	B/2629	25-Sep-15	–

Place of Burial or Commemoration	*Family Information (Where Known)*
YPRES (MENIN GATE) MEMORIAL	
TJSSENTHOEK MILITARY CEMETERY	Brother of Mrs E Howard, of 35 Slater St, Warrington.
YPRES (MENIN GATE) MEMORIAL	
YPRES (MENIN GATE) MEMORIAL	
YPRES (MENIN GATE) MEMORIAL	
YPRES (MENIN GATE) MEMORIAL	
YPRES (MENIN GATE) MEMORIAL	Son of Mrs Elizabeth Bailey; husband of Helena Emma Bailey, of 11 Haldane Rd, Fulham, London.
YPRES (MENIN GATE) MEMORIAL	Son of the late Mr and Mrs Balfour, of 9 Glasshouse Chambers, Aldersgate St, London.
LEICESTER (WELFORD ROAD) CEMETERY	Son of T Barnett, of 37 Woodside Gardens, Tottenham, London; husband of A T Barnett, of 32 Clacton Rd, Walthamstow, Essex.
YPRES (MENIN GATE) MEMORIAL	
YPRES (MENIN GATE) MEMORIAL	Son of the late William Henry and Annie Barrett; husband of Kate J Barrett, of 87 Corbett St, Smethwick, Staffs.
TJSSENTHOEK MILITARY CEMETERY	Son of William and Jane Bartlett, of 55 Westmoreland Place, Nile St, Hoxton, London.
YPRES (MENIN GATE) MEMORIAL	
YPRES (MENIN GATE) MEMORIAL	
YPRES (MENIN GATE) MEMORIAL	
YPRES (MENIN GATE) MEMORIAL	
YPRES (MENIN GATE) MEMORIAL	Son of Tom Edward and Mary Bessant, of 18 Doncaster Rd, Eastleigh, Hants.
YPRES (MENIN GATE) MEMORIAL	
YPRES (MENIN GATE) MEMORIAL	
YPRES (MENIN GATE) MEMORIAL	
YPRES (MENIN GATE) MEMORIAL	
YPRES (MENIN GATE) MEMORIAL	Son of Mr and Mrs F Buder, of White Horse St, Wymondham, Norfolk.
YPRES (MENIN GATE) MEMORIAL	Son of George Montagu Butterworth and Catherine Lucie Butterworth (née Warde), of The Cashmere Hills, Christchurch, New Zealand. Master at Wanganui Collegiate School, New Zealand.
HOOGE CRATER CEMETERY	
YPRES (MENIN GATE) MEMORIAL	Son of Henry and Elizabeth Campbell; husband of Sarah Ann Smith (formerly Campbell), of 6 Warton Rd, Stratford, London.
YPRES (MENIN GATE) MEMORIAL	Son of Sir James Carmichael KBE and Lady Carmichael, of Kingston Hill Place, Kingston-on-Thames.
YPRES (MENIN GATE) MEMORIAL	Son of Thomas and Maria Chapman, of I03 Bloomfield St, Halesowen, Birmingham.
YPRES (MENIN GATE) MEMORIAL	Son of Annie Chatten, of The Row, Tendring, Clacton-on-Sea, Essex.
STAPLES MILITARY CEMETERY	
YPRES (MENIN GATE) MEMORIAL	Son of John George and Rosina Clench, of 3A Shaftesbury St, New North Rd, Hoxton, London.
IMEREUX COMMUNAL CEMETERY	
YPRES (MENIN GATE) MEMORIAL	Son of W H and Louisa Cousins, of 51 Ondine Rd, East Dulwich, London.
YPRES (MENIN GATE) MEMORIAL	Son of Mr and Mrs C C Croome, of 22 Clifton Rd, Aston, Birmingham.
YPRES (MENIN GATE) MEMORIAL	Son of Frederick and Minnie Crowe, of 64 Atheldene Rd, Wandsworth, London.
YPRES (MENIN GATE) MEMORIAL	Son of Annie Elizabeth Dale, of 65 Crawshay Rd, Brixton, London, and the late Henry William Dale.
YPRES (MENIN GATE) MEMORIAL	
HARLEBEKE NEW BRITISH CEMETERY	
YPRES (MENIN GATE) MEMORIAL	
YPRES (MENIN GATE) MEMORIAL	
YPRES (MENIN GATE) MEMORIAL	
YPRES (MENIN GATE) MEMORIAL	
YPRES (MENIN GATE) MEMORIAL	
YPRES (MENIN GATE) MEMORIAL	
YPRES (MENIN GATE) MEMORIAL	Son of Ellen Farrell, of 66 Wyndham Rd, Tower Hamlets, Dover.
YPRES (MENIN GATE) MEMORIAL	

Surname	Initials	Forenames (Where Known)	Rank	Service Number	Date of Death	Age (Where Known)
FLYNN	J	JAMES	Rifleman	6/532	29-Sep-15	18
FORDHAM	G	GEORGE	Serjeant	6205	25-Sep-15	–
GLOVER	G F	GEORGE FREDERICK	Corporal	B/1040	25-Sep-15	21
GODDARD	E J	EMANUEL JOHN	Rifleman	B/3386	25-Sep-15	21
GREEN	F	FREDERICK	Rifleman	S/6559	25-Sep-15	–
GRIMSHAW	S G	SAMUEL G	Rifleman	B/3477	25-Sep-15	–
HAMBROOK	H	HENRY	Rifleman	S/9802	25-Sep-15	–
HENN	E H L	EDWARD HENRY LOVETT	Second Lieutenant		25-Sep-15	23
HOCKLEY	J	JOSEPH	Rifleman	B/1227	25-Sep-15	22
HOPKINS	G	GEORGE	Rifleman	S/9948	25-Sep-15	–
HORTON	T H	THOMAS HENRY	Rifleman	5726	25-Sep-15	–
HOWARTH	A	ARTHUR	Corporal	Z/596	25-Sep-15	23
HULL	G	GEORGE	Rifleman	S/10040	25-Sep-15	–
HUMPHREYS	J G	JOHN GEORGE	Rifleman	B/3005	25-Sep-15	–
HUNT	H	HARRY	Rifleman	S/9709	25-Sep-15	–
HUSSEY	P	PERCY	Rifleman	B/2809	25-Sep-15	–
JAMES	S	SYDNEY	Rifleman	Z/1137	25-Sep-15	–
JONES	J T	JOHN THOMAS	Rifleman	B/1931	25-Sep-15	–
KEMM	F J	FREDERICK JAMES	Rifleman	S/4356	25-Sep-15	–
KNOWLES	E J	EDGAR JOHN	Rifleman	5641	25-Sep-15	–
LAMBERT	H	HERBERT	Rifleman	S/11926	25-Sep-15	–
LANE	A H	ARTHUR HERBERT	Rifleman	S/11294	25-Sep-15	22
LANE	F A	FREDERICK ALBERT	Rifleman	7364	25-Sep-15	36
LEESON	A	ALFRED	Rifleman	S/12934	25-Sep-15	–
LIPSCOMBE	H	HERBERT	Serjeant	S/3942	25-Sep-15	20
LOCKE	W E	WILLIAM ERNEST	Rifleman	Z/1951	25-Sep-15	25
LODGE	J	JAMES	Rifleman	S/12931	25-Sep-15	26
LOWE	A N	ALFRED NORMAN	Corporal	B/1614	25-Sep-15	19
LYMN	T	THOMAS	Rifleman	S/9070	25-Sep-15	20
McANULTY	E	EDWIN	Rifleman	B/2559	25-Sep-15	–
MACE	**J E**	**JOSEPH ERNEST**	**Rifleman**	**S/5975**	**25-Sep-15**	**41**
McLEAR	J	JAMES	Serjeant	S/3593	25-Sep-15	45
MANSFIELD	**H**	**HORACE**	**Rifleman**	**S/8296**	**25-Sep-15**	**23**
MARTIN	C	CHARLES	Corporal	S/6581	25-Sep-15	26
MATTHEWS	M H	MORGAN HENRY	Rifleman	S/3205	25-Sep-15	–
MERRETT	W L	WILLIAM LESLIE	Rifleman	S/8805	25-Sep-15	–
MOBERLY	C G H	CHARLES GORDON HERBERT	Serjeant	B/1179	25-Sep-15	30
MOLL	R	ROBERT	Rifleman	Z/1235	25-Sep-15	–
MOUNSEY	W J	WILLIAM JOHN	Rifleman	6/547	25-Sep-15	18
MULLEY	A V	ALBERT VICTOR	Lance Serjeant	795	25-Sep-15	29
MUNNINGS	J	JOHN	Lance Corporal	B/2546	25-Sep-15	–
MURRELL	E G	ERNEST GEORGE	Rifleman	2910	10-Oct-15	26
NADIN	F	FRANK	Rifleman	5054	25-Sep-15	–
NEYE	C F	CHAS FREDERICK	Rifleman	5/311	29-Sep-15	19
NORTON	J E	JOHN EDWARD	Corporal	B/3089	25-Sep-15	32
O'CONNOR	J	JOHN	Rifleman	S/6089	25-Sep-15	–
OLDRIDGE	H	HARRY	Rifleman	S/6470	25-Sep-15	20
O'REILLY	T		Rifleman	S/10215	28-Sep-15	–
PACKHAM	G	GEORGE	Rifleman	S/11693	25-Sep-15	–
PADWICK	W E	WILLIAM EDWARD	Rifleman	B/1220	25-Sep-15	24
PASK	P H	PHILLIP HENRY	Corporal	S/11947	28-Sep-15	21
PHILPOTT	T B	THOMAS BALLARD	Rifleman	S/9749	25-Sep-15	–
PILLING	W	WILLIAM	Rifleman	B/1116	25-Sep-15	22

Place of Burial or Commemoration	Family Information (Where Known)
PRES (MENIN GATE) MEMORIAL	Son of James and Elizabeth Flynn, of 48 Weaman St, Snow Hill, Birmingham.
PRES (MENIN GATE) MEMORIAL	
PRES (MENIN GATE) MEMORIAL	Son of Edwin and Mary Glover. One of six sons who served.
PRES (MENIN GATE) MEMORIAL	Son of Mr and Mrs William Goddard, of 56 Lawrence St, Canning Town, London.
PRES (MENIN GATE) MEMORIAL	
PRES (MENIN GATE) MEMORIAL	
PRES (MENIN GATE) MEMORIAL	
PRES (MENIN GATE) MEMORIAL	Son of Edward Lovett Henn and Margaret Agnes Vaughan Henry his wife, of Campagne Sidi-Merzoug, El-Biar, Algiers. Educated at Freiburg University, Baden, and Trinity College, Cambridge. B.A., 1913. Qualified for entry to Foreign Office (2nd in Competition)
PRES (MENIN GATE) MEMORIAL	Son of Emma Hockley, of 1 Church Cottages, Alresford, Hants, and the late Frederick Hockley.
PRES (MENIN GATE) MEMORIAL	Son of the late Henry and Annie Hopkins.
PRES (MENIN GATE) MEMORIAL	
PRES (MENIN GATE) MEMORIAL	Son of the late William and Catherine Howarth; husband of Elizabeth Parnell (formerly Howarth), of 5 Thornton St, Collyhurst St, Manchester.
PRES (MENIN GATE) MEMORIAL	
PRES (MENIN GATE) MEMORIAL	
PRES (MENIN GATE) MEMORIAL	
PRES (MENIN GATE) MEMORIAL	
PRES (MENIN GATE) MEMORIAL	Son of William James, of 55 Hume St, Smethwick, Staffs.
PRES (MENIN GATE) MEMORIAL	
PRES (MENIN GATE) MEMORIAL	
PRES (MENIN GATE) MEMORIAL	
PRES (MENIN GATE) MEMORIAL	
PRES (MENIN GATE) MEMORIAL	Son of Herbert and Laura Lane, of 124 Borough High St, London, SE1.
PRES (MENIN GATE) MEMORIAL	Son of John and Sarah Lane, of Gravel Hill, Chalfont St Peter, Bucks; husband of Rose Lane.
PRES (MENIN GATE) MEMORIAL	
PRES (MENIN GATE) MEMORIAL	Son of William and Ellen Lipscombe.
PRES (MENIN GATE) MEMORIAL	Son of Henry Locke, of 12 Orsett Mews, Paddington, London.
PRES (MENIN GATE) MEMORIAL	Son of the late James and Susan Lodge.
PRES (MENIN GATE) MEMORIAL	Son of George William and Jane Ellen Lowe, of 4 Yew Bank, Lower Broughton Rd, Salford, Manchester.
PRES (MENIN GATE) MEMORIAL	Son of John Lymn, of 39 John St, Derby.
PRES (MENIN GATE) MEMORIAL	
PRES (MENIN GATE) MEMORIAL	**Husband of Ethel Grace Young (formerly Mace), of 13 Robson Rd, West Norwood, London.**
PRES (MENIN GATE) MEMORIAL	Son of James and Mary McLear; husband of Mary Ann McLear, of 19 Elm St, West Derby St, Liverpool.
PRES (MENIN GATE) MEMORIAL	**Son of Harry and Mary Anna Mansfield, of 9 Cambria Rd, Camberwell, London.**
PRES (MENIN GATE) MEMORIAL	Son of Mary Martin, of 3 Watlington Grove, Lower Sydenham, London.
PRES (MENIN GATE) MEMORIAL	
PRES (MENIN GATE) MEMORIAL	
PRES (MENIN GATE) MEMORIAL	Son of the late Walter F G and Mary E Moberly.
PRES (MENIN GATE) MEMORIAL	
PRES (MENIN GATE) MEMORIAL	Son of Thomas Craig Mounsey and Hannah Mounsey, of 76 Atlantic Rd, Brixton, London.
PRES (MENIN GATE) MEMORIAL	Son of Mrs E Mulley, of 115 Angel St, Hadleigh, Suffolk.
PRES (MENIN GATE) MEMORIAL	
LE TOUQUET-PARIS PLAGE COMMUNAL CEMETERY	Son of James and Lucy Murrell, of 38 Terminus Place, Eastbourne.
PRES (MENIN GATE) MEMORIAL	Son of Charles and Ellen Beatrice Neye, of 182 New North Rd, Islington, London.
PRES (MENIN GATE) MEMORIAL	Son of Mr H Norton, of 1 Culford Rd, Southgate Rd, London, N1; husband of Mrs C A Norton, of 1 Hill Cottages, Layer Breton, Kelvedon, Essex.
PRES (MENIN GATE) MEMORIAL	
PRES (MENIN GATE) MEMORIAL	Son of Harry and Ellen Oldridge, of 33 Amelia St, Walworth, London.
LIJSSENTHOEK MILITARY CEMETERY	
PRES (MENIN GATE) MEMORIAL	
PRES (MENIN GATE) MEMORIAL	Son of John and Emily Padwick, of Mill Cottage, Bishop's Sutton, Alresford, Hants, husband of the late Mabel Padwick.
LIJSSENTHOEK MILITARY CEMETERY	Son of Arthur and Louisa Pask, of Bury St Edmund's, Suffolk.
PRES (MENIN GATE) MEMORIAL	
PRES (MENIN GATE) MEMORIAL	Son of James Pilling, of 9 Dutton St, Warrington.

Surname	Initials	Forenames (Where Known)	Rank	Service Number	Date of Death	Age (Where Known)
PITCHER	E	ERNEST	Rifleman	S/8727	25-Sep-15	34
PIXTON	J T	JOHN THOMAS	Rifleman	Z/1784	25-Sep-15	–
PLATT	T	THOMAS	Rifleman	S/8803	25-Sep-15	17
PODMORE	S	SAMUEL	Lance Corporal	S/7847	25-Sep-15	–
PROCTOR	W C	WILLIAM CHARLES	Rifleman	S/11948	25-Sep-15	20
PUNTER	H	HENRY	Rifleman	B/2472	25-Sep-15	21
PURVIS	J R	JOHN RALPH	Captain		25-Sep-15	21
PUTMAN	H	HERBERT	Rifleman	S/10107	25-Sep-15	–
QUINN	B T	BERNARD THOMAS	Rifleman	S/8981	25-Sep-15	16
RAPLEY	W	WILLIAM	Corporal	S/7605	25-Sep-15	34
RAY	W	WALTER	Serjeant	S/4125	25-Sep-15	41
REED	H C	HARRY CLAUDE	Rifleman	S/13163	25-Sep-15	23
RESTALL	W	WILLIAM	Rifleman	S/1642	25-Sep-15	18
RICHARDSON	W	WILLIAM	Serjeant	B/974	25-Sep-15	–
ROBINSON	H	HAROLD	Lance Corporal	S/5402	25-Sep-15	18
ROBINSON	R	ROBERT	Rifleman	S/10205	25-Sep-15	36
ROBINSON	W F	WALTER FREDERICK	Rifleman	S/9791	25-Sep-15	–
ROBSON	E	EDWARD	Rifleman	S/10073	25-Sep-15	–
ROSS	D A C	DAVID ARTHUR CECIL	Rifleman	S/7435	25-Sep-15	17
ROWE	J	JAMES	Serjeant	B/903	25-Sep-15	–
ROWE	W B	WILLIAM BERNARD	Rifleman	Z/956	25-Sep-15	30
SALKELD	A E	ALBERT EDWARD	Rifleman	S/11150	02-Oct-15	23
SCHOLEY	C H N	CHARLES HARRY NORMAN	Captain		25-Sep-15	22
SCOULER	J	JOSEPH	Rifleman	S/13158	25-Sep-15	31
SEYMOUR	T W	THOMAS WILLIAM	Rifleman	B/2318	25-Sep-15	20
SHEPHERD	G	GEORGE	Corporal	S/8117	25-Sep-15	–
SHEPHERD	R	ROBERT	Rifleman	S/11563	25-Sep-15	18
SHIPLEY	W A		Rifleman	S/11996	26-Sep-15	–
SHORT	P E	PETER EDWARD	Rifleman	S/12000	25-Sep-15	22
SMITH	A W	ALFRED WILLIAM	Rifleman	S/11998	25-Sep-15	–
SMITH	F A	FRANCIS ARTHUR	Rifleman	S/4103	25-Sep-15	–
SMITH	G A	GORDON ALBERT	Rifleman	S/8321	25-Sep-15	25
SMITH	J J	JAMES JOHN	Rifleman	S/5298	25-Sep-15	23
SPARKS	A	ALFRED	Rifleman	S/12985	25-Sep-15	–
STAINER	G H	GILBERT HOWARD	Rifleman	S/9847	25-Sep-15	19
STEVENS	B	BERT	Rifleman	6072	25-Sep-15	–
STEVENS	J	JOHN	Rifleman	S/1768	25-Sep-15	22
STONE	A	ALBERT	Corporal	S/3731	25-Sep-15	21
STRATFORD	P S	PERCY SAMUEL	Rifleman	B/945	25-Sep-15	–
SUTTON	W	WILLIAM	Rifleman	B/2110	25-Sep-15	21
TALBOT	F	FRANK	Lance Corporal	S/6165	25-Sep-15	20
TAYLOR	W J	WILLIAM JOSEPH	Rifleman	S/342	25-Sep-15	23
TIBBINS	W R	WILLIAM ROBERT	Rifleman	S/9991	25-Sep-15	–
TOWNSEND	T	THOMAS	Rifleman	S/12007	25-Sep-15	23
TURNER	A H	ALBERT HENRY	Rifleman	Z/1420	25-Sep-15	20
UPTON	C	CHARLES	Rifleman	B/2845	25-Sep-15	–
VENABLES	T	THOMAS	Rifleman	S/7746	25-Sep-15	–
WALKER	R	ROBERT	Rifleman	S/11159	25-Sep-15	26
WARD	A	ARTHUR	Corporal	Z/658	25-Sep-15	–
WARREN	E	EDWARD	Rifleman	S/10344	25-Sep-15	22
WATSON	W	WILLIAM	Rifleman	S/5288	25-Sep-15	–

Place of Burial or Commemoration	Family Information (Where Known)
PRES (MENIN GATE) MEMORIAL	Husband of Margaret Pitcher, of 230 Quinn's Square, Russia Lane, Bethnal Green, London.
PRES (MENIN GATE) MEMORIAL	
PRES (MENIN GATE) MEMORIAL	Son of Thomas and Erina E Platt, of 38 Lamprell St, Old Ford, Bow, London.
PRES (MENIN GATE) MEMORIAL	
PRES (MENIN GATE) MEMORIAL	Son of William and Margaret Proctor, of 2 Conislee Cottages, Chase Rd, Old Southgate, London; husband of Annie Rosemary Clarke (formerly Proctor), of 48 Leigh Rd, Highbury Park, London.
PRES (MENIN GATE) MEMORIAL	Son of Mrs E Punter, of 149 Beaumont Rd, Leyton, London.
PRES (MENIN GATE) MEMORIAL	Son of Capt W H Purvis (The Rifle Brigade) and Mabel Vida Purvis, Carphin, Cupar, Fife; educated at Rugby School; Commoner of Trinity College, Oxford.
PRES (MENIN GATE) MEMORIAL	
PRES (MENIN GATE) MEMORIAL	Son of Mrs Annie Quinn, of 7 Stone Terrace, Storer St, Nottingham.
PRES (MENIN GATE) MEMORIAL	Son of Caleb Rapley; husband of Sarah Emily Ledger (formerly Rapley), of 1 Rockfield Cottages, Whyteleafe, Surrey.
PRES (MENIN GATE) MEMORIAL	Son of George Ray, of 9 Rothwell St, London, NW1; husband of the late Sophia Ray; 15 years in 22nd Middlesex Volunteers, finishing in that Regt as Clr Serjt, then joining the National Reserve.
PRES (MENIN GATE) MEMORIAL	Son of Frederick and Linda Reed, of Belgrave Cottage, High St, Wivenhoe, Essex.
PRES (MENIN GATE) MEMORIAL	Son of Benjamin and Sarah Restall, of 76 Armoury Rd, Small Heath, Birmingham.
PRES (MENIN GATE) MEMORIAL	Husband of Kate Rendell (formerly Richardson), of 4 Canal Terrace, Cwmbach, Aberdare, Glam.
PRES (MENIN GATE) MEMORIAL	Son of F W and Rose E Robinson, of 11 Grove Mansions, The Grove, Hammersmith, London.
PRES (MENIN GATE) MEMORIAL	Son of John and Elizabeth Robinson, of Honor Oak Rd, Forest Hill, London; husband of Harriett Robinson, of 20 Guildford Place, Buff Place, Camberwell Green, London.
PRES (MENIN GATE) MEMORIAL	
PRES (MENIN GATE) MEMORIAL	
PRES (MENIN GATE) MEMORIAL	Son of James Ross LRCP, LRCS and Alice Ross, of 'Glengariff', Shore Rd, South Hackney, London.
PRES (MENIN GATE) MEMORIAL	
PRES (MENIN GATE) MEMORIAL	Son of the late William Bernard and Elizabeth Rowe; husband of Mabel Annie Rowe, of 3 Totteridge Rd, Battersea, London.
IJSSENTHOEK MILITARY CEMETERY	Son of John Dodds Salkeld and Isabella Salkeld, of Newcastle-on-Tyne.
PRES (MENIN GATE) MEMORIAL	Son of Harry and Frances Edna Scholey, of 137 Victoria St, London, SW1.
PRES (MENIN GATE) MEMORIAL	Son of Henry and Annie Scouler, of 51 Park Lane, Wembley, Middx.
PRES (MENIN GATE) MEMORIAL	Son of Thomas Henry and Alice Elizabeth Seymour, of 891 Warwick Rd, Tyseley, Birmingham.
PRES (MENIN GATE) MEMORIAL	
PRES (MENIN GATE) MEMORIAL	Son of Mary Crofton Shepherd, of 40 Gladstone St, Monkwearmouth, Sunderland, and the late Robert Shepherd.
EDFORD HOUSE CEMETERY	
PRES (MENIN GATE) MEMORIAL	Son of Mrs Ann Caroline Short, of 75 Marner St, Bromley, Bow, London.
PRES (MENIN GATE) MEMORIAL	
PRES (MENIN GATE) MEMORIAL	
PRES (MENIN GATE) MEMORIAL	Son of William E and Sarah E A Smith, of 22 South Rd, Faversham, Kent.
PRES (MENIN GATE) MEMORIAL	Husband of Annie Maria Smith, of 54 Northumberland St, Poplar, London.
PRES (MENIN GATE) MEMORIAL	Husband of Caroline Agnes Sparks, of 7 Heathwood Gardens, Charlton, London.
PRES (MENIN GATE) MEMORIAL	Son of Charles Edward Stainer, of The Halfway, Kintbury, Berks.
PRES (MENIN GATE) MEMORIAL	
PRES (MENIN GATE) MEMORIAL	Son of Mrs Clare Stevens, of 193 New John St, West Birmingham; husband of Annie Hodges (formerly Stevens), of 192 Great Russell St, Birmingham.
PRES (MENIN GATE) MEMORIAL	Son of Mr and Mrs Stone, of 29 Herbert St, Stockton-on-Tees.
PRES (MENIN GATE) MEMORIAL	
PRES (MENIN GATE) MEMORIAL	Son of Mrs Rose Sutton, of Muss Lane, King's Somborne, Hants.
PRES (MENIN GATE) MEMORIAL	Son of Edward James Cecil and Elizabeth Mary Talbot, of 35 Granfield St, Battersea, London.
PRES (MENIN GATE) MEMORIAL	Son of Samuel James and Elizabeth Taylor, of 25 South St, New North Rd, Islington, London.
PRES (MENIN GATE) MEMORIAL	
PRES (MENIN GATE) MEMORIAL	Son of Thomas Townsend, of 65 Andover Rd, Holloway, London.
PRES (MENIN GATE) MEMORIAL	Son of Arthur and Louisa Emily Turner, of 71 Tanner St, Barking, Essex.
PRES (MENIN GATE) MEMORIAL	
PRES (MENIN GATE) MEMORIAL	
PRES (MENIN GATE) MEMORIAL	Son of Thomas and Annie E Walker, of Rose Cottage, Harden, Bingley, Yorks.
PRES (MENIN GATE) MEMORIAL	
PRES (MENIN GATE) MEMORIAL	Son of the late James and Alice Warren.
PRES (MENIN GATE) MEMORIAL	

Surname	Initials	Forenames (Where Known)	Rank	Service Number	Date of Death	Age (Where Known)
WILLIAMS	A F	ARTHUR FREDERICK	Rifleman	6198	25-Sep-15	–
WILLIS	F S	FRED S	Rifleman	7787	25-Sep-15	–
WILSON	E	ERNEST	Corporal	S/13122	25-Sep-15	19
WILSON	W J	WILLIAM JAMES	Rifleman	S/8723	25-Sep-15	31
WINCH	A B	ALBERT BERTRAM	Rifleman	B/152	26-Sep-15	–
WRIGHT	G E	GEORGE EDWARD	Rifleman	S/12033	25-Sep-15	32
WRIGHT	J	JOHN	Rifleman	6/608	25-Sep-15	–
YOUNG	W H	WILLIAM HAROLD	Rifleman	S/12045	25-Sep-15	21

PRES (MENIN GATE) MEMORIAL
PRES (MENIN GATE) MEMORIAL
PRES (MENIN GATE) MEMORIAL   Son of James and Alice Beatrice Wilson, of Castle House, Lower Cambridge St, Castleford, Yorks.
PRES (MENIN GATE) MEMORIAL   Son of William and Esther Wilson; husband of Helena Petronela Wilson, of 7 Pollard Row, Bethnal Green, London.

EDFORD HOUSE CEMETERY
PRES (MENIN GATE) MEMORIAL   Son of Mr and Mrs Edward Wright, of Nottingham.
PRES (MENIN GATE) MEMORIAL
PRES (MENIN GATE) MEMORIAL   Son of Joseph Henry and Eliza Alice Young, of 46 Durham Rd, South Ealing, London.

German Reserve Infantry Regiment No. 289, 25 October 1915

German Reserve Infantry Regiment 248 *Verlustlisten* No. 289, 25 October 1915

Name	Rank	Coy	Birthplace	Details
LEGL, FRANZ VON	Hauptmann a.D.	I Bn Staff	München	Slightly wounded, remained with the regiment
KNÖLLER, KARL	Leutnant der Reserve	1	Stuttgart	Severely wounded
KRAFT, JOSEF	Leutnant der Landwehr	1	Hachtel, Mergentheim	KIA 25.9.15
ROLL, WILHELM	Offizier Stellvertreter	1	Botnang, Stuttgart	MIA 25.9.15 Declared KIA
HERBERT, ERNST	Vizefeldwebel	1	Berlin	KIA 25.9.15
WEISS, JOHANNES	Unteroffizier	1	Grossfussen, Geislingen	Severely wounded
KLAIBER, CHRISTIAN	Unteroffizier	1	Waldbach, Weinsberg	Severely wounded
WELT, ANTON	Unteroffizier	1	Wasseralfingen	KIA 25.9.15
ROSENBERGER, KARL	Unteroffizier	1	Stuttgart	KIA 25.9.15
MARKGRAF, OTTO	Unteroffizier	1	Villingen	MIA 25.9.15 Declared KIA
FREY, FRIEDRICH	Unteroffizier	1	Feuerbach, Stuttgart	MIA KIA 25.9.15
KRUASS, KARL	Unteroffizier	1	Gerlingen, Leonberg	MIA
MAIER, NIKOLAUS	Unteroffizier	1	Sauggart, Riedlingen	MIA 25.9.15 Declared KIA
ZARTMANN, ALOIS	Unteroffizier	1	Neckarsulm	Slightly wounded
MENGIS, JOHANN	Gefreiter	1	Nendingen, Tuttlingen	Slightly wounded
BRÄNDLE, RUDOLF	Gefreiter	1	Backnang	Severely wounded
SIGLE, KARL	Gefreiter	1	Schorndorf	KIA 25.9.15
GANZER, FRITZ	Gefreiter	1	Ludwigsburg	MIA 25.9.15 Declared KIA
HAUG, ROBERT	Gefreiter	1	Mettingen, Esslingen	MIA 25.9.15 Declared KIA
KRAUSS, FRIEDRICH	Gefreiter	1	Gerlingen, Leonberg	MIA 25.9.15 Declared KIA
WEGMER, OTTO	Gefreiter	1	Oelbronn, Maulbronn	MIA 25.9.15 Declared KIA
ARNOLD, ALFRED	Gefreiter	1	Lauterbach, Oberndorf	KIA 25.9.15 Also shown as Ersatz Reservist
HELLER, REINHOLD	Infanterist	1	Steinbach, Backnang	Slightly wounded
HOFMANN, GEORG	Infanterist	1	Rotenhar, Gaildorf	Severely wounded
WELTE, KARL	Infanterist	1	Stetten, Tuttlingen	Severely wounded
STOLZ, JAKOB	Infanterist	1	Weiler, Blaubeuren	Severely wounded
STORZ, EMIL	Landsturmmann	1	Esslingen	KIA 25.9.15
BETZ, JOHANNES	Infanterist	1	Laichingen, Münsingen	Slightly wounded

Name	Rank	Coy	Birthplace	Details
BECK, KARL	Infanterist	1	Oberböbingen, Gmünd	Slightly wounded
WEISS, KARL	Infanterist	1	Malmsheim, Leonberg	Severely wounded
ZIESEL, KARL	Infanterist	1	Erolzheim, Biberach	Slightly wounded
KLOTZ, KARL	Infanterist	1	Neckarwestheim, Besigheim	Slightly wounded
SCHAD, MICHAEL	Infanterist	1	Hürbel, Biberach	Severely wounded
GEIGER, GOTTLIEB	Infanterist	1	Hösslinswart, Schorndorf	Slightly wounded
PFLÜGER, RICHARD	Infanterist	1	Stuttgart	Severely wounded
HÄFELE, KARL	Infanterist	1	Nordheim, Brackenheim	Slightly wounded
NOLL, ANTON	Infanterist	1	Ebersbach, Saulgau	Severely wounded
RÜHLE, OTTO	Infanterist	1	Stuttgart	Severely wounded WIA 25.9.15
SCHÄFER, KARL	Ersatz Reservist	1	Murrhardt, Backnang	Died from wounds 26.9.15
ROHMER, KASIMIR	Infanterist	1	Burgrieden, Laupheim	Severely wounded
WILHELM, ALFRED	Infanterist	1	Duisburg	Severely wounded
NECKEL, KARL	Infanterist	1	Kirchrosin, Mecklenburg	Slightly wounded
GRAU, WILHELM	Infanterist	1	Stuttgart-Cannstatt	Slightly wounded
SCHUPP, FRIEDRICH	Infanterist	1	Möckmühl, Neckarsulm	Severely wounded
BÜHLER, FRITZ	Infanterist	1	Geringwalde, Sachsen	Slightly wounded
RUESS, GOTTLIEB	Infanterist	1	Backnang	Died from wounds 26.9.15 WIA 25.9.15
WILD, ANTON	Infanterist	1	Ebersberg, Backnang	Severely wounded
GEBHARD, WILHELM	Infanterist	1	Stuttgart	Slightly wounded
MÄGERLE, PETER	Infanterist	1	Böttingen, Spaichingen	Severely wounded
KIPP, EUGEN	Infanterist	1	Stuttgart	Severely wounded
HARTMANN, JOHANN	Infanterist	1	Wittensweiler, Freudenstadt	Severely wounded
NEUFFER, EUGEN	Infanterist	1	Bietigheim, Besigheim	Severely wounded
MÜLLER, WENDELIN	Infanterist	1	Sulgen, Oberndorf	Slightly wounded
SATTLER, JOSEF	Infanterist	1	Friedingen, Tuttlingen	Slightly wounded
KUBACH, WILHELM	Infanterist	1	Waldbach, Weinsberg	Severely wounded
KÄSTLE, ALBERT	Landsturmmann	1	Messstetten, Balingen	KIA 25.9.15
WITZELMAIER, OTTO	Landsturmmann	1	Lützenhardt, Horb	KIA 25.9.15
KELLER I, PAUL	Kriegsfreiwilliger	1	Seedorf, Oberndorf	KIA 25.9.15
ROMETSCH, ANDREAS	Reservist	1	Liebelsberg, Calw	KIA 25.9.15
WIRTH, KARL	Ersatz Reservist	1	Ulm	KIA 25.9.15
SCHMIED, FRIEDRICH	Ersatz Reservist	1	Schopfloch, Freudenstadt	KIA 25.9.15

Name	Rank	Coy	Birthplace	Details
HAUG, PAUL	Ersatz Reservist	1	Mettingen, Esslingen	KIA 25.9.15
WOLF, FRANZ	Ersatz Reservist	1	Heilbronn	KIA 25.9.15
HUBSCHNEIDER, GOTTLOB	Landsturmmann	1	Beutelsbach, Schorndorf	KIA 25.9.15
GURT, KARL	Fusilier	1	Tiefenbach, Neckarsulm	KIA 25.9.15
RIETHGRAF, WILHELM	Ersatz Reservist	1	Rietenau, Backnang	KIA 25.9.15
KAMM, GOTTLOB	Reservist	1	Winnenden, Waiblingen	KIA 25.9.15
ZIELFLEISCH, RICHARD	Musketier	1	Stuttgart	KIA 25.9.15
MAIER I, Karl	Ersatz Reservist	1	Grossheppach, Waiblingen	KIA 25.9.15
SCHRODE, MAX	Kriegsfreiwilliger	1	Berkach, Ehingen	KIA 25.9.15
WÖHRLE, GEORG	Musketier	1	Schramberg, Oberndorf	KIA 25.9.15
NOTHDURFT II, CHRISTIAN	Landsturmmann	1	Kleindeinbach, Welzheim	KIA 25.9.15
RENNER, GOTTLOB	Infanterist	1	Willsbach, Weinsberg	Severely wounded
VÖSTE, KARL	Musketier	1	Sossmar, Peine, Hannover	KIA 25.9.15
RÜDT, PAUL	Ersatz Reservist	1	Kornwestheim, Ludwigsburg	KIA 25.9.15
WITTMANN, JOSEF	Ersatz Reservist	1	Grossallmerspann, Hall	KIA 25.9.15
NUFER, JOHANN	Landsturmmann	1	Rosswangen, Rottweil	KIA 25.9.15
FICHTINGER, JOHANN	Reservist	1	Falkenberg, Oberbayern	KIA 25.9.15
REHFUSS, ADOLF	Musketier	1	Dürrwangen, Balingen	KIA 25.9.15
BÖHMERLE, KARL	Musketier	1	Serach, Esslingen	KIA 25.9.15
NOTHDURFT I, CHRISTIAN	Landsturmmann	1	Pfahlbronn, Welzheim	KIA 25.9.15
MAZETH, JOSEF	Reservist	1	Harthausen, Günzburg	KIA 25.9.15
SCHREIBER, LUDWIG	Landsturmmann	1	Fridingen, Tuttlingen	KIA 25.9.15
ADIS, OTTO	Landwehrmann	1	Rottenburg	MIA 25.9.15	Declared KIA
BAUER, HERMANN	Ersatz Reservist	1	Feldrennach, Neuenbürg	MIA 25.9.15	Declared KIA
BAUER, ARTUR	Infanterist	1	Mannheim	MIA
BIESER, JOSEF	Infanterist	1	Strassdorf, Gmünd	MIA
BRÖSAMLE, SIMON	Ersatz Reservist	1	Affstätt, Herrenberg	MIA	KIA 25.9.15
CHUR, FRIEDRICH	Ersatz Reservist	1	Büchelberg, Oehringen	KIA 25.9.15
ESSIG, HEINRICH	Infanterist	1	Flach, Leonberg	KIA	Possibly in error
FUTTER, FRIEDRICH	Musketier	1	Dusslingen, Tübingen	KIA 25.9.15
SPEHRER, FRIEDRICH	Landsturmmann	1	Neuhaus, Crailsheim	KIA 25.9.15
GRESSER, KARL	Ersatz Reservist	1	Hohenacker, Waiblingen	MIA 25.9.15	Declared KIA
HEINER, HERMANN	Landwehrmann	1	Hall	MIA	KIA 25.9.15

Name	Rank	Coy	Birthplace	Details	
HUTT, HERMANN	Landsturmmann	1	Winterbach, Schorndorf	KIA 25.9.15	KIA 25.9.15
KELLER II, PAUL	Landwehrmann	1	Ravensburg	MIA	KIA 25.9.15
KIRCHER, ERNST	Ersatz Reservist	1	Orendelfall, Oehringen	MIA	
KLOTZ, HERMANN	Musketier	1	Grunbach, Neunbürg	MIA 25.9.15	Declared KIA
KNÖPFLER, JOHANN	Ersatz Reservist	1	Schlegel, Wangen	MIA 25.9.15	Declared KIA
KRAFT, ADAM	Ersatz Reservist	1	Steinberg, Backnang	MIA 25.9.15	Declared KIA
KRANICH, WILHELM	Landsturmmann	1	Grossbotwar, Marbach	MIA	KIA 25.9.15
KUGLER, JOHANN	Landsturmmann	1	Unterriflingen, Freudenstadt	MIA	KIA 25.9.15
KLINK, KARL	Landsturmmann	1	Unterurbach, Schorndorf	MIA 25.9.15	Declared KIA
KÖLLREUTTER, PAUL	Ersatz Reservist	1	Bietigheim, Besigheim	KIA 25.9.15	
LOBMÜLLER, OTTO	Landsturmmann	1	Talheim, Heilbronn	MIA	KIA 25.9.15
MAILÄNDER, KARL	Landsturmmann	1	Hildrizhausen, Herrenberg	MIA 25.9.15	Declared KIA
METZGER, ANTON	Landsturmmann	1	Ramsenstrut, Ellwangen	MIA	KIA 25.9.15
MÜHLBERGER, GEORG	Landwehrmann	1	Ulm	KIA 25.9.15	
MÜNZ, JOSEF	Ersatz Reservist	1	Laupertshausen, Biberach	MIA 25.9.15	Declared KIA
REMPEL, ADOLF	Ersatz Reservist	1	Göppingen	MIA 25.9.15	Declared KIA
RÖSCH, JOHANNES	Landsturmmann	1	Seissen, Blaubeuren	KIA 25.9.15	
RAPP, KONRAD	Landsturmmann	1	Bärenbach, Schorndorf	MIA 25.9.15	Declared KIA
SALZER, GUSTAV	Reservist	1	Oberhausen, Reutlingen	MIA	KIA 25.9.15
SEITZ, GOTTLOB	Landsturmmann	1	Winterbach, Schorndorf	MIA 25.9.15	Declared KIA
SAMMET, WILHELM	Musketier	1	Sechselberg, Backnang	MIA 25.9.15	Declared KIA
SCHELLING, ULRICH	Infanterist	1	Nehren, Tübingen	MIA	
SCHRECKENHÖFER, JOSEF	Landsturmmann	1	Lautenhof, Ellwangen	MIA 25.9.15	Declared KIA
SCHUPPERT, FRIEDRICH	Landsturmmann	1	Breitenfürst, Welzheim	KIA 25.9.15	
SCHMIDT, HEINRICH	Landsturmmann	1	Gutendorf, Gaildorf	KIA 25.9.15	
SCHNAITH, KARL	Ersatz Reservist	1	Tübingen	KIA 25.9.15	
SCHUSTER, FLORIAN	Landsturmmann	1	Tiefenbach, Neckarsulm	KIA 25.9.15	
SCHÜCKLE, AUGUST	Infanterist	1	Bauschlott, Pforzheim	MIA	
STORZ, WILHELM	Infanterist	1	Benningen, Ludwigsburg	MIA	
STEINBACH, KARL	Landsturmmann	1	Bayreuth	KIA 25.9.15	
WECKENMANN, CLEMENS	Landsturmmann	1	Dotternhausen, Tottweil	MIA 25.9.15	Declared KIA
WOHLWENDER, KARL	Ersatz Reservist	1	Herbertingen, Daulgau	KIA 25.9.15	
ZIMMERMANN, JULIUS	Kriegsfreiwilliger	1	Harthausen, Stuttgart	MIA 25.9.15	Declared KIA

Name	Rank	Coy	Birthplace	Details	
ZELLER, BERNHARD	Landsturmmann	1	Bärenhof, Göppingen	MIA 25.9.15	Declared KIA
BETZ, GUSTAV	Landwehrmann	1	Talheim, Rottenburg	KIA 25.9.15	
ÖSER, RUDOLF	Kriegsfreiwilliger	1	Ohlau, Schlesien	MIA 25.9.15	Declared KIA
KRAUSS, WILLY	Infanterist	1	Wittershausen, Sulz	MIA 25.9.15	Declared KIA
PUMMER, ALOIS	Kriegsfreiwilliger	1	Dillisheim, Bayern	MIA	KIA 25.9.15
NASER, ALFRED	Kriegsfreiwilliger	1	Hedelfingen, Cannstatt	KIA 25.9.15	
LEUCHT, WILHELM	Musketier	1	Mühlheim, Sulz	MIA 25.9.15	Declared KIA
LIPPUS, KONRAD	Musketier	1	Schwenningen, Rottweil	KIA 25.9.15	
OST, HANS	Infanterist	1	Stuttgart	MIA 25.9.15	Declared KIA
MÜLLER, WILHELM	Landwehrmann	1	Neuenbürg	Died from sickness 26.9.15	
WELKER, HELMUT	Vizefeldwebel	2	Altensteig, Nagold	Slightly wounded	
KLEIN, LUDWIG	Unteroffizier	2	Kirchheim u.T.	Slightly wounded	
BALBACH, GEORG	Musketier	2	Ruppertshofen, Gerabronn	KIA 25.9.15	
HÖRNLEN, KARL	Ersatz Reservist	2	Meissach, Vaihingen	KIA 25.9.15	
STEFANZ, JOSEF	Infanterist	2	Havingen, Münsingen	Severely wounded	
AUGENSTEIN, EUGEN	Infanterist	2	Ludwigsburg	Severely wounded	
STRITZELBERGER, JOHANN	Infanterist	2	Härdtsfeldhausen, Neresheim	Slightly wounded	
HOFREUTER, JOHANN	Infanterist	2	Jagstberg, Künzelsau	Slightly wounded	
STREINER, FRIEDRICH	Landsturmmann	2	Neufels, Oehringen	Died from wounds 26.9.15	WIA 25.9.15
SCHULER, GEORG	Ersatz Reservist	2	Niedersweiler, Ravensburg	KIA 25.9.15	
RAMME, HEINRICH	Infanterist	2	Wilsche, Preussen	Slightly wounded	
KÖNGETER, HEINRICH	Infanterist	3	Imberg, Gaildorf	Died from wounds	
THUM, JOSEF	Musketier	3	Heiligenberg, Baden	KIA 25.9.15	
SPIEGEL, JOHANN	Landwehrmann	3	Isingen, Sulz	KIA 6.9.15	
FRITZ, CHRISTOPH	Kriegsfreiwilliger	3	Dettingen, Urach	KIA 25.9.15	
BRUNS, HEINRICH	Infanterist	3	Wernigerode, Harz	Slightly wounded	
NIESS, EDUARD	Infanterist	3	Ulm	Slightly wounded	
RIST, JULIUS	Infanterist	3	Neussen, Nürtingen	Slightly wounded	
KATZ, KARL	Infanterist	3	Remmingsheim, Rottenburg	Slightly wounded	
WACKER, GOTTLIEB	Infanterist	3	Schömberg, Neuenbürg	Slightly wounded	
KRAFT, KARL	Landsturmmann	3	Höfingen, Leonberg	Severely wounded	KIA 25.9.15
BREISCHAFT, ADOLF	Infanterist	3	Neckarwestheim, Besigheim	Severely wounded	
BEISSWENGER, GEORG	Infanterist	3	Lusthof, Aalen	Slightly wounded	

Name	Rank	Coy	Birthplace	Details	
SEEGER, GOTTLIEB	Infanterist	3	Rohrdorf, Nagold	Slightly wounded	
WÖRNER, CHRISTIAN	Infanterist	3	Hülben, Urach	Slightly wounded	
SCHILL, ANDREAS	Infanterist	3	Bleichstetten, Urach	Slightly wounded	
MÜHLICH, KARL	Infanterist	3	Ulm	Severely wounded	
NAGEL, JOHANN	Infanterist	3	Bergerhausen, Biberach	Severely wounded	
STEMMER, HEINRICH	Infanterist	3	Rohrbach, Waldsee	Slightly wounded	
FISCHER, ERNST	Infanterist	3	Schorndorf	Slightly wounded	
SCHWÄMMLE, GUSTAV	Infanterist	3	Calw	Slightly wounded	
BRAUN, EUGEN	Infanterist	3	Nellmersbach, Waiblingen	Slightly wounded	
PFEIL, TRAUGOTT	Infanterist	3	Ochsenberg, Heidenheim	Slightly wounded	
HERZOG, GEORG	Infanterist	3	Oepfingen, Ehingen	Slightly wounded	
STAIGER, PAUL	Leutnant	4	Düneberg, Lauenburg	Slightly wounded	
SCHMID, MAX	Leutnant	4	Tübingen	KIA	Possibly in error
NEU, EUGEN	Gefreiter	4	Rottenburg	Slightly wounded	
HAMPP, KARL	Gefreiter	4	Leonbronn, Brackenheim	Slightly wounded	
MÜLLER, FRIEDRICH	Gefreiter	4	Hösselinshof, Neckarsulm	MIA	
VÖLMLE, JULIUS	Infanterist	4	Kornwestheim, Ludwigsburg	Slightly wounded	
NÄGELE, FRIEDRICH	Infanterist	4	Hessigheim, Besigheim	Slightly wounded	
BAUST, PANKRATZ	Infanterist	4	Hilbertshausen, Bayern	Slightly wounded	
FRITZ, GEORG	Infanterist	4	Schillinghof, Welzheim	Slightly wounded	
MÜNZMAIER, PAUL	Infanterist	4	Sillenbuch, Cannstatt	Slightly wounded	
MAYER, BERNHARD	Musketier	4	Ravensburg	KIA 25.9.15	
KRAUSS, FRIEDRICH	Landsturmmann	4	Heilbronn	KIA 25.9.15	
AMMANN, KARL	Infanterist	4	Beihingen, Ludwigsburg	Slightly wounded	
FETZER, FRIEDRICH	Infanterist	4	Stuttgart	Slightly wounded	
MOHRING, MATTHÄUS	Infanterist	4	Heiningen, Göppingen	Slightly wounded	
SAUTER, GEORG	Infanterist	4	Bitzenhofen, Tettnang	Slightly wounded	
SCHREIBER, CHRISTIAN	Infanterist	4	Plattenhardt, Stuttgart	Slightly wounded	
GANZHORN, EUGEN	Infanterist	4	Magstadt, Böblingen	Slightly wounded	
BREITLING, OTTO	Infanterist	4	Gächingen, Calw	Slightly wounded	
SCHIMPF, GOTTLIEB	Infanterist	4	Schönaich, Böblingen	Slightly wounded	
WALTER, GEORG	Infanterist	4	Degerschlacht, Tübingen	Slightly wounded	
LANG, PAUL	Infanterist	4	Esslingen	Slightly wounded	

Name	Rank	Coy	Birthplace	Details
KLEINER, JOSEF	Infanterist	4	Hardthöfle, Spaichingen	Slightly wounded
EBERHARDT, JOHANN	Infanterist	4	Lossburg, Freudenstadt	Slightly wounded
STRÄHLE, WILHELM	Infanterist	4	Oberstenfeld, Marbach	Slightly wounded
MURSCHEL, ERNST	Infanterist	4	Sersheim, Vaihingen	Slightly wounded
FAHRION, HERMANN	Infanterist	4	Göppingen	Slightly wounded
RUPP, THOMAS	Infanterist	4	Oberstetten, Münsingen	Slightly wounded
HAUSSMANN, WILHELM	Infanterist	4	Nürtingen	Slightly wounded
SCHMID, KARL	Infanterist	4	Vaihingen a.Enz	Slightly wounded
KIRCHNER, KARL	Infanterist	4	Weingarten, Ravensburg	Slightly wounded
SCHABEL, PAUL	Kriegsfreiwilliger	4	Esslingen	KIA 25.9.15
SCHENK, KARL	Infanterist	4	Wolfenbrück, Gaildorf	Slightly wounded
LOHRMANN, KARL	Infanterist	4	Waiblingen	Slightly wounded
BRENZEL, ANTON	Infanterist	4	Stuttgart	Slightly wounded
STEPHAN, KARL	Infanterist	4	Stuttgart	Slightly wounded
SCHÄDLER, ANTON	Infanterist	4	Ravensburg	Slightly wounded
MAYER, KARL	Infanterist	4	Cleebronn, Brackenheim	Severely wounded
FICHTER, EMIL	Infanterist	4	Sulgau, Oberndorf	Slightly wounded
STAHL, GEORG	Infanterist	4	Blaufelden, Gerabronn	Slightly wounded
KOST, ADOLF	Infanterist	4	Stuttgart-Cannstatt	Severely wounded
STEIGMANN, AUGUST	Infanterist	4	Bitzfeld, Weinsberg	Slightly wounded
FISCHER, OLTMANN	Infanterist	4	Jemgum, Hannover	Severely wounded
SELLNER, WILHELM	Infanterist	4	Gerlingen, Leonberg	Slightly wounded
MOSSLER, ERWIN	Infanterist	4	Obercrinitz, Sachsen	Injured
FINK, JULIUS	Infanterist	4	Feldkirch, Vorarlberg	Slightly wounded
SCHIEFER, ERNST	Infanterist	4	Oberbrüden, Backnang	Severely wounded
FALKE, WILHELM	Infanterist	4	Oldendorf, Hildesheim	Slightly wounded
REINHARDT, FRIEDRICH	Infanterist	4	Ingersheim, Crailsheim	Slightly wounded
STREICHER, GOTTLIEB	Infanterist	4	Beilstein, Marbach	Severely wounded
FAUSER, FRIEDRICH	Infanterist	4	Gerlingen, Leonberg	Severely wounded
ROLLER, GOTTLOB	Infanterist	4	Effringen, Leonberg	Slightly wounded
KÜGLER, PAUL	Infanterist	4	Parchwitz, Liegnitz	Slightly wounded
WIDMANN, HERMANN	Infanterist	4	Tailfingen, Balingen	Severely wounded
WILLIG, JOHANNES	Musketier	4	Kirchheimbolanden, Bayern	KIA 25.9.15

Name	Rank	Coy	Birthplace	Details
KRÄMER, IMANUEL	Ersatz Reservist	4	Schwieberdingen, Ludwigsburg	KIA 25.9.15
WAHL, HERMANN	Ersatz Reservist	4	Murrhardt, Backnang	KIA 25.9.15
JANSSEN, FRERICH	Infanterist	4	Moordorf, Hannover	MIA
IMLE, MAX	Kriegsfreiwilliger	4	Stuttgart	KIA 25.9.15
SCHLENKER, ANDREAS	Infanterist	4	Schwenningen, Rottweil	MIA
RÖHRLE, OTTO	Landsturmmann	4	Waiblingen	KIA 25.9.15
GLÜCK, ADOLF	Landsturmmann	4	Backnang	KIA 25.9.15
SCHWARZKOPF, ROBERT	Landsturmmann	4	Stuttgart-Cannstatt	KIA 25.9.15
WAIDELICH, GUSTAV	Landsturmmann	4	Edelweiler, Freudenstadt	KIA 25.9.15
LÖHNER, GEORG	Landsturmmann	4	Happurg, Bayern	KIA 25.9.15
HELLER, WILHELM	Landsturmmann	4	Kleineislingen, Göppingen	KIA 25.9.15
BUCK, CHRISTIAN	Infanterist	4	Langenau, Ulm	WIA
STEGMAIER, JOSEF	Musketier	4	Schw. Gmünd	MIA 25.9.15, Declared KIA
VAIHINGER, HERMANN	Vizefeldwebel	5	Hochdorf, Vaihingen	Slightly wounded
BIHN, KARL	Infanterist	5	Menzingen, Bretten	Slightly wounded
LETZKUS, MAX	Infanterist	5	Mühringen, Horb	WIA
BERGER, EUGEN	Infanterist	5	Stuttgart	Slightly wounded
SCHAUFLER, HUGO	Infanterist	5	Lippoldsweiler, Backnang	Slightly wounded
HAAG, EUGEN	Infanterist	5	Unterberken, Schorndorf	Slightly wounded
DÄMERER, KARL	Infanterist	5	Aalen	Slightly wounded
REISINGER, KARL	Infanterist	5	Regensburg	Slightly wounded
MAYER, JOHANN	Infanterist	5	Rohrdorf, Wangen	Severely wounded
BEILHARZ, KARL.	Musketier	5	Baiersbronn, Freudenstadt	Died from wounds 28.9.15, WIA 27.9.15
SCHUH, ERNST	Infanterist	5	Kurzach, Marbach	Severely wounded
BERGER, ALBERT	Gefreiter	6	Gross Neundorf, Schlesien	Slightly wounded
IMLE, ERNST	Musketier	6	Markgröningen, Ludwigsburg	Died from wounds 23.9.15, WIA 22.9.15
EISENHARDT, WILHELM	Landsturmmann	6	Rutesheim, Leonberg	KIA 25.9.15
HALDENWANGER, JAKOB	Infanterist	6	Geislingen-Altenstadt	Slightly wounded
TREIBER, JOHANN	Ersatz Reservist	6	Jesingen	Died from wounds 27.9.15, WIA 27.9.15
MÖSSLER, FRIEDRICH	Landsturmmann	6	Tennstedt, Erfurt	Died from wounds 27.9.15, WIA 27.9.15
MOSER, EDUAR	Landsturmmann	7	Obernheim, Spaichingen	KIA 25.9.15
SEMMLER, GOTTLIEB	Ersatz Reservist	7	Oberlenningen, Kirchheim	KIA 25.9.15
HELD, CHRISTIAN	Landwehrmann	7	Schönaich, Böblingen	KIA 26.9.15

Name	Rank	Coy	Birthplace	Details	
WEIPPERT, PAUL	Landsturmmann	7	Ludwigsburg	Died from wounds 27.9.15	WIA 26.9.15
KNODEL, WILHELM	Feldwebel	8	Bönnigheim, Besigheim	Slightly wounded	
EHRHARDT, FRIEDRICH	Unteroffizier	8	Horb	Slightly wounded	
WOLF, ALFRED	Gefreiter	8	Heilbronn	MIA	KIA 25.9.15
MODEST, HEINRICH	Infanterist	8	Dornweiler, Bayern	Slightly wounded	
HORLACHER, FRIEDRICH	Infanterist	8	Sulzbach, Gaildorf	Slightly wounded	
SCHULZ, BERNHARD	Hornist	8	Biberach, Heilbronn	Slightly wounded	
SCHATZ, GOTTLIEB	Infanterist	8	Burgfelden, Balingen	Slightly wounded	
BAUER, GEORG	Infanterist	8	Beuerlbach, Crailsheim	Slightly wounded	
WEISS, HEINRICH	Infanterist	8	Deilingen, Spaichingen	Slightly wounded	
ASSING, DIRK	Musketier	8	Ostgrossefehn, Hannover	KIA 25.9.15	
NICK, PAUL	Infanterist	8	Mengen, Saulgau	Slightly wounded	
DURST, ALBERT	Infanterist	8	Faurnbau, Göppingen	Severely wounded	
GÖTZ, JOHANNES	Infanterist	8	Tuningen, Tuttlingen	Slightly wounded	
MÜNCH, CHRISTOF	Infanterist	8	Bayreuth	Injured	
VON FLATOW, HANS	Major	Staff III Bn	Berlin	KIA 25.9.15	
SCHÄFER, JAKOB	Gefreiter	9	Sauserhof, Marbach	Severely wounded	
HASS, WILHELM	Musketier	9	Ditzumer-Verlaat, Hannover	KIA 25.9.15	
PFERSICH, GOTTLOB	Ersatz Reservist	9	Geyerbad, Balingen	KIA 25.9.15	
WEGGENMANN, XAVER	Landwehrmann	9	Brackenheim	KIA 25.9.15	
RETTENMEIER, JAKOB	Ersatz Reservist	9	Krettenbach, Crailsheim	KIA 25.9.15	
DRAUTZ, HERMANN	Infanterist	9	Heilbronn	Severely wounded	
FRÜH, EUGEN	Infanterist	9	Stuttgart	Severely wounded	
ENGELHARDT, KARL	Infanterist	9	Wallhausen, Gerabronn	Severely wounded	
GEIGER, RICHARD	Infanterist	9	Magstadt, Böblingen	Severely wounded	
STREULE, KARL	Infanterist	9	Oberensingen, Nürtingen	Severely wounded	
SCHMAUSS, THADDÄUS	Infanterist	9	Vogelhaus, Ehingen	Severely wounded	
RIEDMAIER, EDUARD	Infanterist	9	Heilbronn	Slightly wounded	
KÜMMEL, CHRISTIAN	Infanterist	9	Linbach, Gmünd	Slightly wounded	
WANDERER, ROBERT	Musketier	9	Vaihingen a.F.	Died from wounds 26.9.15	WIA 25.9.15
EGGENSPERGER, EUGEN	Offizier Stellvertreter	10	Stuttgart	Slightly wounded	
SCHWARZ, KARL	Unteroffizier	10	Tübingen	Slightly wounded	
BECK, OSKAR	Unteroffizier	10	Obertal, Freudenstadt	KIA 25.9.15	

Name	Rank	Coy	Birthplace	Details
DRECHSLER, HEINRICH	Infanterist	10	Vellberg, Hall	Slightly wounded
SEIFERT, WILHELM	Infanterist	10	Schwieberdingen, Ludwigsburg	KIA 22.9.15
EHINGER, RUDOLF	Landsturmmann	10	Balingen	KIA 25.9.15
KÜMMERER, FRIEDRICH	Landsturmmann	10	Hohenberg, Hall	KIA 25.9.15
MARQUARDT, MARTIN	Ersatz Reservist	10	Rietheim, Tittlingen	KIA 25.9.15
HUB, FRIEDRICH	Infanterist	10	Rieden, Hall	Slightly wounded
SCHMID, CHRISTIAN	Landwehrmann	10	Kirchheim	Died from wounds 28.9.15 WIA 25.9.15
SCHMIDT, SIEBEND	Infanterist	10	Holtrop, Hannover	Slightly wounded
BOSCH, WILHELM	Infanterist	10	Truchtelfingen, Balingen	Slightly wounded
MAYER, CHRISTIAN	Infanterist	10	Ohmenhausen, Reutlingen	Severely wounded
KANTENWEIN, JOHANN	Infanterist	10	Heimhausen, Künzelsau	Severely wounded
SCHÖNLE, OTTO	Infanterist	10	Laupheim	Slightly wounded
SCHWENK, JORDAN	Infanterist	10	Schönberg, Balingen	Slightly wounded
FREY, HUGO	Infanterist	10	Britzingen, Baden	Severely wounded
JÄGER, ALBERT	Infanterist	10	Mainhardt, Weinsberg	Injured
ZEISER, ANTON	Infanterist	10	Binsdorf, Sulz	Slightly wounded
BADER, KARL	Infanterist	10	Aalen	Slightly wounded
STROBEL, WILHELM	Infanterist	10	Frommern, Balingen	Slightly wounded
HETZEL, FRANZ	Ersatz Reservist	10	Herrenzimmern, Rottweil	KIA 25.9.15
BLEHER, EMIL	Infanterist	10	Hedelfingen, Cannstatt	WIA
DRESEN, JOHANN	Infanterist	10	Bachem, Preussen	WIA
WOLF, CHRISTIAN	Infanterist	10	Erzingen, Balingen	WIA
EBERLE, ERNST	Landsturmmann	10	Freudenstadt	KIA 25.9.15
BAUER, GUSTAV	Hauptmann	11	Heilbronn	Slightly wounded
SCHWIRZKE, PAUL	Leutnant der Reserve	11	Berlin	Severely wounded
BEUTEL, RUDOLF	Leutnant der Reserve	11	Mehrstetten, Münsingen	Severely wounded
SCHWARZ, HERMANN	Leutnant der Reserve	11	Hohebach, Künzelsau	Severely wounded
MÜLLER, PAUL	Vizefeldwebel	11	Tuttlingen	Severely wounded
EPPLER, ERNST	Unteroffizier	11	Hossingen, Balingen	Slightly wounded
GESSINGER, KARL	Unteroffizier	11	Kupferzell, Oehringen	Severely wounded
MINK, ANTON	Unteroffizier	11	Rottweil	Slightly wounded
DÖRNER, AUGUST	Gefreiter	11	Hohebach, Künzelsau	Slightly wounded
HÄRDTWECK, GEORG	Ersatz Reservist	11	Buchenmühle, Künzelsau	KIA 25.9.15

Name	Rank	Coy	Birthplace	Details
GOTH, KARL	Infanterist	11	Maienfels, Weinsberg	Slightly wounded
KING, JOHANNES	Infanterist	11	Aichhalden, Oberndorf	Slightly wounded
ESSLINGER, RICHARD	Landsturmmann	11	Backnang	KIA 25.9.15
GOLL, WILHELM	Infanterist	11	Schwaikheim, Waiblingen	Severely wounded
HÄUSSERMANN, KARL	Infanterist	11	Fellbach, Cannstatt	Slightly wounded
WURSTER, ALBERT	Infanterist	11	Sauerhöfle, Backnang	Slightly wounded
RAUSCHER, EMIL	Infanterist	11	Asperg, Ludwigsburg	Slightly wounded
HÖRN, JAKOB	Infanterist	11	Richen, Baden	Severely wounded
ILG, JOHANNES	Infanterist	11	Saverwang, Ellwangen	Slightly wounded
RECK, ULFERT	Musketier	11	Moordorf, Hannover	KIA 25.9.15
SCHLIENZ, GOTTLOB	Ersatz Reservist	11	Feuerbach, Stuttgart	KIA 25.9.15
OEHLER, MARKUS	Landwehrmann	11	Nordrach, Baden	KIA 25.9.15
DÖTTERER, FRIEDRICH	Ersatz Reservist	11	Beihingen, Ludwigsburg	KIA 25.9.15
LEHMANN, EUGEN	Landwehrmann	11	Worms	KIA 25.9.15
DUPPEL, JAKOB	Landsturmmann	11	Rutesheim, Leonberg	KIA 25.9.15
MÜNDLEIN, GEORG	Landsturmmann	11	Elpersheim, Mergentheim	KIA 25.9.15
LÄSSING, KARL	Ersatz Reservist	11	Kirchheim u.T.	KIA 25.9.15
KERN, ALFONS	Reservist	11	Sontheim, Heilbronn	KIA 25.9.15
KRAPF, XAVER	Landwehrmann	11	Oberessendorf, Waldsee	MIA
KNECHT, JOHANNES	Fusilier	11	Altmannsrot, Ellwangen	KIA 25.9.15
STECK, ANDREAS	Reservist	11	Schalksstetten, Geislingen	KIA 25.9.15
PFISTERER, GOTTLOB	Ersatz Reservist	11	Zuffenhausen, Ludwigsburg	KIA 25.9.15
MARQUARDT, FRIEDRICH	Infanterist	11	Oberjesingen, Herrenberg	Severely wounded
SCHEU, ALBERT	Infanterist	11	Owen, Kirchheim	Severely wounded
ATZ, ALBERT	Infanterist	11	Nassach	Severely wounded
BINDER, SEBASTIAN	Infanterist	11	Lechhausen, Augsburg	Severely wounded
KÖHNLEIN, GEORG	Infanterist	11	Neustädtlein, Crailsheim	Slightly wounded
SCHICK, FRIEDRICH	Infanterist	11	Böhringsweiler, Weinsberg	Slightly wounded
KNÖDLER, ALBERT	Infanterist	11	Oberheinriet, Weinsberg	Slightly wounded
URICH, KARL	Infanterist	11	Ulrichsberg, Oehringen	Slightly wounded
BRAUN, JOHANN	Infanterist	11	Buchhorn, Oehringen	Severely wounded
BETTING, JAKOB	Infanterist	11	Denkingen, Spaichingen	Severely wounded
KRÄMER, PAUL	Infanterist	11	Steinach, Waiblingen	Slightly wounded

KIA 25.9.15

Name	Coy	Birthplace	Rank	Details
SÄNGER, KARL	11	Lautenbach, Crailsheim	Infanterist	Slightly wounded
TEUFEL, ADOLF	11	Tuttlingen	Infanterist	Slightly wounded
KÖRBER, ERNST	11	Böblingen	Infanterist	Severely wounded
MORLOCK, ADOLF	11	Mötzingen, Herrenberg	Infanterist	Severely wounded
GERBING, CHRISTIAN	11	Tübingen	Infanterist	Slightly wounded
RUF, HERMANN	11	Münchingen, Leonberg	Infanterist	Severely wounded
HIRSCH, GEORG	11	Berndshausen, Künzelsau	Infanterist	Severely wounded
PROSS, FRIEDRICH	11	Reutlingen	Infanterist	Severely wounded
BURKHARDT, FRIEDRICH	11	Erfurt	Infanterist	Slightly wounded
LAUSTER, JULIUS	11	Münster, Cannstatt	Infanterist	Severely wounded
EPPINGER, JOHANNES	11	Notzingen, Kirchheim	Infanterist	Severely wounded
MAISCH, KARL	11	Gerlingen, Leonberg	Infanterist	Slightly wounded
SPÄTH, KARL	11	Sondernach, Ehingen	Musketier	Died from wounds 26.9.15
OF, KARL	11	Stuttgart	Infanterist	Severely wounded
HARR, ERNST	12	Cleversulzbach, Neckarsulm	Leutnant der Reserve	KIA 25.9.15
GÖLTENBOTH, FRIEDRICH	12	Grosshirschbach, Oehringen	Unteroffizier	Severely wounded
BÜRKLE, KARL	12	Schmiden, Cannstatt	Infanterist	Severely wounded
VOLLMER, CHRISTIAN	12	Stuttgart-Untertürkheim	Ersatz Reservist	KIA 20.9.15
UNFRIED, DAVID	12	Rappoltshofen, Gaildorf	Landsturmmann	KIA 20.9.15
LAYER, KARL	12	Stuttgart	Infanterist	Slightly wounded
RAIBER, JAKOB	12	Hütten, Münsingen	Infanterist	Slightly wounded
WAGENPFEIL, JOSEPH	12	München	Infanterist	Severely wounded
BODE, FRANZ	12	Weimar	Landsturmmann	KIA 25.9.15
EBINGER, GOTTHILF	12	Waldenbuch, Stuttgart	Landsturmmann	KIA 20.9.15
SCHMID, CHRISTIAN	12	Hochdorf, Kirchheim	Infanterist	Severely wounded
SCHLUMBERGER, KASPAR	12	Lehr, Ulm	Infanterist	Severely wounded
BÖLZ, LUDWIG	12	Wagrain, Hall	Tambour	KIA 25.9.15
BREY, ADOLF	12	Schelklingen, Blaubeuren	Kriegsfreiwilliger	Died from wounds 21.9.15
WELTE, OTTO	12	Stuttgart	Kriegsfreiwilliger	KIA 22.9.15
FISCHER, GEORG	12	Dörrenzimmern, Künzelsau	Infanterist	Slightly wounded
ABELEIN, WILHELM	12	Unterampfrach, Mittelfranken	Infanterist	Slightly wounded
LABOUTE, KONRAD	12	Siegelbach, Rheinpfalz	Infanterist	Slightly wounded
FAISST, FRIEDRICH	12	Glatten, Freudenstadt	Infanterist	Died from wounds

Additional notes:
- SPÄTH, KARL: WIA 25.9.15
- SCHLUMBERGER, KASPAR: Fusilier?
- BREY, ADOLF: WIA 20.9.15

Name	Rank	Coy	Birthplace	Details
HERRMANN, JOSEPH	Infanterist	12	Grosstissen, Saulgau	Slightly wounded
WAHL, KARL	Infanterist	12	Engelsbrand, Neuenbürg	Severely wounded
TROSTEL, GOTTLOB	Ersatz Reservist	12	Ossweil, Ludwigsburg	Died from wounds WIA 25.9.15
WOLPER, MARTIN	Infanterist	12	Neueneck, Freudenstadt	Slightly wounded
WEBER, JOSEPH	Infanterist	12	Dorfmerkingen, Neresheim	Slightly wounded
HIRZEL, GOTTFRIED	Landwehrmann	12	Vordersteinberg, Gaildorf	KIA 25.9.15
ULLRICH, KARL	Landsturmmann	12	Erfurt	KIA 25.9.15
MACK, GEORG	Infanterist	12	Oelmühle, Aalen	WIA
SCHEIBLE, WILHELM	Infanterist	12	Mengen, Saulgau	Severely wounded
SCHWARZ, KARL	Infanterist	12	Göppingen	WIA
BÜTTNER, KARL	Infanterist	12	Lassbach, Künzelsau	WIA
LÄMMLE, ALBERT	Infanterist	12	Murr, Marbach	Severely wounded
KÜBLER, MARZELLUS	Krankenträger	12	Geishausen, Elsass	Severely wounded
MERK, PAUL	Musketier	12	Donzdorf, Geislingen	KIA 25.9.15
SEIFERT, HERMANN	Infanterist	12	Mellenbach, Schwarzb.-Rud.	MIA
OTTENBACHER, ERWIN	Reservist	12	Stuttgart	KIA 22.9.15
RENTSCHLER, GOTTLOB	Landsturmmann	12	Teinach, Calw	Died from wounds 27.9.15 WIA 25.9.15
SCHMID, MARTIN	Infanterist	12	Wollbach, Zusmarshausen	Slightly wounded
UNSÖLT, ERWIN	Gefreiter	MG Coy	Marbach a.N.	KIA 25.9.15
FRANK, PAUL	Schütze	MG Coy	Jaffa, Palästina	Severely wounded
KALMBACH, CHRISTIAN	Schütze	MG Coy	Beuren, Nagold	Slightly wounded
EHMER, KARL	Schütze	MG Coy	Grossingersheim, Besigheim	Slightly wounded (previously reported)

Notes

Introduction

1. See the excellent Great War Forum site for the following threads that include mention of Hugh Butterworth: http://1914–1918.invisionzone.com/forums/index .php?showtopic=101846&hl=butterworth; http://1914–1918.invisionzone.com/ forums/index.php?showtopic=74583&hl=butterworth; http://1914–1918 .invisionzone.com/forums/index.php?showtopic=146158&hl=butterworth; accessed to confirm availability 16 June 2010.
2. It is interesting to note that amongst the most famous of the musical works of Hugh's cousin George Butterworth are his settings to the collection of poems 'A Shropshire Lad' by Laurence Housman's elder brother A E Housman.
3. Laurence Housman (ed.), *War Letters of Fallen Englishmen* (Philadelphia: Pine Street Books, 2002), p. xxiii.
4. Ibid., p. xxiv.
5. Ibid., p. vii.
6. John Laffin, *British Butchers and Bunglers of World War One* (Stroud: Sutton, 2003), p. 179.
7. Susan Thyne, 'O Captain My Captain – The Relationship between Officers and Enlisted Men in World War One', *Rochester University Journal of Undergraduate Research* (JUR), Vol. 4 (Spring, 2006), 36–39.

Chapter 1

1. Sydney H Pardon (ed.), *John Wisden's Cricketers' Almanack for 1916* (London: John Wisden and Co. Ltd, 1916), p. 152.
2. 1881 census. Information on the Butterworth family tree kindly supplied by Michael Barlow, author of *Whom the Gods Love: The Life and Music of George Butterworth* (London: Toccata Press, 2009).
3. *London Gazette*, 16 November 1886, p. 5515 and 8 March 1887, p. 1222.
4. *The Times*, 14 July 1880, p. 11.
5. Irene Butterworth, *He that has once been happy is, for aye, out of destruction's reach* (Bath: The Mendip Press, 1975), p. 21.

Chapter 2

1. The *Nutshell– The Hazelwood Gazette*, No. 26, August 1899, p. 14.
2. Ibid., p. 16.
3. Ibid., No. 75, January 1916, p. 1.
4. *Marlborough College Register 1843–1933*, 8th edn (Marlborough: The Bursar, Marlborough College, 1936).
5. Butterworth, *He that has once been happy*, p. 6.
6. Summary of Hugh Montagu Butterworth's academic record at Marlborough College compiled by and with grateful thanks to Mr Terry Rogers, Honorary Archivist, Marlborough College.
7. The *Marlburian*, 7 October 1903, p. 131.
8. Leslie Woodroffe also went on to serve with the Rifle Brigade and wrote Hugh's eulogy in the *Marlburian* of November 1916. His award of the Military Cross appeared in the same *London Gazette* list of 11 January 1916 as that of William La Touche Congreve (later Victoria Cross) and Noel Chavasse (later Victoria Cross and bar). Woodroffe was killed in action on 4 June 1916 and thus became the third of four Woodroffe brothers to die in action. Middle brother Kenneth was killed on 9 May 1915 and 19-year-old Sidney was lost in the German liquid-fire attack at Hooge on 30 July 1915, just a few kilometres south of Hugh, who was in the trenches at the time. For his actions on 30 July 1915, Sidney Woodroffe was also awarded the Victoria Cross.
9. Butterworth, *He that has once been happy*, p. 43.
10. Ibid.
11. www.cliftonrfchistory.co.uk; accessed 20 October 2009.
12. The *Marlburian*, 17 December 1903, p. 186.
13. *The Times*, 14 April 1904, p. 9.
14. Ibid., 15 April 1904, p. 5.
15. The *Marlburian*, 10 October 1904, p. 135.
16. Butterworth, *He that has once been happy*, p. 44.
17. Letter from Mr Terry Rogers, Honorary Archivist of Marlborough College, 19 January 2010.
18. *The Times*, 28 July 1904, p. 6.
19. Butterworth, *He that has once been happy*, p. 43.
20. Hugh should have played in a game against Monmouthshire at Rodney Parade, Newport on 8 and 9 August 1906 but is listed eleventh on the first innings scorecard as 'absent'. See www.rammyarchive.co.uk/Archive/Scorecards/87/87289.html; accessed 20 October 2009.
21. See www.rammyarchive.co.uk/Archive/Scorecards/87/87120.html; accessed 20 October 2009. Full details of all the Minor Counties matches in which Hugh played for Wiltshire can be found at the excellent cricket archive website www.

rammyarchive.co.uk/Archive/Players/28/28372/Minor_Counties_Championship
_Matches.html; accessed 20 October 2009.

Chapter 3

1. Butterworth, *He that has once been happy*, p. 21.
2. Ibid., p. 32.
3. *The Times*, 9 November 1904, p. 7 and 11 November 1904, p. 9. Both Christopher and Noel Chavasse went on to gain running blues in 1907. Christopher Chavasse was also the first of the Chavasse boys to don uniform in the Great War. Accepted in August 1914 by the Army Chaplain's department as a Temporary Chaplain 4th Class, he was later attached to IV Army Corps. See Ann Clayton, *Chavasse Double VC* (Barnsley: Pen and Sword, 1997), pp. 56–61.
4. *The Times*, 13 November 1905, p. 11.
5. Ibid., 15 February 1906, p. 11.
6. Ibid., 21 February 1906, p. 12.
7. The Right Hon. Lord Desborough, *Fifty Years of Sport at Oxford, Cambridge and the Great Public Schools. Vols I and II, Oxford and Cambridge*, edited by A C L Croome (London: Walter Southwood and Co. Ltd, 1913), p. 110.
8. *The Times*, 21 February 1907, p. 11.
9. The *Marlburian*, 2 November 1915, p. 164.
10. Desborough, *Fifty Years of Sport at Oxford, Cambridge and the Great Public Schools*, p. 11.
11. Ibid.
12. Lieutenant Wilfred Stanley Bird, 5th, attached 2nd Battalion, the King's Royal Rifle Corps, was killed in action on the opening day of the Battle of Aubers Ridge on 9 May 1915, south of Richebourg St Vaast, France. He is commemorated on the Le Touret Memorial to the Missing, France panels 32–33.
13. *The Times*, 11 May 1905, p. 7.
14. *The Times*, 2 May 1906, p. 11. Hugh's opening partner Charles George Edgar Farmer was killed serving as a lieutenant in the 7th Battalion, the King's Royal Rifle Corps near Longueval on the Somme on 18 August 1916. He has no known grave and is commemorated on the Thiepval Memorial to the Missing Pier and Face 13 A and B.
15. See the exhaustive cricket archive at www.rammyarchive.co.uk/Archive/.
16. Butterworth, *He that has once been happy*, p. 44.
17. In an email from the MCC on 29 October 2009, Mr Neil Robinson wrote, 'Although I can confirm that Stephen Green was curator here in 1975, I am unable to confirm the story of Butterworth catching out W G Grace. There was indeed a match at Swindon on that date between Swindon and MCC & Ground (i.e. the groundstaff), but neither Butterworth nor Grace was playing. Butterworth did play for Wiltshire v MCC on three occasions, including once later in 1906, but on none of these occasions was W G involved'.

18. Ollivierre had already represented St Vincent and went on to play for the now-politically incorrect sounding West Indian Coloured XI in 1913. The taker of Hugh's scalp that day, Sydney Smith, went on to represent Northamptonshire the following year until the outbreak of war in 1914 then, like Hugh had done before him, he emigrated to Auckland in New Zealand where he lived until his death in 1963.

19. Letter from University College Oxford Archivist Dr Robin Darwall-Smith, 26 January 2010.

20. Butterworth, *He that has once been happy*, p. 21.

21. They sailed from London bound for Wellington – with a final onward destination cited as Lyttelton – on board the New Zealand Shipping Company vessel *Rimutaka*, arriving on 12 March 1908. See http://web.ukonline.co.uk/sheila.jones/Passa-c.txt; accessed 7 November 2009.

22. Butterworth, *He that has once been happy*, p. 46.

23. Bruce and Don Hamilton, *Never a Footstep Back – A History of the Wanganui Collegiate School, 1854–2003* (Wanganui: Wanganui Collegiate School Board of Trustees, 2003), p. 127.

24. Wanganui Collegiate School website: www.collegiate.school.nz/main.cfm?id=6347; accessed 7 November 2009. In 2004, Wanganui Collegiate School celebrated its 150th anniversary, which included a visit from Prince Edward, His Royal Highness The Earl of Wessex, who had spent two terms at the school in 1982 as a junior master whilst on a 'gap year'.

25. John Allen was commissioned into the 2nd Volunteer Battalion of the King's Own Royal Lancaster Regiment on 3 October 1900. He became a temporary lieutenant with the 2nd Active Service Volunteer Company from 24 March 1901 and served in the war in South Africa. The Active Service Companies of the Volunteer Battalions of the King's Own Royal Lancaster Regiment served in the South African War in support of the 2nd Battalion of the King's Own. Lieutenant Allen's name appears on a memorial of those who served and he is shown as having served in the 2nd Company under Captain Wadham. He was made an Honorary Lieutenant on 26 July 1902.

26. 10200, Private Charles Bramwell Allen, age 30 of the 2nd Battalion, Canterbury Regiment, NZEF. Son of John Allen Senior of Lancaster, England, he was killed on 15 September 1916 but has no known grave and is commemorated on the Caterpillar Valley NZ Memorial, Longueval, France.

27. Kenneth Macfarlane Gresson became the leading member of one of New Zealand's foremost legal families. He was wounded whilst serving as an officer in Gallipoli with the New Zealand forces and after the Second World War was appointed as a judge of the Supreme Court of New Zealand. When a separate and permanent Court of Appeal was created in 1957, Gresson was appointed its first president, serving until his retirement in 1963. He was mentioned by Hugh in one of his letters.

28. Arthur Espie Porritt, Baron Porritt, was a renowned New Zealand physician, military surgeon, statesman and athlete – he represented New Zealand at the 1924

Olympic Games in Paris and won a bronze in the 100yd, a race later immortalised in the film *Chariots of Fire*. He served as the 11th Governor-General of New Zealand from 1967–1972 and died in 1994 at the age of 93. His son is Jonathan Porritt, the well-known writer, broadcaster and advisor to a variety of bodies on environmental issues.

29. Butterworth, *He that has once been happy*, p. 48.
30. Hamilton and Hamilton, *Never a Footstep Back*, p. 138.
31. In addition to Hugh, 10 other masters of the school served in the Great War and of these, a further 6 – E L Wells, T D Long, P F Armstrong, L S Jennings, A S Reid and A G Hodges – gave their lives, along with 4 of the domestic staff. In all, 668 Old Boys served in the Great War – a hugely significant number considering that barely 2,000 boys had passed through the school between 1854 and 1914, of which some 1,700 would have been eligible to fight. Of those 668 who served – almost half of those eligible – 152 lost their lives. The school is, quite rightly, very proud of its record of service to Britain during the Great War.

Chapter 4

1. See the *London Gazette* of 7 August 1914, p. 6209. Amongst other works, Farquharson, who was later promoted to brevet lieutenant colonel and received the CBE, is perhaps best known for his celebrated translation of the *Meditations of Marcus Aurelius*. He became Chief Postal Censor for the War Office and in that capacity produced, in March 1920, the *Report on Postal Censorship during the Great War (1914–1918)*. He was decorated with the Palmes Academie Officier by the President of the French Republic on 30 September 1920.
2. Service record of Hugh Montagu Butterworth. TNA, WO 339/38677.
3. Michael Haines, *The Rifle Brigade – A Critical Bibliography* (privately published, 1995), p. 104.
4. Robert M Maxwell, *Villiers-Stuart Goes to War* (Edinburgh: The Pentland Press, 1990), p. 4.
5. Ibid.
6. Ibid., p. 18.
7. Ibid., p. 14.
8. Ibid., p. i.
9. Ibid., p. 36.
10. Ibid., p. 48.
11. Butterworth, *He that has once been happy*, p. 50.
12. Ibid.
13. Total British Empire and Dominions casualties for the battles of Neuve Chapelle, Second Ypres, Aubers Ridge and Festubert amounted to around 100,000 men, of which some 21,000–22,000 were killed. 22-year-old Lieutenant Kenneth Herbert Clayton Woodroffe, 6th Battalion, the Welsh Regiment attached 2nd Battalion, the

Rifle Brigade and Captain Anthony Wilding (31) of the Royal Marines – serving with the Armoured Car Section of the Royal Naval Air Service – were killed within a few kilometres of each other on the opening day of the Battle of Aubers Ridge. Hugh knew both men personally; Woodroffe being the brother of his great friend Leslie, whilst the dashing Tony Wilding – the reigning Wimbledon men's singles champion of 1913 – was a family friend. Wilding's family had, like Hugh's, moved to Christchurch in New Zealand in the late 1800s. Naturally, with tennis being such an obsession in both households, the families had got to know each other very well and often played tennis together when Wilding returned home.

Chapter 5

1. Maxwell, *Villiers-Stuart Goes to War*, p. 57.
2. 9/RB War Diary, TNA WO 95/1901. Thankfully there were no deaths amongst the total of six casualties suffered during the battalion's induction.
3. The action on the Bellewaarde Ridge on 16 June was recorded in several photographs by Private F A Fyfe of the Liverpool Scottish. Very few photographs taken in the heat of combat exist but those taken by Fyfe, a press photographer in civilian life, showing men advancing or taking cover under the parapet of the German front-line trench are remarkable documents indeed.
4. The 14th Division War Diary gives the following casualty breakdown for 16/17 June 1915: 4 officers and 19 OR killed, 4 officers and 158 OR wounded, 1 officer and 7 OR slightly wounded, 2 OR gassed, 8 OR missing. TNA WO 95/1864.
5. 14th (Light) Division Headquarters War Diary, TNA WO95/1864.
6. Lieutenant Colonel L H Thornton CMG, DSO and Pamela Fraser, *The Congreves – Father and Son* (London: John Murray, 1930), p. 290.
7. Maxwell, *Villiers-Stuart Goes to War*, p. 74.
8. Ibid., p. 73.
9. Ibid., p. 82. Hugh Cecil Benson was the son of Cecil and Constance Benson, of 12 Sumner Place, Kensington, London. Second Lieutenant Bernard Rissik, the other officer killed, was the son of the Hon. Johann Friedrich Bernhardt Rissik (Administrator of the Transvaal) and Mrs Rissik, of 'Linschoten', Park Street, Pretoria, South Africa. Educated at Trinity College, Oxford, Rissik had joined the Oxford OTC at the outbreak of war and had been commissioned into the 8th Battalion, the Middlesex Regiment in November 1914. Both men are commemorated on panels 46–48 and 50 of the Menin Gate Memorial to the Missing along with Hugh.
10. This was one of the letters selected by Laurence Housman for his volume *War Letters of Fallen Englishmen* in 1930.
11. This was Major G J Davis who had been Second in Command of 9/RB under Lieutenant Colonel Villiers-Stuart. Davis had moved up to take temporary command of 9/King's Royal Rifle Corps after the death of Lieutenant Colonel Chaplin amid the chaos following the German liquid fire attack near Hooge on 30 July 1915.

12. The exact location is uncertain. The War Diary is unclear for the date given as the map reference is ambiguous but the location cited immediately prior to this is specific and points to a location halfway between Vlamertinghe and Brandhoek, west of Ypres.

13. Brigadier General Sir James E Edmonds, *Military Operations France and Belgium, 1915, Vol. II* (London: Macmillan, 1928 – corrected to 19 June 1936), p. v. Hereafter *Official History*.

14. Ibid., pp. ix, vii.

15. Richard Holmes, *The Little Field Marshal – A Life of Sir John French* (London: Weidenfeld and Nicolson, 2004), p. 294.

16. John Hughes-Wilson, '1915 – The Forgotten Year on the Western Front', *Battlefields Review*, No. 19 *(2002)*, 33.

17. *The Times*, Monday 27 September 1915, p. 8.

18. Ibid.

19. Holmes, *The Little Field Marshal*, p. 305.

20. *Official History*, p. 136.

21. The total casualties of the Meerut Division during 25, 26 and 27 September 1915 were 107 officers, 1,172 British other ranks and 1,738 Indian other ranks killed, wounded or missing. The bulk of these occurred on 25 September. The losses of the 8th Division at Bois Grenier totalled 52 officers and 1,283 other ranks. *Official History*, pp. 261–263.

22. The notification reads: 'Temp. 2nd Lt. H M Butterworth (since killed in action) to be temp. Capt. whilst comdg. a Co. 6 Sep. 1915.', *London Gazette*, 14 April 1916, p. 3921.

23. The two men – not mentioned by name by Hugh – were B/2079 Sergeant F Bunstead and D/1518 Acting Corporal D Brown. The wording of the citations for the award of the Distinguished Conduct Medal for both is exactly the same: 'For conspicuous gallantry and devotion to duty near Hooge, during operations from 31st July to 2nd August, 1915. He carried out his duty as a stretcher bearer under heavy shell fire with the utmost bravery. On several previous occasions his coolness and gallantry have been noticed.', *Supplement to the London Gazette*, 15 September 1915, p. 9171.

24. *London Gazette*, 26 March 1915, p. 2991.

25. Marquis de Ruvigny, *The Roll of Honour – A Biographical Record of All Members of His Majesty's Naval and Military Forces Who Have Fallen in the War*, Vol. 2 (London: The Standard Art Book Co. Ltd, n.d.), p. 58.

26. From the references given in this document it has been possible to track down copies of four of the five photographs in the Imperial War Museum photographic archive. Grateful thanks to IWM Principal Historian Nigel Steel and Alan Wakefield of the department of photographs for assisting in their rediscovery.

27. 9/RB War Diary, TNA WO 95/1901.

28. Maxwell, *Villiers-Stuart Goes to War*, p. 135.

Chapter 6

1. Maxwell, *Villiers-Stuart Goes to War*, p. 141.
2. Typescript of interview with Captain Basil Sawers, 177 Tunnelling Company (TC) Royal Engineers (RE), the Barrie Papers, Royal Engineers' Museum, Chatham, pp. 3–4.
3. 177 TC RE War Diary, TNA WO95/404. The crater blown on 25 September later became known as the 'Bliss Crater' after Captain Bliss the CO of 177 TC. It appears as such on mining maps of Railway Wood compiled by 177 TC in 1917. I am indebted to Iain McHenry for allowing me access to his research material and for his advice and comments regarding the mining operations of 177 TC.
4. This charge was never blown due to the failure of 9/RB's left column to hold its gains on 25 September. The 177 TC War Diary states that 'the gallery filled with water and was left so'. One assumes the charges are still in situ. 177 Tunnelling Company RE War Diary, TNA WO95/404.
5. 14th (Light) Division Headquarters War Diary, TNA WO95/1864.
6. 9/RB War Diary, TNA WO 95/1901.
7. Maxwell, *Villiers-Stuart Goes to War*, p. 142.
8. Ibid.
9. 9/RB War Diary, TNA WO 95/1901.
10. Maxwell, *Villiers-Stuart Goes to War*, p. 143.
11. Part of the 54th Reserve Division, RIR 248 was formed in Ludwigsburg (Regimental Staff, I Battalion from Ersatz Battalion, Württemberg Infantry Regiment No. 121), Heilbronn (II Battalion from Ersatz Battalion, Württemberg Füsilier Regiment No. 122) and Bietigheim (III Battalion From Ersatz Battalion, Württemberg Infantry Regiment No. 126). The Regiment became part of the XV Army Corps. It consisted of about 50 per cent men with previous service and 50 per cent *Kriegsfreiwilligen* (War Volunteers).
    Commander: *Oberst* a. D. Frhr. v. Hügel
    I: *Major* z. D. v. Lützow   (Bezirks Offizier. Hall)
    II: *Major* a. D. Burgund
    III: *Major* z. D. Jordan   (Bezirks Offizier I Stuttgart) killed: 30.10.14
    Fatal war losses: 80 officers, 2,726 non-commissioned officers and men.
12. *Generalleutnant* a. D. Ernst Reinhardt, *Das Württembergische Reserve Inf. Regiment Nr. 248 im Weltkrieg 1914–1918* (Stuttgart: Chr. Belser A.G., Verlagsbuchhandlung, 1924), p. 30. My grateful thanks to Ralph Whitehead, who has been a font of knowledge, given sound advice on translations and provided unfailing encouragement during the research of the German accounts of the battle of 25 September, must be recorded here.
13. 14th Division War Diary, September 1915, WO 95/1864.
14. Reinhardt, *Das Württembergische Reserve Inf. Regiment Nr. 248*, p. 30.

15. Ibid., p. 31. The Württemberg *Verlustlisten* 289 of 25 October 1915 lists the following men of RIR 248 – mostly from the 12th Company of the III Battalion – killed in action or died of wounds received between 17 and 24 September 1915. It is reasonable to assume that they died under the British bombardment. There are no dates given against wounded men but again it is reasonable to assume that at least a similar number of men were wounded, if not more, as many are listed as 'slightly wounded'.
Ersatz Reservist Christian Vollmer of 12 Company from Stuttgart Unterturkheim. Killed 20.9.15.
Landsturmmann David Unfried of 12 Company from Rappoltshofen, Gaildorf. Killed 20.9.15.
Landsturmmann Gotthilf Ebinger of 12 Company from Waldenbuch, Stuttgart. Killed 20.9.15.
Kriegsfreiwilliger Adolf Brey of 12 Company from Schelklingen, Blaubeuren. Died of wounds 21.9.15.
Infanterist Wilhelm Seifert of 10 Company from Schwieberdingen, Ludwigsburg. Killed 22.9.15.
Kriegsfreiwilliger Otto Welte of 12 Company from Stuttgart. Killed 22.9.15.
Reservist Erwin Ottenbacher of 12 Company from Stuttgart. Killed 22.9.15.
Musketier Ernst Imle of 6 Company from Markgröningen, Ludwigsburg. Died of wounds 23.9.15.
16. 14th Division Report on Operations on 25 September 1915, WO 95/1864.
17. Reinhardt, *Das Württembergische Reserve Inf. Regiment Nr. 248*, p. 31. Note that the timings used by the German Army – and therefore cited in their diaries and accounts – were an hour ahead of that used by the British.
18. General Otto von Moser, *Die Württemberger im Weltkrieg* (Stuttgart: Chr. Belser, 1938), p. 374.
19. *Ibid.*, p. 374.
20. Maxwell, *Villiers-Stuart Goes to War*, p. 144.
21. Moser, *Die Württemberger im Weltkrieg*, p. 373.
22. Maxwell, *Villiers-Stuart Goes to War*, p. 141.
23. Reinhardt, *Das Württembergische Reserve Inf. Regiment Nr. 248*, p. 31.
24. Maxwell, *Villiers-Stuart Goes to War*, pp. 142–143.
25. Ibid., p. 146. Although Villiers-Stuart claims he 'pressed the key', it is unlikely that he did so. This task would have been in the hands of an officer of 177 TC.
26. Reinhardt, *Das Württembergische Reserve Inf. Regiment Nr. 248*, p. 31.
27. Ibid., p. 32.
28. Moser, *Die Württemberger im Weltkrieg*, p. 374.
29. Reinhardt, *Das Württembergische Reserve Inf. Regiment Nr. 248*, p. 32.
30. Lieutenant C Thatcher, 'Report of the action fought on 25 September in area 0.4, 2.4, 3.0, 1.0', 14th (Light) Division Headquarters War Diary, TNA WO95/1864.
31. There was such a bewildering array of bombs – hand grenades – then in use by the

British Army that not all men could be spared to be trained in their use. Each battalion had 'specialist' teams consisting of bombers, carriers and spare men – protected by their own bayonet men. The bayonet men provided cover for and advanced ahead of the bombers whose job was to bomb hostile dug-outs and around the corners of the traverses of the German trenches to clear and secure them. Serious problems occurred during intense fighting in unfamiliar trenches when trained bombers and the spare men were killed and wounded as the men who were left often did not know how to use the bombs available.

32. Moser, *Die Württemberger im Weltkrieg*, p. 374.
33. Ibid., p. 374.
34. Reinhardt, *Das Württembergische Reserve Inf. Regiment Nr. 248*, p. 32.
35. *London Gazette*, 16 November 1915, pp. 11433, 11428, 11421.
36. Temporary Major Henry Howard's younger brother Lieutenant Lyulph Walter Mowbray Howard was killed on the Somme, aged 29, just ten days before the attack on the Bellewaarde Ridge. He is buried in the Norfolk Cemetery in Becordel-Becourt, east of Albert. Howard must have known of his brother's death by the time 9/RB went over the top on 25 September 1915.
37. Service Number 25, CSM George Goodey, survived the day and died just ten days short of a year later on 15 September 1916 on the opening day of the Battle of Flers-Courcelette on the Somme. He has no known grave and is commemorated on the Thiepval Memorial to the Missing of the Somme, Pier and Face 16b and C. Interestingly the CWGC Commission Debt of Honour Register records him as being the recipient of the Military Cross!
38. Reinhardt, *Das Württembergische Reserve Inf. Regiment Nr. 248*, p. 32.
39. Ibid., p. 33.
40. Thatcher, 'Report of the action fought on 25 September in area 0.4, 2.4, 3.0, 1.0'.
41. 9/RB War Diary, TNA WO 95/1901.
42. Reinhardt, *Das Württembergische Reserve Inf. Regiment Nr. 248*, p. 33.
43. Villiers-Stuart was as scathing of Captain John Christie as he was of other 'school-master' officers he knew, referring to him as an 'Eton master of some age and though very brave quite useless as a soldier . . . I found him reading Shakespeare to his platoon commanders while the Germans were working nearer and nearer'. The cultured Christie survived the war and went on to found the Glyndebourne Opera House and the Glyndebourne Festival Opera at his home at Glyndebourne, near Lewes in Sussex in 1934. Educated at Eton College and Trinity College, Cambridge, he later spent seven years at Eton as a master. Despite his partial blindness, he was awarded the Military Cross; his award appearing on p. 577 of the *Supplement to the London Gazette* of 14 January 1916 along with many others; just two entries below that of Noel Chavasse and eight above that of Billy Congreve. In 1954 John Christie was made a Companion of Honour for his achievements at Glyndebourne and died in 1962.
44. Thatcher, 'Report of the action fought on 25 September in area 0.4, 2.4, 3.0, 1.0'.

45. 14th (Light) Division Headquarters War Diary, TNA WO95/1864.
46. Reinhardt, *Das Württembergische Reserve Inf. Regiment Nr. 248*, p. 33.
47. Ibid.
48. Maxwell, *Villiers-Stuart Goes to War*, p. 150.
49. Ibid., p. 151.

Chapter 7
1. E S Craig, MA and W M Gibson, MA (eds), *Oxford University Roll of Service* (Oxford: Clarendon Press, 1920), p. 4.
2. *Official History*, p. 267.
3. Figures for those killed, compiled using the databases *Officers and Soldiers Died in the Great War* and the Commonwealth War Graves Commission Debt of Honour Register, return the following for the four battalions of 42 Brigade between the dates 25 September and 12 October 1915, which is the day before the brigade effectively returned to active service: 5/Oxfordshire and Buckinghamshire Light Infantry – 5 officers and 192 OR; 9/Rifle Brigade – 5 officers and 153 OR; 5/King's Shropshire Light Infantry – 6 officers and 143 OR; 9/King's Royal Rifle Corps – 5 officers and 72 OR. Of the men of 62 Field Company RE who attacked with the units of 42 Brigade, ten went missing and were later recorded as killed; eight are remembered on the Menin Gate and one each on the Ploegsteert and, strangely, the Loos Memorials to the Missing. It should be noted, however, that neither database is infallible.
4. Second Report on the Operations of 25 September, 1915, dated 30 September, 1915. 14th (Light) Division Headquarters War Diary, TNA WO95/1864.
5. First Report on the Operations of 25 September, 1915, dated 26 September, 1915. 14th (Light) Division Headquarters War Diary, TNA WO95/1864.
6. Second Report on the Operations of 25 September, 1915, dated 30 September, 1915.
7. 'Notes on Deductions to be made from the Attack about Hooge, 25th September, 1915' – V Corps Headquarters to Second Army. 14th (Light) Division Headquarters War Diary, TNA WO95/1864.
8. *Official History*, p. 264.
9. Reichsarchiv, *Der Weltkrieg 1914–1918, Vol. 9* (Berlin: Mittler and Sohn, 1933), p. 51.
10. General a. D. Artur Baumgarten-Crusius, *Sachsen in großer Zeit – Geschichte der Sachsen im Weltkrieg, Vol. II* (Leipzig: Buchhandlung Max Lippold, 1919).
11. Heinz Lehmann, *Das Königlich Sächsische Reserve-Jaeger-Bataillon Nr. 26, Erinnerungsblaetter deutscher Regimenter, Heft 11 der Schriftfolge* (Dresden: Wilhelm und Bertha Baensch-Stiftung, 1923), p. 57.
12. *Das Königlich Sächsische Reserve-Infanterie-Regiment Nr. 241* (Dresden: Wilhelm Limpert, 1936), pp. 137–139.
13. *Das Königlich Sächsische Reserve-Infanterie-Regiment Nr. 243 im Weltkriege 1914–1918* (Dresden: Wilhelm und Bertha von Baensch Stiftung, 1927), p. 67.

14. Reichsarchiv, *Der Weltkrieg 1914–1918, Vol. 9*, p. 67.
15. Lehmann, *Das Königlich Sächsische Reserve-Jaeger-Bataillon Nr. 26*, p. 55.
16. See *Das Königlich Sächsische Reserve-Infanterie-Regiment Nr. 241*, p. 142, *Das Königlich Sächsische Reserve-Infanterie-Regiment Nr. 243 im Weltkriege 1914–1918*, p. 69 and *Das Königlich Sächsische Reserve-Jäger-Bataillon Nr. 25 im Weltkriege* (Dresden: Wilhelm und Bertha von Baensch Stiftung, 1927), pp. 64–65. The Order of Battle of the units in the 53rd Reserve Division posed a puzzle when studying the movements of its subordinate units towards the end of September, early October 1915. Several sources indicate that RIR 241 and RIR 242 constituted the German 105 Reserve Infantry Brigade, whilst RIR 243 and RIR 244 along with RJB 25 were part of 106 Reserve Infantry Brigade. The standard work on the Saxon Army – written by a Saxon general just after the war – describes the organisation of the 53rd Reserve Division without reference to brigades at the outbreak of hostilities and adds a note that 'later' two brigades were formed; 105 (RIR 241 and 243) and 106 (RIR 242 and 244). None of the individual unit histories refer to brigades before the autumn of 1915 except that of RJB 25, which refers to it being part of 106 Brigade from August 1914. Whatever the order, what is not in doubt is that RIR 241, RIR 243 and RJB 25 were moved to Champagne, while RIR 242 and RIR 244 made the shorter journey to the valleys of the Rivers Douve and Lys. I am indebted to Sebastian Laudan for his thoughts on the above.
17. Reinhardt, *Das Württembergische Reserve Inf. Regiment Nr. 248*, p. 44.
18. Lehmann, *Das Königlich Sächsische Reserve-Jaeger-Bataillon Nr. 26*, pp. 55–58. There is no record in any of the British official war diaries of any wounded officers being rescued from no-man's-land. If the German accounts are to be believed, there may well have been one or several very localised truces after the battle in order to recover some of the bodies of the dead.
19. Reinhardt, *Das Württembergische Reserve Inf. Regiment Nr. 248*, p. 34.
20. 8/RB War Diary, TNA WO95/1895.
21. Ibid.
22. Service record of Hugh Montagu Butterworth. TNA, WO 339/38677. A report of Hugh's death, sent by the New Armies Infantry Section at GHQ 3rd Echelon to the War Office after receiving official notification from Lieutenant Colonel Villiers-Stuart, has a note to the effect that a place of burial was 'not forthcoming'.
23. *The Times*, Tuesday 5 October 1915, p. 6.
24. Ibid., Monday 11 October 1915, p. 6.
25. *Auckland Weekly News*, 7 October 1915, p. 21.
26. Hamilton and Hamilton, *Never a Footstep Back*, p. 179.
27. The *Marlburian*, 2 November 1915, pp. 164–165.
28. The *Nutshell – The Hazelwood Gazette*, No. 75, January 1916, p. 1.
29. Service record of Hugh Montagu Butterworth. TNA, WO 339/38677.
30. Ibid.

31. Probate of the Will of H M Butterworth, Archives New Zealand, AAOM 6029/284, record 18024.
32. Wanganui *Collegian*, No. 99, December 1915, pp. 4–6.
33. Butterworth, *He that has once been happy*, p. 39.
34. Lieutenant George Sainton Kaye Butterworth MC is remembered on the Thiepval Memorial to the Missing, Pier and Face 14A and 15C.
35. *In Memoriam 1914–1918*, Wanganui Collegiate School Old Boys' Association (Wanganui, NZ: Wanganui Chronicle Co., 1919), p. 1.

Bibliography

Barlow, Michael. *Whom the Gods Love: The Life and Music of George Butterworth*, London: Toccata Press, 2009

Barton, Peter, Peter Doyle and Johan Vandewalle. *Beneath Flanders Fields – The Tunnellers' War 1914–1918*, Stapelehurst: Spellmount, 2004

Butterworth, Irene. *He that has once been happy is, for aye, out of destruction's reach*, Bath: The Mendip Press, 1975

Clayton, Ann. *Chavasse Double VC*, Barnsley: Pen and Sword, 1997

Craig, E S, MA, and W M Gibson, MA (eds). *Oxford University Roll of Service*, Oxford: Clarendon Press, 1920

Desborough, the Right Hon. Lord. *Fifty Years of Sport at Oxford, Cambridge and the Great Public Schools. Vols I and II, Oxford and Cambridge*, edited by A C L Croome, London: Walter Southwood and Co. Ltd, 1913

Edmonds, Brigadier General Sir James E. *Military Operations France and Belgium, 1915, Vol. II*, London: Macmillan, 1928 – corrected to 19 June 1936

Fussell, Paul. *The Great War and Modern Memory*, London: Oxford University Press, 1977

Haines, Michael. *The Rifle Brigade – A Critical Bibliography*, privately published, 1995

Hamilton, Bruce and Don. *Never a Footstep Back – A History of the Wanganui Collegiate School, 1854–2003*, Wanganui: Wanganui Collegiate School Board of Trustees, 2003

Holmes, Richard. *The Little Field Marshal – A Life of Sir John French*, London:Weidenfeld and Nicolson, 2004

Housman, Laurence (ed.). *War Letters of Fallen Englishmen*, Philadelphia: Pine Street Books, 2002

Hughes-Wilson, John. '1915 – The Forgotten Year on the Western Front', *Battlefields Review*, No. 19 *(2002)*, 33

In Memoriam 1914–1918, Wanganui Collegiate School Old Boys' Association, Wanganui, NZ: Wanganui Chronicle Co., 1919

Laffin, John. *British Butchers and Bunglers of World War One*, Stroud: Sutton, 2003

Marlborough College Register 1843–1933, 8th edn, Marlborough: The Bursar, Marlborough College, 1936

Maxwell, Robert M. *Villiers-Stuart Goes to War*, Edinburgh: The Pentland Press, 1990

Pardon, Sydney H (ed.). *John Wisden's Cricketers' Almanack for 1916*, London: John Wisden and Co. Ltd, 1916

de Ruvigny, Marquis. *The Roll of Honour – A Biographical Record of All Members of His*

Majesty's Naval and Military Forces Who Have Fallen in the War, Vol. 2, London: The Standard Art Book Co. Ltd, n.d.

Thornton, Lieutenant Colonel L H, CMG, DSO, and Pamela Fraser. *The Congreves – Father and Son*, London: John Murray, 1930

Thyne, Susan. 'O Captain My Captain – The Relationship between Officers and Enlisted Men in World War One', *Rochester University Journal of Undergraduate Research* (JUR), Vol. 4 (Spring, 2006)

Wanganui Collegiate School Register 1854 to 1947, 3rd edn, Dunedin and Wellington, NZ: A H & A W Reed under the Auspices of the Wanganui Collegiate School Old Boys' Association, 1948

German Secondary Sources

Baumgarten-Crusius, General a. D. Artur. *Sachsen in großer Zeit – Geschichte der Sachsen im Weltkrieg, Vol. II*, Leipzig: Buchhandlung Max Lippold, 1919

Geschichte des Königlich Sächsischen Reserve-Infanterie-Regiments 242, Dresden: Reinhold Mönch, Inhaber Georg Lippold, 1924

Die Geschichte des Königlich Sächsischen Reserve-Infanterie-Regiments 244 im Weltkriege 1914–1918, Chemnitz: Vereinigung ehemaliger Offiziere des R.I.R. 244, 1920

Das Königlich Sächsische Reserve-Jäger-Bataillon Nr. 25 im Weltkriege, Dresden: Wilhelm und Bertha von Baensch Stiftung, 1927

Das Königlich Sächsische Reserve-Infanterie-Regiment Nr. 241, Dresden: Wilhelm Limpert, 1936

Das Königlich Sächsische Reserve-Infanterie-Regiment Nr. 241, Kriegserinnerungen eines Truppenarztes von Stabsarzt d. L. Dr. Grill, Dresden: Wilhelm Limpert, 1922

Das Königlich Sächsische Reserve-Infanterie-Regiment Nr. 243 im Weltkriege 1914–1918, Dresden: Wilhelm und Bertha von Baensch Stiftung, 1927

Lehmann, Heinz. *Das Königlich Sächsische Reserve-Jaeger-Bataillon Nr. 26, Erinnerungsblaetter deutscher Regimenter, Heft 11 der Schriftfolge*, Dresden: Wilhelm und Bertha Baensch-Stiftung, 1923

Moser, General Otto von. *Die Württemberger im Weltkrieg*, Stuttgart: Chr. Belser, 1938

Reichsarchiv. *Der Weltkrieg 1914–1918, Vol. 9*, Berlin: Mittler and Sohn, 1933

Reinhardt, Generalleutnant a. D. Ernst. *Das Württembergische Reserve Inf. Regiment Nr. 248 im Weltkrieg 1914–1918*, Stuttgart: Chr. Belser A.G., Verlagsbuchhandlung, 1924

Newspapers and Periodicals

Battlefields Review

London Gazette

Marlburian – the Journal of Marlborough School

Nutshell – The Hazelwood School Gazette

The Times
Wanganui *Collegian*

Unpublished Sources

9th Battalion, the Rifle Brigade War Diary. TNA WO 95/1901
5th Battalion, the Oxfordshire and Buckinghamshire Light Infantry War Diary. TNA WO95/1900
9th Battalion, the King's Royal Rifle Corps War Diary. TNA WO95/1900
42 Infantry Brigade Headquarters War Diary. TNA WO95/1897
14th (Light) Division Headquarters War Diary. TNA WO95/1864
14th (Light) Division Report on Operations on 25 September 1915. TNA WO 95/1864
Hugh Montagu Butterworth, Service Record. TNA WO 339/38677
The Württemberg *Verlustlisten* 289 of 25 October 1915

Websites

Clifton Rugby Club History – www.cliftonrfchistory.co.uk
The Long, Long Trail – The British Army of 1914–18 for Family Historians – www.1914–1918.net
Rammy Cricket Archive – www.rammyarchive.co.uk/Archive/
Wanganui Collegiate School New Zealand official website –www.collegiate .school.nz/main.cfm?id=6347

Index